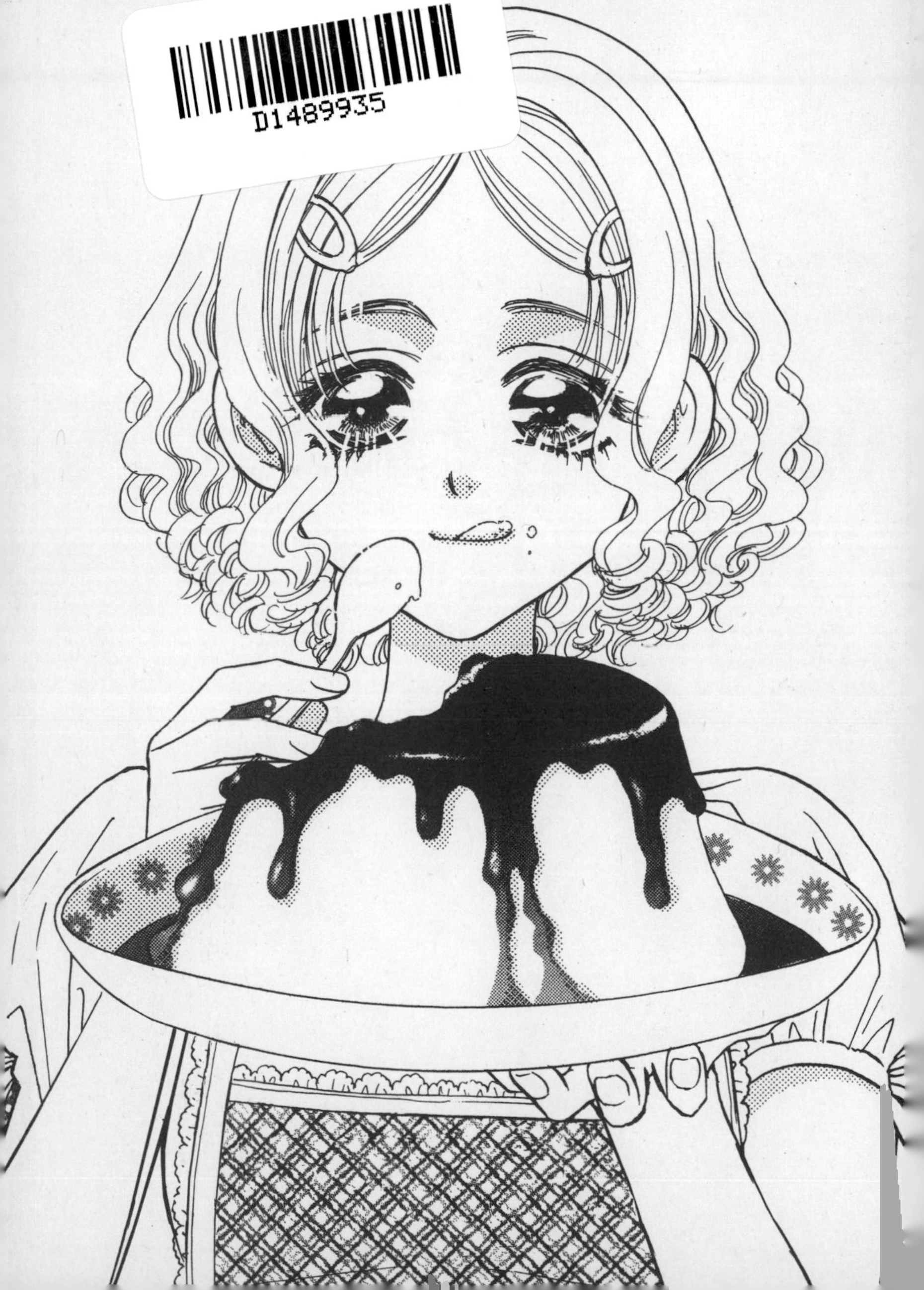

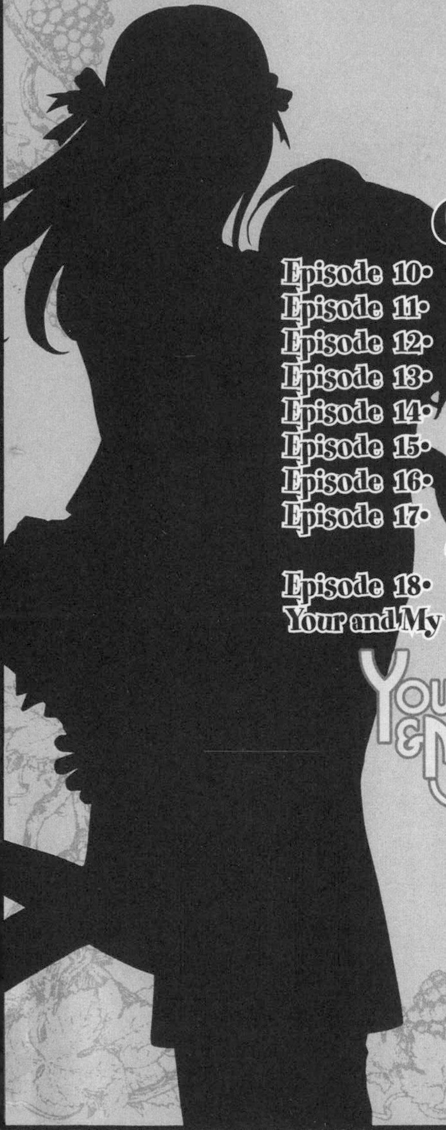

Contents

YOUR & MY SECRET ×××

2

Your & My Secret

Secret

Volume 2
by
Ai Morinaga

HAMBURG // LONDON // LOS ANGELES // TOKYO

Your & My Secret Volume 2
Created by Ai Morinaga

Translation - Yuya Otake
English Adaptaion - Jamie S. Rich
Copy Editor - Jessica Chavez
Retouch and Lettering - Star Print Brokers
Production Artist - Vicente Rivera, Jr.
Graphic Designers - Niyaz Mahmud & Jose Macasocol, Jr.

Editor - Nikhil Burman
Digital Imaging Manager - Chris Buford
Pre-Production Supervisor - Lucas Rivera
Production Manager - Elisabeth Brizzi
Managing Editor - Vy Nguyen
Creative Director - Anne Marie Horne
Editor-in-Chief - Rob Tokar
Publisher - Mike Kiley
President and C.O.O. - John Parker
C.E.O. and Chief Creative Officer - Stu Levy

A  Manga

TOKYOPOP and  are trademarks or registered trademarks of TOKYOPOP Inc.

TOKYOPOP Inc.
5900 Wilshire Blvd. Suite 2000
Los Angeles, CA 90036

E-mail: info@TOKYOPOP.com
Come visit us online at www.TOKYOPOP.com

ISBN: 978-1-4278-0523-2

First TOKYOPOP printing: July 2008

10 9 8 7 6 5 4 3 2 1

Printed in the USA

Story so far...

It's not that Akira Uehara is ugly. Girls don't acknowledge him because his personality is about as interesting as a dishrag. He's got a private crush on his tomboyish classmate, Nanako Momoi, who is undeniably attractive but whom others avoid like the plague, thanks to her sometimes violent and usually cantankerous disposition.

Nanako lives with her wacky scientist grandfather, and when his newest invention goes haywire, it causes a body swap for the two ill-matched teenagers. Unfortunately, Grandpa's machine is now broken, so Akira and Nanako must learn to live in each other's bodies for the time being. Akira, in Nanako's body, has taken a job to pay for Nanako's grandfather to fix the machine. But between trips to Hawaii and time spent with his new mail-order hula hoop, Grandpa doesn't seem to be spending a lot of time in the lab.

Meanwhile, Akira's best friend, Senbongi, has taken a liking to the now tamer Nanako (really Akira), and Shiina, Nanako's best friend, has a thing for the suddenly more virile Akira (Nanako). Gender confusion abounds!

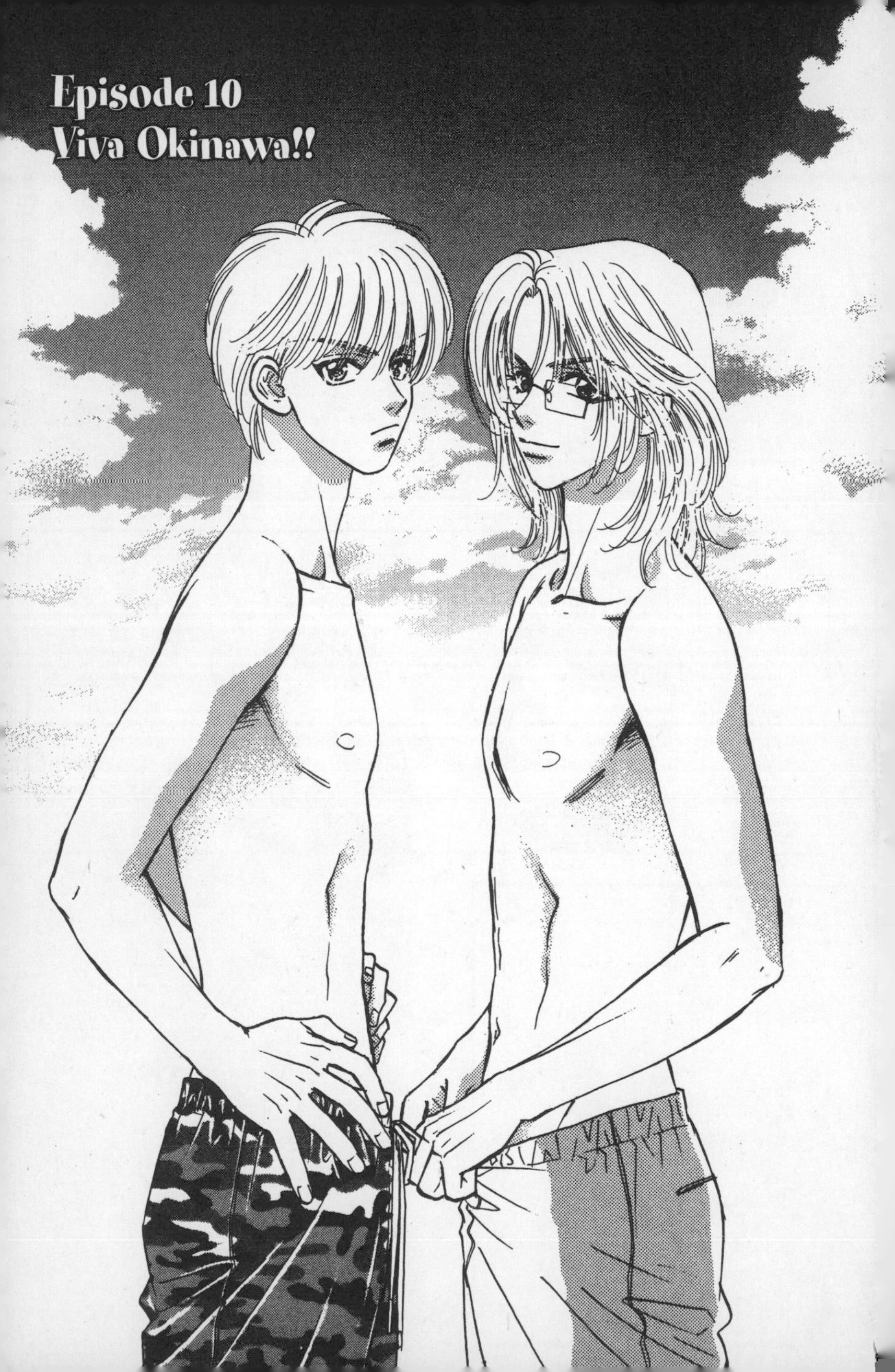
Episode 10
Viva Okinawa!!

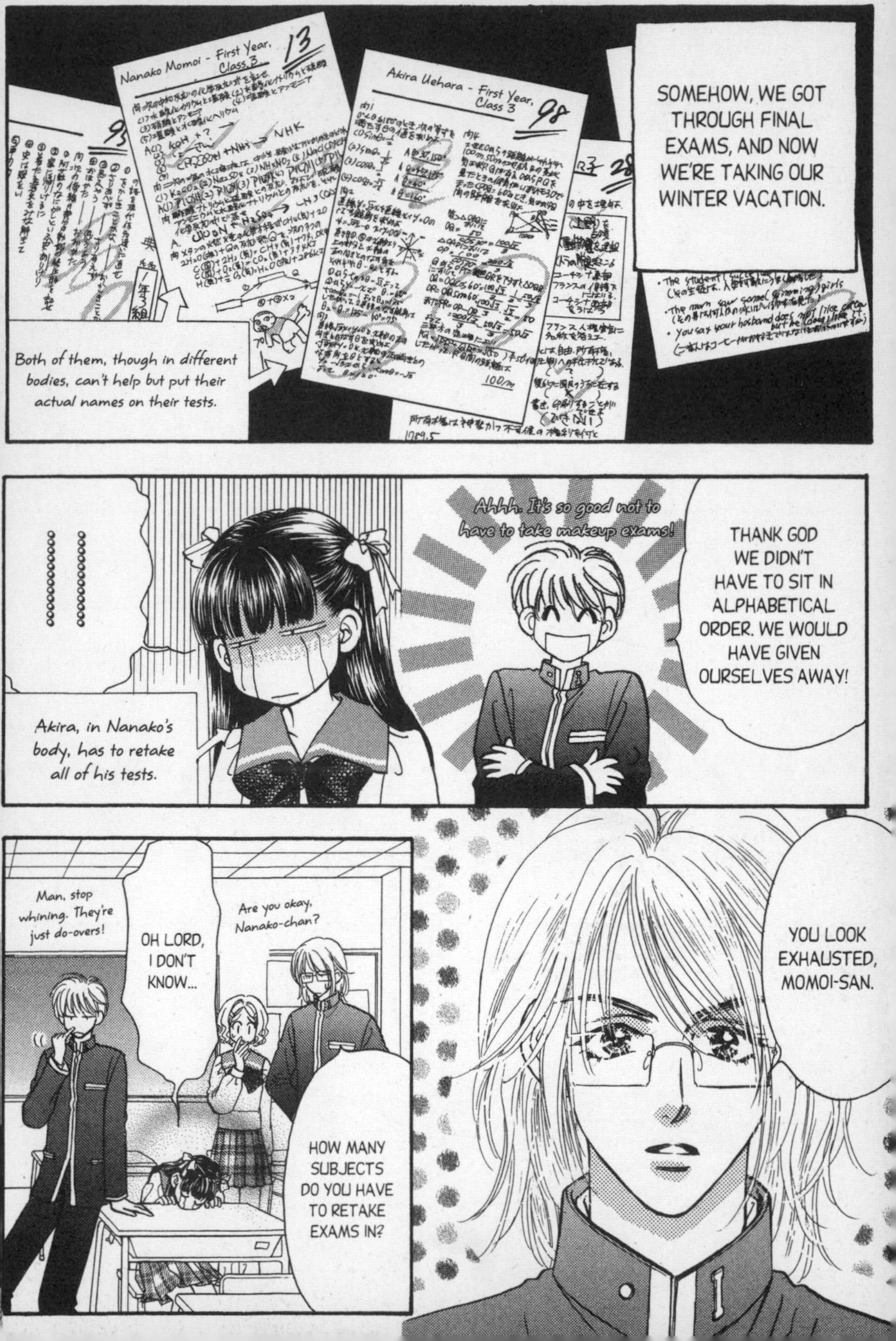
SOMEHOW, WE GOT THROUGH FINAL EXAMS, AND NOW WE'RE TAKING OUR WINTER VACATION.
Akira Uehara - First Year, Class 3
98
100m
Nanako Momoi - First Year, Class 3
13
NHK
Both of them, though in different bodies, can't help but put their actual names on their tests.
THANK GOD WE DIDN'T HAVE TO SIT IN ALPHABETICAL ORDER. WE WOULD HAVE GIVEN OURSELVES AWAY!
Ahhh. It's so good not to have to take makeup exams!
....
Akira, in Nanako's body, has to retake all of his tests.
YOU LOOK EXHAUSTED, MOMOI-SAN.
HOW MANY SUBJECTS DO YOU HAVE TO RETAKE EXAMS IN?
Are you okay, Nanako-chan?
OH LORD, I DON'T KNOW...
Man, stop whining. They're just do-overs!

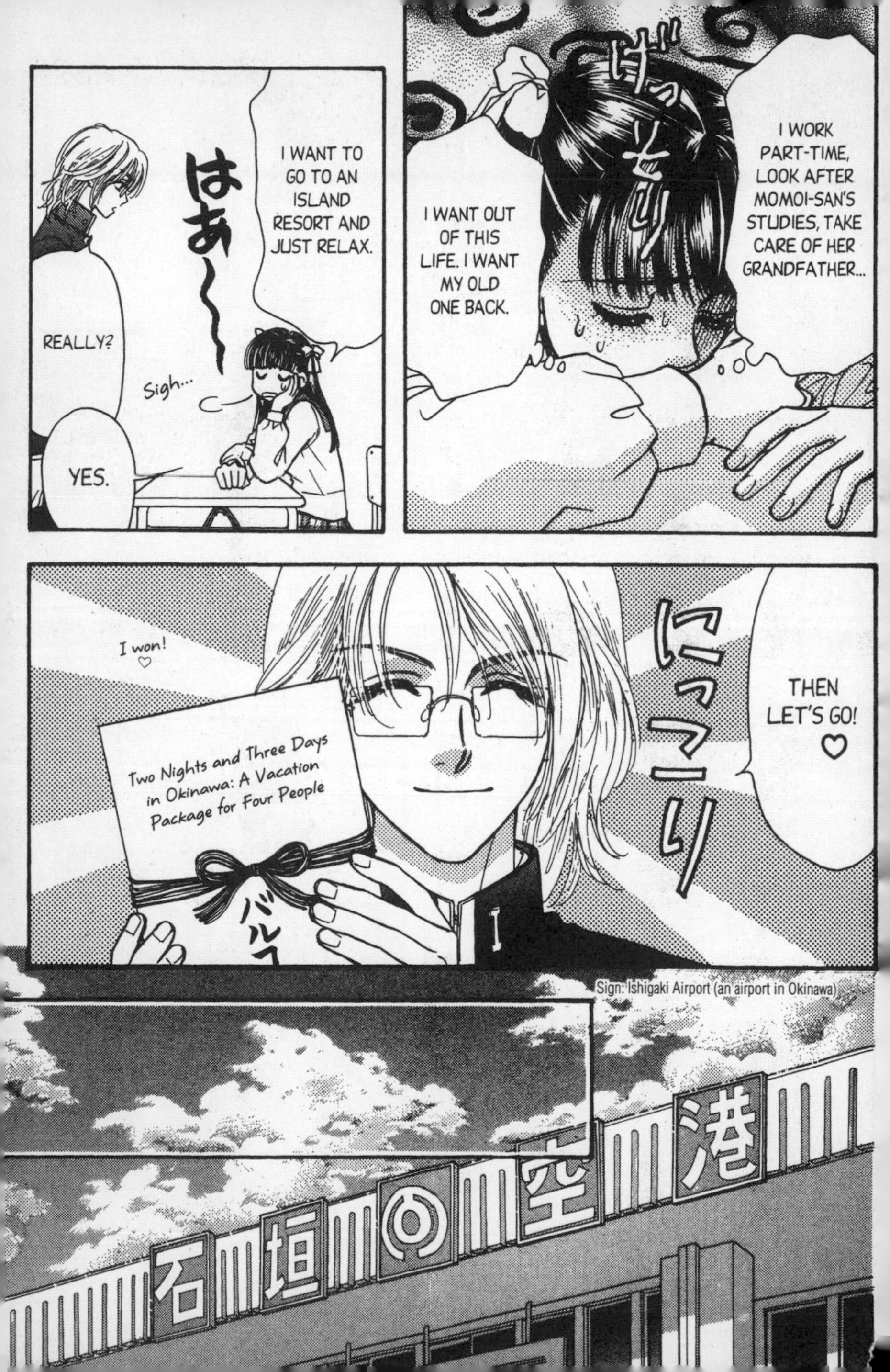
I WORK PART-TIME, LOOK AFTER MOMOI-SAN'S STUDIES, TAKE CARE OF HER GRANDFATHER...
げっそり
I WANT OUT OF THIS LIFE. I WANT MY OLD ONE BACK.
I WANT TO GO TO AN ISLAND RESORT AND JUST RELAX.
はあ〜〜
Sigh...
REALLY?
YES.
THEN LET'S GO! ♡
にっこーり
I won! ♡
Two Nights and Three Days in Okinawa: A Vacation Package for Four People
Sign: Ishigaki Airport (an airport in Okinawa)
石垣空港

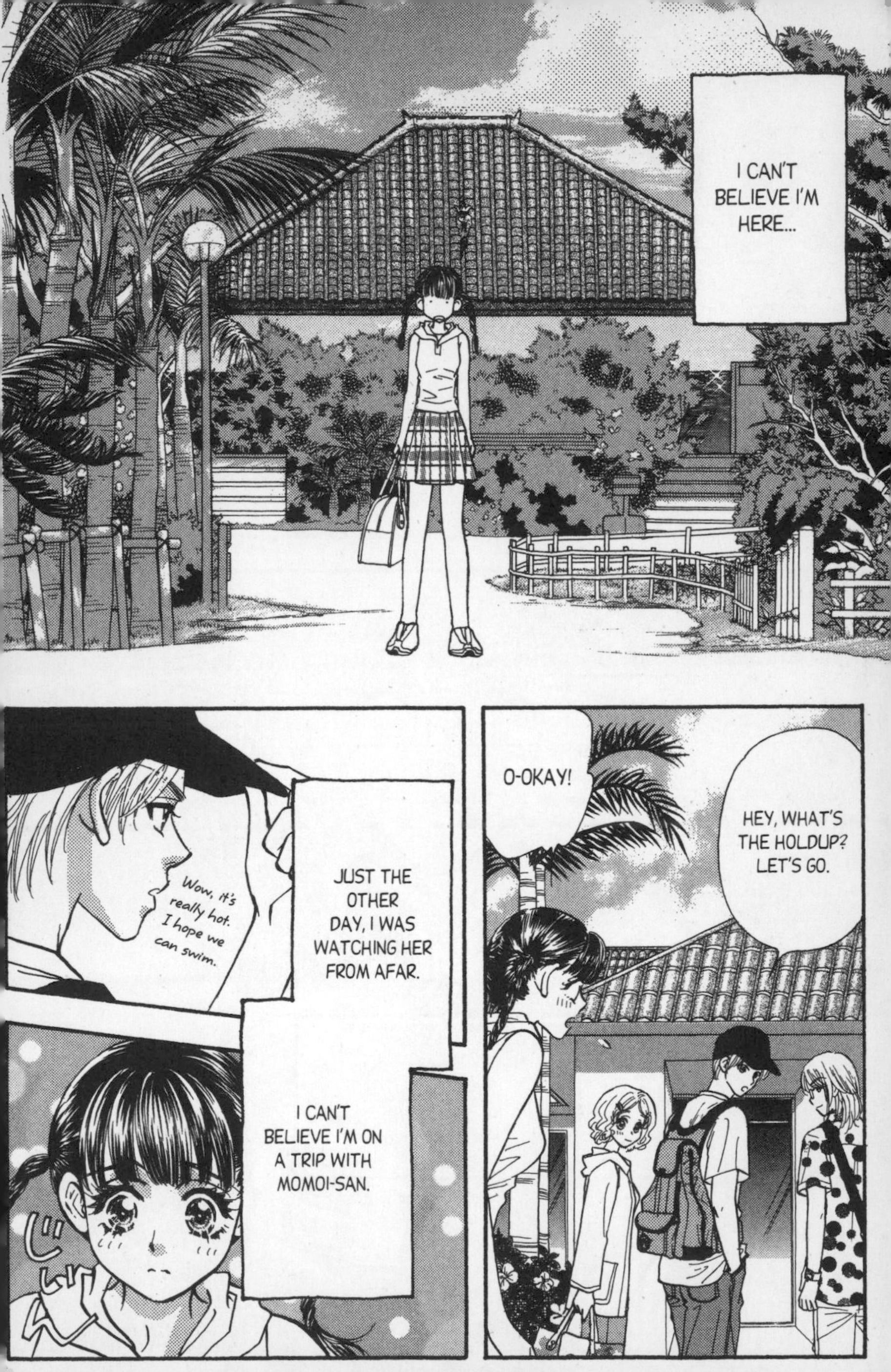
I CAN'T BELIEVE I'M HERE...
HEY, WHAT'S THE HOLDUP? LET'S GO.
O-OKAY!
JUST THE OTHER DAY, I WAS WATCHING HER FROM AFAR.
Wow, it's really hot. I hope we can swim.
I CAN'T BELIEVE I'M ON A TRIP WITH MOMOI-SAN.
じぃ

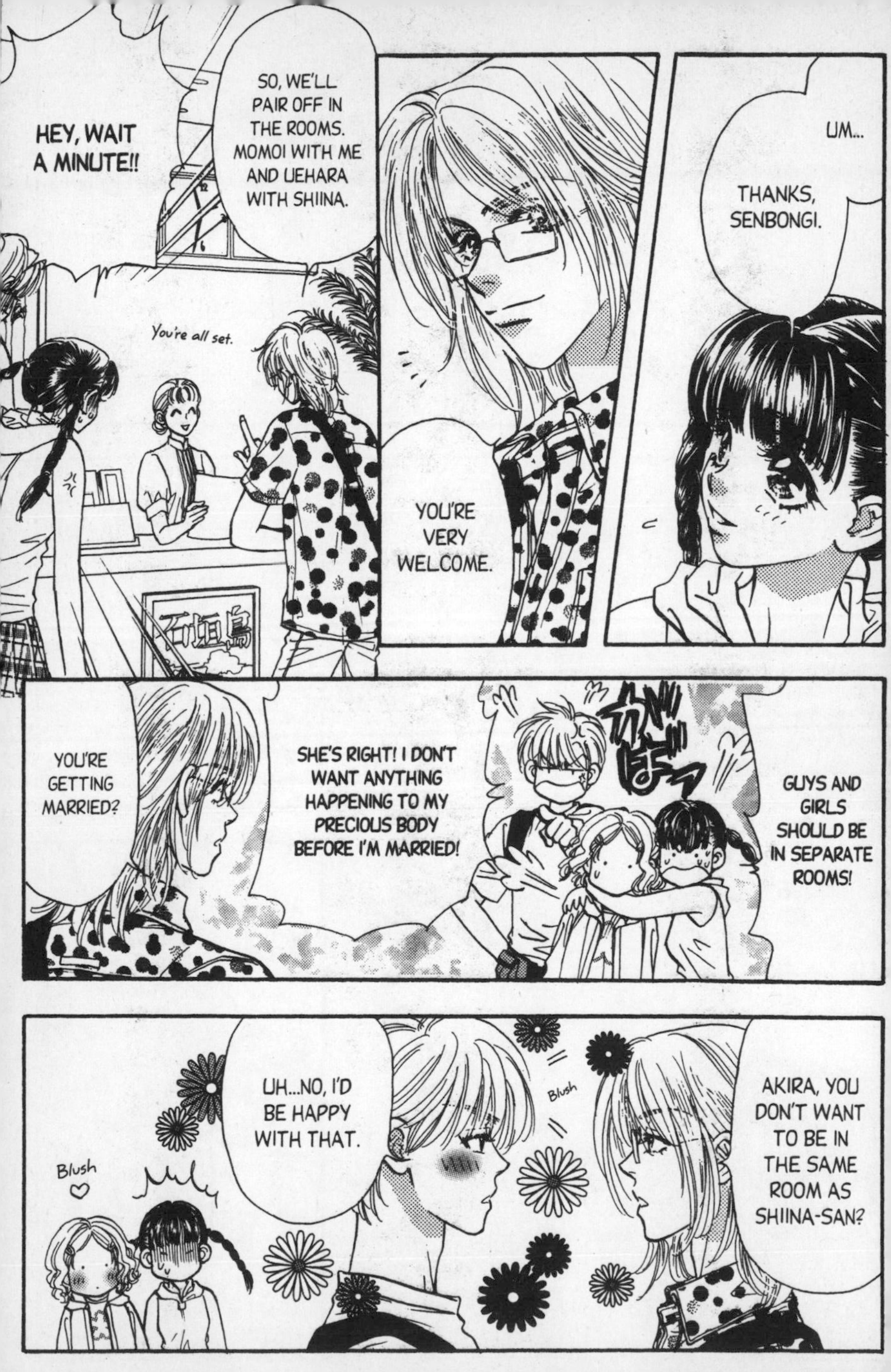
UM...
THANKS, SENBONGI.
YOU'RE VERY WELCOME.
SO, WE'LL PAIR OFF IN THE ROOMS. MOMOI WITH ME AND UEHARA WITH SHIINA.
HEY, WAIT A MINUTE!!
You're all set.
GUYS AND GIRLS SHOULD BE IN SEPARATE ROOMS!
SHE'S RIGHT! I DON'T WANT ANYTHING HAPPENING TO MY PRECIOUS BODY BEFORE I'M MARRIED!
YOU'RE GETTING MARRIED?
AKIRA, YOU DON'T WANT TO BE IN THE SAME ROOM AS SHIINA-SAN?
Blush
UH...NO, I'D BE HAPPY WITH THAT.
Blush ♡

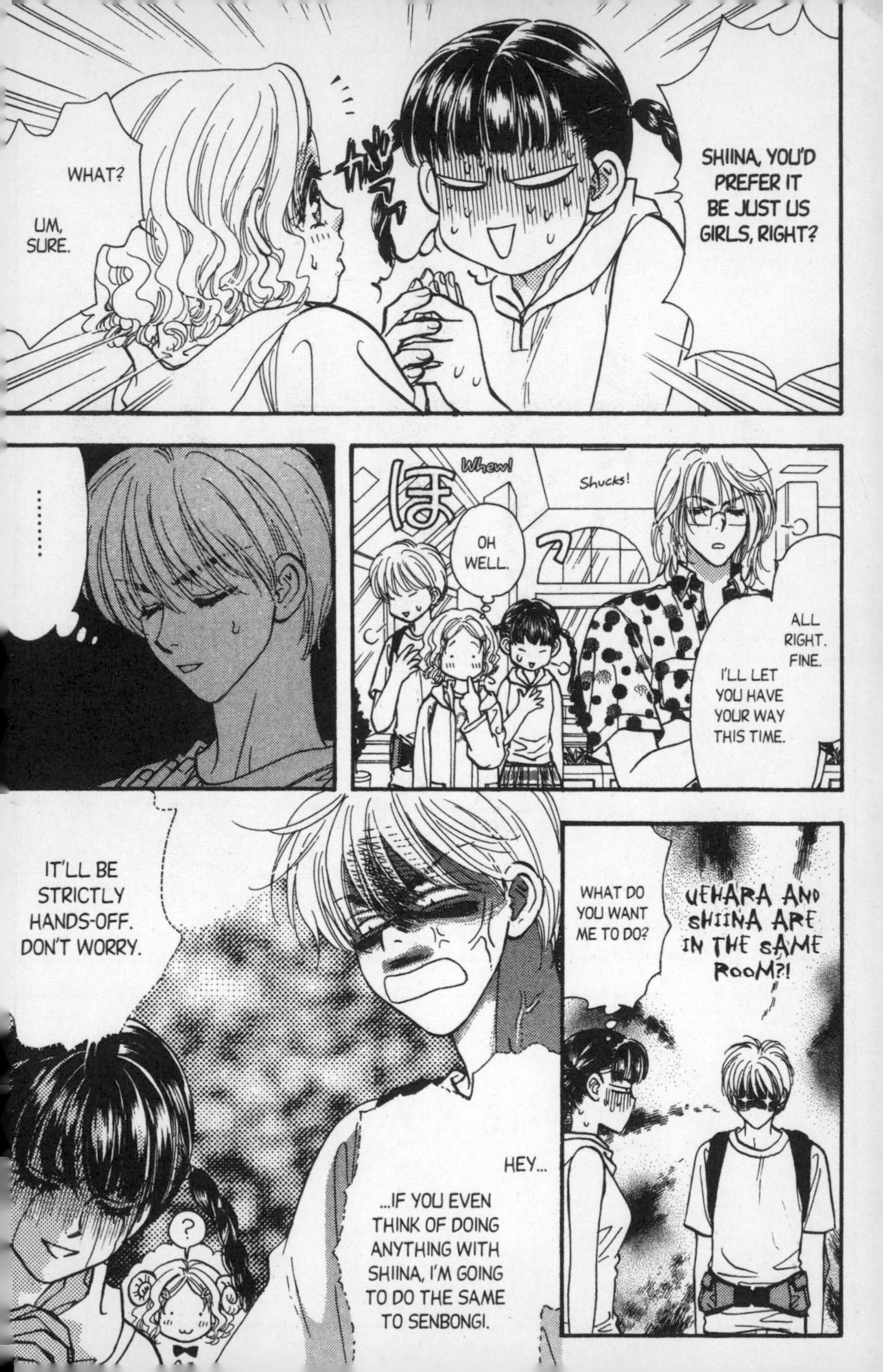
SHIINA, YOU'D PREFER IT BE JUST US GIRLS, RIGHT?
WHAT?
UM, SURE.
ALL RIGHT. FINE.
I'LL LET YOU HAVE YOUR WAY THIS TIME.
Shucks!
Whew!
OH WELL.
......
UEHARA AND SHIINA ARE IN THE SAME ROOM?!
WHAT DO YOU WANT ME TO DO?
HEY...
...IF YOU EVEN THINK OF DOING ANYTHING WITH SHIINA, I'M GOING TO DO THE SAME TO SENBONGI.
IT'LL BE STRICTLY HANDS-OFF. DON'T WORRY.
?

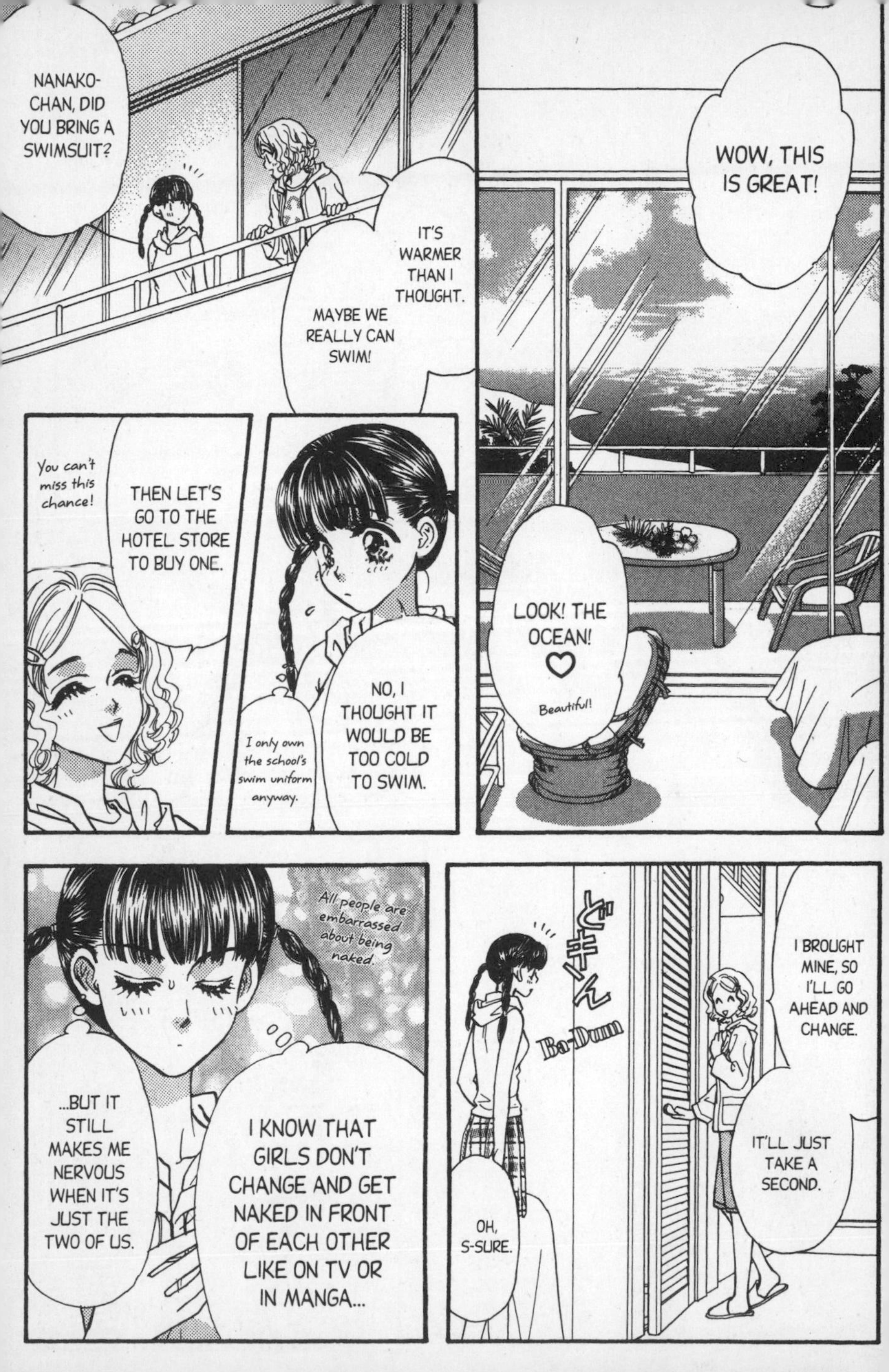
WOW, THIS IS GREAT!
LOOK! THE OCEAN! ♥
Beautiful!
IT'S WARMER THAN I THOUGHT.
MAYBE WE REALLY CAN SWIM!
NANAKO-CHAN, DID YOU BRING A SWIMSUIT?
NO, I THOUGHT IT WOULD BE TOO COLD TO SWIM.
I only own the school's swim uniform anyway.
THEN LET'S GO TO THE HOTEL STORE TO BUY ONE.
You can't miss this chance!
I BROUGHT MINE, SO I'LL GO AHEAD AND CHANGE.
IT'LL JUST TAKE A SECOND.
どきん
Ba-Dum
OH, S-SURE.
All people are embarrassed about being naked.
I KNOW THAT GIRLS DON'T CHANGE AND GET NAKED IN FRONT OF EACH OTHER LIKE ON TV OR IN MANGA...
...BUT IT STILL MAKES ME NERVOUS WHEN IT'S JUST THE TWO OF US.

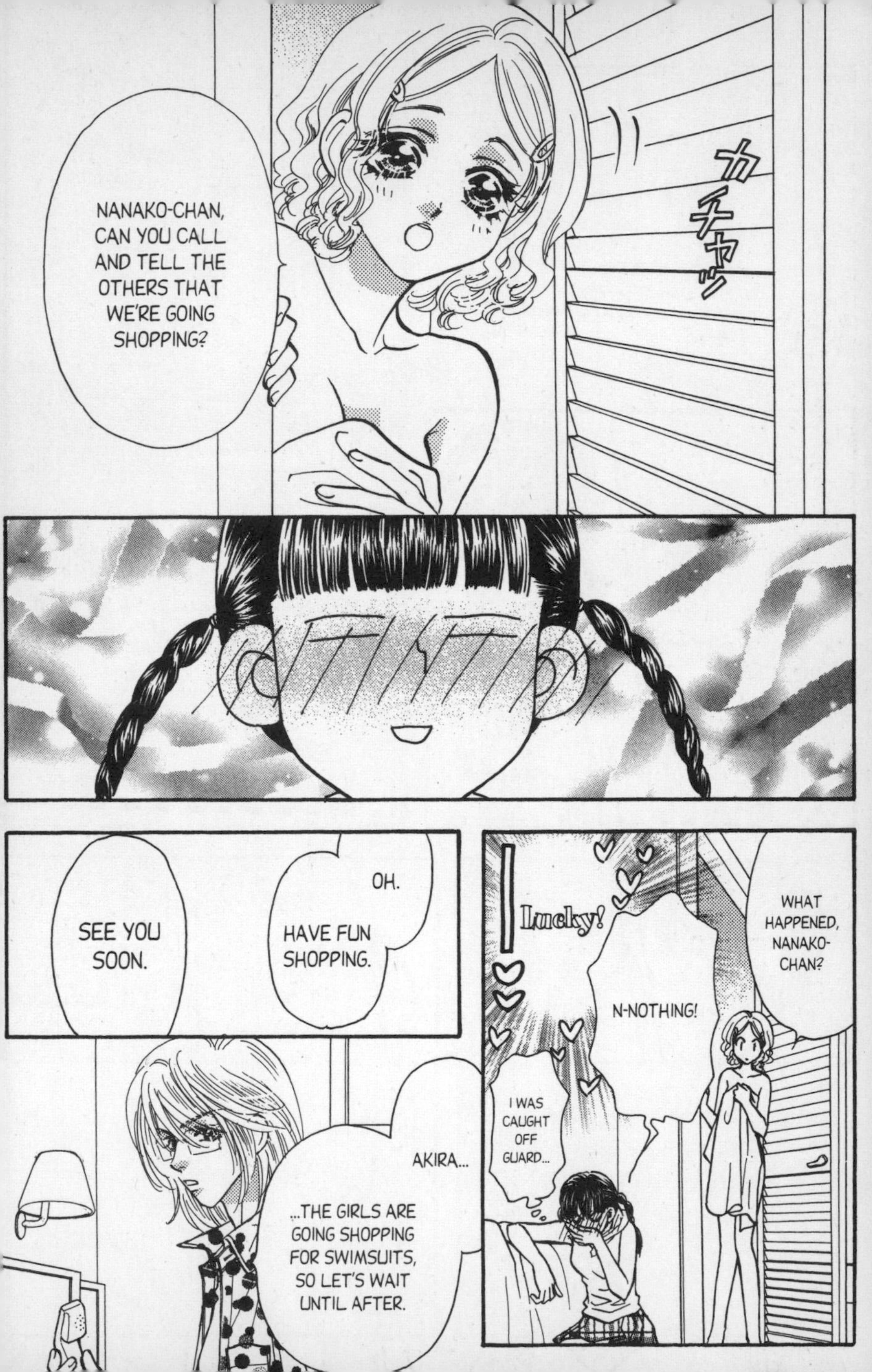
カチャッ
NANAKO-CHAN, CAN YOU CALL AND TELL THE OTHERS THAT WE'RE GOING SHOPPING?
WHAT HAPPENED, NANAKO-CHAN?
N-NOTHING!
Lucky!
I WAS CAUGHT OFF GUARD...
OH.
HAVE FUN SHOPPING.
SEE YOU SOON.
AKIRA...
...THE GIRLS ARE GOING SHOPPING FOR SWIMSUITS, SO LET'S WAIT UNTIL AFTER.

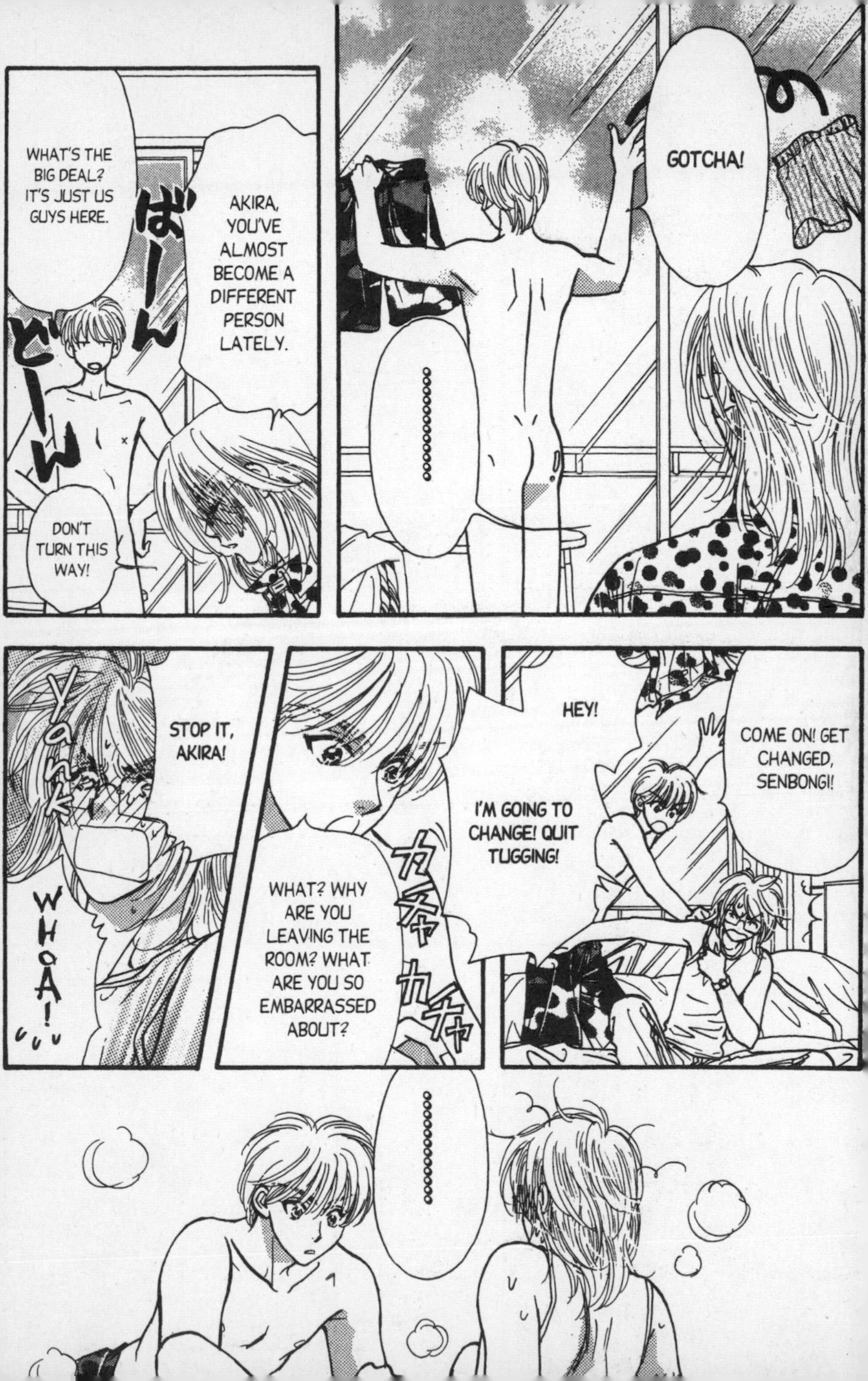
GOTCHA!
......
AKIRA, YOU'VE ALMOST BECOME A DIFFERENT PERSON LATELY.
ばーん
どーん
WHAT'S THE BIG DEAL? IT'S JUST US GUYS HERE.
DON'T TURN THIS WAY!
COME ON! GET CHANGED, SENBONGI!
HEY!
I'M GOING TO CHANGE! QUIT TUGGING!
WHAT? WHY ARE YOU LEAVING THE ROOM? WHAT ARE YOU SO EMBARRASSED ABOUT?
STOP IT, AKIRA!
yank
WHOA!
......

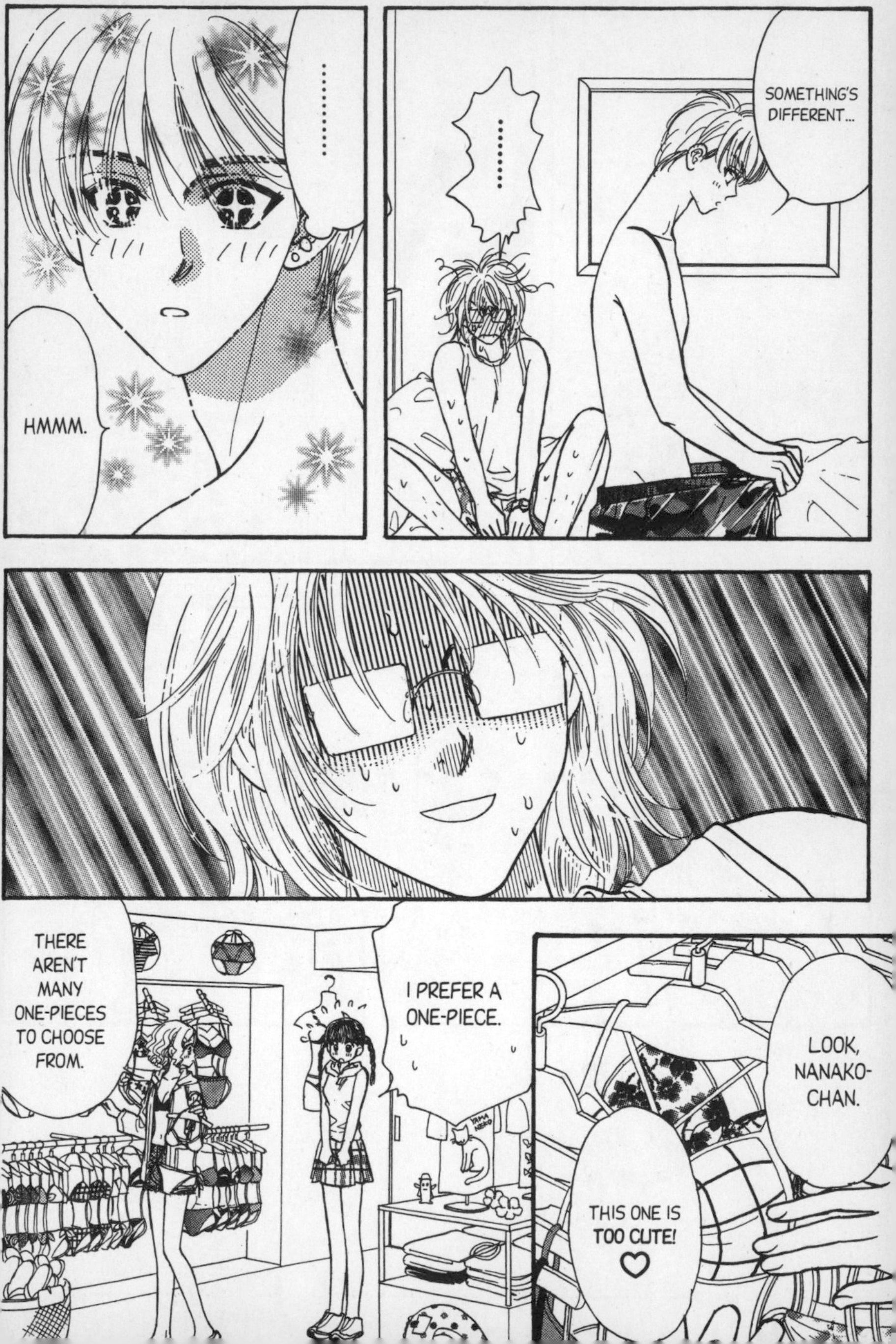
SOMETHING'S DIFFERENT...
......
......
HMMM.
LOOK, NANAKO-CHAN.
THIS ONE IS TOO CUTE! ♥
I PREFER A ONE-PIECE.
THERE AREN'T MANY ONE-PIECES TO CHOOSE FROM.
YAMA NEKO

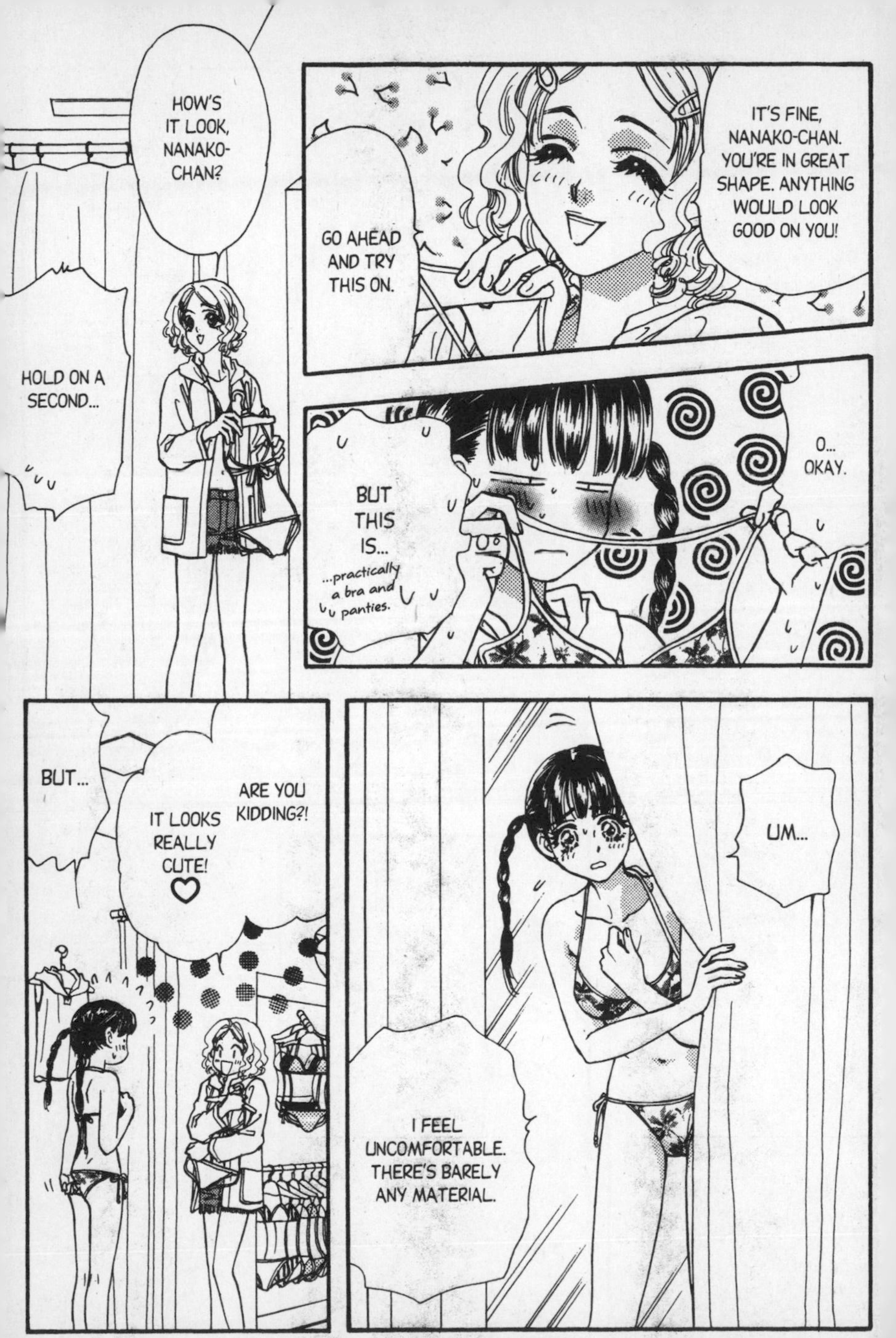
IT'S FINE, NANAKO-CHAN. YOU'RE IN GREAT SHAPE. ANYTHING WOULD LOOK GOOD ON YOU!
GO AHEAD AND TRY THIS ON.
O... OKAY.
BUT THIS IS...
...practically a bra and panties.
HOW'S IT LOOK, NANAKO-CHAN?
HOLD ON A SECOND...
UM...
I FEEL UNCOMFORTABLE. THERE'S BARELY ANY MATERIAL.
ARE YOU KIDDING?!
IT LOOKS REALLY CUTE! ♡
BUT...

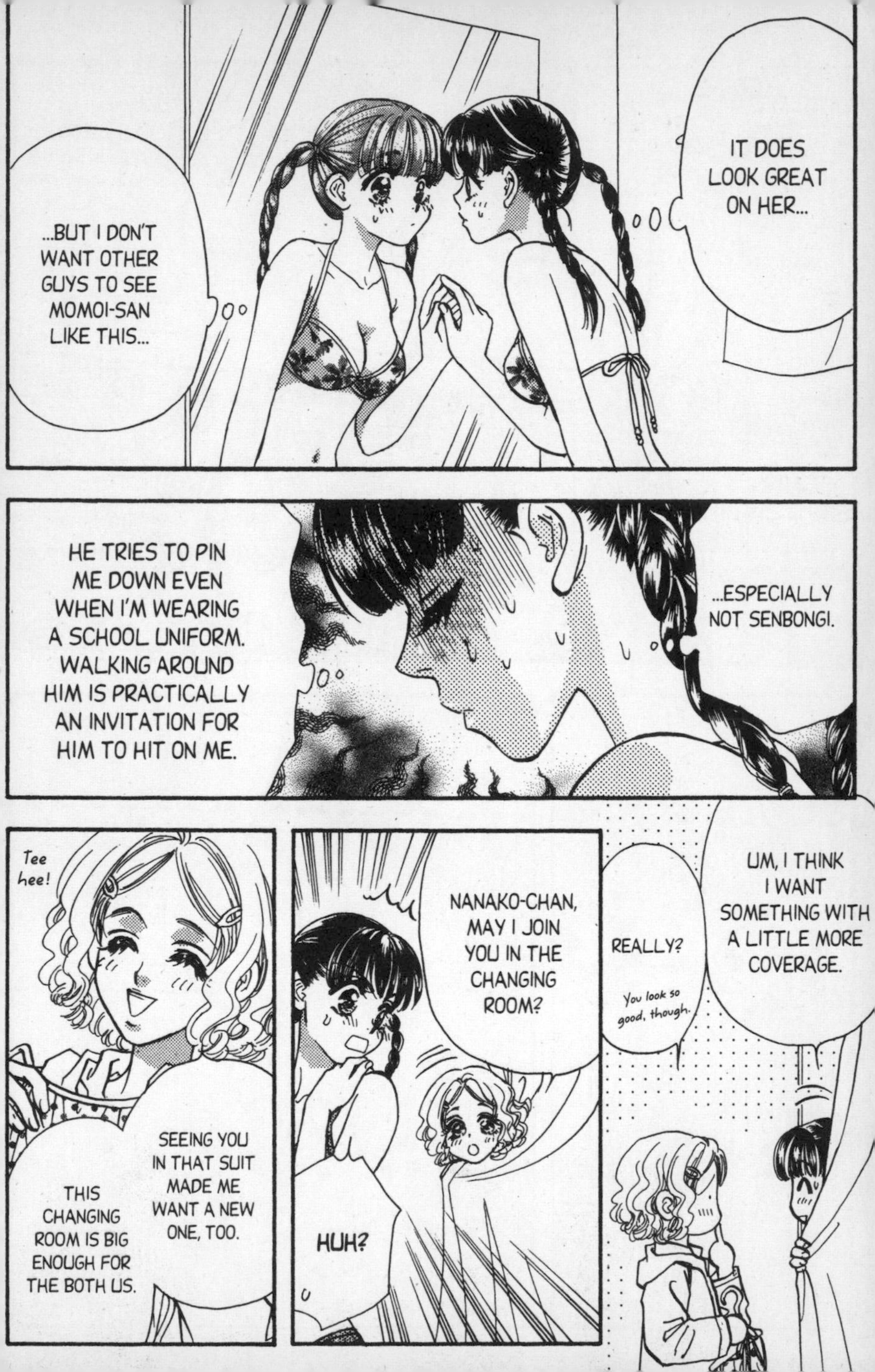
IT DOES LOOK GREAT ON HER...
...BUT I DON'T WANT OTHER GUYS TO SEE MOMOI-SAN LIKE THIS...
...ESPECIALLY NOT SENBONGI.
HE TRIES TO PIN ME DOWN EVEN WHEN I'M WEARING A SCHOOL UNIFORM. WALKING AROUND HIM IS PRACTICALLY AN INVITATION FOR HIM TO HIT ON ME.
UM, I THINK I WANT SOMETHING WITH A LITTLE MORE COVERAGE.
REALLY?
You look so good, though.
NANAKO-CHAN, MAY I JOIN YOU IN THE CHANGING ROOM?
HUH?
Tee hee!
SEEING YOU IN THAT SUIT MADE ME WANT A NEW ONE, TOO.
THIS CHANGING ROOM IS BIG ENOUGH FOR THE BOTH US.

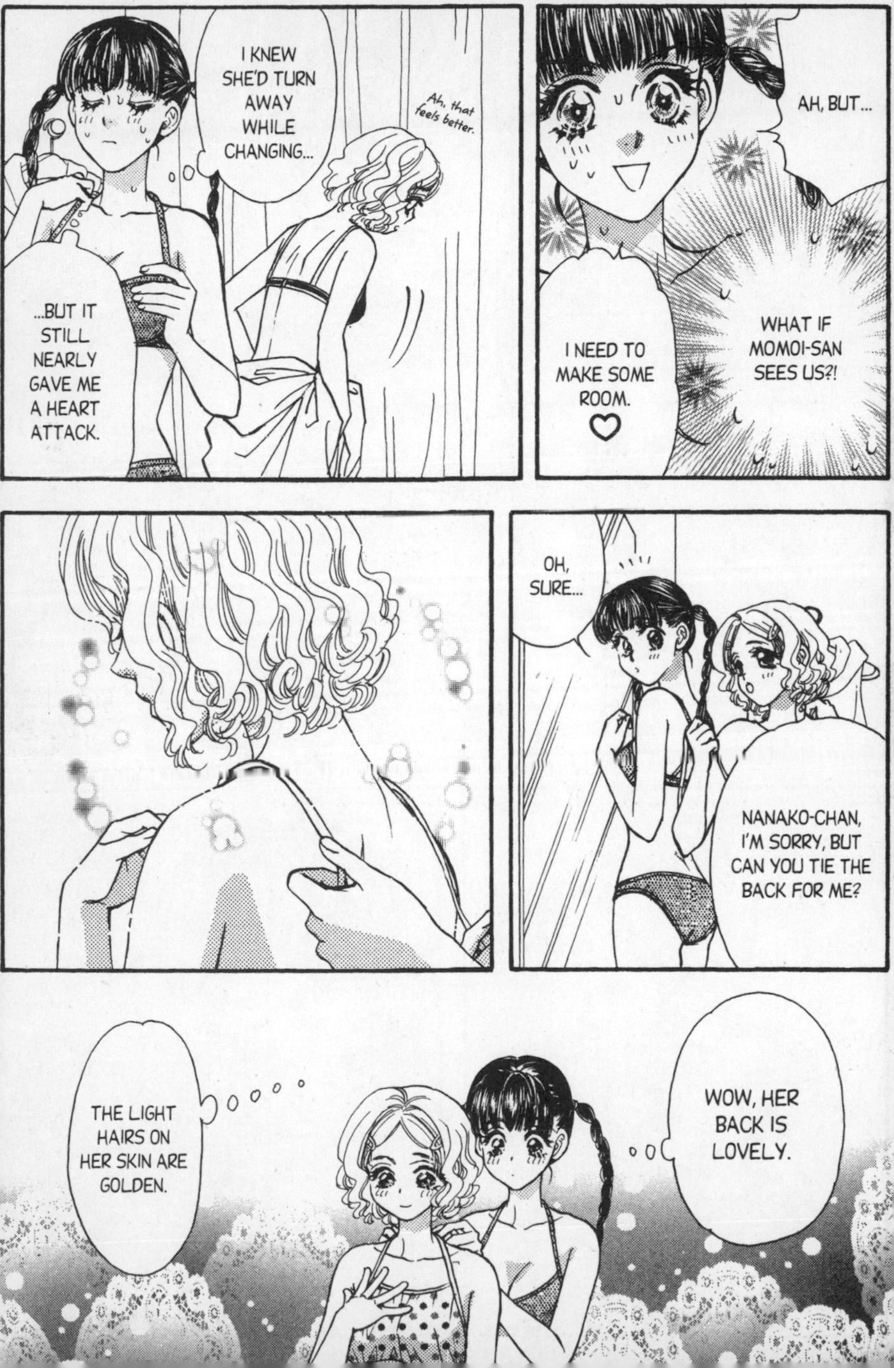
AH, BUT...
WHAT IF MOMOI-SAN SEES US?!
I NEED TO MAKE SOME ROOM. ♡
Ah, that feels better.
I KNEW SHE'D TURN AWAY WHILE CHANGING...
...BUT IT STILL NEARLY GAVE ME A HEART ATTACK.
NANAKO-CHAN, I'M SORRY, BUT CAN YOU TIE THE BACK FOR ME?
OH, SURE...
WOW, HER BACK IS LOVELY.
THE LIGHT HAIRS ON HER SKIN ARE GOLDEN.

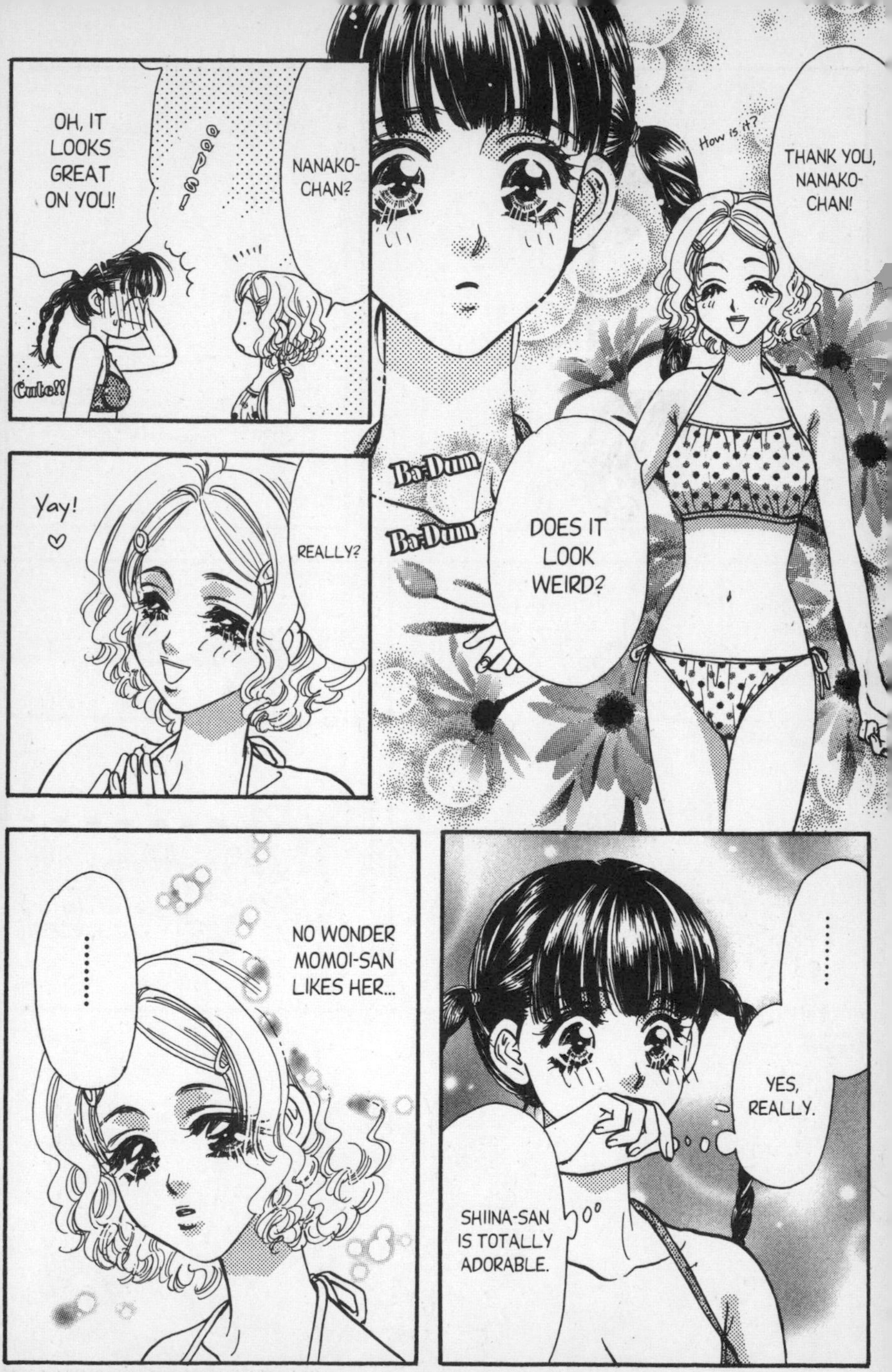
How is it?
THANK YOU, NANAKO-CHAN!
Ba-Dum
Ba-Dum
DOES IT LOOK WEIRD?
NANAKO-CHAN?
OH, IT LOOKS GREAT ON YOU!
Cute!!
REALLY?
Yay! ♡
......
YES, REALLY.
SHIINA-SAN IS TOTALLY ADORABLE.
NO WONDER MOMOI-SAN LIKES HER...
......

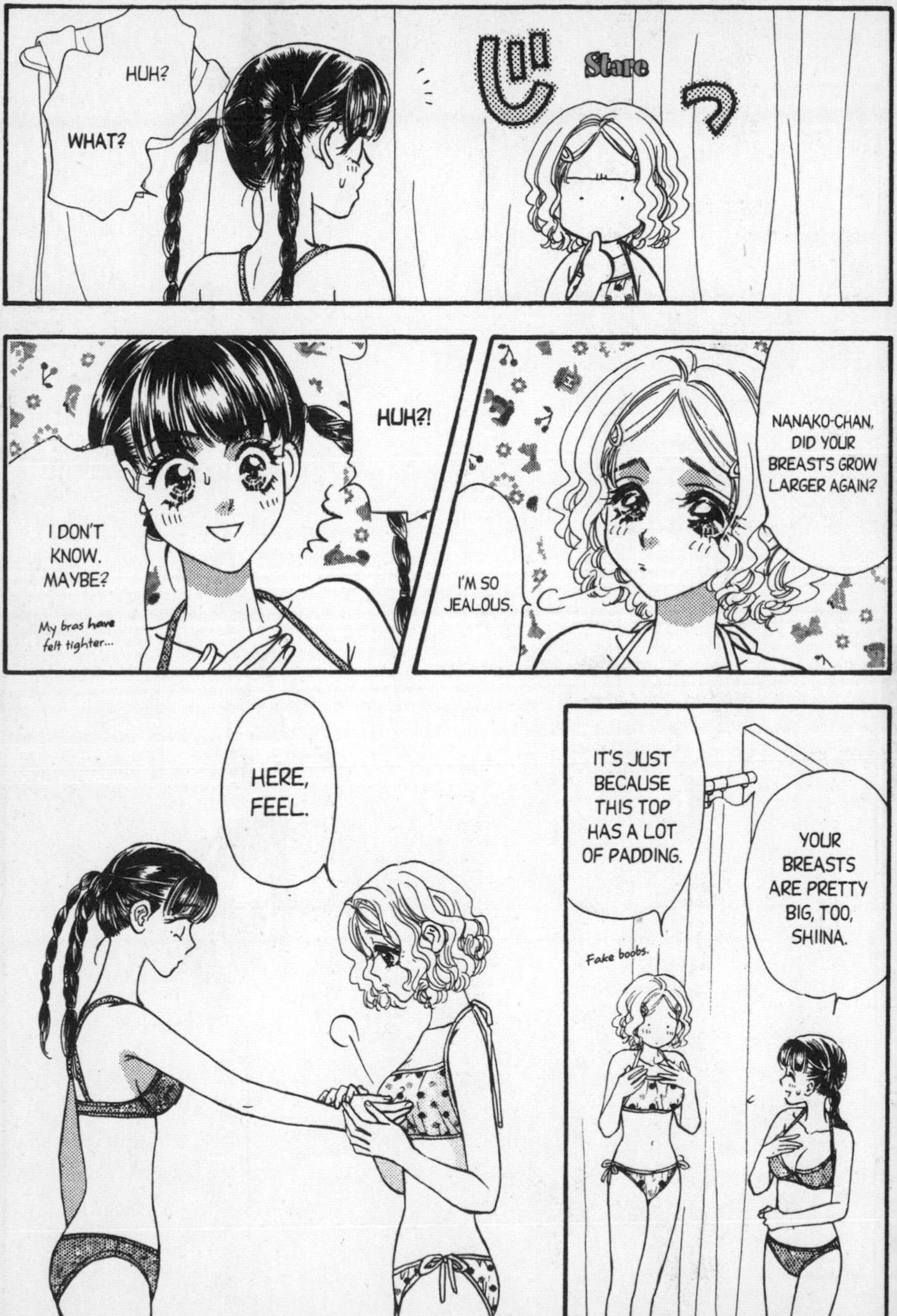
じっ
Stare
HUH?
WHAT?
NANAKO-CHAN, DID YOUR BREASTS GROW LARGER AGAIN?
I'M SO JEALOUS.
HUH?!
I DON'T KNOW. MAYBE?
My bras have felt tighter...
YOUR BREASTS ARE PRETTY BIG, TOO, SHIINA.
IT'S JUST BECAUSE THIS TOP HAS A LOT OF PADDING.
Fake boobs.
HERE, FEEL.

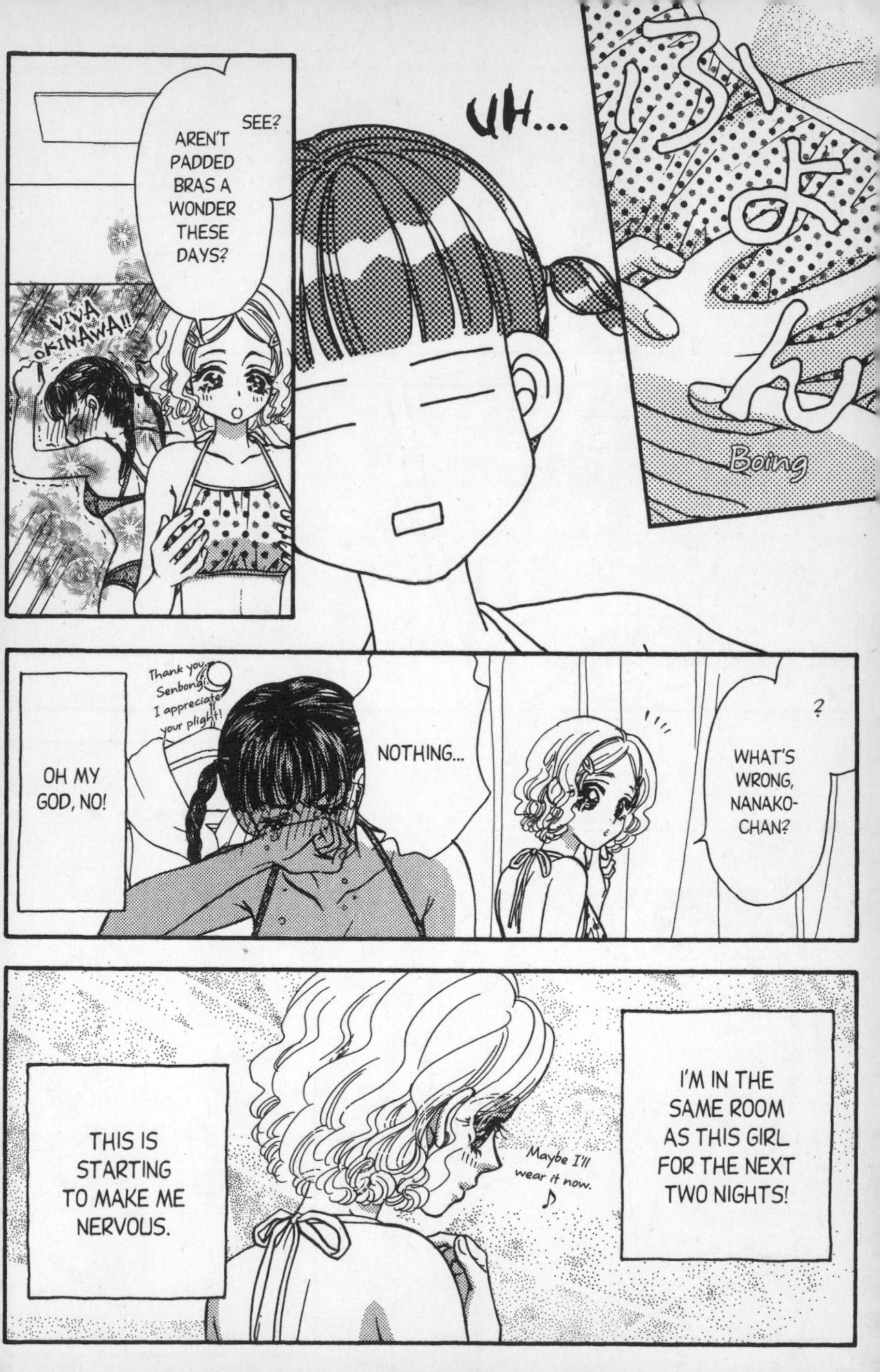
ふよん
Boing
UH...
SEE?
AREN'T PADDED BRAS A WONDER THESE DAYS?
VIVA OKINAWA!!
?
WHAT'S WRONG, NANAKO-CHAN?
NOTHING...
Thank you, Senbongi! I appreciate your plight!
OH MY GOD, NO!
I'M IN THE SAME ROOM AS THIS GIRL FOR THE NEXT TWO NIGHTS!
Maybe I'll wear it now. ♪
THIS IS STARTING TO MAKE ME NERVOUS.

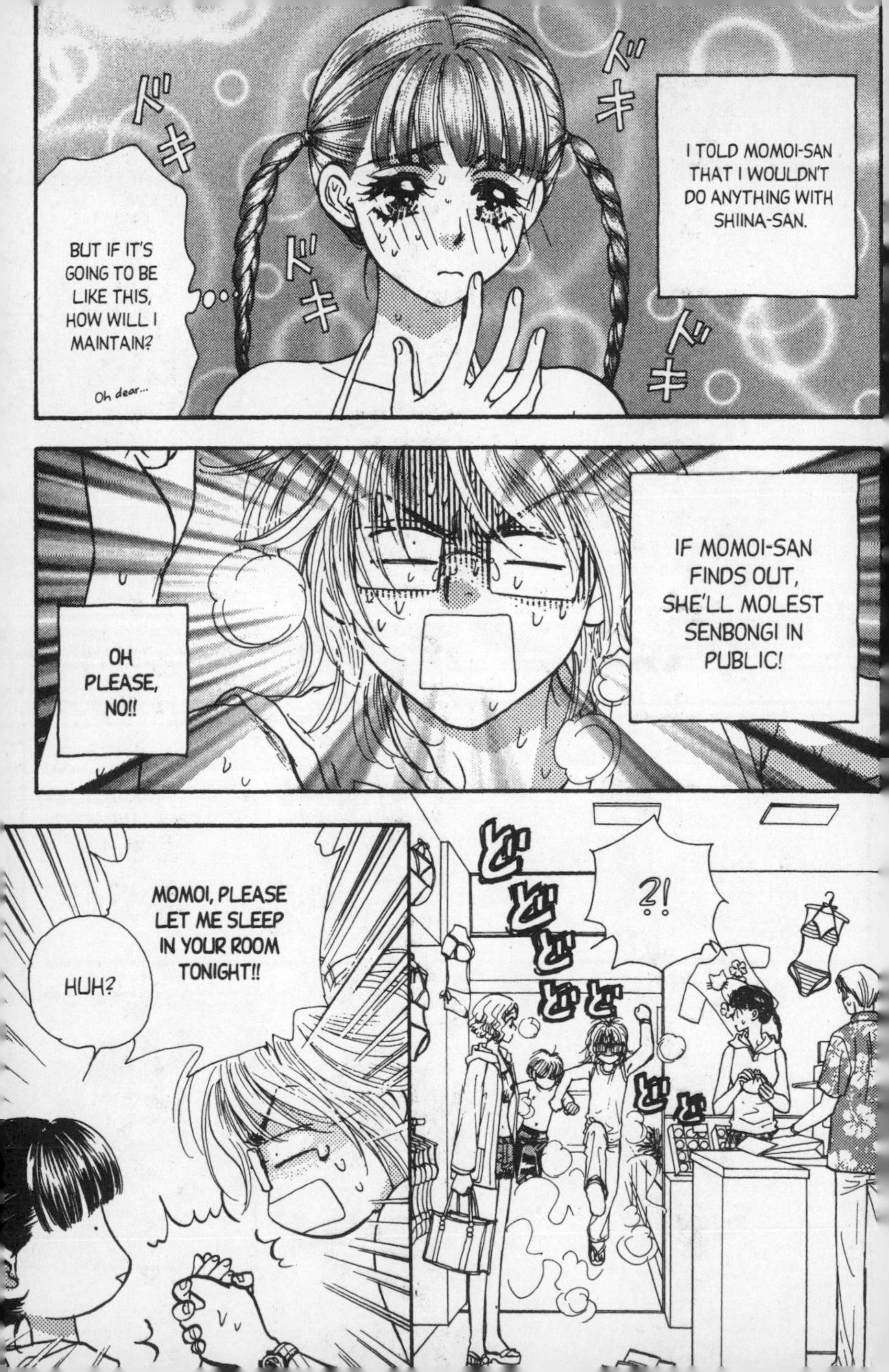

I TOLD MOMOI-SAN THAT I WOULDN'T DO ANYTHING WITH SHIINA-SAN.
BUT IF IT'S GOING TO BE LIKE THIS, HOW WILL I MAINTAIN?
Oh dear...
IF MOMOI-SAN FINDS OUT, SHE'LL MOLEST SENBONGI IN PUBLIC!
OH PLEASE, NO!!
?!
MOMOI, PLEASE LET ME SLEEP IN YOUR ROOM TONIGHT!!
HUH?

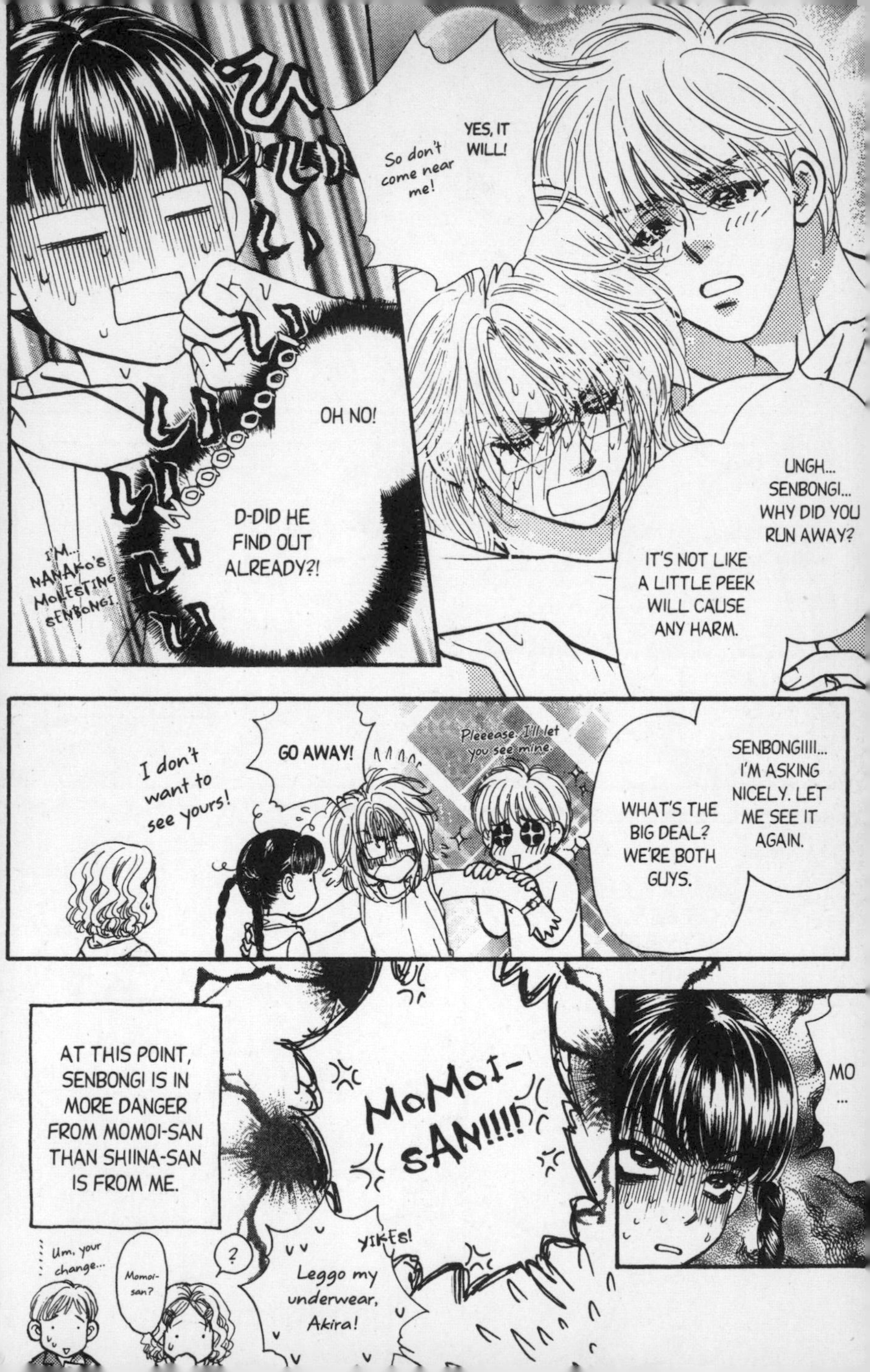
UNGH... SENBONGI... WHY DID YOU RUN AWAY?
IT'S NOT LIKE A LITTLE PEEK WILL CAUSE ANY HARM.
YES, IT WILL!
So don't come near me!
OH NO!
D-DID HE FIND OUT ALREADY?!
I'M... NANAKO's MOLESTING SENBONGI.
SENBONGIIII... I'M ASKING NICELY. LET ME SEE IT AGAIN.
WHAT'S THE BIG DEAL? WE'RE BOTH GUYS.
Pleeease. I'll let you see mine.
GO AWAY!
I don't want to see yours!
MO ...
MOMOI-SAN!!!!
AT THIS POINT, SENBONGI IS IN MORE DANGER FROM MOMOI-SAN THAN SHIINA-SAN IS FROM ME.
YIKES!
Leggo my underwear, Akira!
?
Momoi-san?
Um, your change...

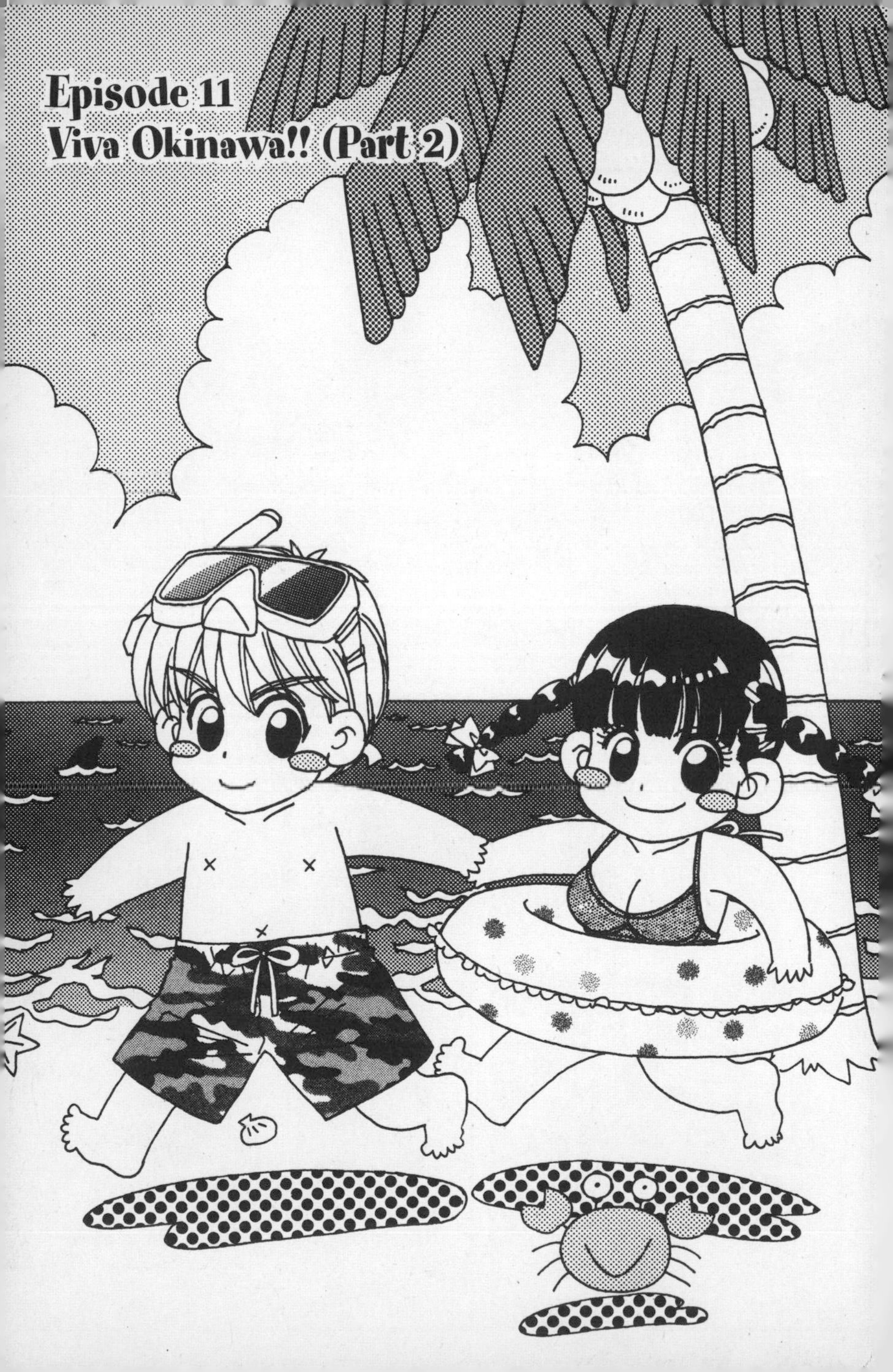
Episode 11
Viva Okinawa!! (Part 2)

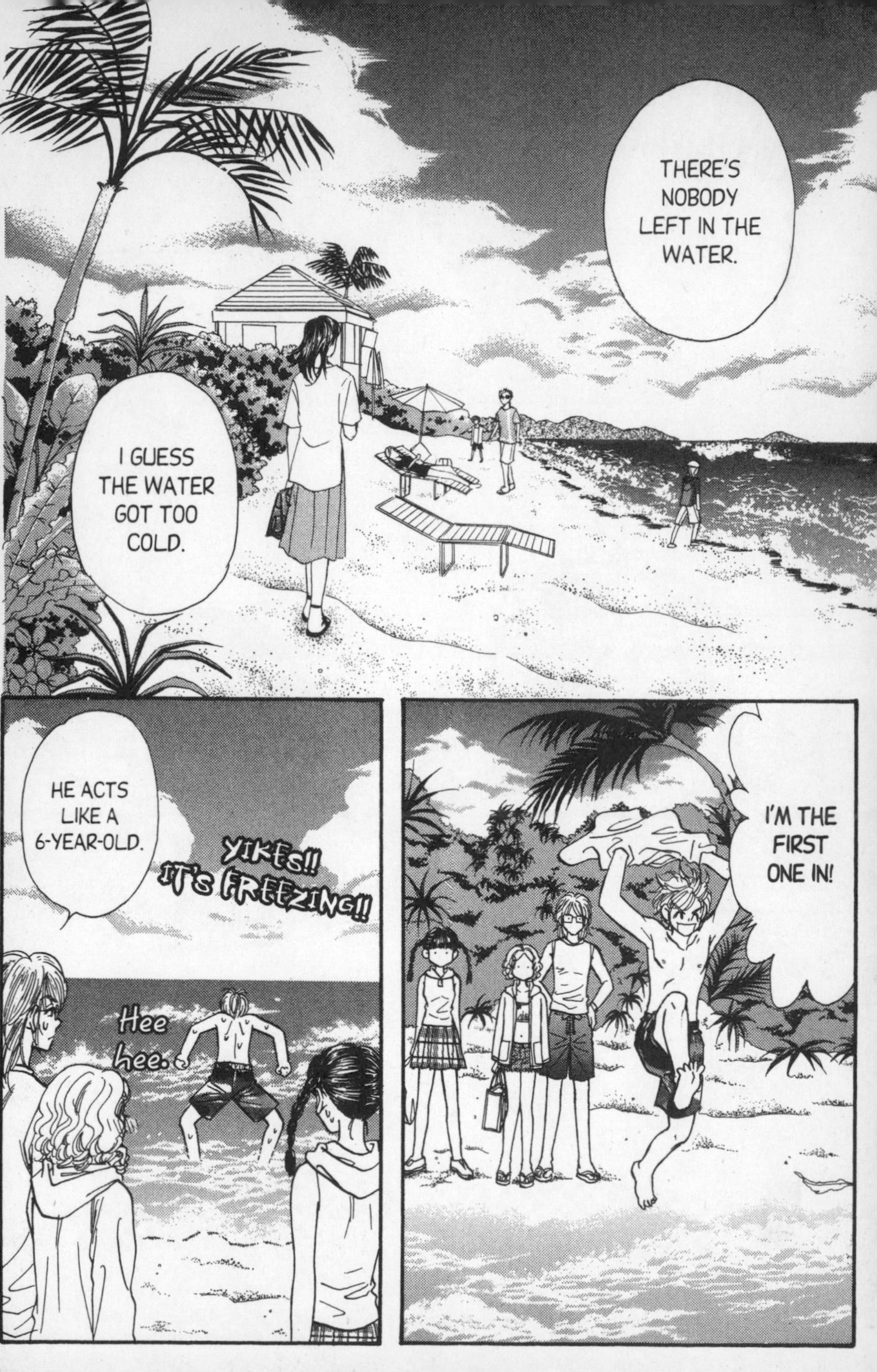
THERE'S NOBODY LEFT IN THE WATER.
I GUESS THE WATER GOT TOO COLD.
I'M THE FIRST ONE IN!
YIKES!! IT'S FREEZING!!
HE ACTS LIKE A 6-YEAR-OLD.
Hee hee.

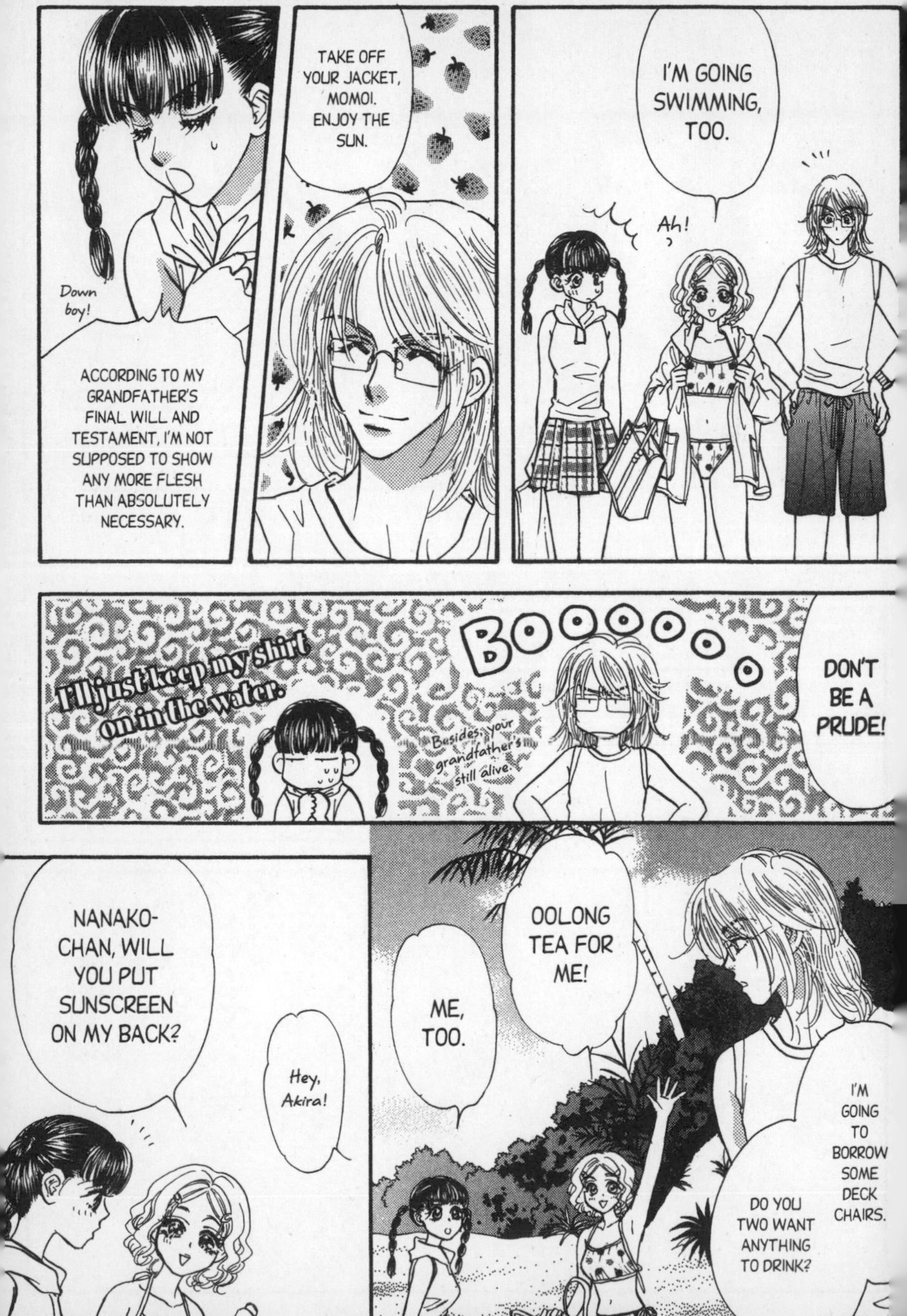
I'M GOING SWIMMING, TOO.
Ah!
TAKE OFF YOUR JACKET, MOMOI. ENJOY THE SUN.
Down boy!
ACCORDING TO MY GRANDFATHER'S FINAL WILL AND TESTAMENT, I'M NOT SUPPOSED TO SHOW ANY MORE FLESH THAN ABSOLUTELY NECESSARY.
DON'T BE A PRUDE!
BOOOOOO
Besides, your grandfather's still alive.
I'll just keep my shirt on in the water.
I'M GOING TO BORROW SOME DECK CHAIRS.
DO YOU TWO WANT ANYTHING TO DRINK?
OOLONG TEA FOR ME!
ME, TOO.
NANAKO-CHAN, WILL YOU PUT SUNSCREEN ON MY BACK?
Hey, Akira!

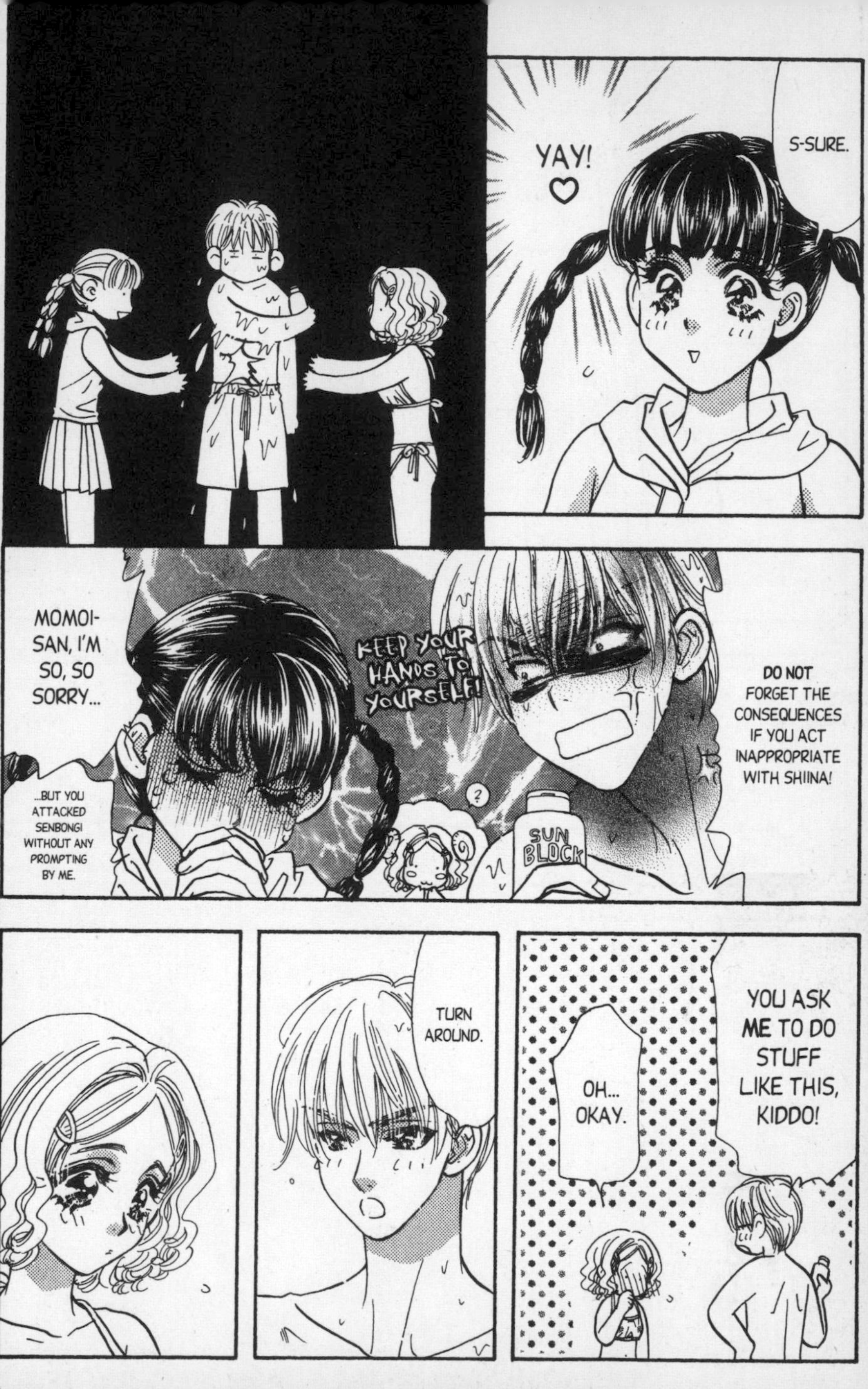
S-SURE.
YAY! ♡
DO NOT FORGET THE CONSEQUENCES IF YOU ACT INAPPROPRIATE WITH SHIINA!
KEEP YOUR HANDS TO YOURSELF!
MOMOI-SAN, I'M SO, SO SORRY...
?
...BUT YOU ATTACKED SENBONGI WITHOUT ANY PROMPTING BY ME.
SUN BLOCK
YOU ASK ME TO DO STUFF LIKE THIS, KIDDO!
OH... OKAY.
TURN AROUND.

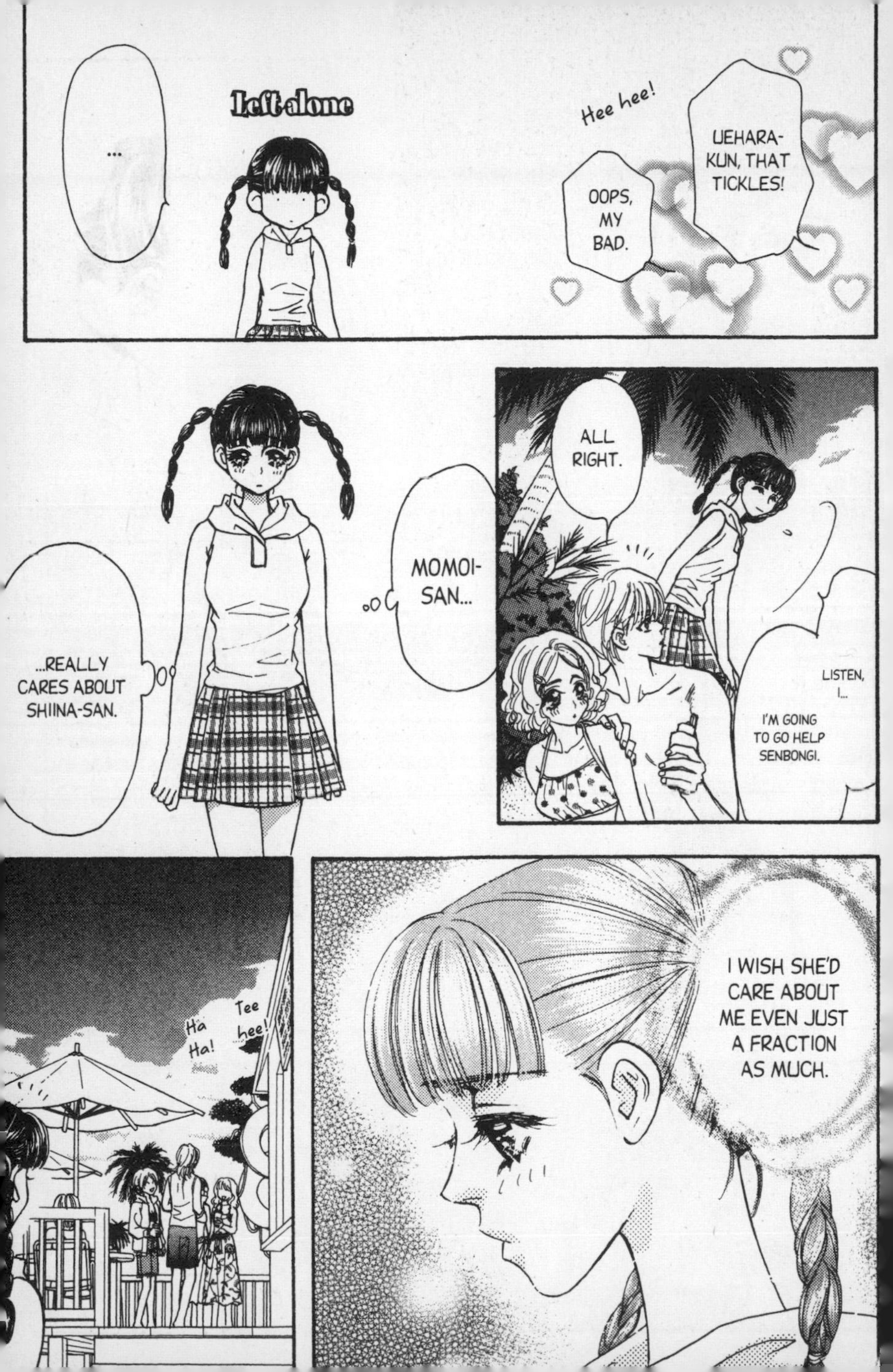
UEHARA-KUN, THAT TICKLES!
Hee hee!
OOPS, MY BAD.
Left alone
...
LISTEN, I...
I'M GOING TO GO HELP SENBONGI.
ALL RIGHT.
MOMOI-SAN...
...REALLY CARES ABOUT SHIINA-SAN.
I WISH SHE'D CARE ABOUT ME EVEN JUST A FRACTION AS MUCH.
Tee hee!
Ha Ha!

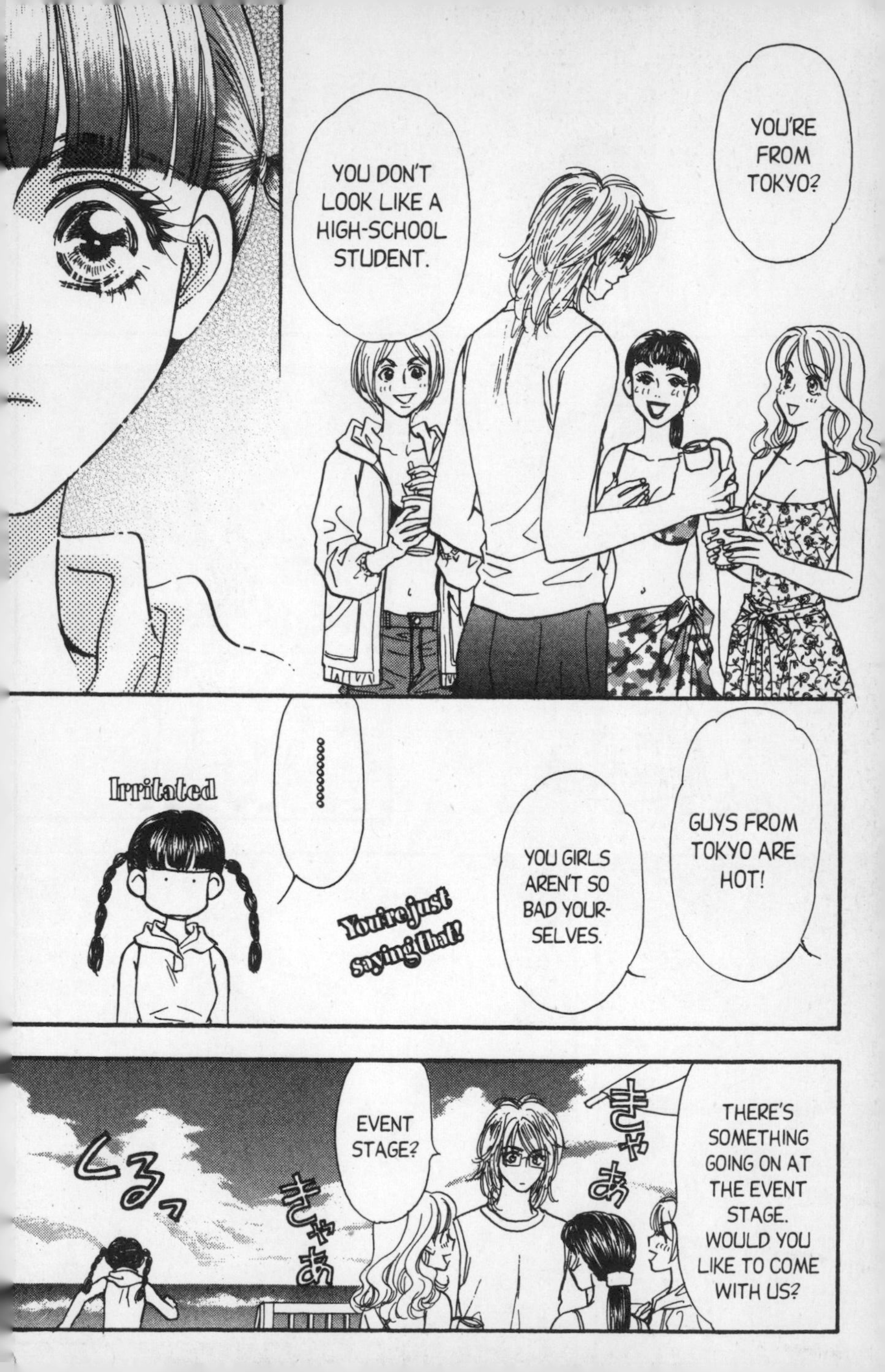
YOU'RE FROM TOKYO?
YOU DON'T LOOK LIKE A HIGH-SCHOOL STUDENT.
GUYS FROM TOKYO ARE HOT!
YOU GIRLS AREN'T SO BAD YOUR-SELVES.
You're just saying that!
....
Irritated
THERE'S SOMETHING GOING ON AT THE EVENT STAGE. WOULD YOU LIKE TO COME WITH US?
きゃあ
EVENT STAGE?
きゃあ
くるっ

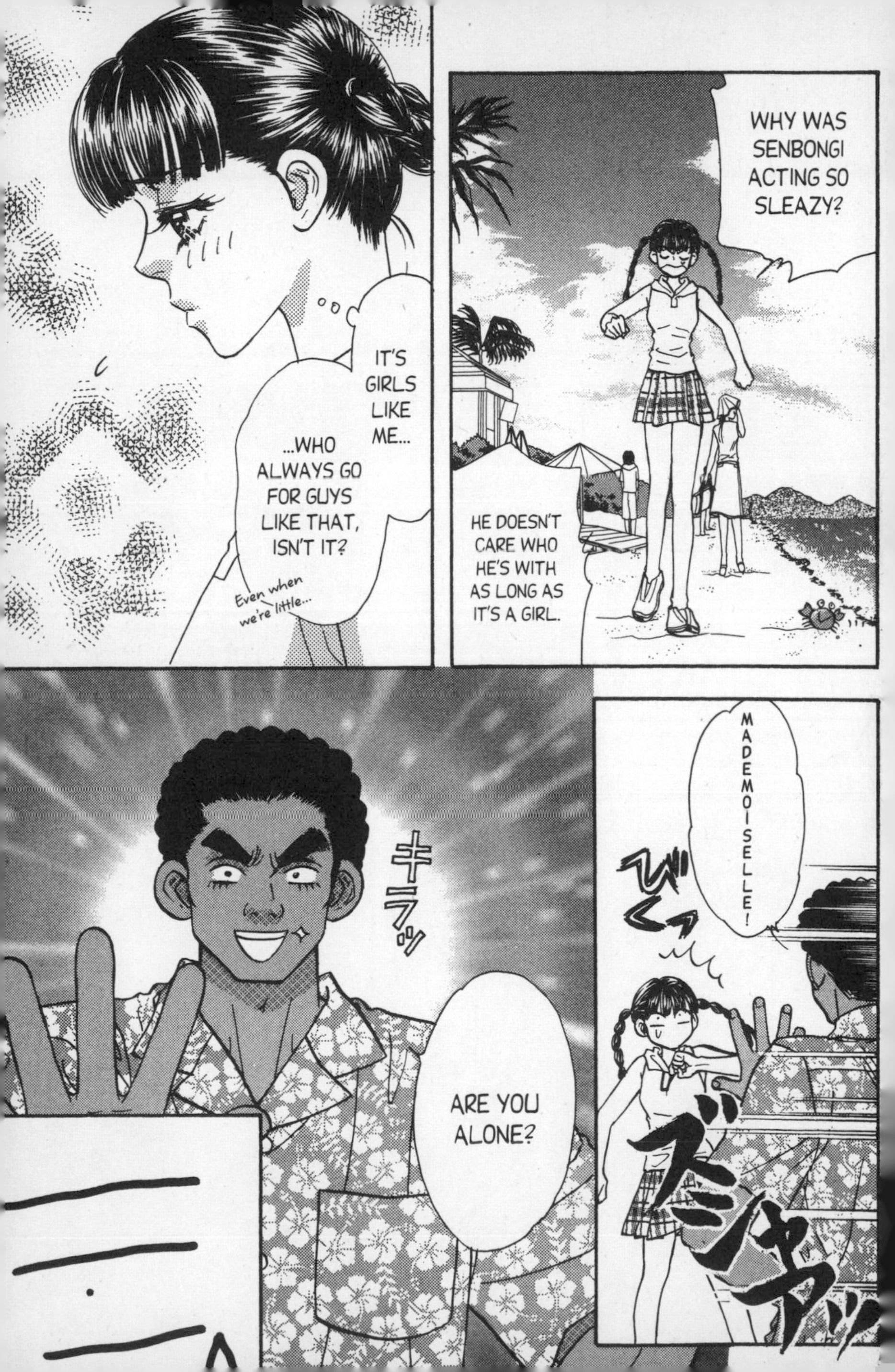

WHY WAS SENBONGI ACTING SO SLEAZY?
HE DOESN'T CARE WHO HE'S WITH AS LONG AS IT'S A GIRL.
IT'S GIRLS LIKE ME...
...WHO ALWAYS GO FOR GUYS LIKE THAT, ISN'T IT?
Even when we're little...
MADEMOISELLE!
キラッ
ARE YOU ALONE?

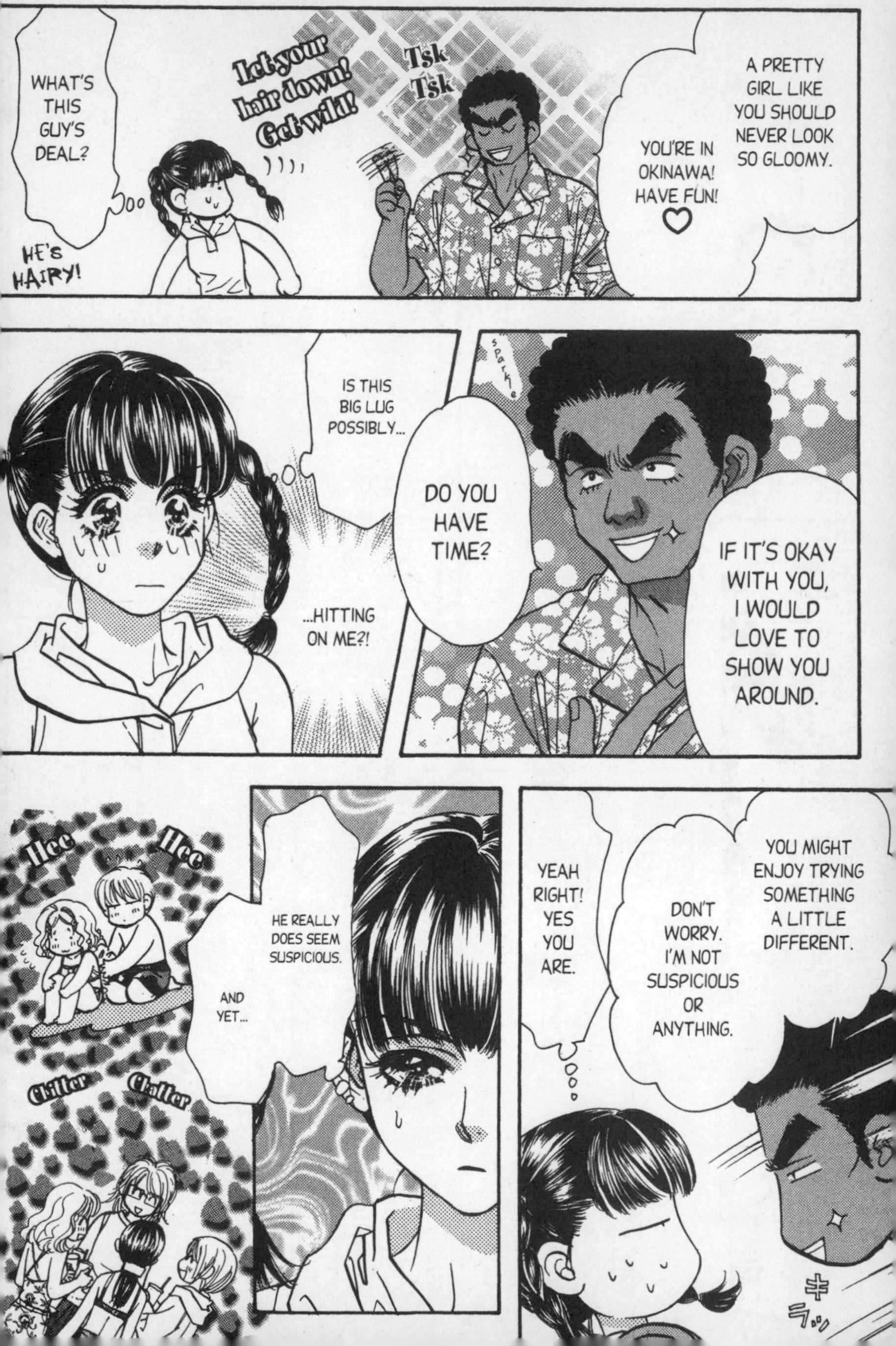
A PRETTY GIRL LIKE YOU SHOULD NEVER LOOK SO GLOOMY.
YOU'RE IN OKINAWA! HAVE FUN! ♡
Tsk Tsk
Let your hair down! Get wild!
WHAT'S THIS GUY'S DEAL?
HE'S HAIRY!
sparkle
IF IT'S OKAY WITH YOU, I WOULD LOVE TO SHOW YOU AROUND.
DO YOU HAVE TIME?
IS THIS BIG LUG POSSIBLY...
...HITTING ON ME?!
YOU MIGHT ENJOY TRYING SOMETHING A LITTLE DIFFERENT.
DON'T WORRY. I'M NOT SUSPICIOUS OR ANYTHING.
YEAH RIGHT! YES YOU ARE.
HE REALLY DOES SEEM SUSPICIOUS.
AND YET...
Hee Hee
Chitter Chatter

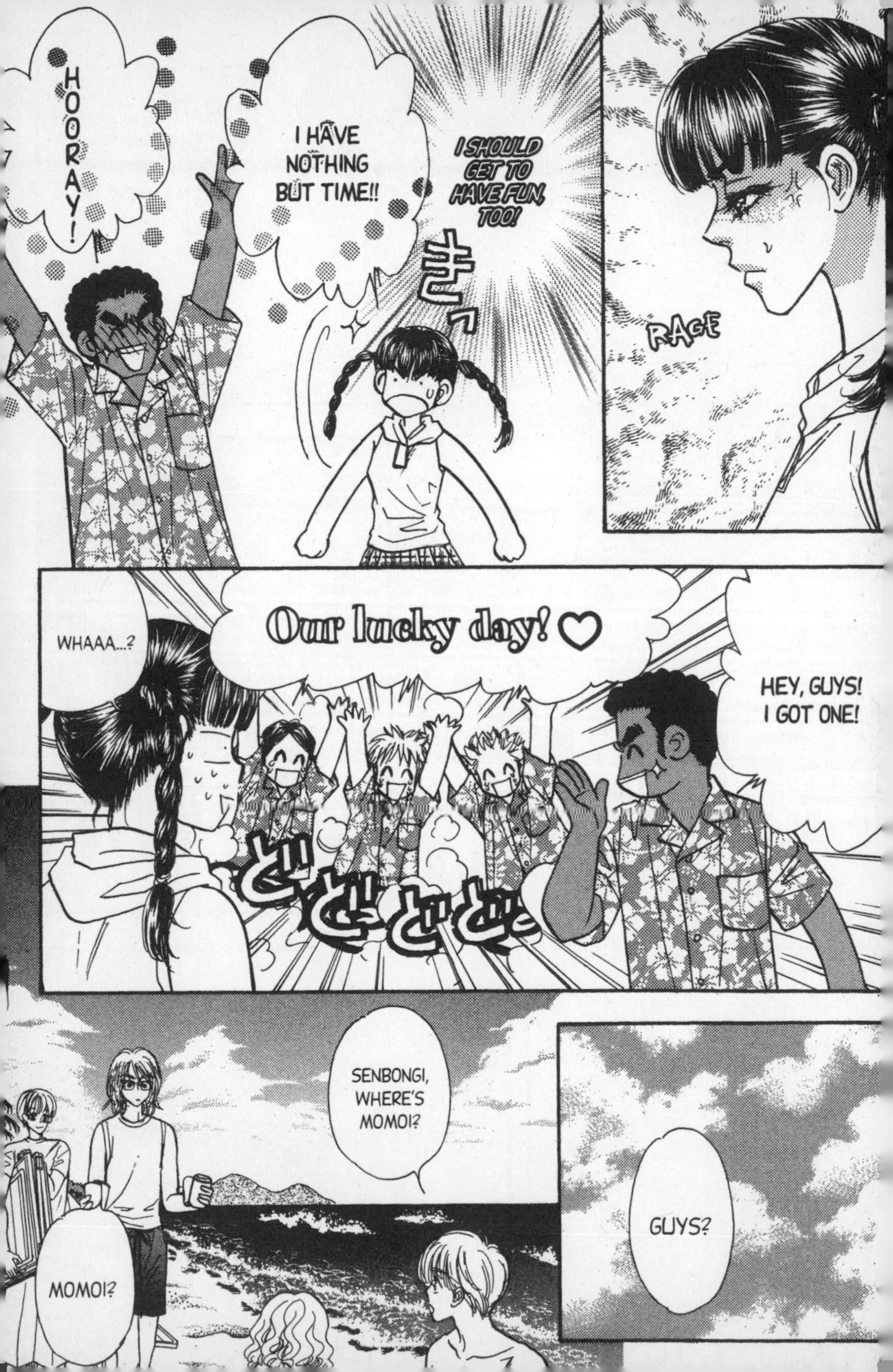
RAGE
I SHOULD GET TO HAVE FUN, TOO!
き
I HAVE NOTHING BUT TIME!!
HOORAY!
HEY, GUYS! I GOT ONE!
Our lucky day! ♡
WHAAA...?
どどどど
GUYS?
SENBONGI, WHERE'S MOMOI?
MOMOI?

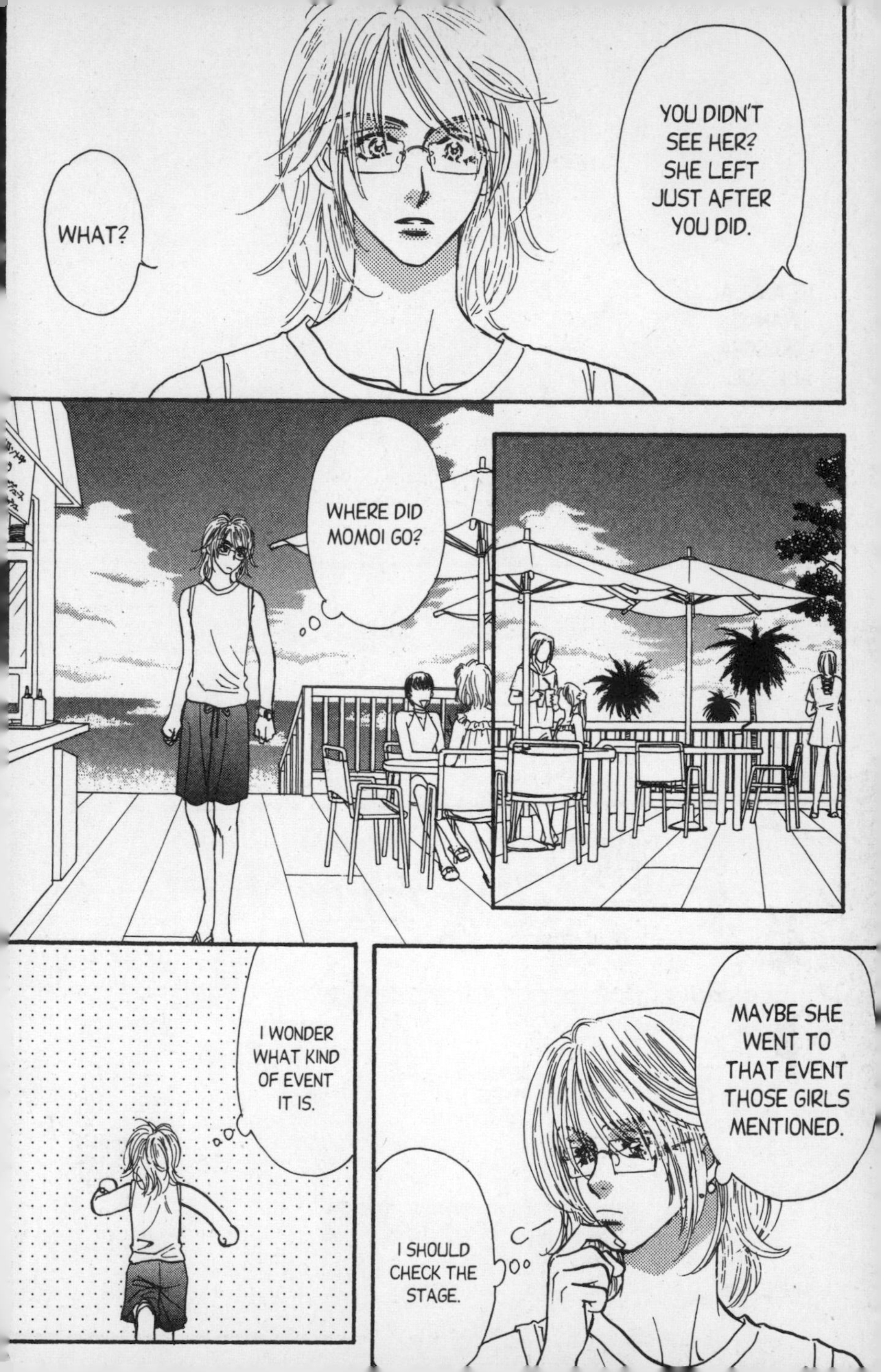
YOU DIDN'T SEE HER? SHE LEFT JUST AFTER YOU DID.
WHAT?
WHERE DID MOMOI GO?
MAYBE SHE WENT TO THAT EVENT THOSE GIRLS MENTIONED.
I SHOULD CHECK THE STAGE.
I WONDER WHAT KIND OF EVENT IT IS.

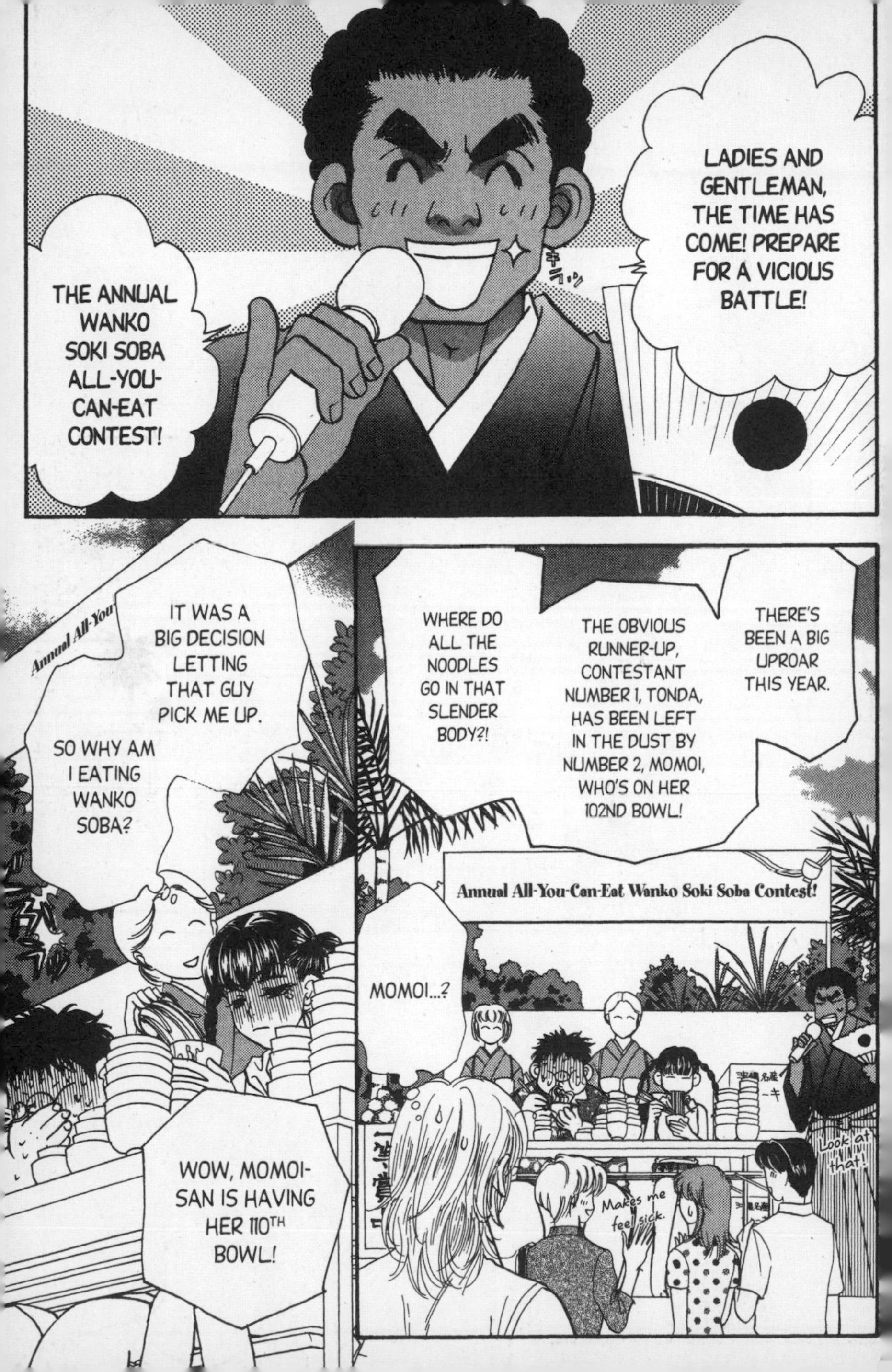

LADIES AND GENTLEMAN, THE TIME HAS COME! PREPARE FOR A VICIOUS BATTLE!
THE ANNUAL WANKO SOKI SOBA ALL-YOU-CAN-EAT CONTEST!
THERE'S BEEN A BIG UPROAR THIS YEAR.
THE OBVIOUS RUNNER-UP, CONTESTANT NUMBER 1, TONDA, HAS BEEN LEFT IN THE DUST BY NUMBER 2, MOMOI, WHO'S ON HER 102ND BOWL!
WHERE DO ALL THE NOODLES GO IN THAT SLENDER BODY?!
Annual All-You-Can-Eat Wanko Soki Soba Contest!
MOMOI...?
Look at that!
Makes me feel sick.
Annual All-You
IT WAS A BIG DECISION LETTING THAT GUY PICK ME UP.
SO WHY AM I EATING WANKO SOBA?
WOW, MOMOI-SAN IS HAVING HER 110TH BOWL!

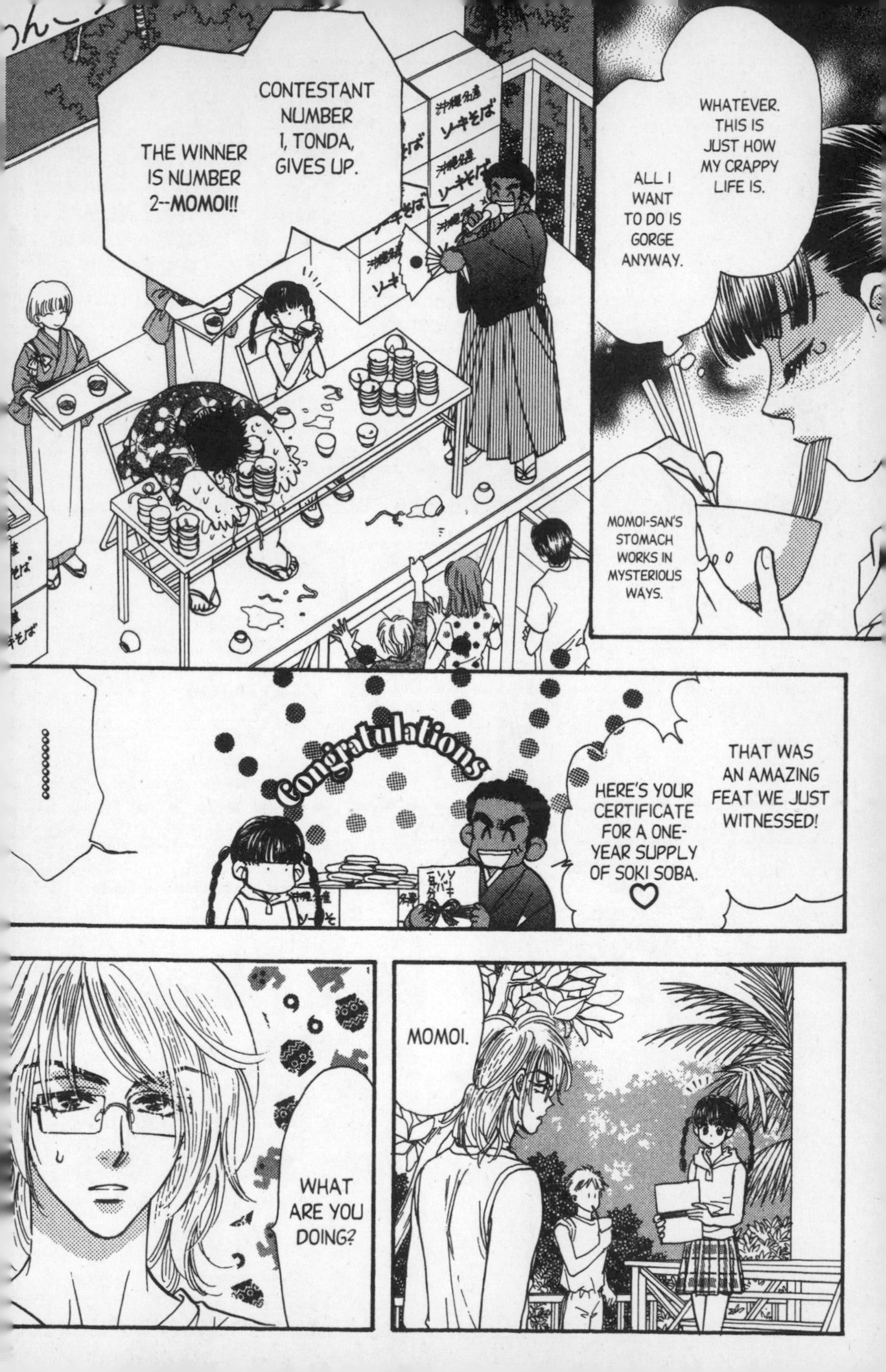
WHATEVER. THIS IS JUST HOW MY CRAPPY LIFE IS.
ALL I WANT TO DO IS GORGE ANYWAY.
MOMOI-SAN'S STOMACH WORKS IN MYSTERIOUS WAYS.
CONTESTANT NUMBER 1, TONDA, GIVES UP.
THE WINNER IS NUMBER 2--MOMOI!!
沖縄名産
ソーキそば
THAT WAS AN AMAZING FEAT WE JUST WITNESSED!
HERE'S YOUR CERTIFICATE FOR A ONE-YEAR SUPPLY OF SOKI SOBA. ♡
Congratulations
OOOOOOOOOOO...
MOMOI.
WHAT ARE YOU DOING?

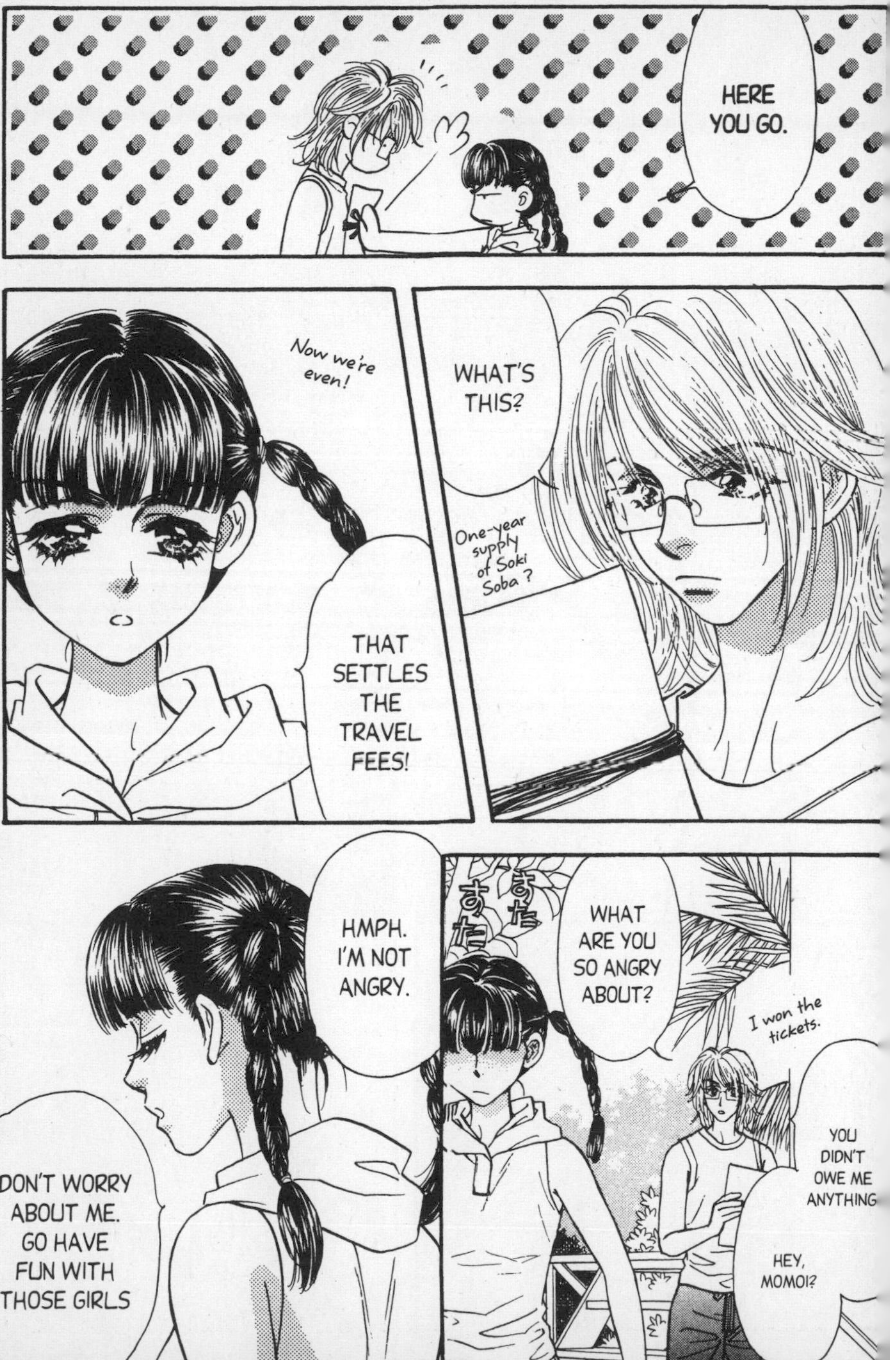
HERE YOU GO.
WHAT'S THIS?
One-year supply of Soki Soba?
Now we're even!
THAT SETTLES THE TRAVEL FEES!
I won the tickets.
YOU DIDN'T OWE ME ANYTHING
HEY, MOMOI?
WHAT ARE YOU SO ANGRY ABOUT?
すたすた
HMPH. I'M NOT ANGRY.
DON'T WORRY ABOUT ME. GO HAVE FUN WITH THOSE GIRLS

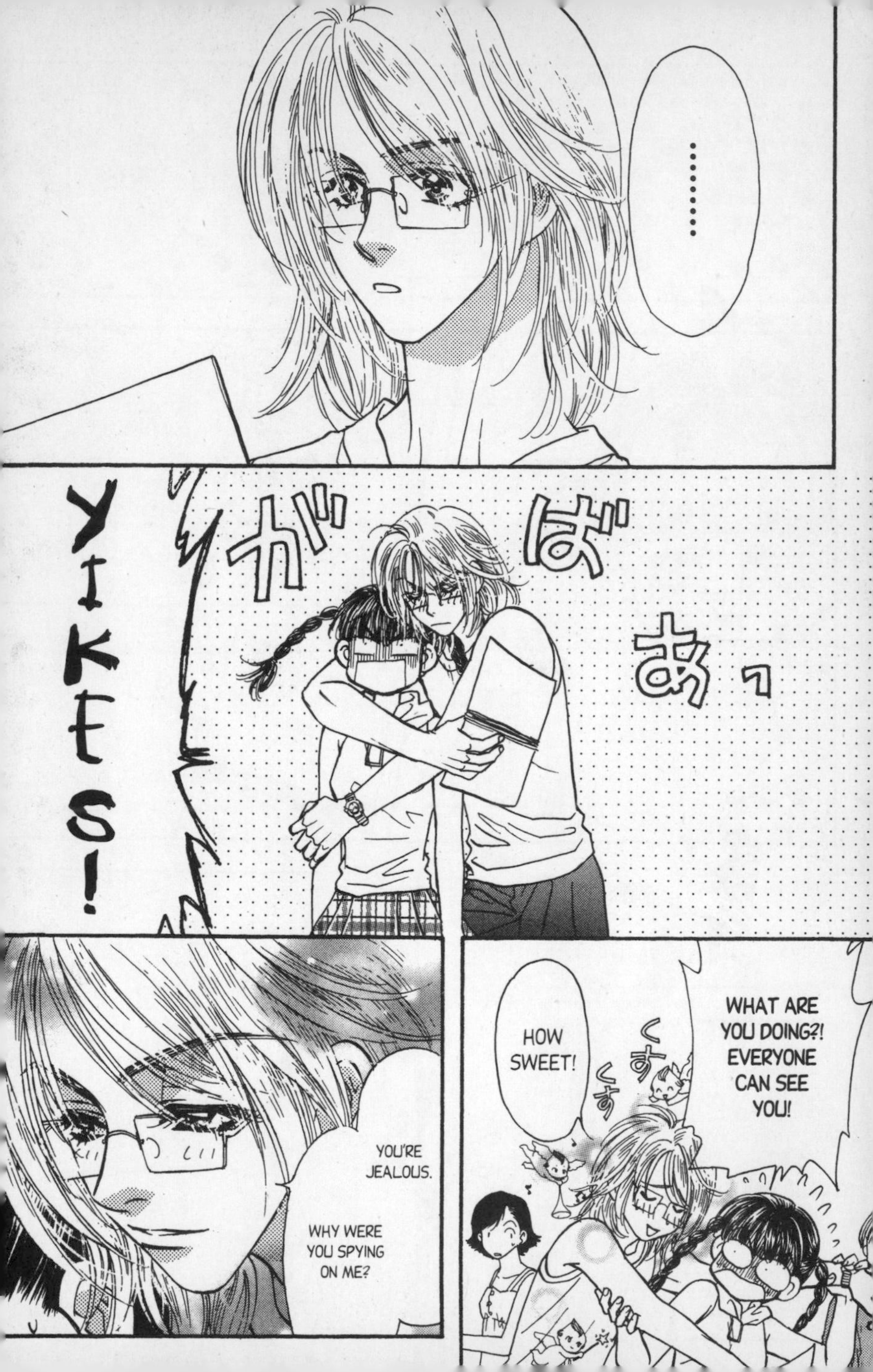
......
がばあっ
YIKES!
WHAT ARE YOU DOING?! EVERYONE CAN SEE YOU!
くすくす
HOW SWEET!
YOU'RE JEALOUS.
WHY WERE YOU SPYING ON ME?

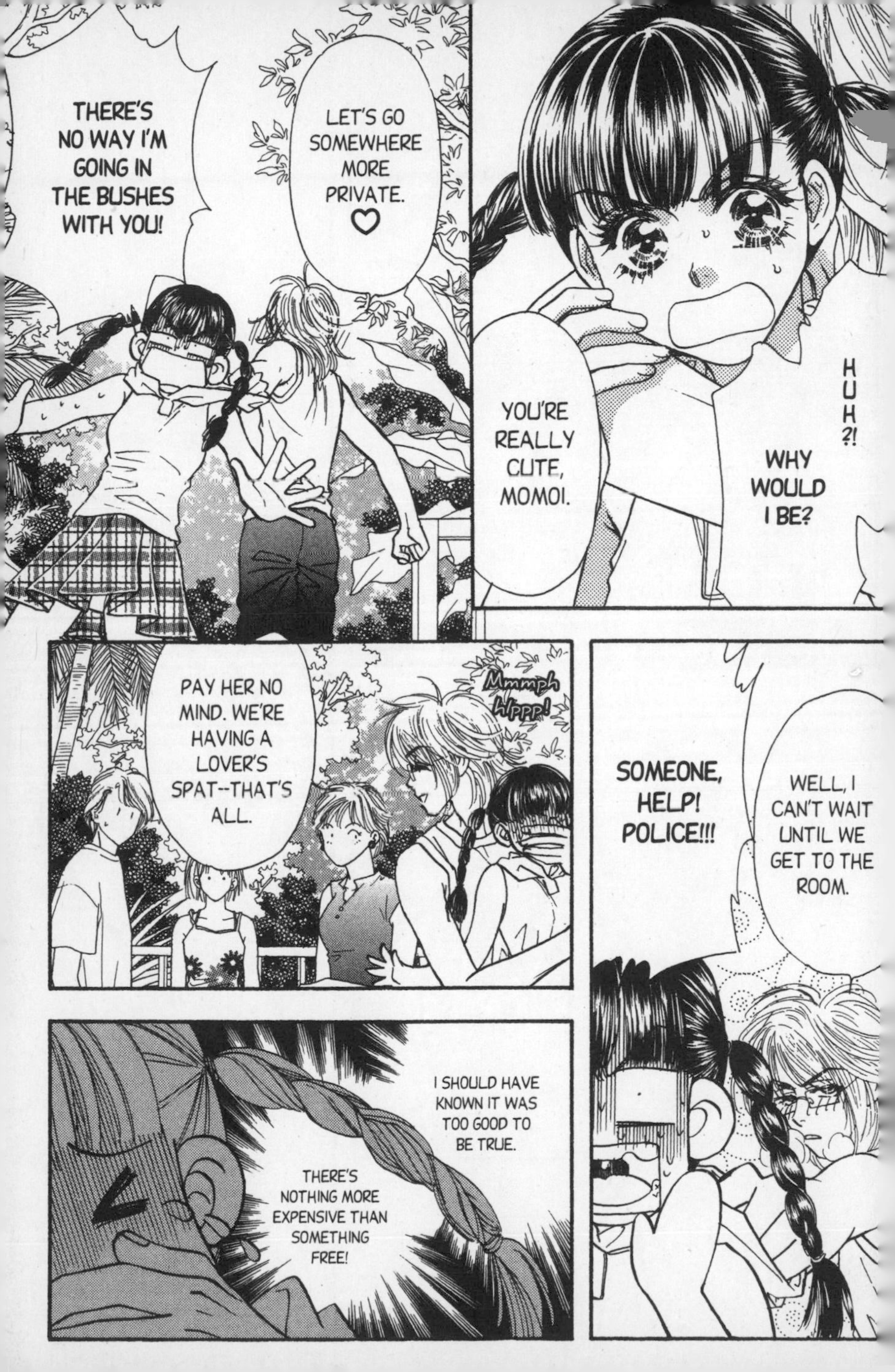

YOU'RE REALLY CUTE, MOMOI.
HUH?!
WHY WOULD I BE?
LET'S GO SOMEWHERE MORE PRIVATE. ♡
THERE'S NO WAY I'M GOING IN THE BUSHES WITH YOU!
WELL, I CAN'T WAIT UNTIL WE GET TO THE ROOM.
SOMEONE, HELP! POLICE!!!
Mmmph hlppp!
PAY HER NO MIND. WE'RE HAVING A LOVER'S SPAT--THAT'S ALL.
I SHOULD HAVE KNOWN IT WAS TOO GOOD TO BE TRUE.
THERE'S NOTHING MORE EXPENSIVE THAN SOMETHING FREE!

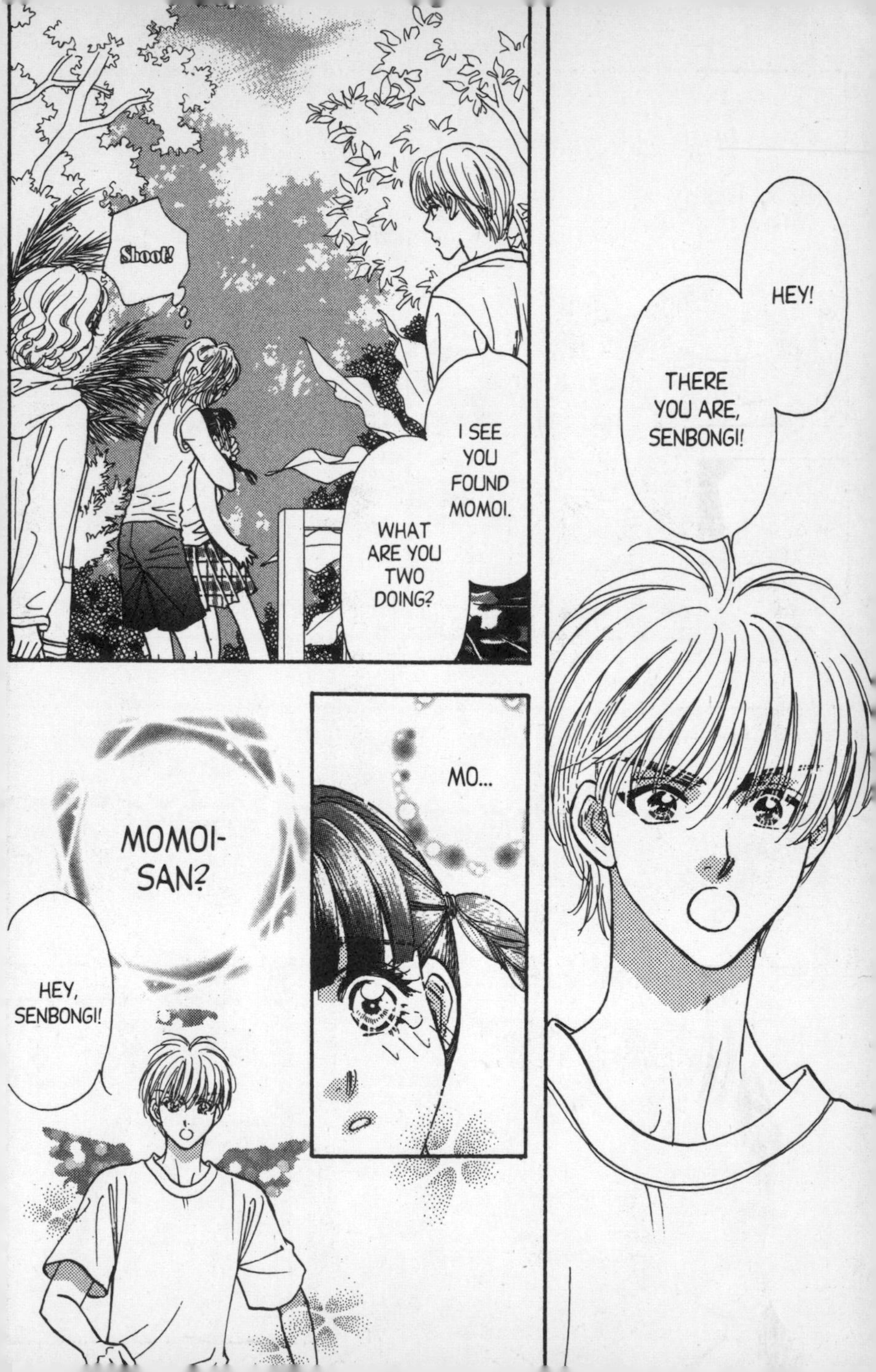
HEY!
THERE YOU ARE, SENBONGI!
I SEE YOU FOUND MOMOI.
WHAT ARE YOU TWO DOING?
Shoot!
MO...
MOMOI-SAN?
HEY, SENBONGI!

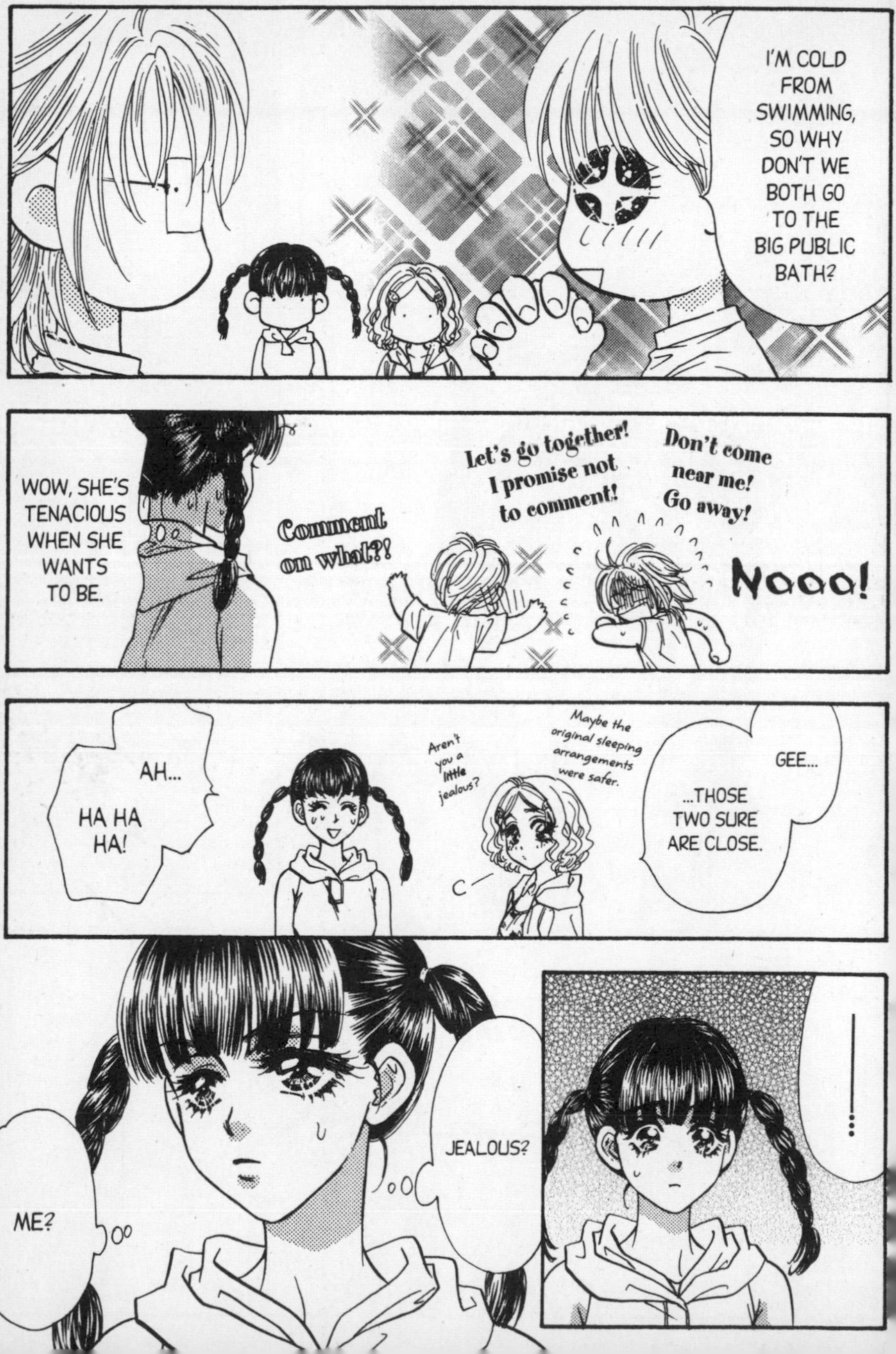
I'M COLD FROM SWIMMING, SO WHY DON'T WE BOTH GO TO THE BIG PUBLIC BATH?
Naaa!
Don't come near me! Go away!
Let's go together! I promise not to comment!
Comment on what?!
WOW, SHE'S TENACIOUS WHEN SHE WANTS TO BE.
GEE...
...THOSE TWO SURE ARE CLOSE.
Maybe the original sleeping arrangements were safer.
Aren't you a little jealous?
AH...
HA HA HA!
JEALOUS?
ME?

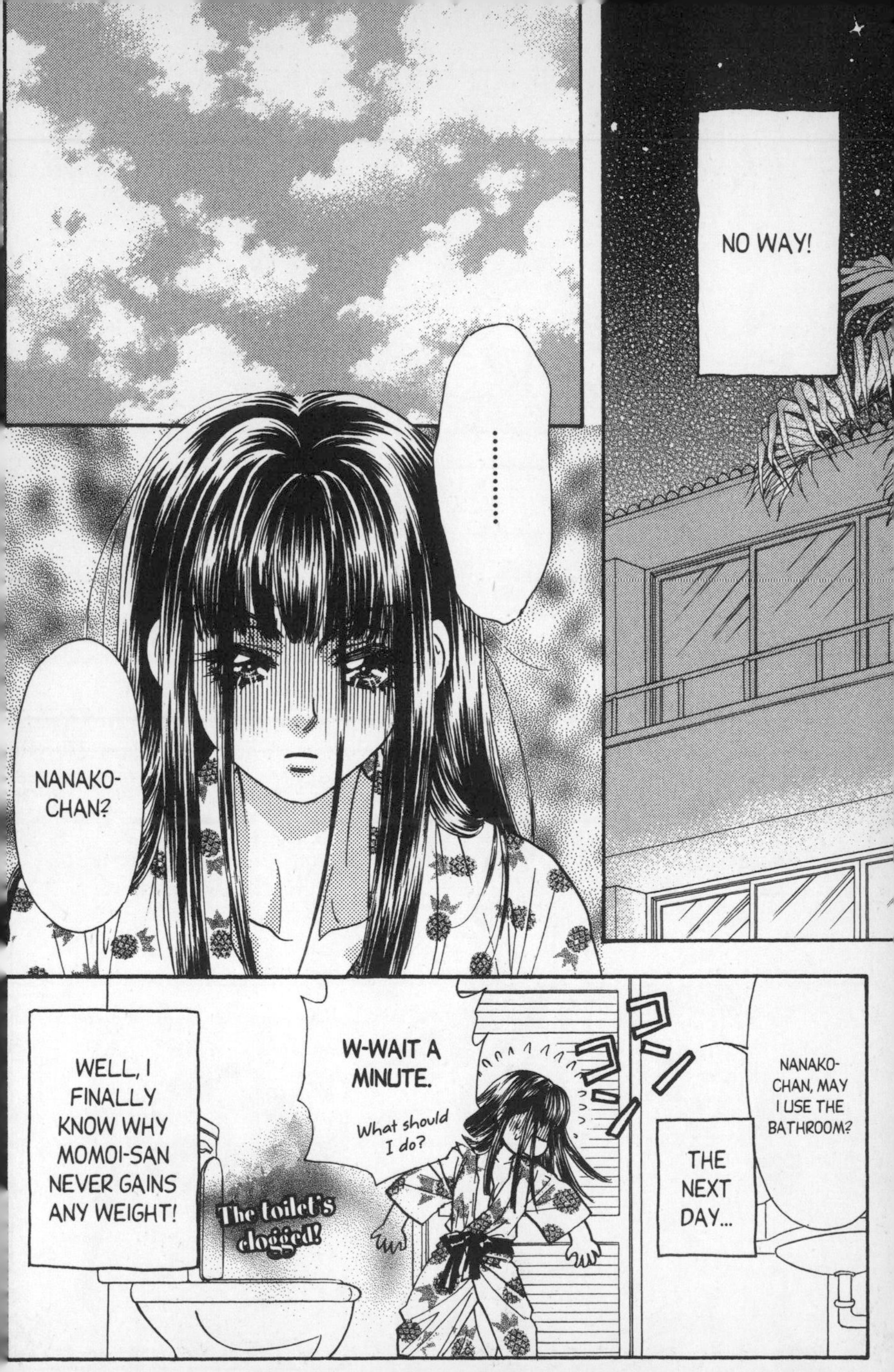
NO WAY!
......
NANAKO-CHAN?
NANAKO-CHAN, MAY I USE THE BATHROOM?
THE NEXT DAY...
W-WAIT A MINUTE.
What should I do?
The toilet's clogged!
WELL, I FINALLY KNOW WHY MOMOI-SAN NEVER GAINS ANY WEIGHT!

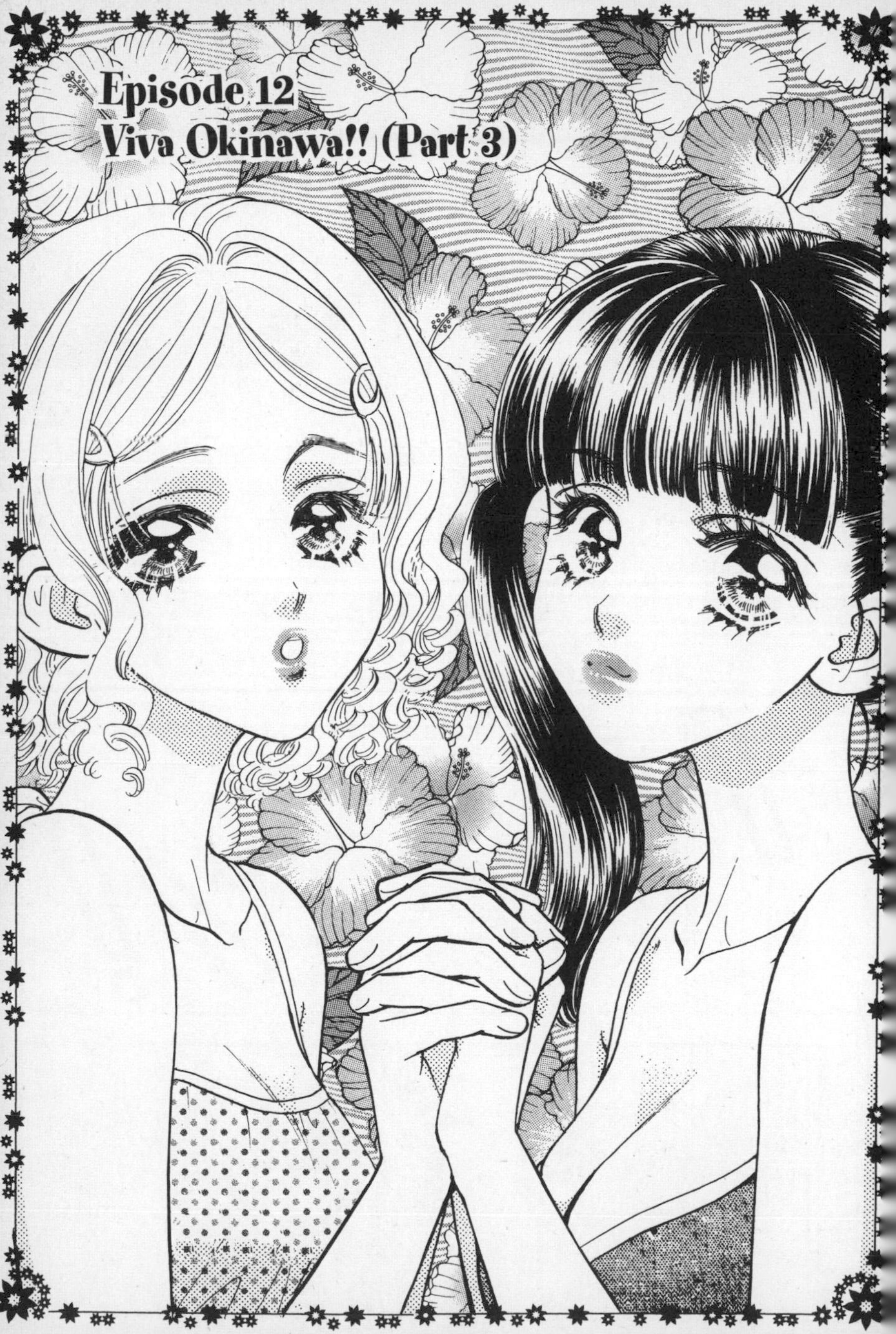
Episode 12
Viva Okinawa!! (Part 3)

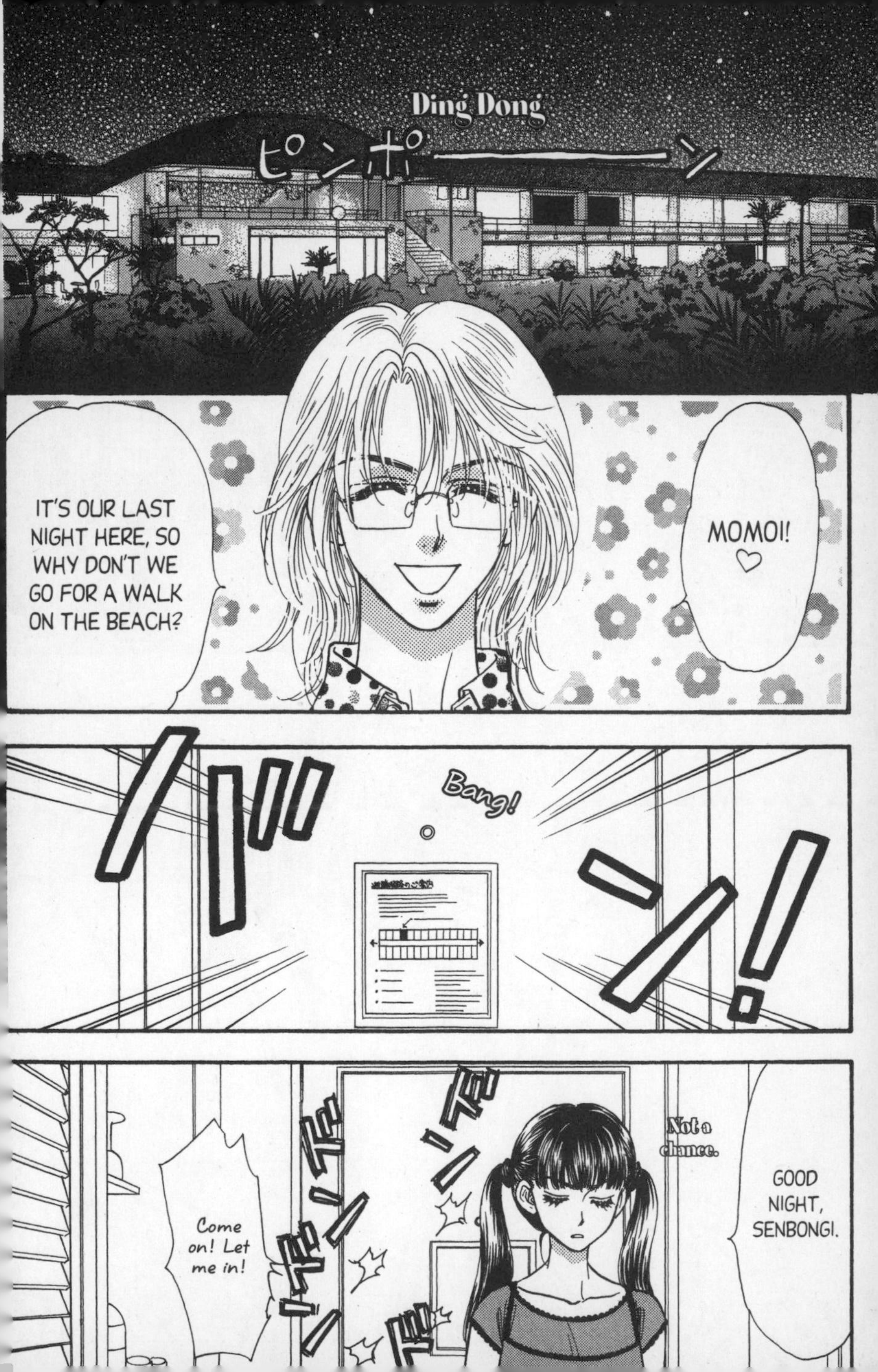
Ding Dong
ピンポーーン
MOMOI! ♡
IT'S OUR LAST NIGHT HERE, SO WHY DON'T WE GO FOR A WALK ON THE BEACH?
Bang!
GOOD NIGHT, SENBONGI.
Not a chance.
Come on! Let me in!

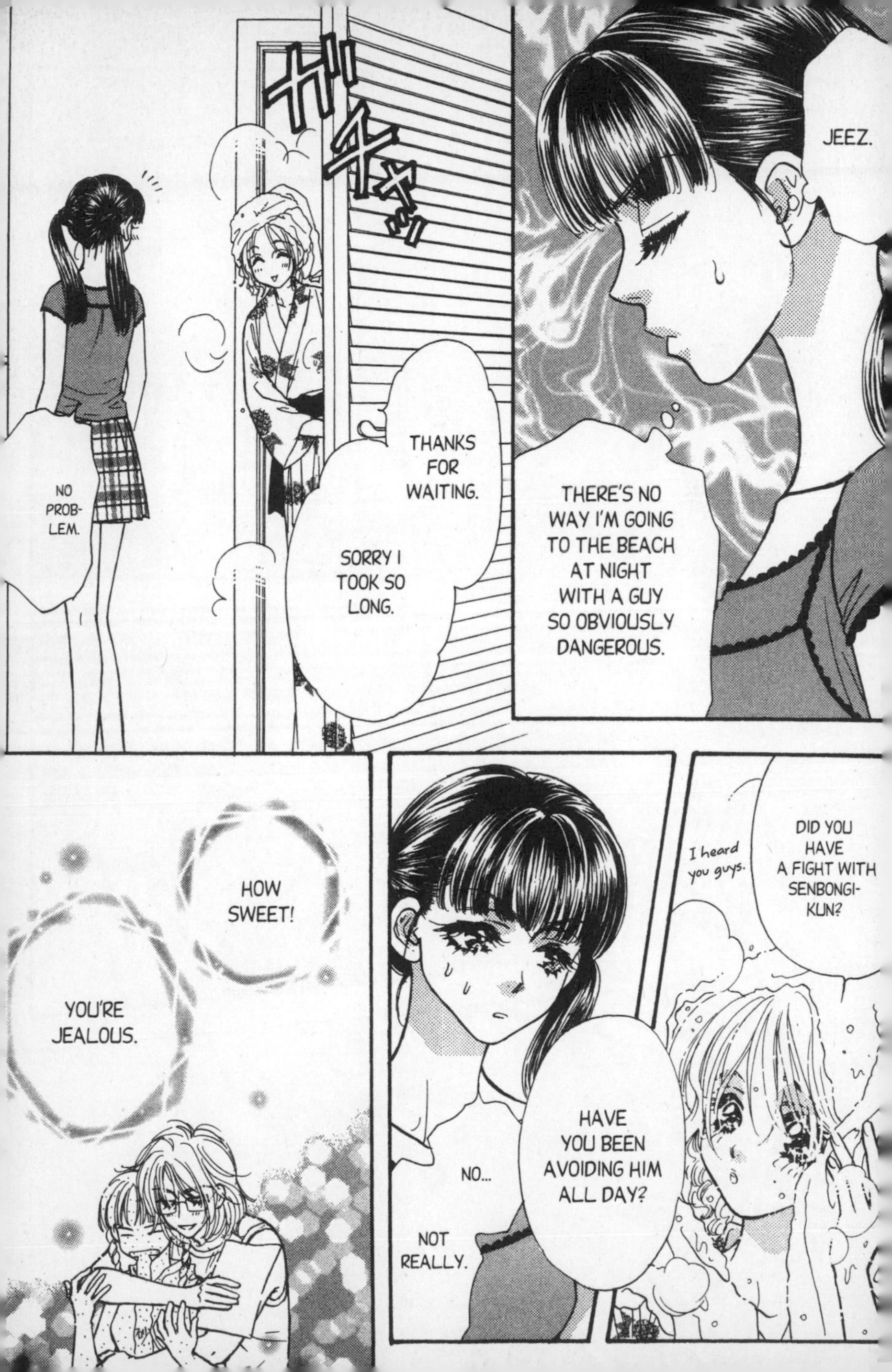
JEEZ.
THERE'S NO WAY I'M GOING TO THE BEACH AT NIGHT WITH A GUY SO OBVIOUSLY DANGEROUS.
THANKS FOR WAITING.
SORRY I TOOK SO LONG.
NO PROB-LEM.
DID YOU HAVE A FIGHT WITH SENBONGI-KUN?
I heard you guys.
HAVE YOU BEEN AVOIDING HIM ALL DAY?
NO...
NOT REALLY.
HOW SWEET!
YOU'RE JEALOUS.

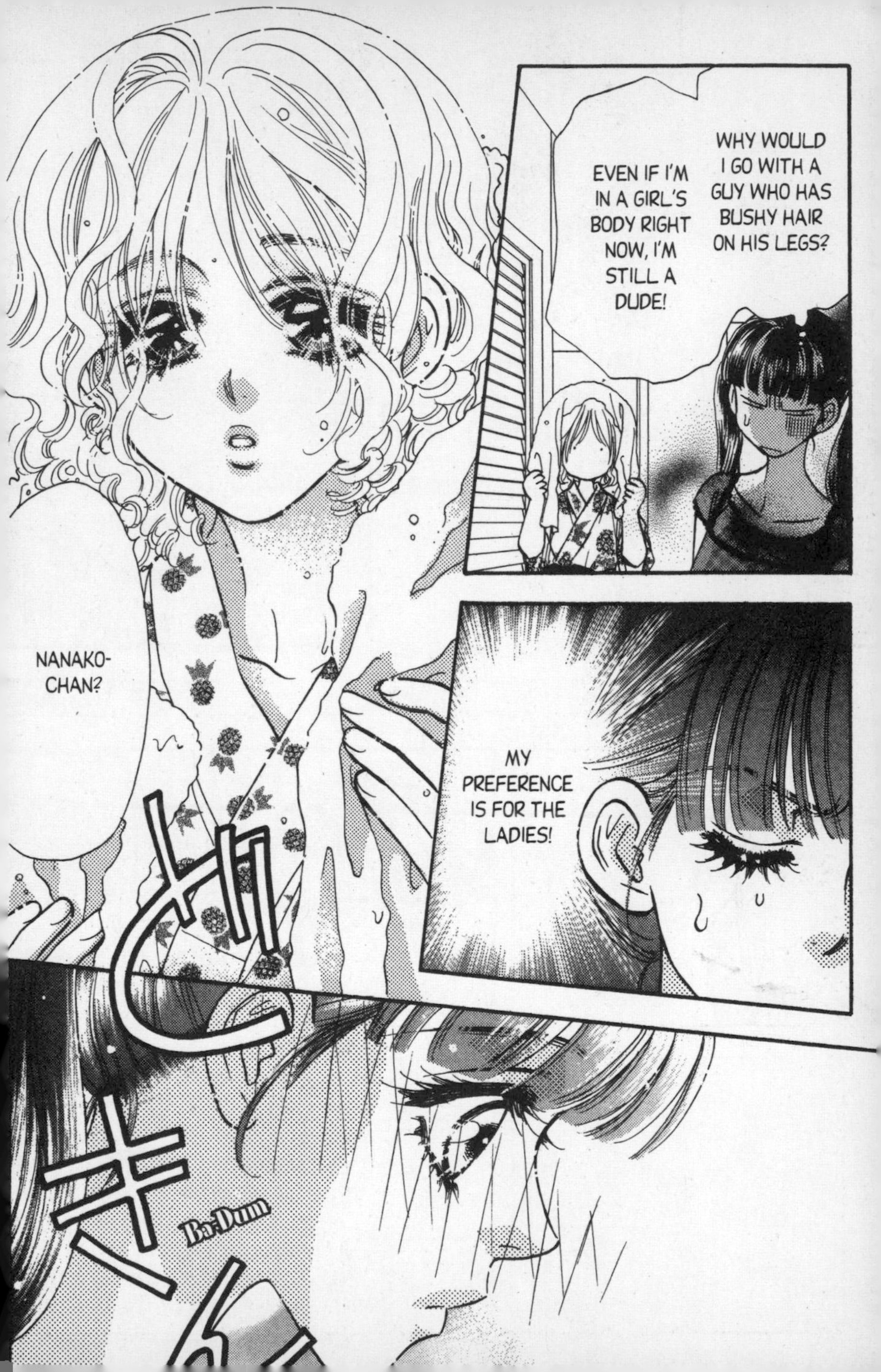
WHY WOULD I GO WITH A GUY WHO HAS BUSHY HAIR ON HIS LEGS?
EVEN IF I'M IN A GIRL'S BODY RIGHT NOW, I'M STILL A DUDE!
MY PREFERENCE IS FOR THE LADIES!
NANAKO-CHAN?
Ba-Dum

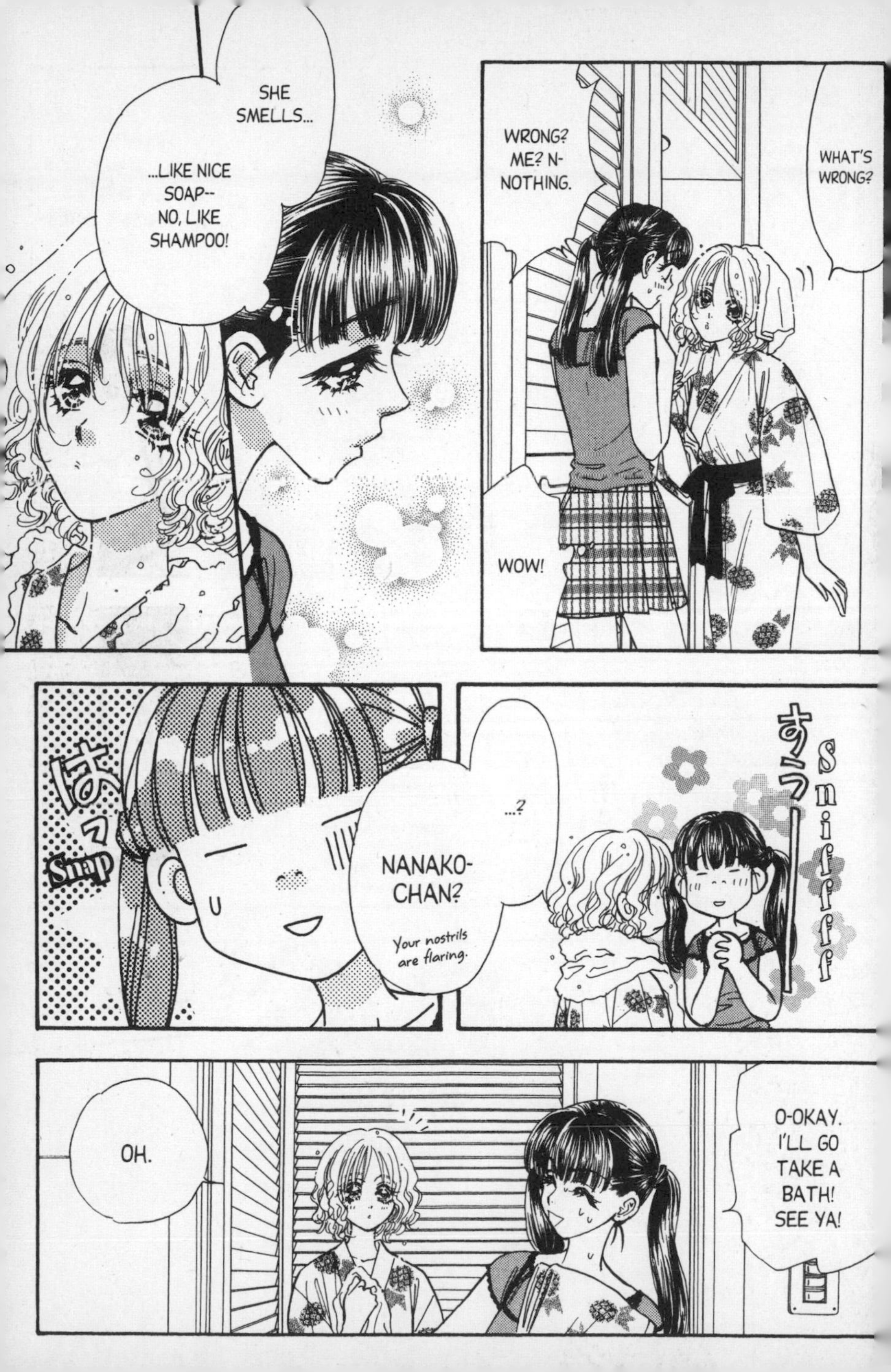
WHAT'S WRONG?
WRONG? ME? N-NOTHING.
WOW!
SHE SMELLS...
...LIKE NICE SOAP-- NO, LIKE SHAMPOO!
すう
Sniffff
...?
NANAKO-CHAN?
Your nostrils are flaring.
はっ
Snap
O-OKAY. I'LL GO TAKE A BATH! SEE YA!
OH.

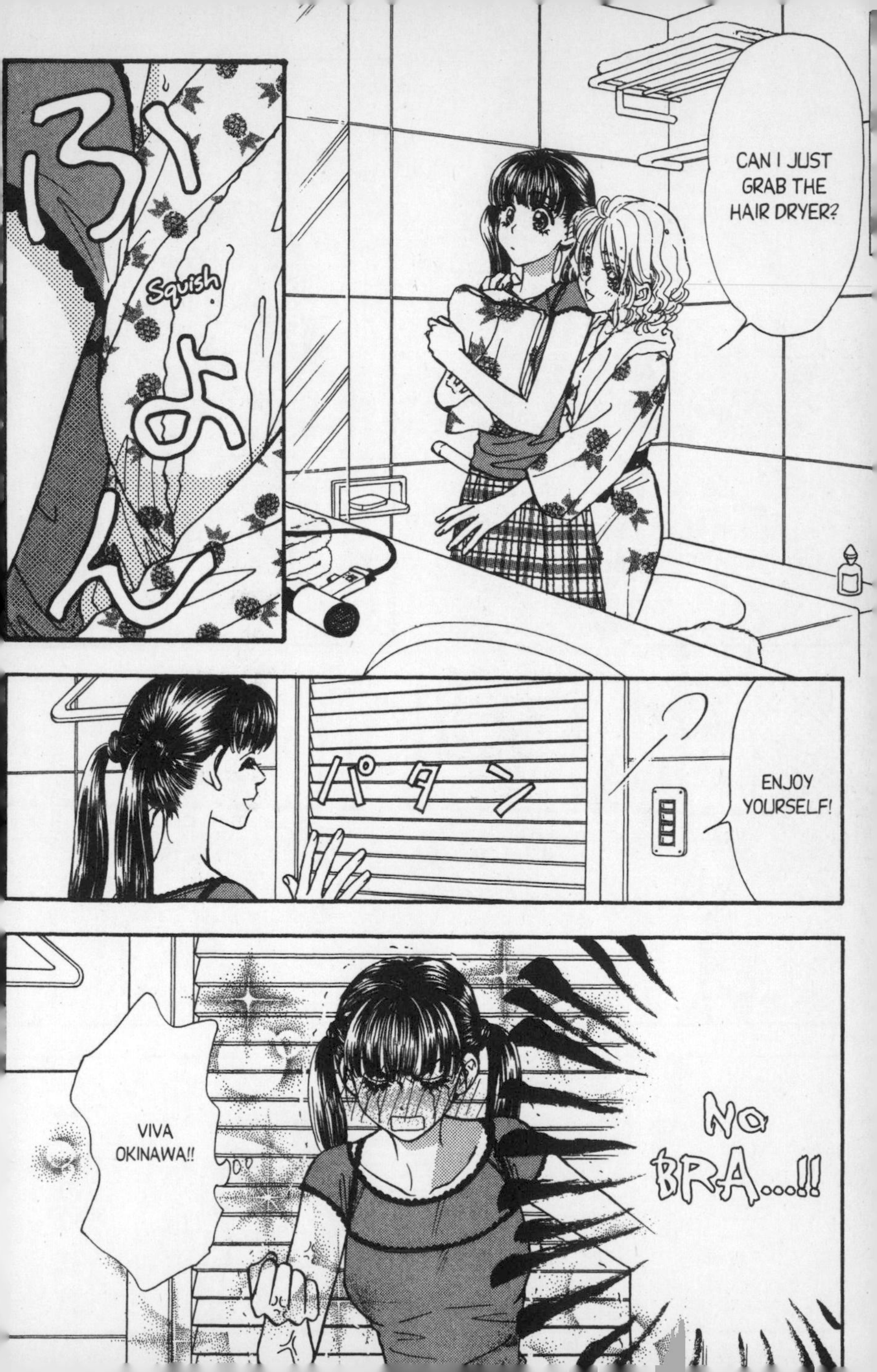
CAN I JUST GRAB THE HAIR DRYER?
ふよん
Squish
パタン
ENJOY YOURSELF!
No BRA...!!
VIVA OKINAWA!!

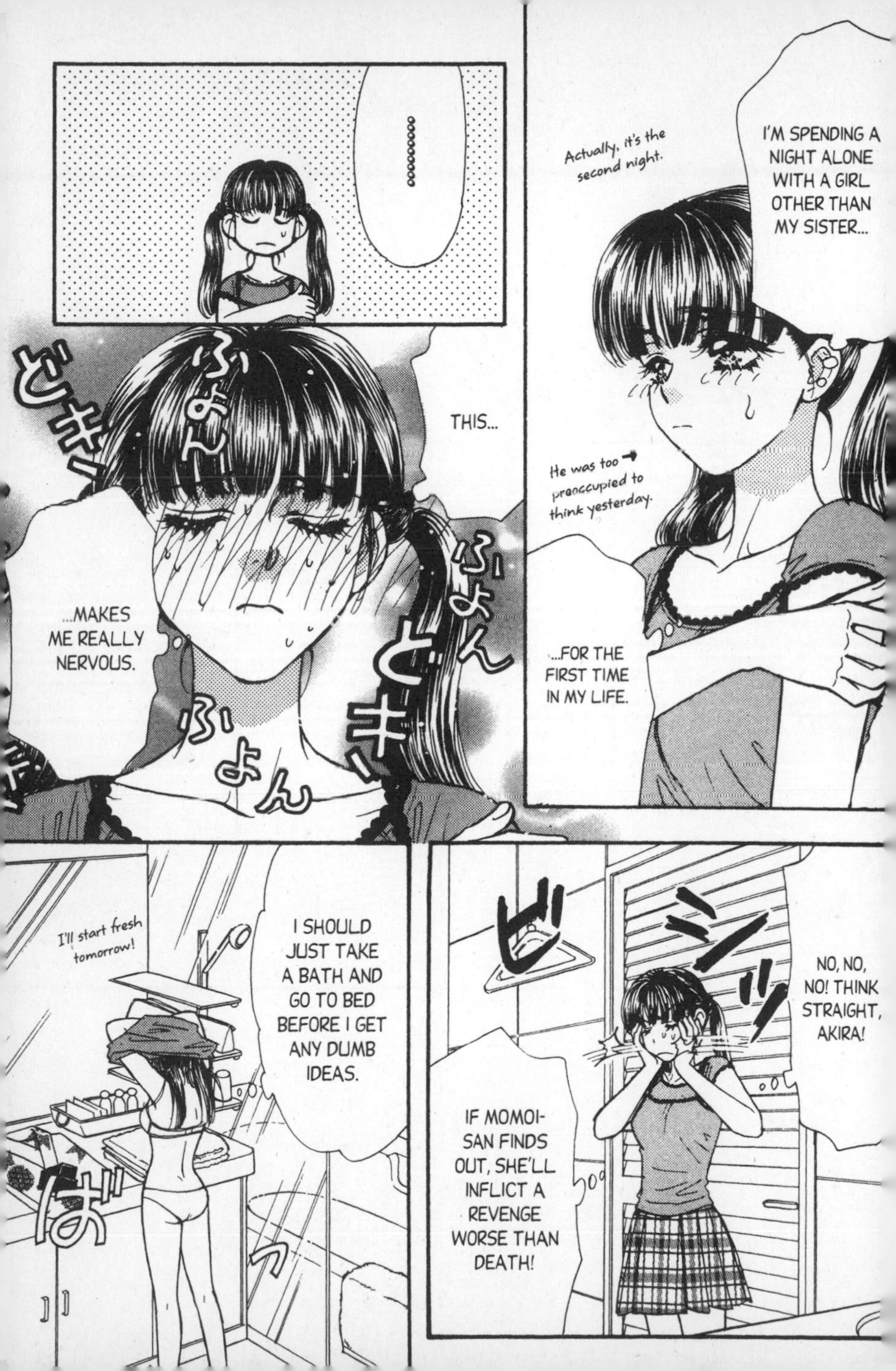
I'M SPENDING A NIGHT ALONE WITH A GIRL OTHER THAN MY SISTER...
Actually, it's the second night.
He was too preoccupied to think yesterday.
...FOR THE FIRST TIME IN MY LIFE.
....
THIS...
...MAKES ME REALLY NERVOUS.
ふよん
ふよん
どき
ふよん
ビ
シッ
NO, NO, NO! THINK STRAIGHT, AKIRA!
IF MOMOI-SAN FINDS OUT, SHE'LL INFLICT A REVENGE WORSE THAN DEATH!
I SHOULD JUST TAKE A BATH AND GO TO BED BEFORE I GET ANY DUMB IDEAS.
I'll start fresh tomorrow!
ばっ

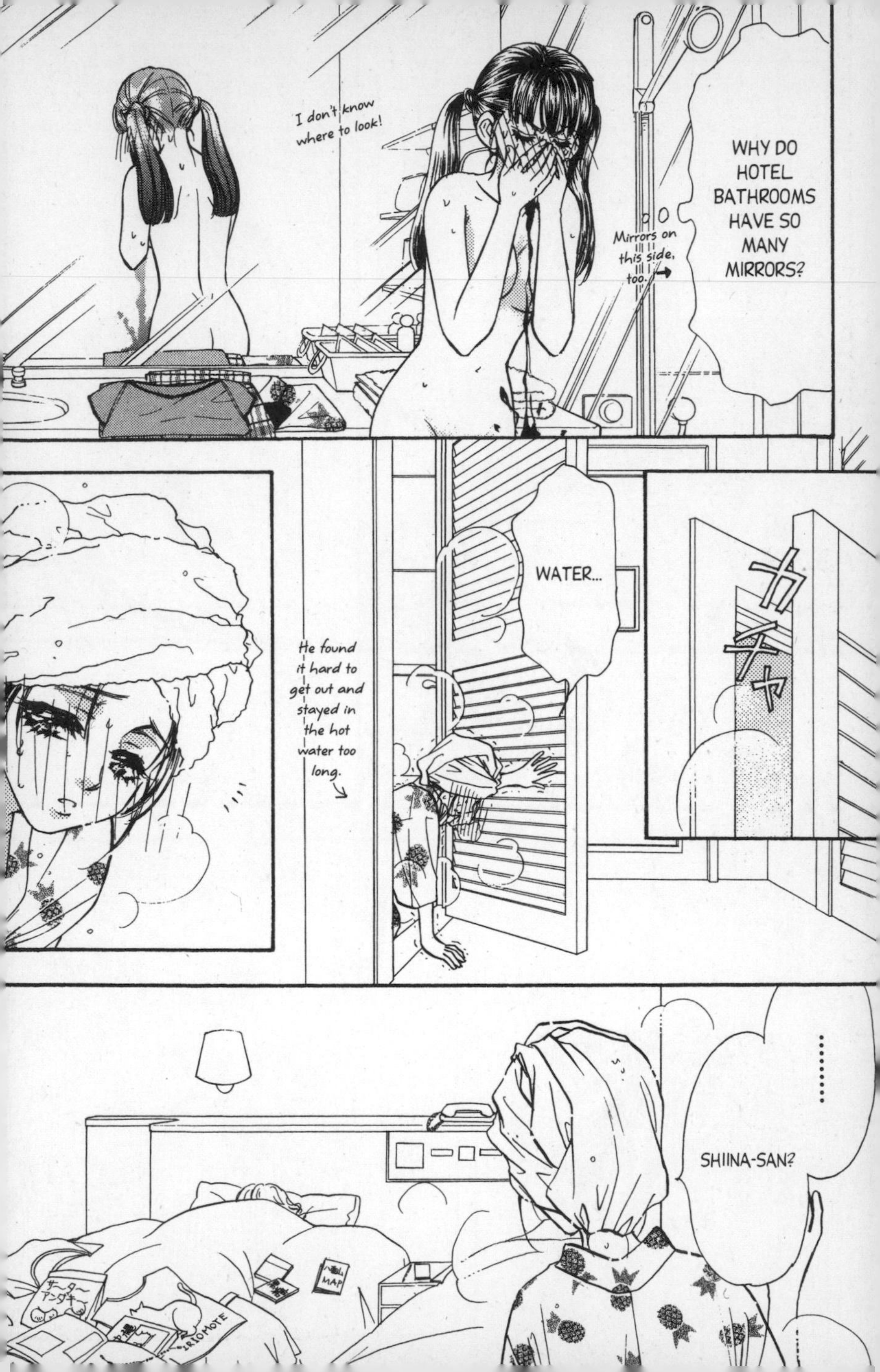
WHY DO HOTEL BATHROOMS HAVE SO MANY MIRRORS?
Mirrors on this side, too.
I don't know where to look!
カチャ
WATER...
He found it hard to get out and stayed in the hot water too long.
......
SHIINA-SAN?
サーターアンダギー
MAP
IRIOMOTE

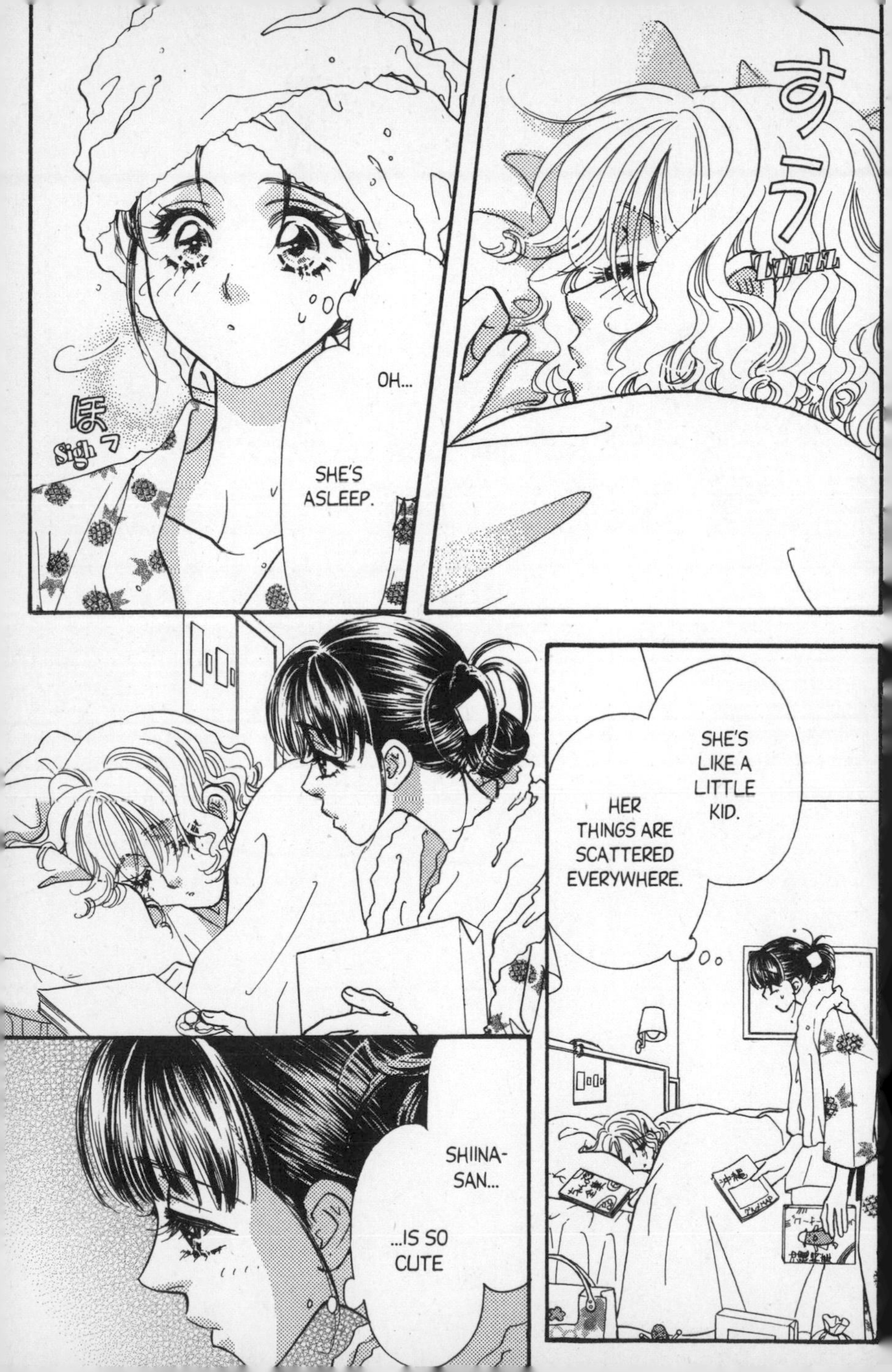
すう
Zzzzz
OH...
SHE'S ASLEEP.
ほっ
Sigh
SHE'S LIKE A LITTLE KID.
HER THINGS ARE SCATTERED EVERYWHERE.
SHIINA-SAN...
...IS SO CUTE

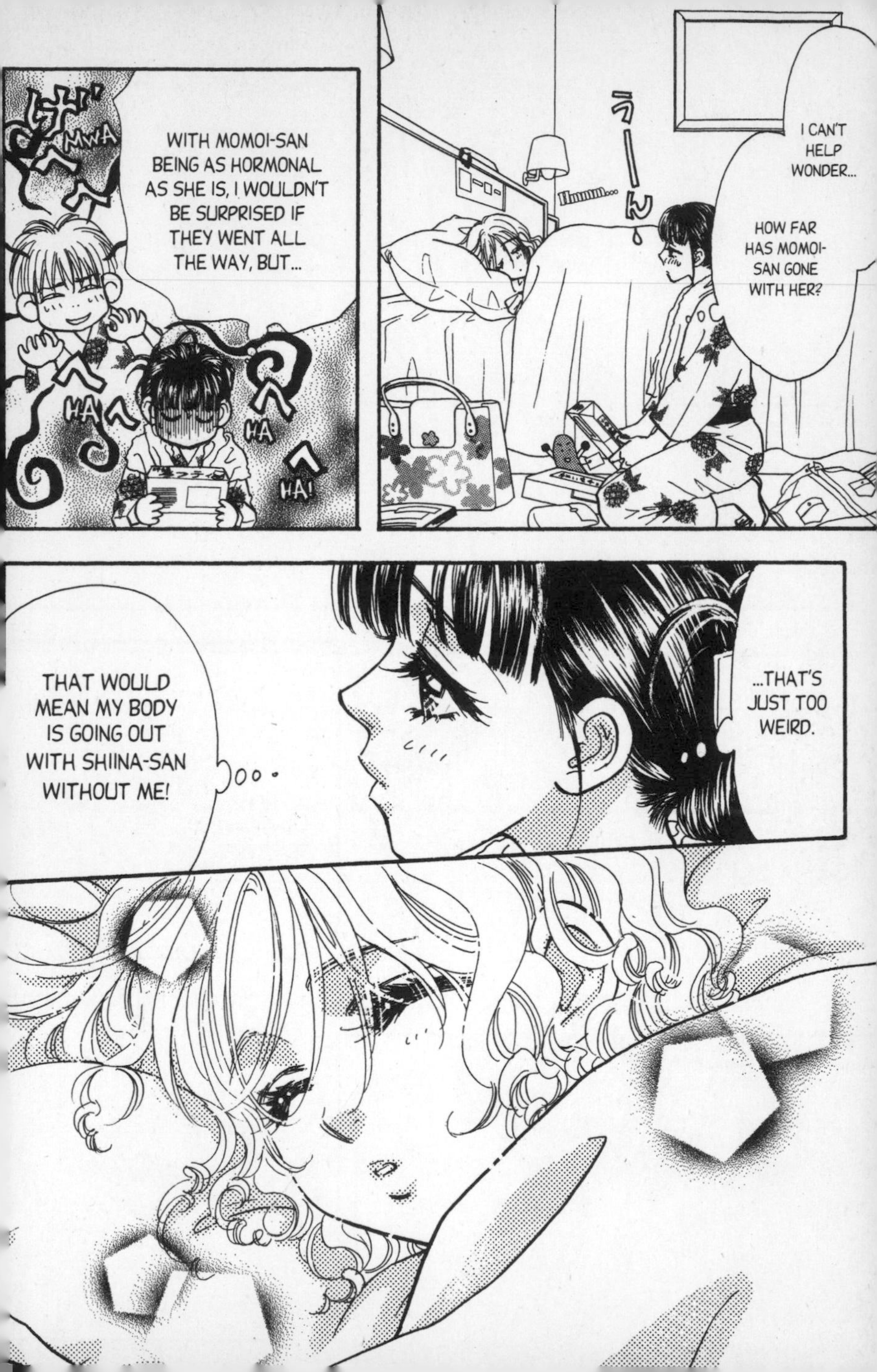
I CAN'T HELP WONDER...
HOW FAR HAS MOMOI-SAN GONE WITH HER?
Hmmm...
WITH MOMOI-SAN BEING AS HORMONAL AS SHE IS, I WOULDN'T BE SURPRISED IF THEY WENT ALL THE WAY, BUT...
MWA
HA
HA
HA!
THAT WOULD MEAN MY BODY IS GOING OUT WITH SHIINA-SAN WITHOUT ME!
...THAT'S JUST TOO WEIRD.

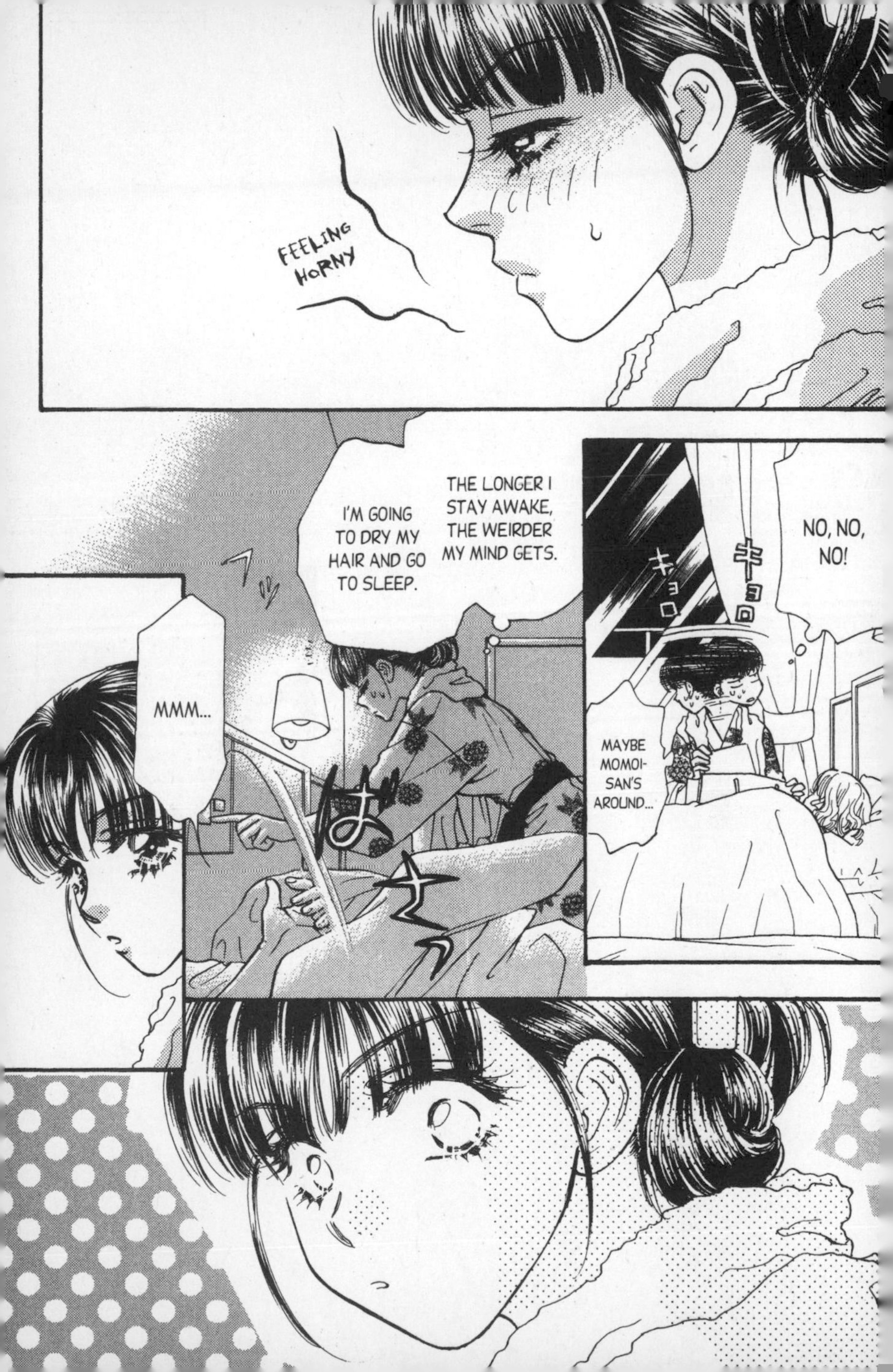
FEELING HORNY
NO, NO, NO!
キョロ
キョロ
MAYBE MOMOI-SAN'S AROUND...
THE LONGER I STAY AWAKE, THE WEIRDER MY MIND GETS.
I'M GOING TO DRY MY HAIR AND GO TO SLEEP.
はっ
MMM...

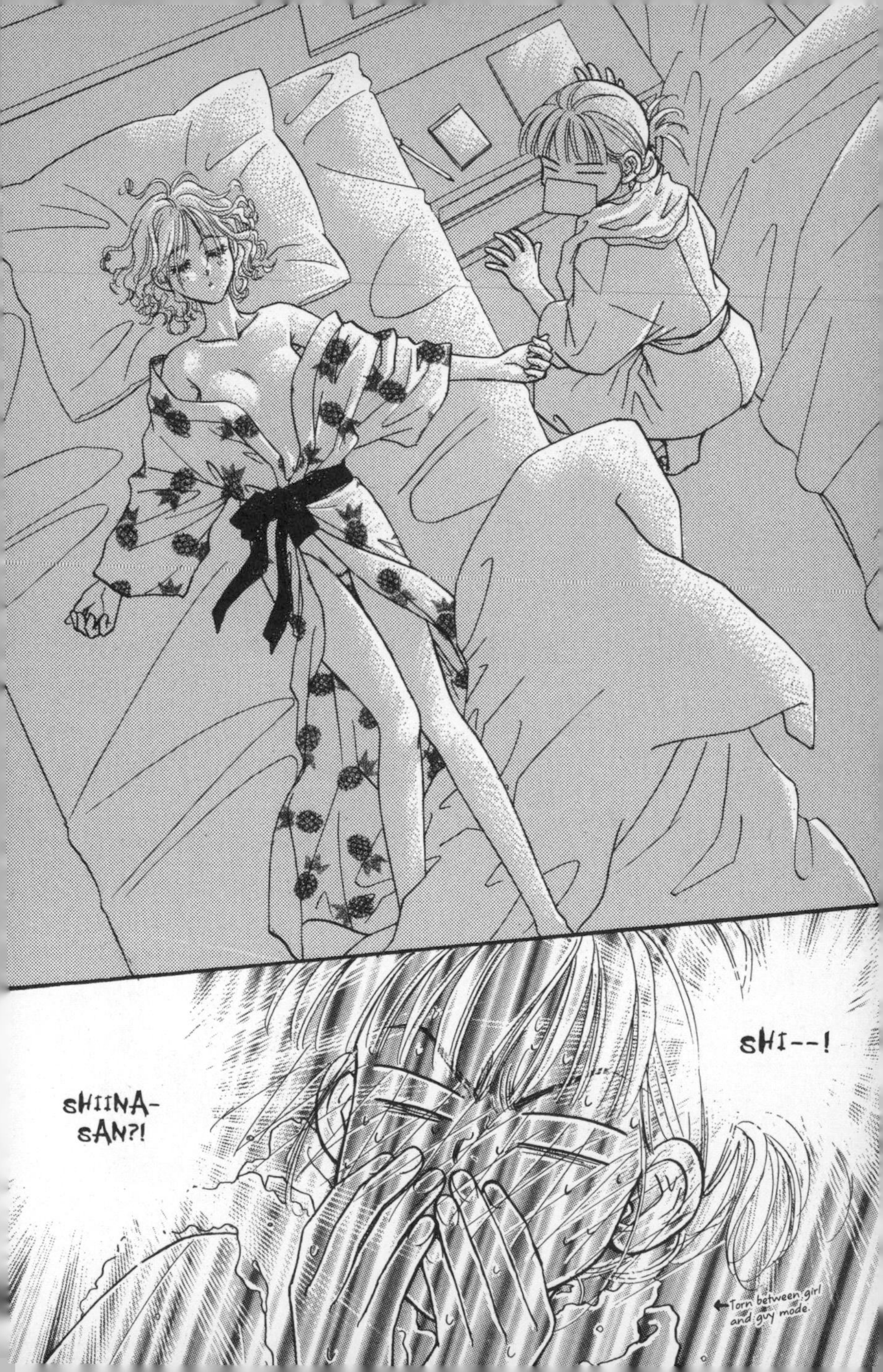
SHI--!
SHIINA-SAN?!
←Torn between girl and guy mode.

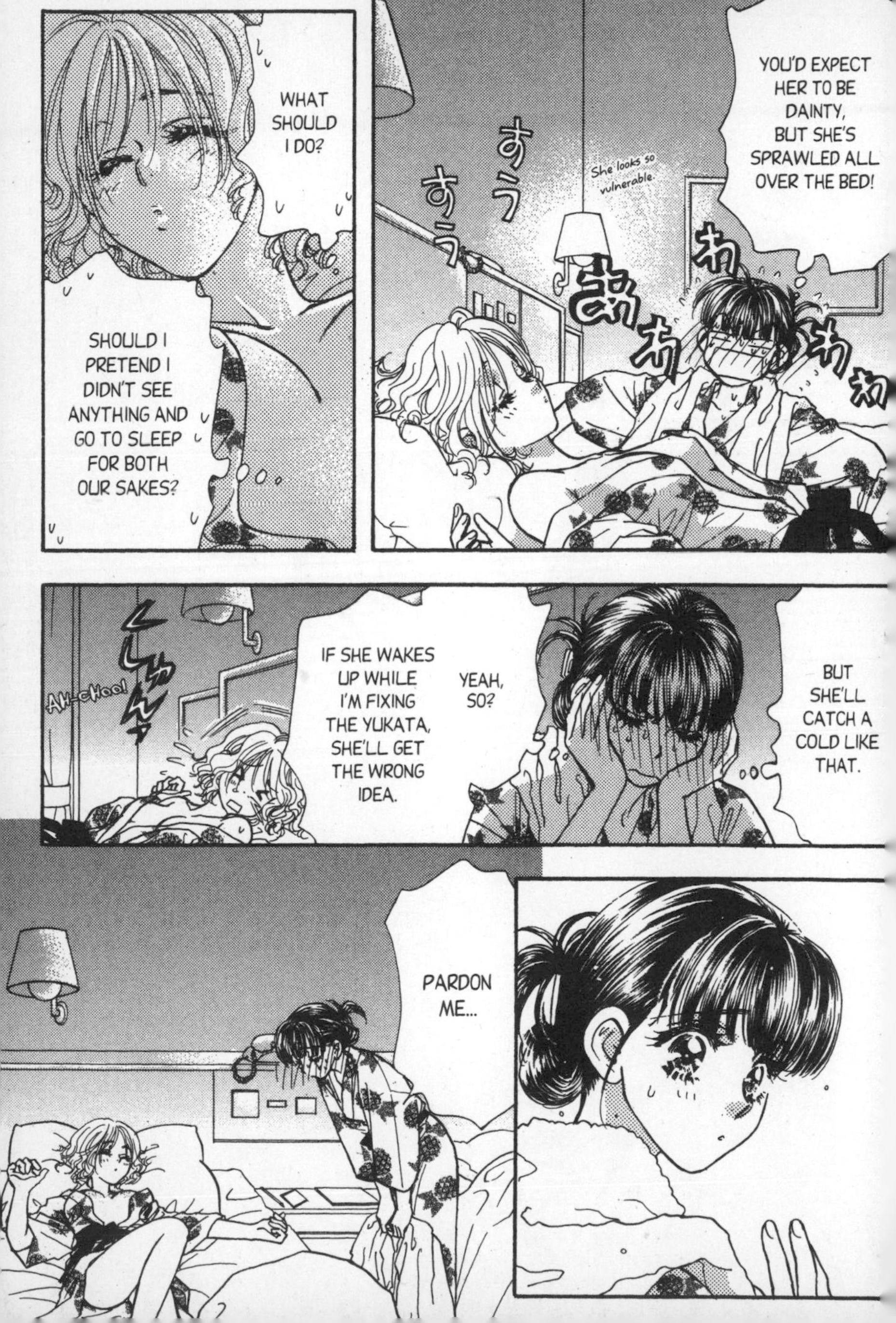
YOU'D EXPECT HER TO BE DAINTY, BUT SHE'S SPRAWLED ALL OVER THE BED!
She looks so vulnerable.
すう
すう
WHAT SHOULD I DO?
SHOULD I PRETEND I DIDN'T SEE ANYTHING AND GO TO SLEEP FOR BOTH OUR SAKES?
BUT SHE'LL CATCH A COLD LIKE THAT.
YEAH, SO?
IF SHE WAKES UP WHILE I'M FIXING THE YUKATA, SHE'LL GET THE WRONG IDEA.
くしゅん
AH-CHOO!
PARDON ME...

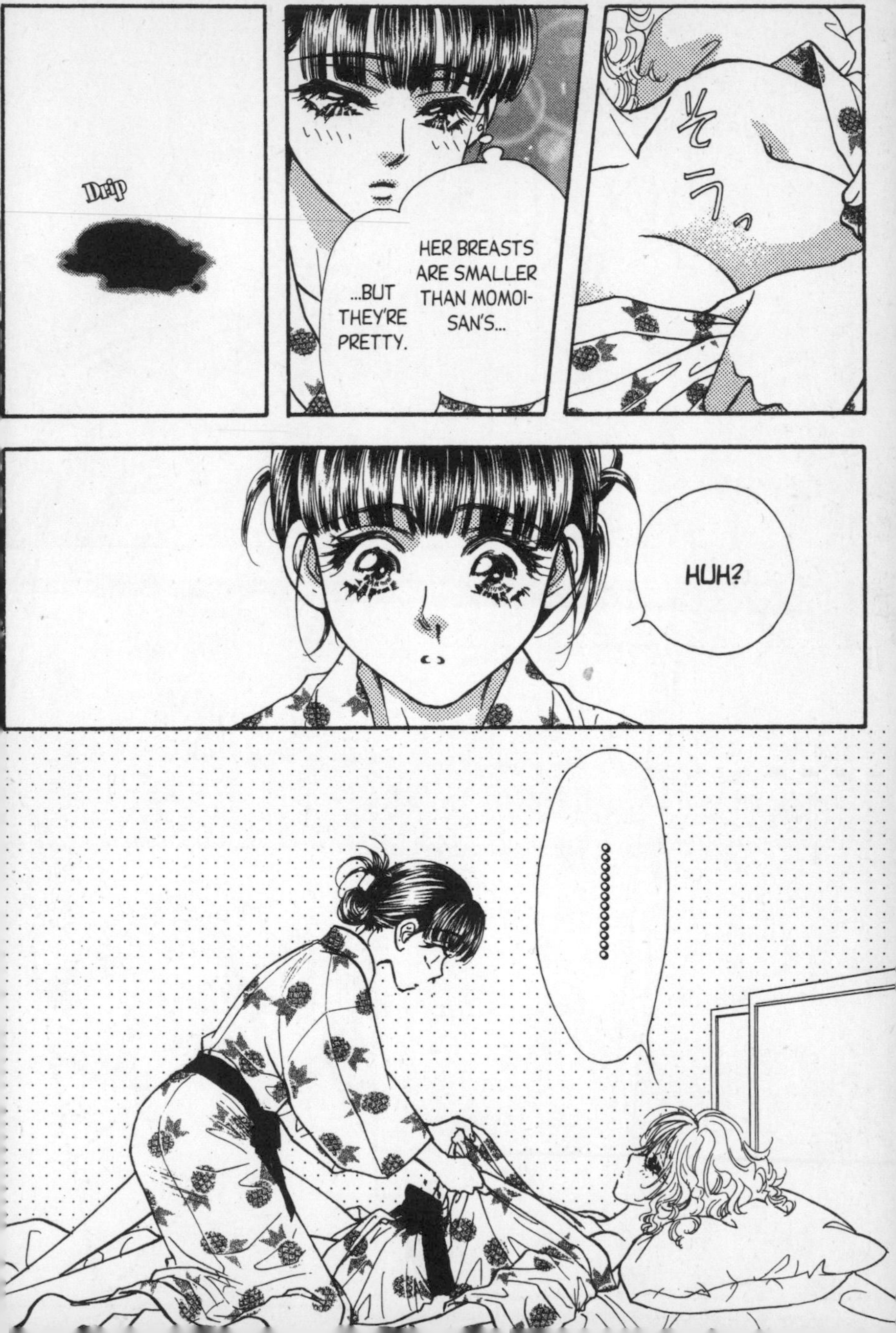
HER BREASTS ARE SMALLER THAN MOMOI-SAN'S...
...BUT THEY'RE PRETTY.
Drip
HUH?
....

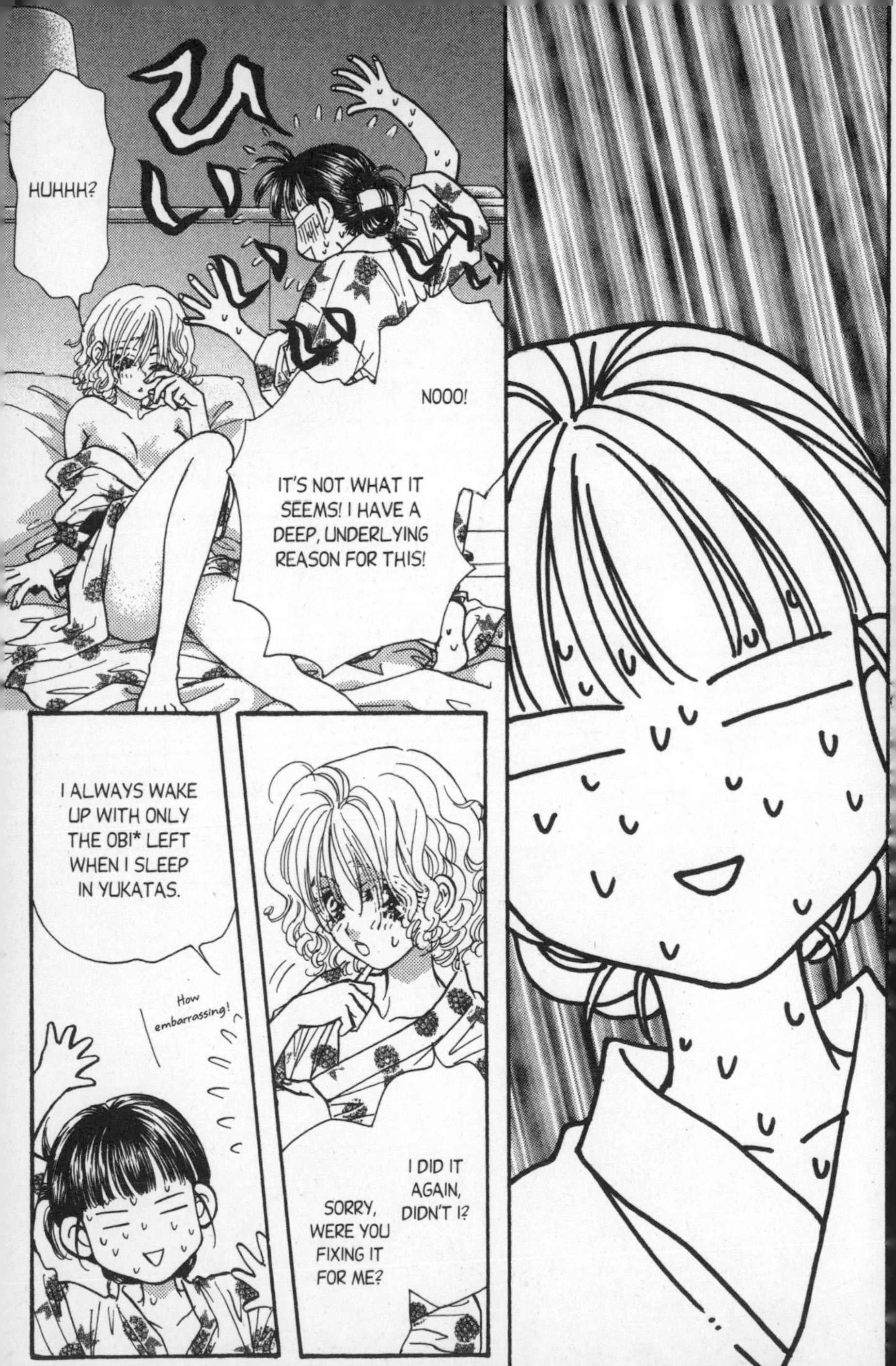
HUHHH?
NOOO!
IT'S NOT WHAT IT SEEMS! I HAVE A DEEP, UNDERLYING REASON FOR THIS!
I DID IT AGAIN, DIDN'T I?
SORRY, WERE YOU FIXING IT FOR ME?
I ALWAYS WAKE UP WITH ONLY THE OBI* LEFT WHEN I SLEEP IN YUKATAS.
How embarrassing!

*Obi is the band you tie around your waist to keep the Yukata in place.

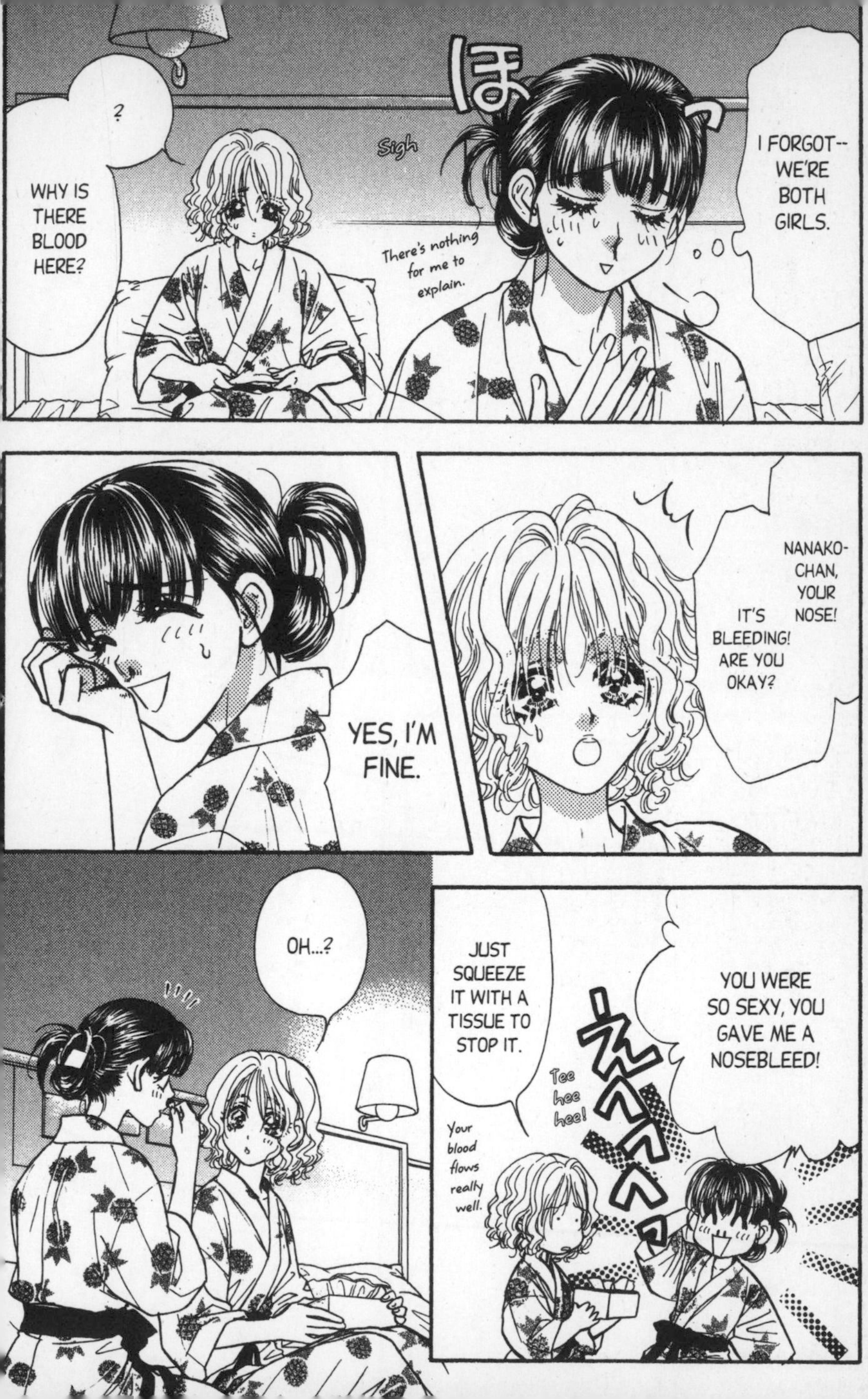
I FORGOT--WE'RE BOTH GIRLS.
ほっ
Sigh
There's nothing for me to explain.
?
WHY IS THERE BLOOD HERE?
NANAKO-CHAN, YOUR NOSE!
IT'S BLEEDING! ARE YOU OKAY?
YES, I'M FINE.
YOU WERE SO SEXY, YOU GAVE ME A NOSEBLEED!
えへへへ
Tee hee hee!
JUST SQUEEZE IT WITH A TISSUE TO STOP IT.
Your blood flows really well.
OH...?

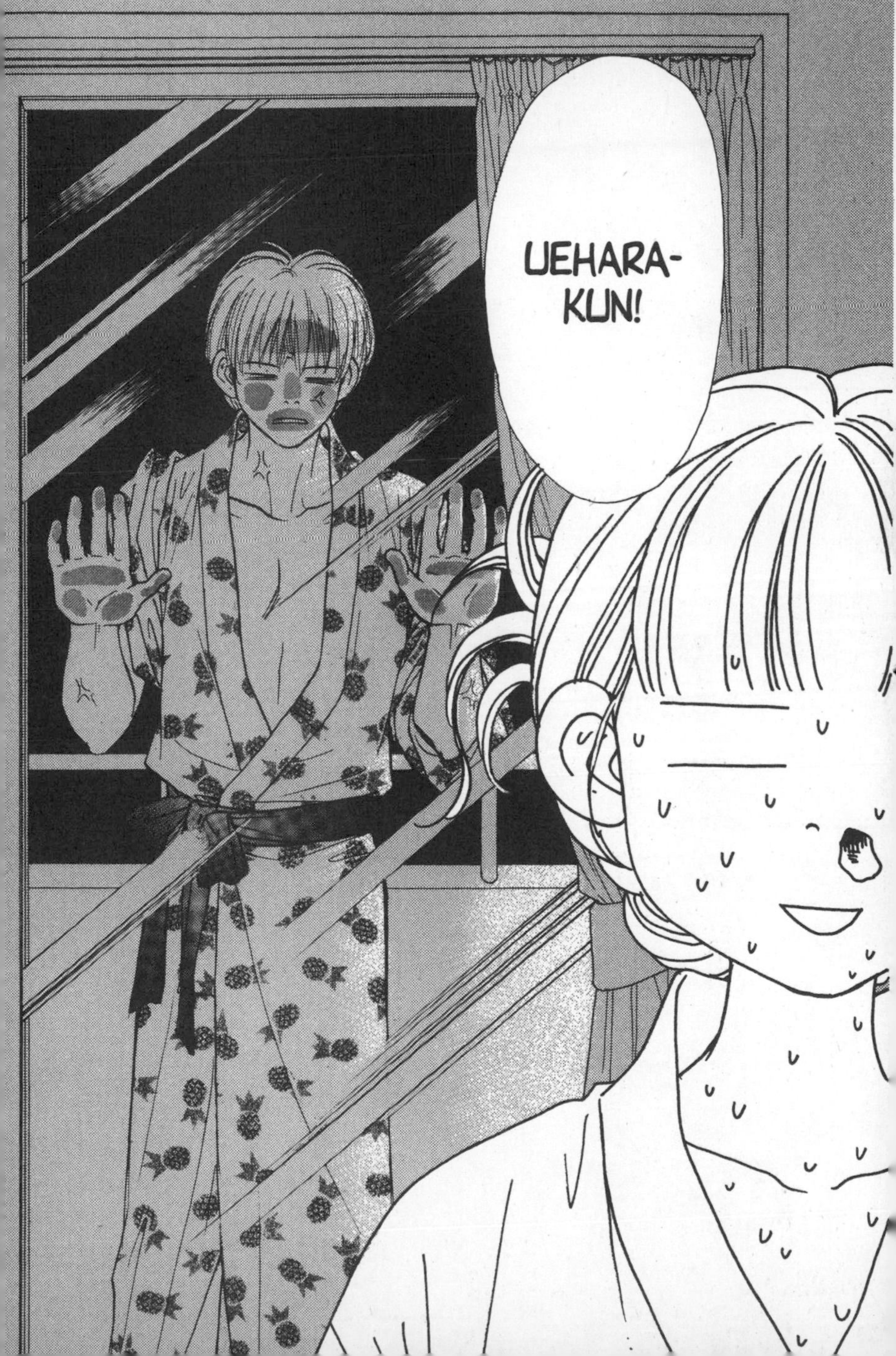
UEHARA-KUN!

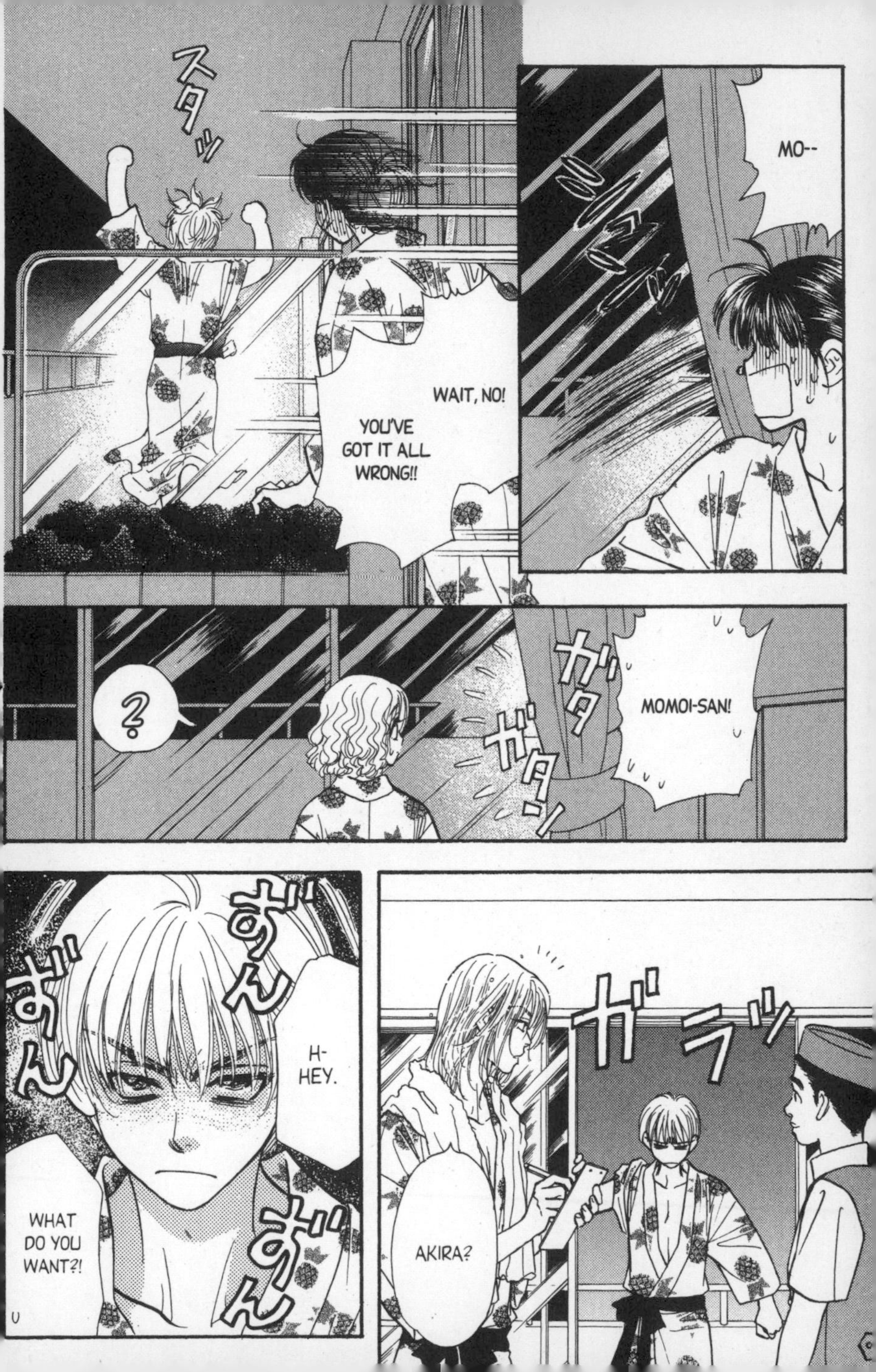
MO--
スタッ
WAIT, NO!
YOU'VE GOT IT ALL WRONG!!
MOMOI-SAN!
ガタ ガタン
?
ガラッ
AKIRA?
H- HEY.
ずん ずん ずん
WHAT DO YOU WANT?!

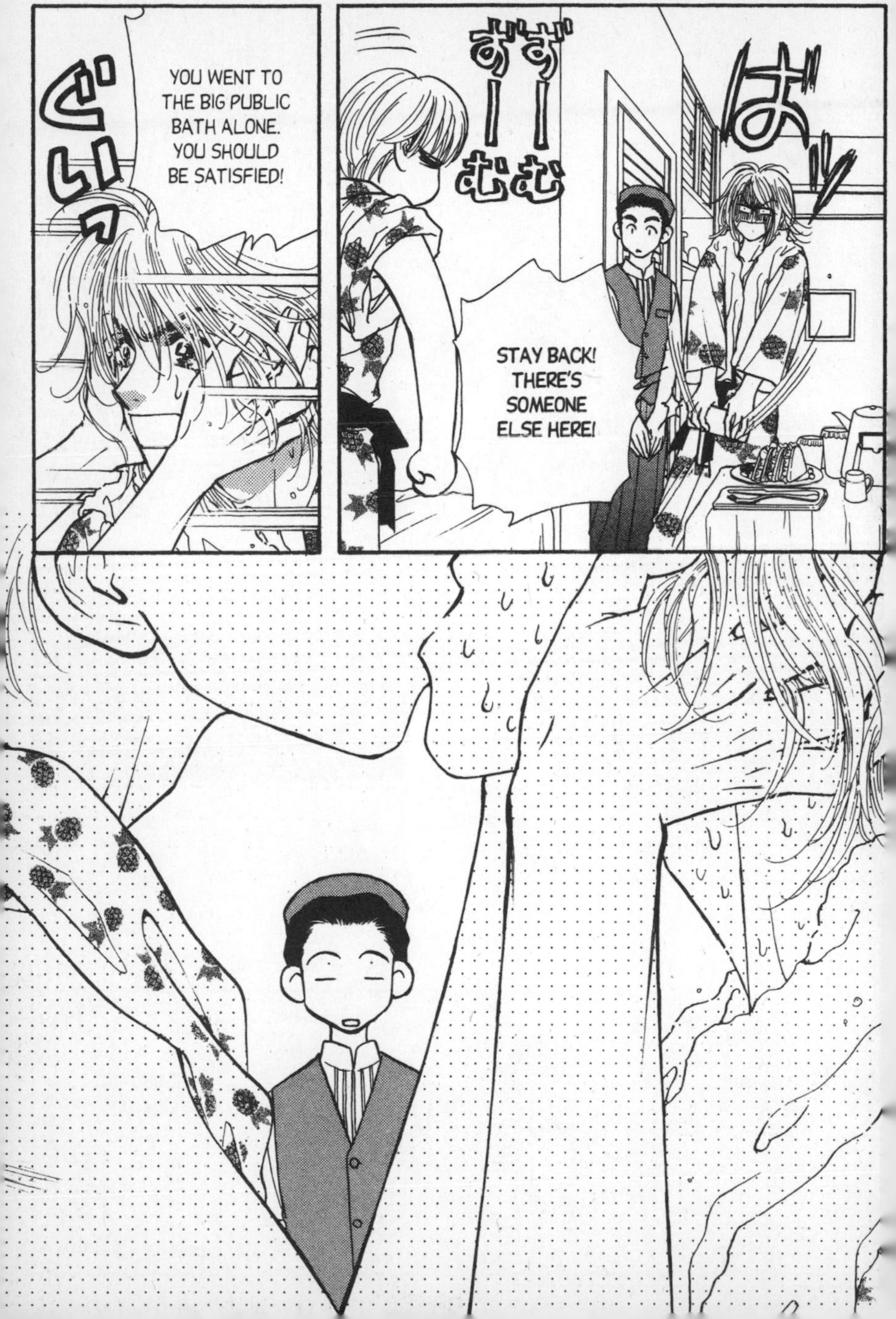
ばッ
STAY BACK! THERE'S SOMEONE ELSE HERE!
YOU WENT TO THE BIG PUBLIC BATH ALONE. YOU SHOULD BE SATISFIED!
ぐいっ

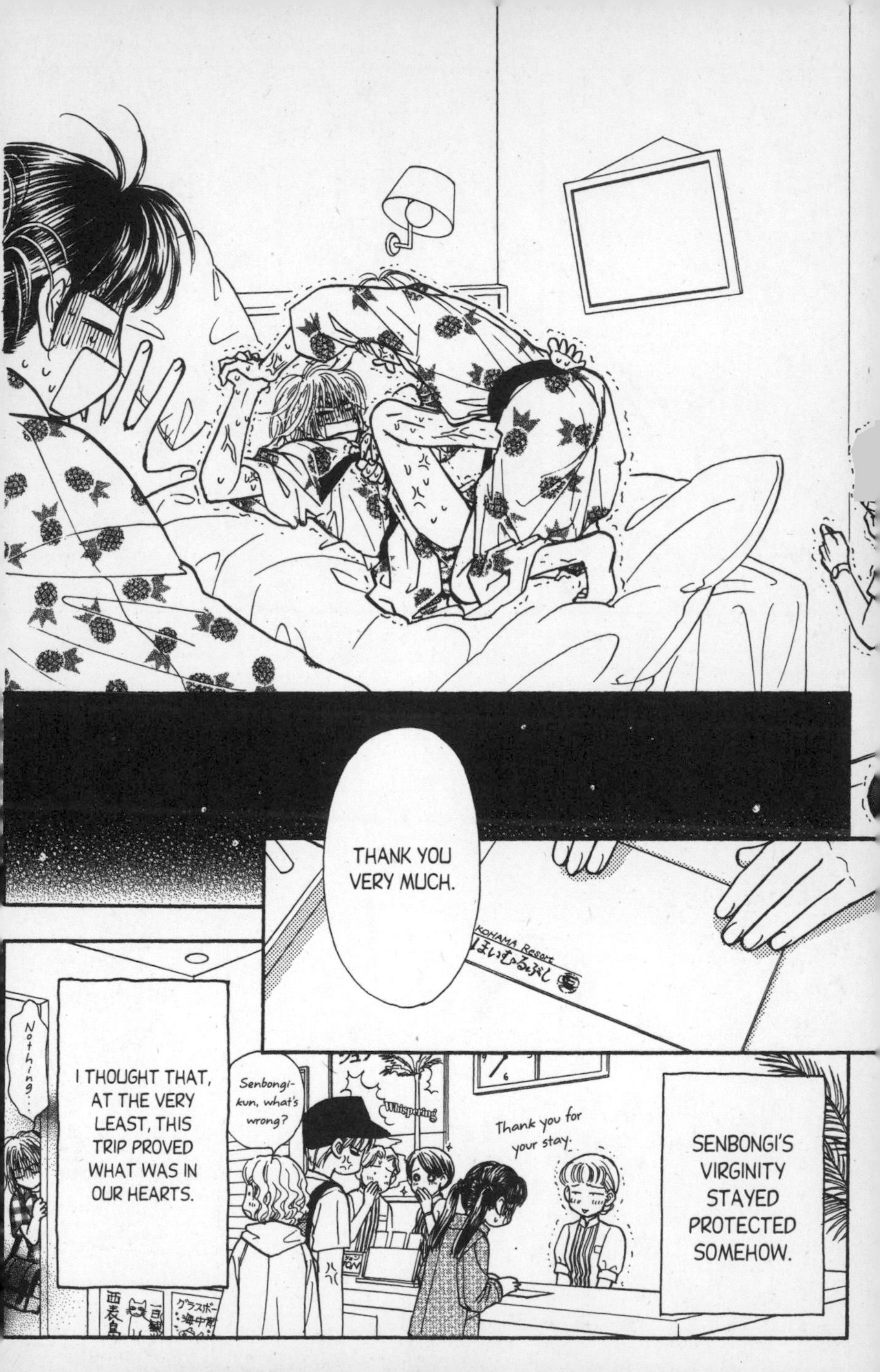
THANK YOU VERY MUCH.
KOHAMA Resort
はいむるぶし
SENBONGI'S VIRGINITY STAYED PROTECTED SOMEHOW.
Thank you for your stay.
Whispering
Senbongi-kun, what's wrong?
I THOUGHT THAT, AT THE VERY LEAST, THIS TRIP PROVED WHAT WAS IN OUR HEARTS.
Nothing...

Episode 13
A Girl's Feelings

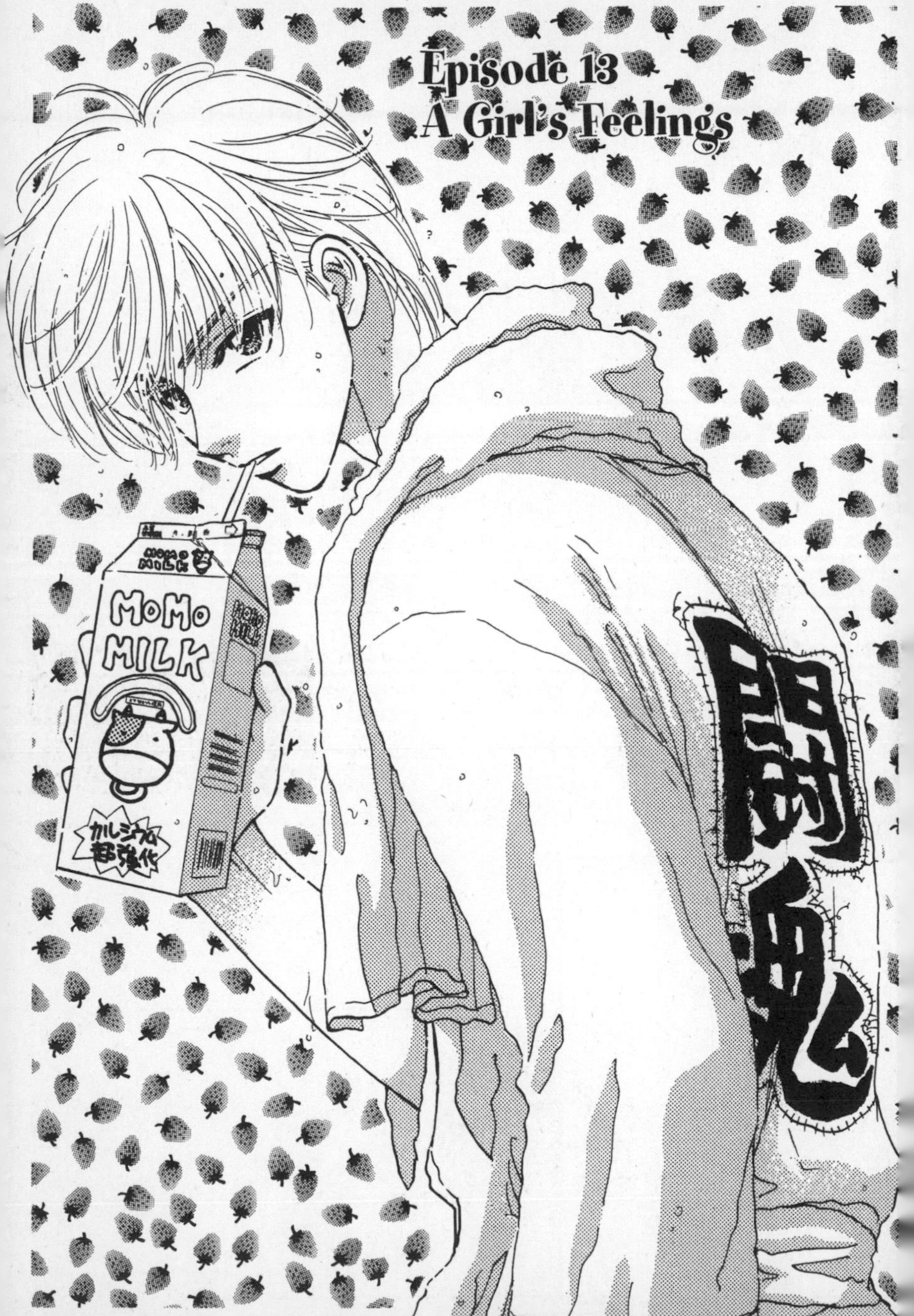
MoMo MILK
カルシウム超強化
闘魂

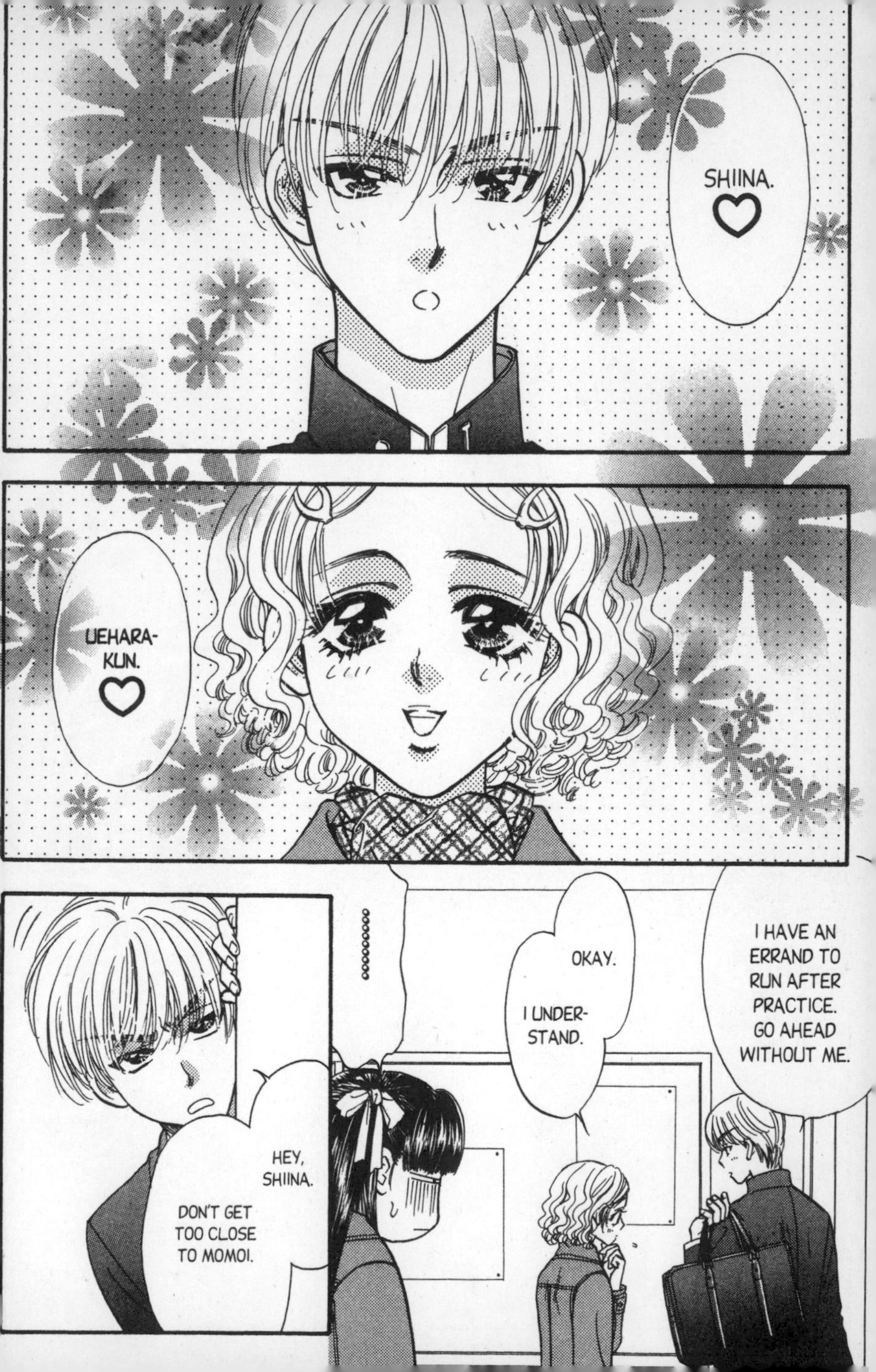
SHIINA. ♥
UEHARA-KUN. ♥
I HAVE AN ERRAND TO RUN AFTER PRACTICE. GO AHEAD WITHOUT ME.
OKAY. I UNDERSTAND.
....
HEY, SHIINA. DON'T GET TOO CLOSE TO MOMOI.

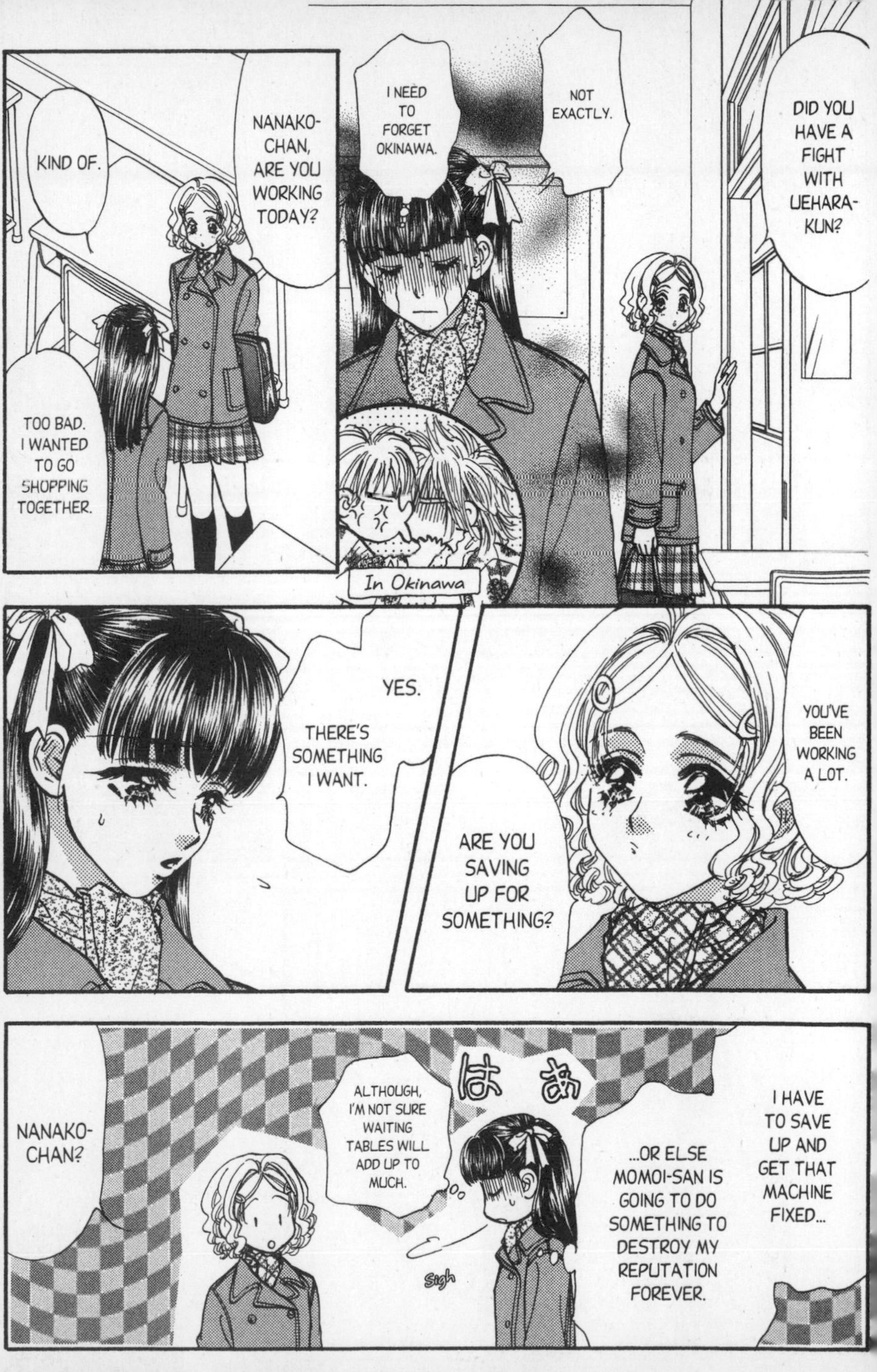
DID YOU HAVE A FIGHT WITH UEHARA-KUN?
NOT EXACTLY.
I NEED TO FORGET OKINAWA.
In Okinawa
NANAKO-CHAN, ARE YOU WORKING TODAY?
KIND OF.
TOO BAD. I WANTED TO GO SHOPPING TOGETHER.
YOU'VE BEEN WORKING A LOT.
ARE YOU SAVING UP FOR SOMETHING?
YES.
THERE'S SOMETHING I WANT.
I HAVE TO SAVE UP AND GET THAT MACHINE FIXED...
...OR ELSE MOMOI-SAN IS GOING TO DO SOMETHING TO DESTROY MY REPUTATION FOREVER.
はあ
Sigh
ALTHOUGH, I'M NOT SURE WAITING TABLES WILL ADD UP TO MUCH.
NANAKO-CHAN?

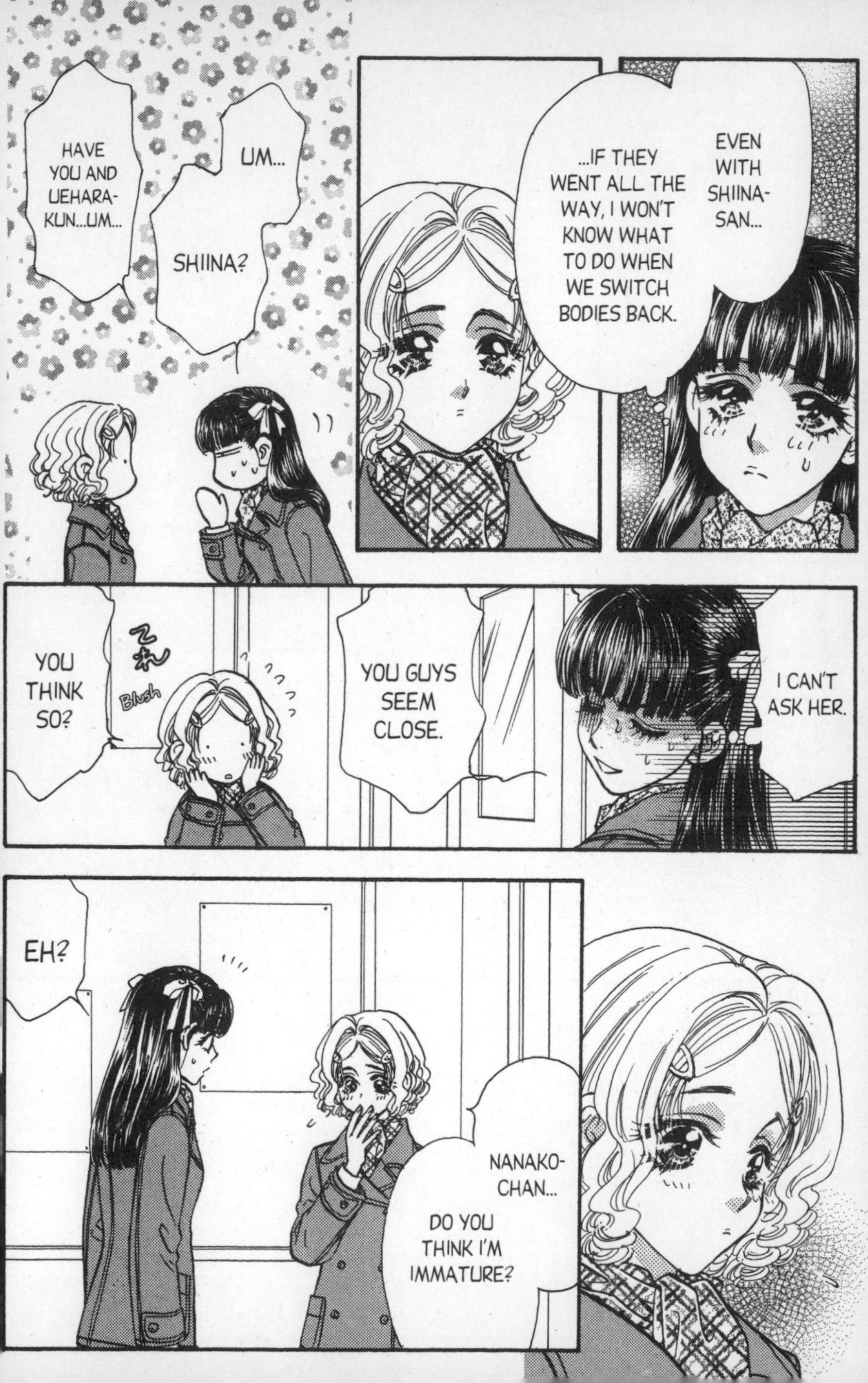
EVEN WITH SHIINA-SAN...
...IF THEY WENT ALL THE WAY, I WON'T KNOW WHAT TO DO WHEN WE SWITCH BODIES BACK.
UM...
SHIINA?
HAVE YOU AND UEHARA-KUN...UM...
I CAN'T ASK HER.
YOU GUYS SEEM CLOSE.
YOU THINK SO?
Blush
NANAKO-CHAN...
DO YOU THINK I'M IMMATURE?
EH?

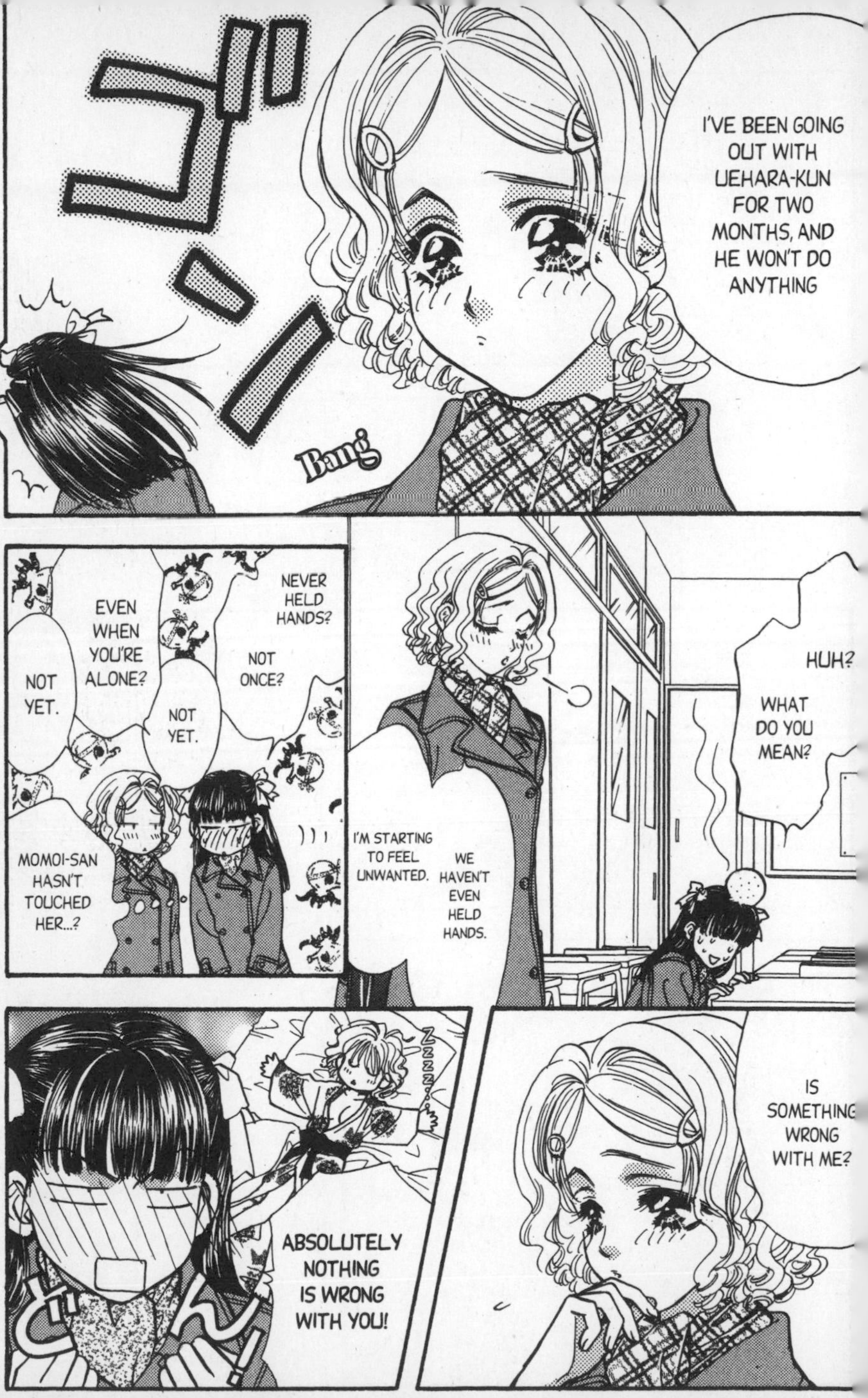
I'VE BEEN GOING OUT WITH UEHARA-KUN FOR TWO MONTHS, AND HE WON'T DO ANYTHING
ゴン
Bang
HUH?
WHAT DO YOU MEAN?
WE HAVEN'T EVEN HELD HANDS.
I'M STARTING TO FEEL UNWANTED.
NEVER HELD HANDS?
NOT ONCE?
EVEN WHEN YOU'RE ALONE?
NOT YET.
NOT YET.
MOMOI-SAN HASN'T TOUCHED HER...?
IS SOMETHING WRONG WITH ME?
ZZZZ...
ABSOLUTELY NOTHING IS WRONG WITH YOU!

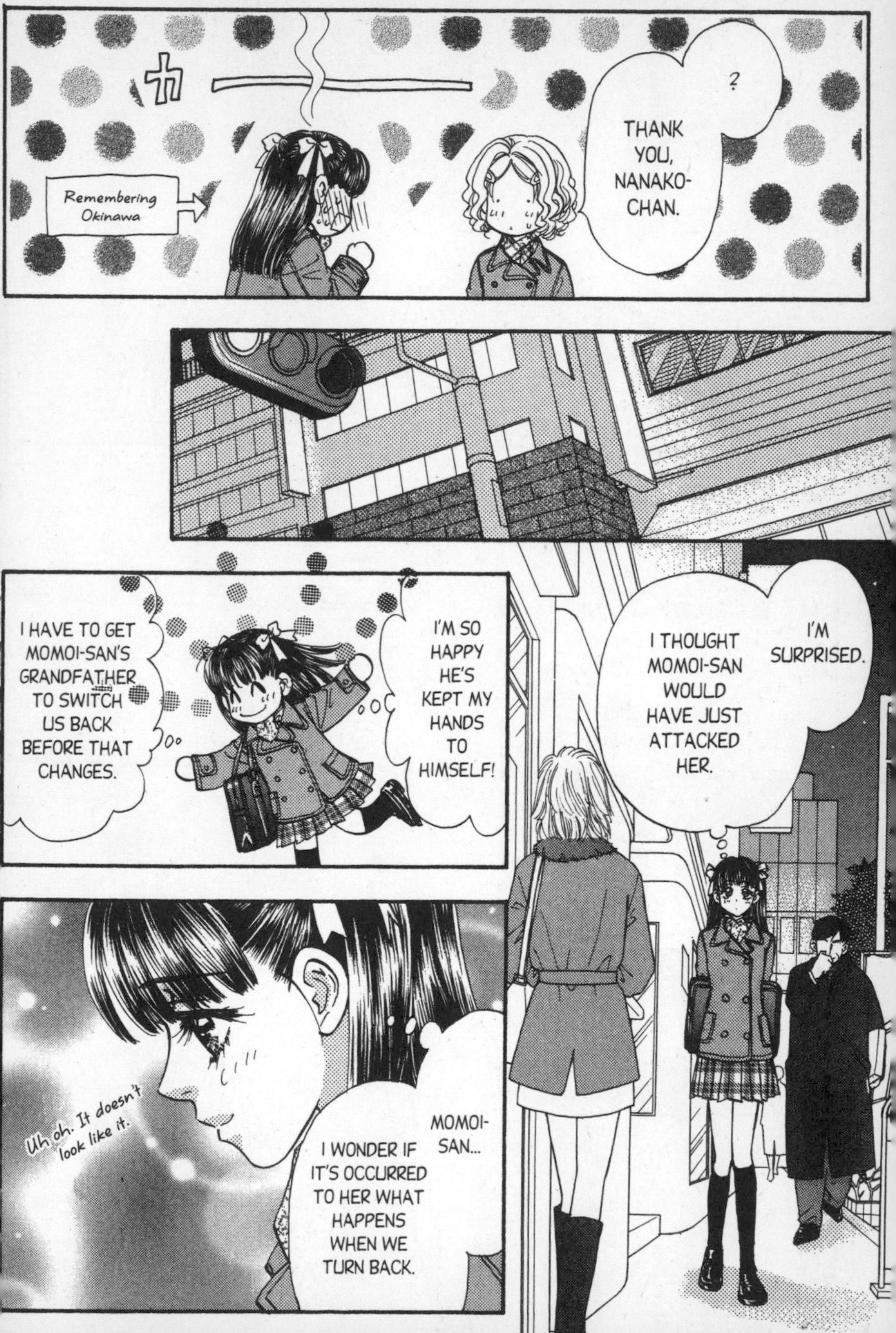
?
THANK YOU, NANAKO-CHAN.
Remembering Okinawa
カ
I'M SURPRISED.
I THOUGHT MOMOI-SAN WOULD HAVE JUST ATTACKED HER.
I'M SO HAPPY HE'S KEPT MY HANDS TO HIMSELF!
I HAVE TO GET MOMOI-SAN'S GRANDFATHER TO SWITCH US BACK BEFORE THAT CHANGES.
MOMOI-SAN...
I WONDER IF IT'S OCCURRED TO HER WHAT HAPPENS WHEN WE TURN BACK.
Uh oh. It doesn't look like it.

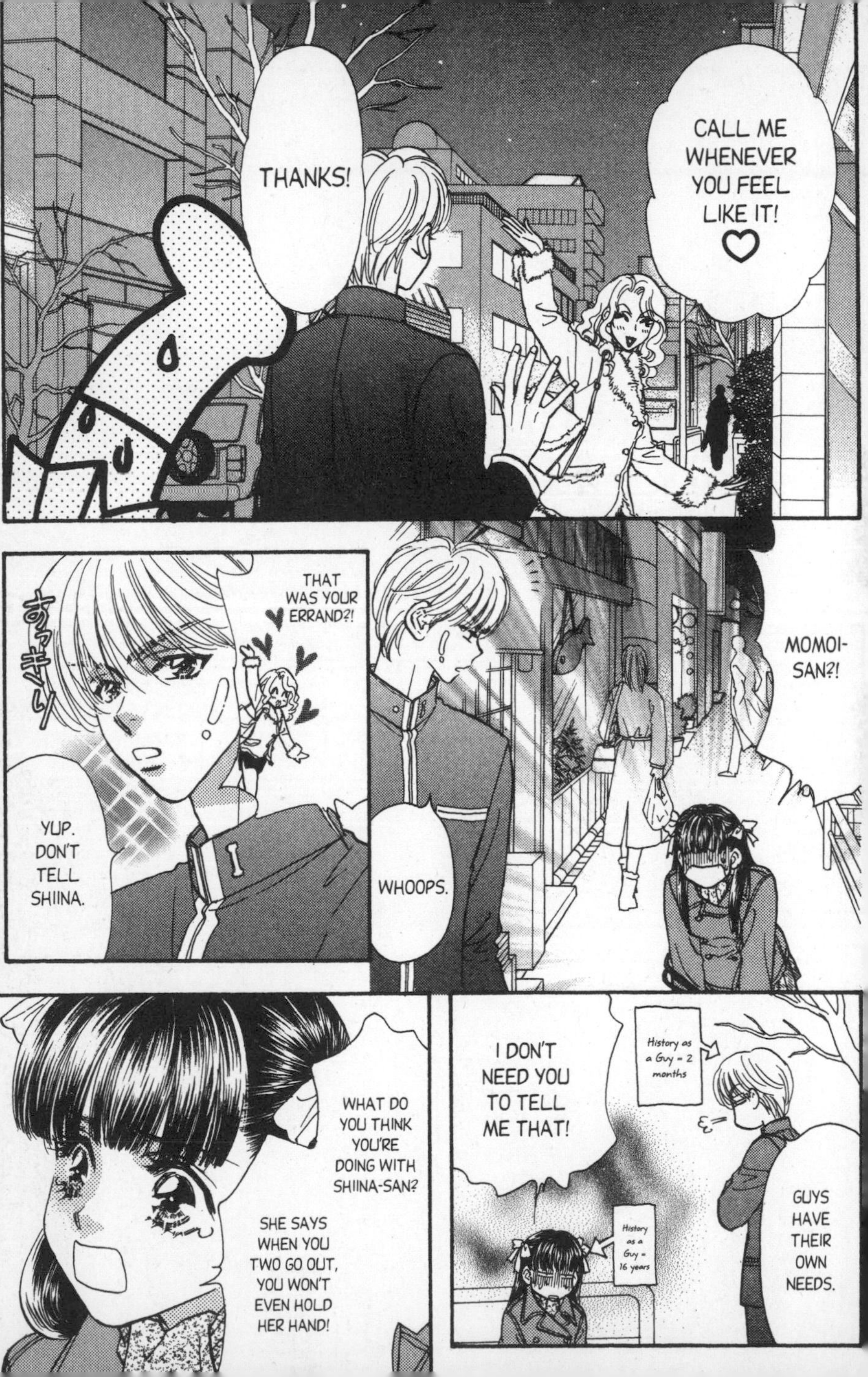
CALL ME WHENEVER YOU FEEL LIKE IT! ♡
THANKS!
MOMOI-SAN?!
WHOOPS.
THAT WAS YOUR ERRAND?!
YUP. DON'T TELL SHIINA.
History as a Guy = 2 months
I DON'T NEED YOU TO TELL ME THAT!
GUYS HAVE THEIR OWN NEEDS.
History as a Guy = 16 years
WHAT DO YOU THINK YOU'RE DOING WITH SHIINA-SAN?
SHE SAYS WHEN YOU TWO GO OUT, YOU WON'T EVEN HOLD HER HAND!

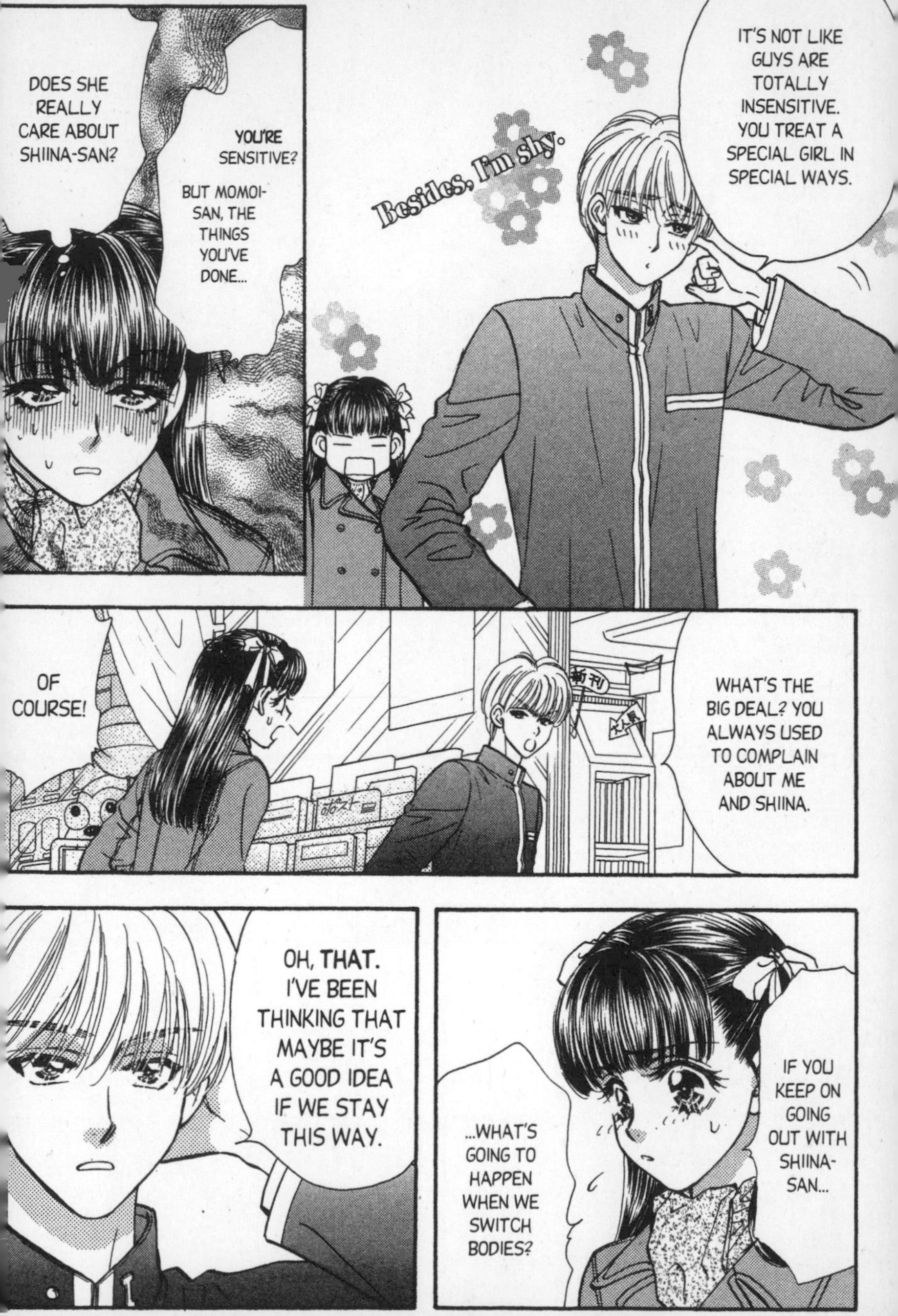
IT'S NOT LIKE GUYS ARE TOTALLY INSENSITIVE. YOU TREAT A SPECIAL GIRL IN SPECIAL WAYS.
Besides, I'm shy.
YOU'RE SENSITIVE?
BUT MOMOI-SAN, THE THINGS YOU'VE DONE...
DOES SHE REALLY CARE ABOUT SHIINA-SAN?
WHAT'S THE BIG DEAL? YOU ALWAYS USED TO COMPLAIN ABOUT ME AND SHIINA.
OF COURSE!
IF YOU KEEP ON GOING OUT WITH SHIINA-SAN...
...WHAT'S GOING TO HAPPEN WHEN WE SWITCH BODIES?
OH, THAT. I'VE BEEN THINKING THAT MAYBE IT'S A GOOD IDEA IF WE STAY THIS WAY.

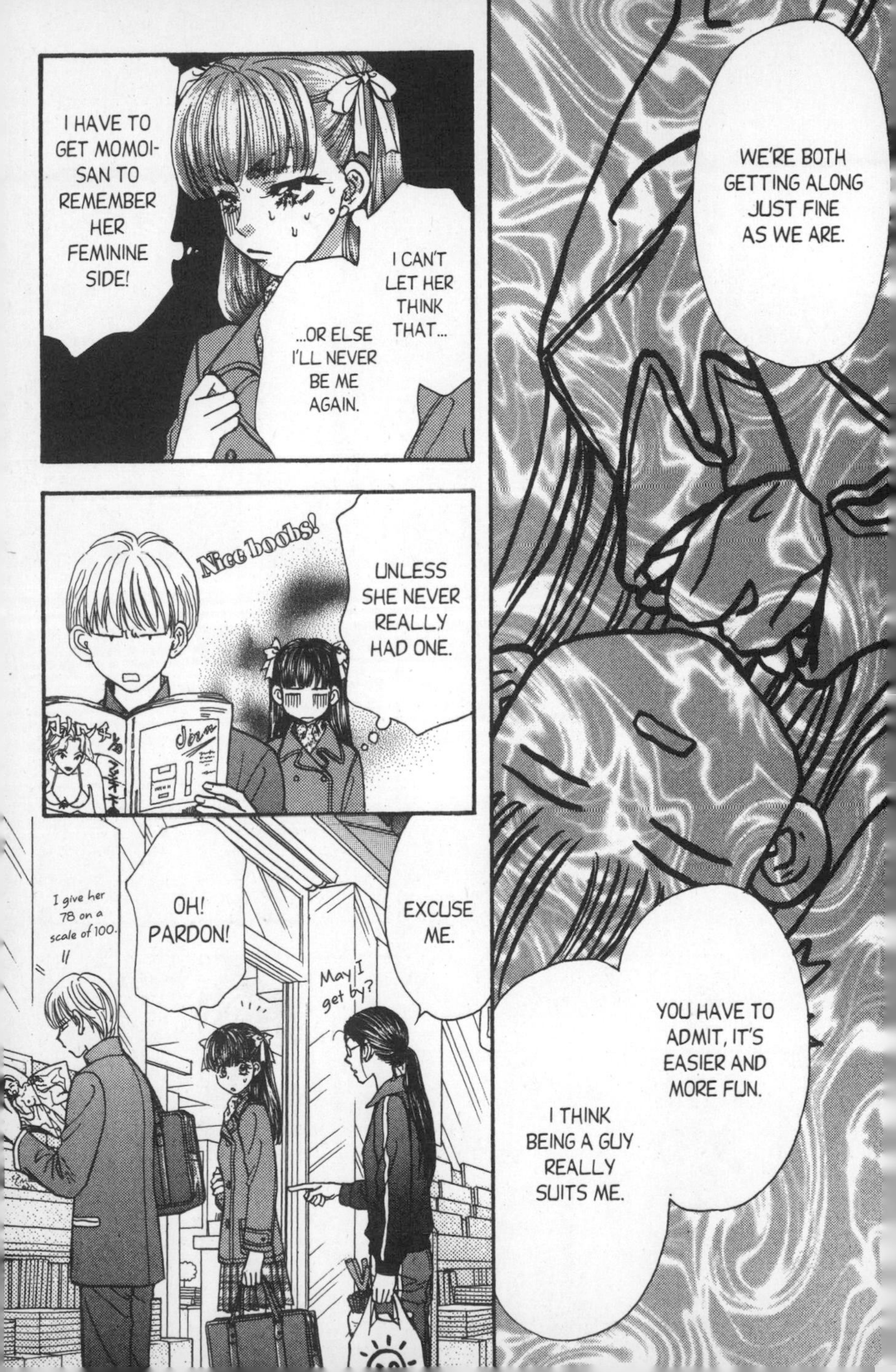
WE'RE BOTH GETTING ALONG JUST FINE AS WE ARE.
YOU HAVE TO ADMIT, IT'S EASIER AND MORE FUN.
I THINK BEING A GUY REALLY SUITS ME.
I CAN'T LET HER THINK THAT...
...OR ELSE I'LL NEVER BE ME AGAIN.
I HAVE TO GET MOMOI-SAN TO REMEMBER HER FEMININE SIDE!
UNLESS SHE NEVER REALLY HAD ONE.
Nice boobs!
EXCUSE ME.
May I get by?
OH! PARDON!
I give her 78 on a scale of 100.

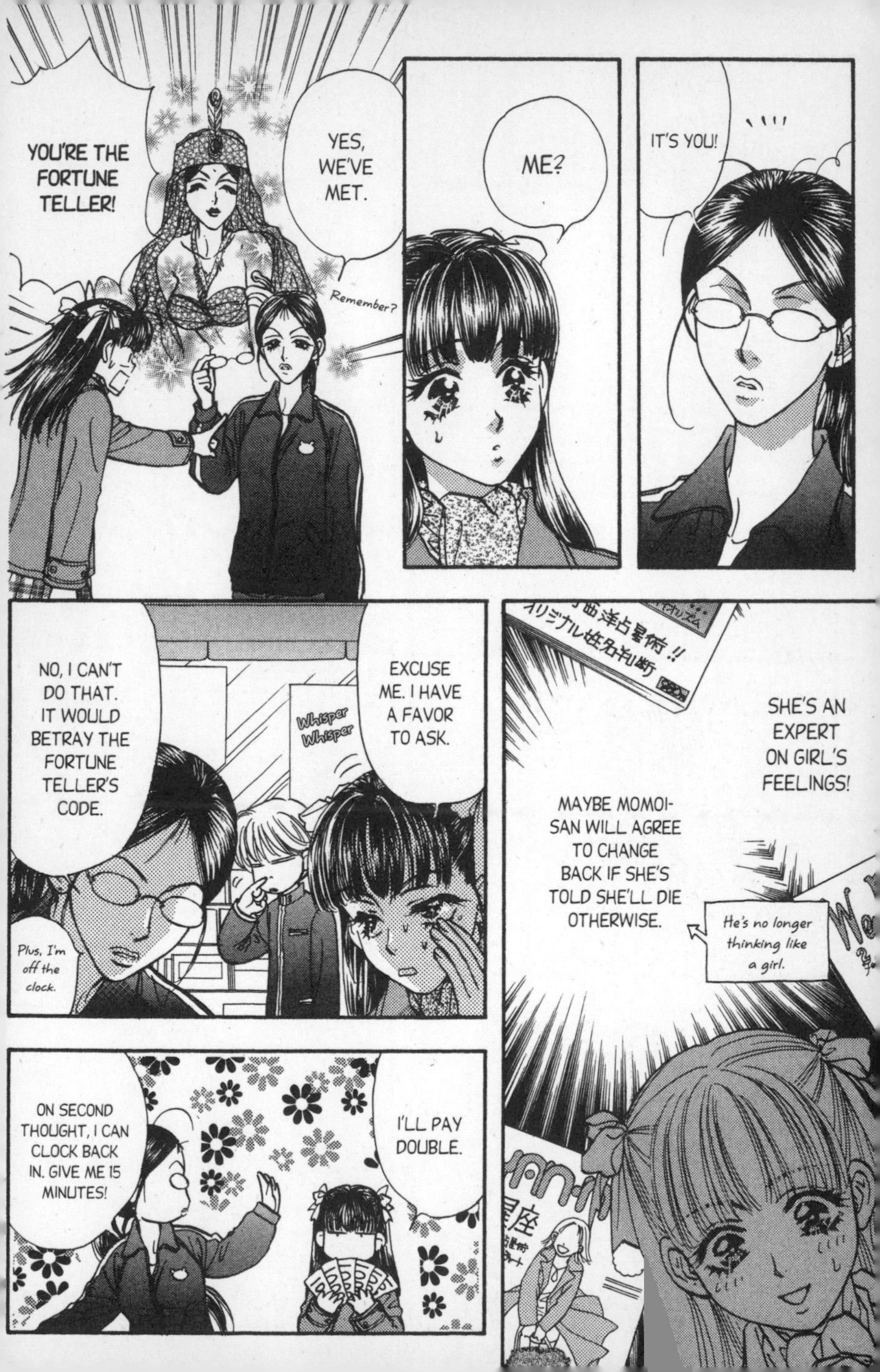

IT'S YOU!
ME?
YES, WE'VE MET.
Remember?
YOU'RE THE FORTUNE TELLER!
西洋占星術!!
オリジナル姓名判断
SHE'S AN EXPERT ON GIRL'S FEELINGS!
MAYBE MOMOI-SAN WILL AGREE TO CHANGE BACK IF SHE'S TOLD SHE'LL DIE OTHERWISE.
He's no longer thinking like a girl.
EXCUSE ME. I HAVE A FAVOR TO ASK.
Whisper Whisper
NO, I CAN'T DO THAT. IT WOULD BETRAY THE FORTUNE TELLER'S CODE.
Plus, I'm off the clock.
I'LL PAY DOUBLE.
ON SECOND THOUGHT, I CAN CLOCK BACK IN. GIVE ME 15 MINUTES!

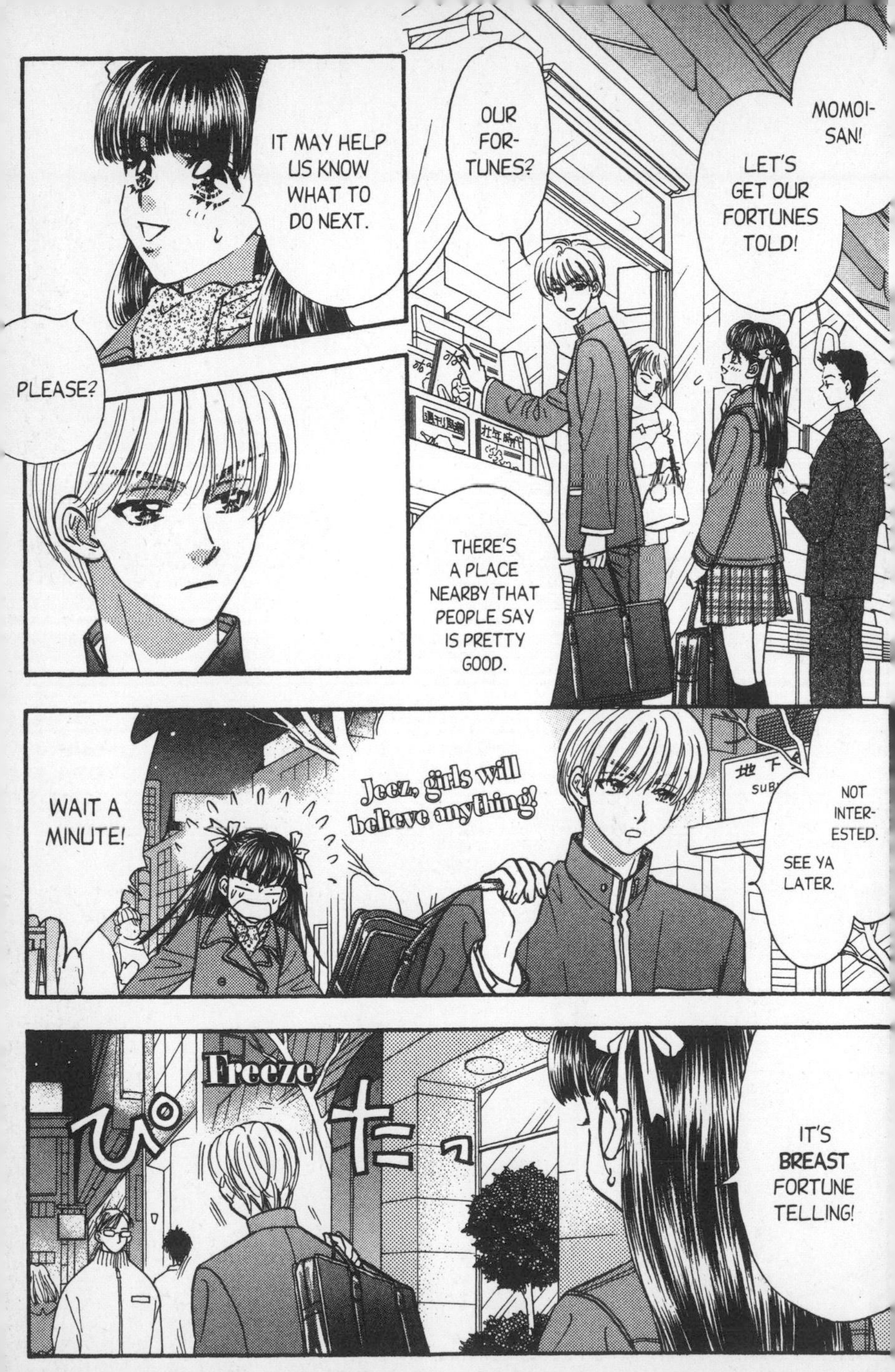
MOMOI-SAN!
LET'S GET OUR FORTUNES TOLD!
OUR FOR-TUNES?
THERE'S A PLACE NEARBY THAT PEOPLE SAY IS PRETTY GOOD.
IT MAY HELP US KNOW WHAT TO DO NEXT.
PLEASE?
NOT INTER-ESTED.
SEE YA LATER.
Jeez, girls will believe anything!
WAIT A MINUTE!
IT'S **BREAST** FORTUNE TELLING!
Freeze
ぴたっ

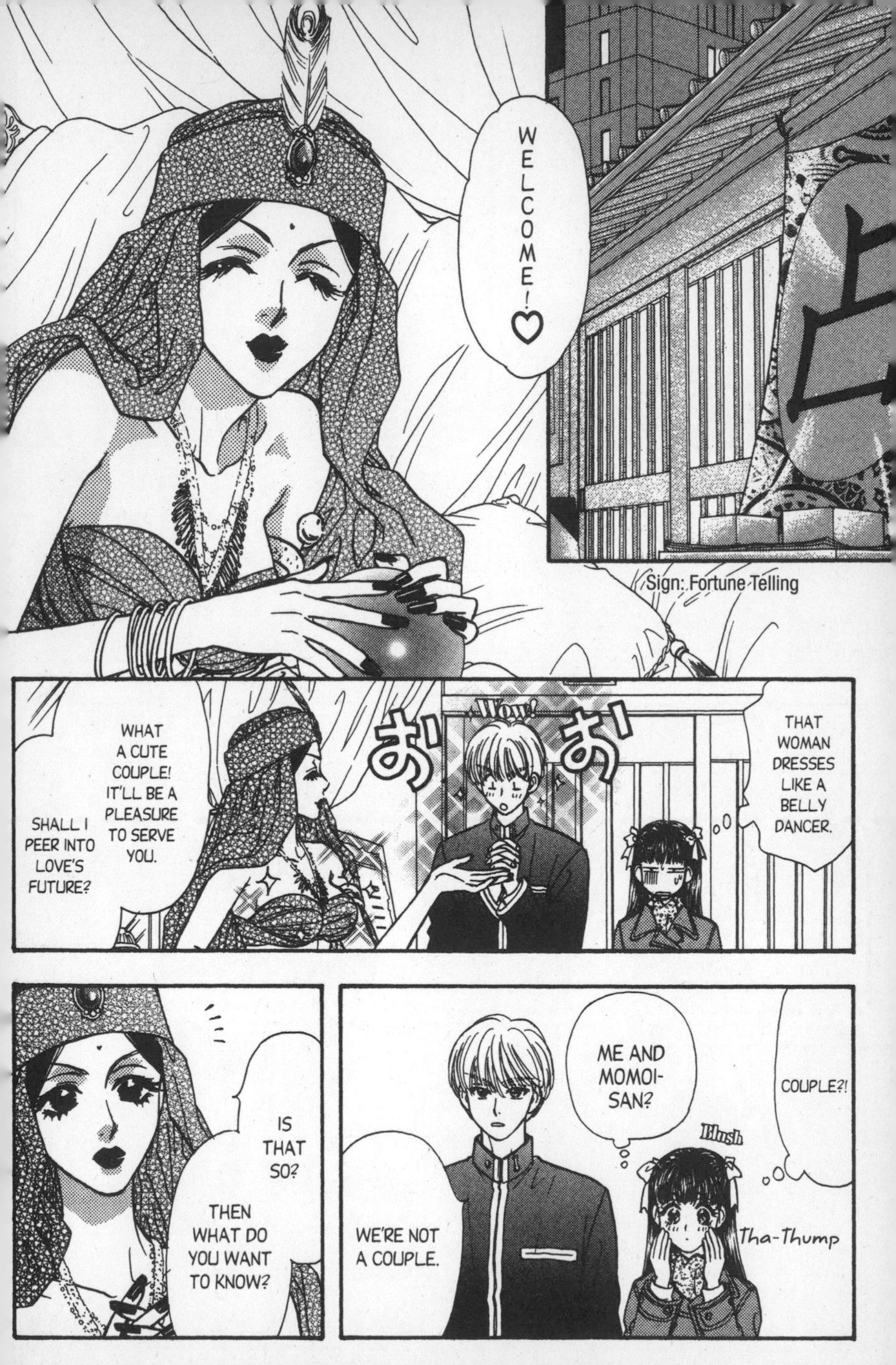
Sign: Fortune Telling
WELCOME! ♥
THAT WOMAN DRESSES LIKE A BELLY DANCER.
Wow!
おお
WHAT A CUTE COUPLE! IT'LL BE A PLEASURE TO SERVE YOU.
SHALL I PEER INTO LOVE'S FUTURE?
COUPLE?!
Blush
ME AND MOMOI-SAN?
Tha-Thump
WE'RE NOT A COUPLE.
IS THAT SO?
THEN WHAT DO YOU WANT TO KNOW?

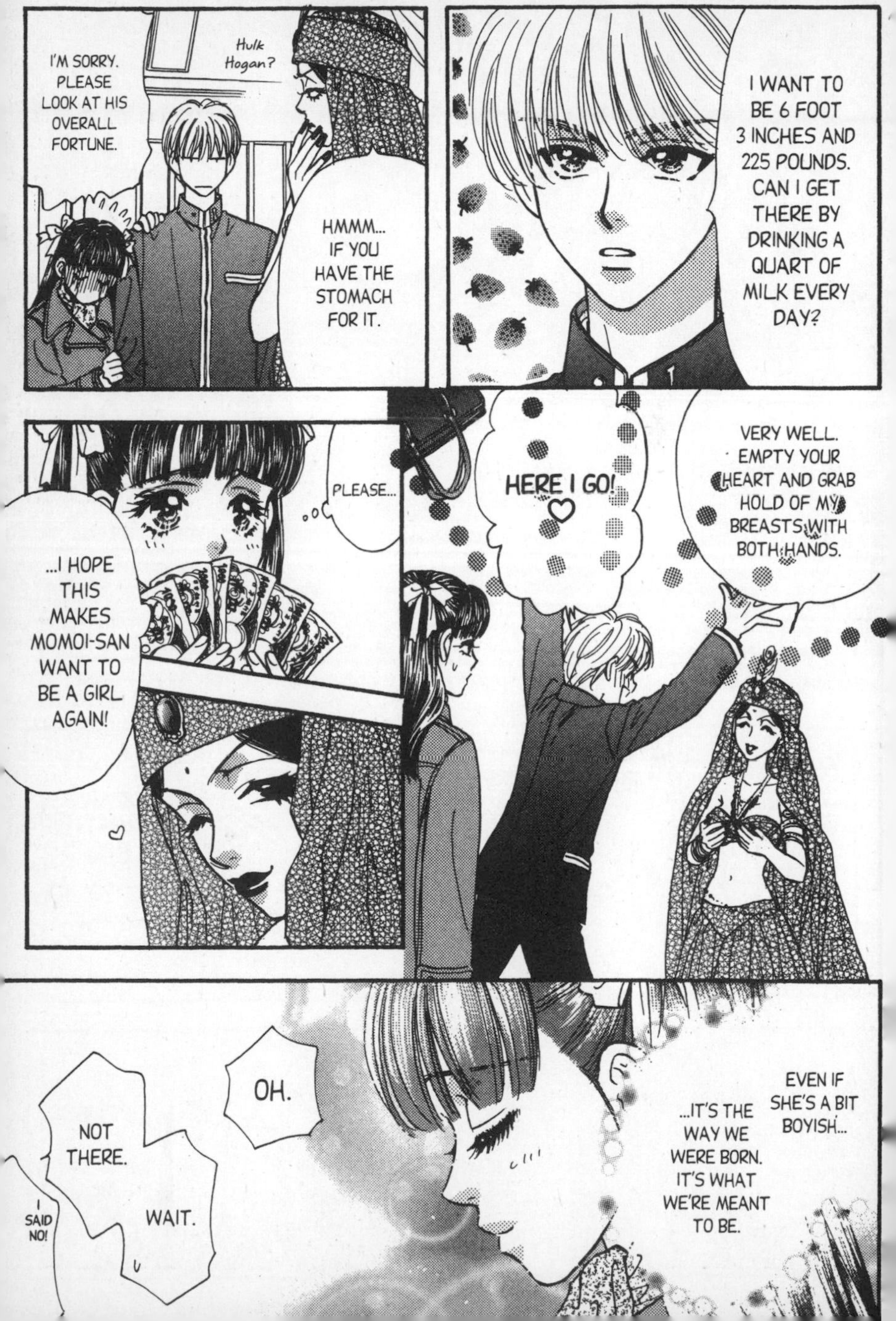
I WANT TO BE 6 FOOT 3 INCHES AND 225 POUNDS. CAN I GET THERE BY DRINKING A QUART OF MILK EVERY DAY?
I'M SORRY. PLEASE LOOK AT HIS OVERALL FORTUNE.
Hulk Hogan?
HMMM... IF YOU HAVE THE STOMACH FOR IT.
VERY WELL. EMPTY YOUR HEART AND GRAB HOLD OF MY BREASTS WITH BOTH HANDS.
HERE I GO! ♡
PLEASE...
...I HOPE THIS MAKES MOMOI-SAN WANT TO BE A GIRL AGAIN!
EVEN IF SHE'S A BIT BOYISH...
...IT'S THE WAY WE WERE BORN. IT'S WHAT WE'RE MEANT TO BE.
OH.
WAIT.
NOT THERE.
I SAID NO!

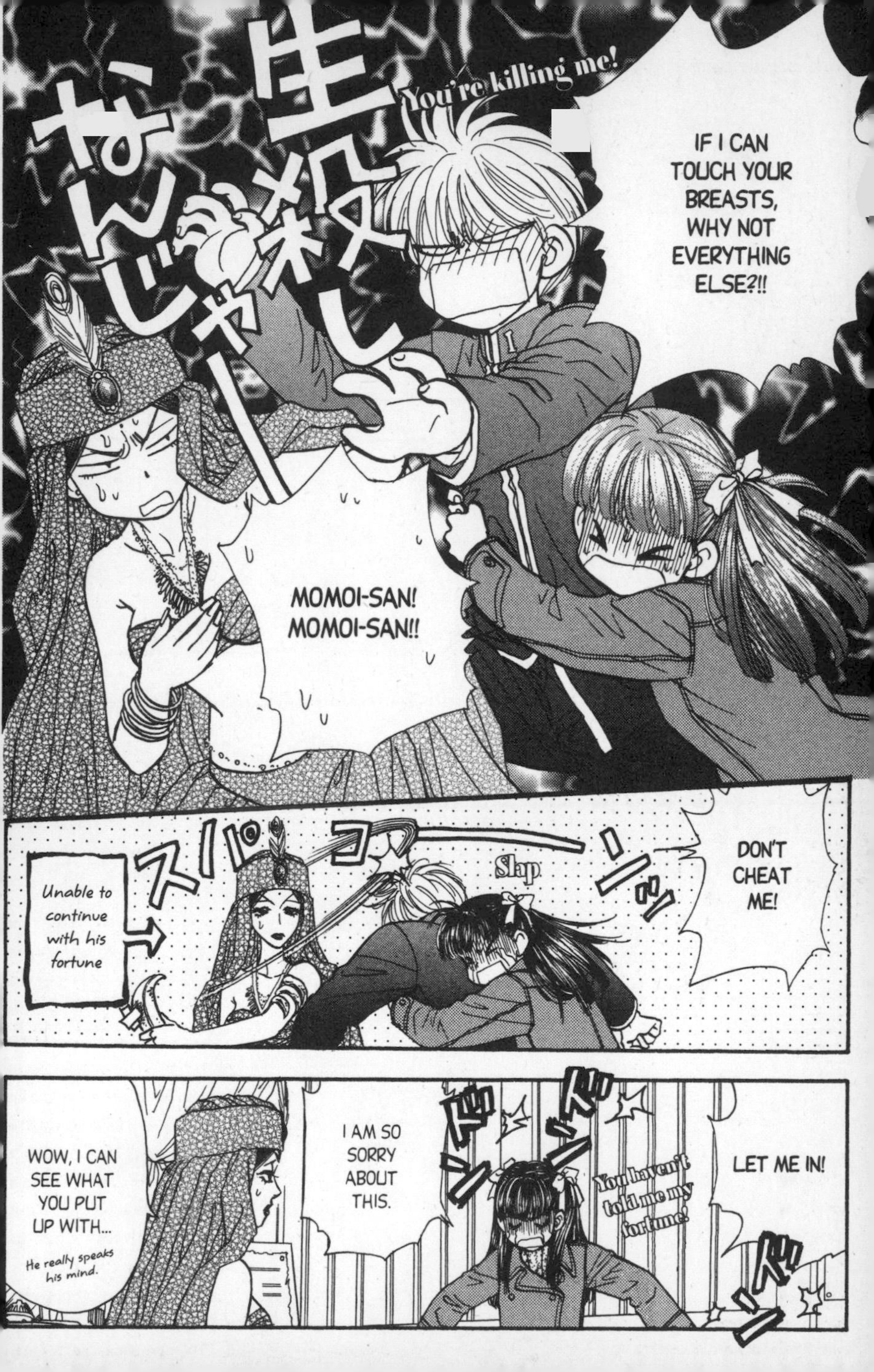
You're killing me!
IF I CAN TOUCH YOUR BREASTS, WHY NOT EVERYTHING ELSE?!!
MOMOI-SAN! MOMOI-SAN!!
DON'T CHEAT ME!
Slap
Unable to continue with his fortune
LET ME IN!
You haven't told me my fortune!
I AM SO SORRY ABOUT THIS.
WOW, I CAN SEE WHAT YOU PUT UP WITH...
He really speaks his mind.

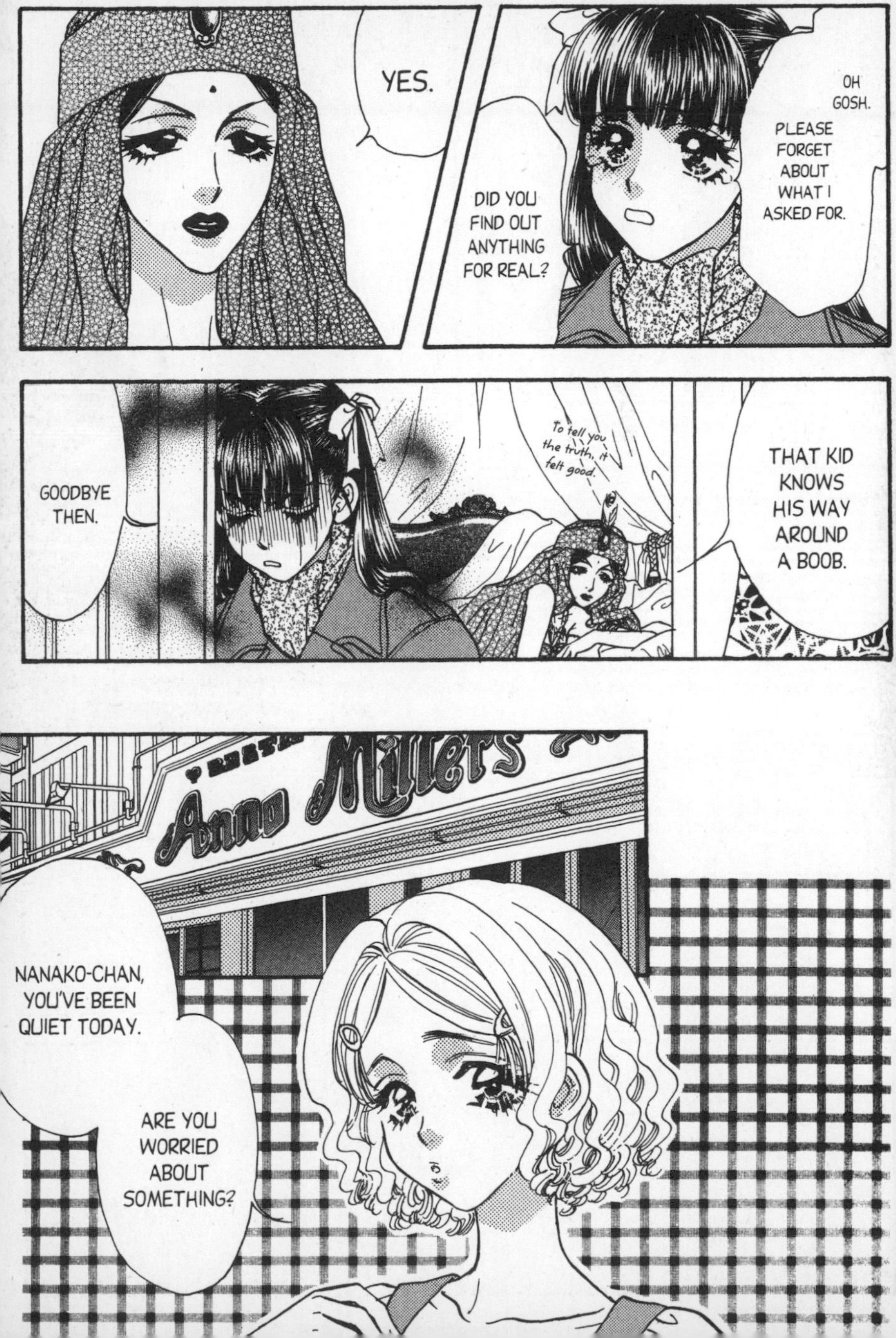
OH GOSH.
PLEASE FORGET ABOUT WHAT I ASKED FOR.
DID YOU FIND OUT ANYTHING FOR REAL?
YES.
THAT KID KNOWS HIS WAY AROUND A BOOB.
To tell you the truth, it felt good.
GOODBYE THEN.
Anna Millers
NANAKO-CHAN, YOU'VE BEEN QUIET TODAY.
ARE YOU WORRIED ABOUT SOMETHING?

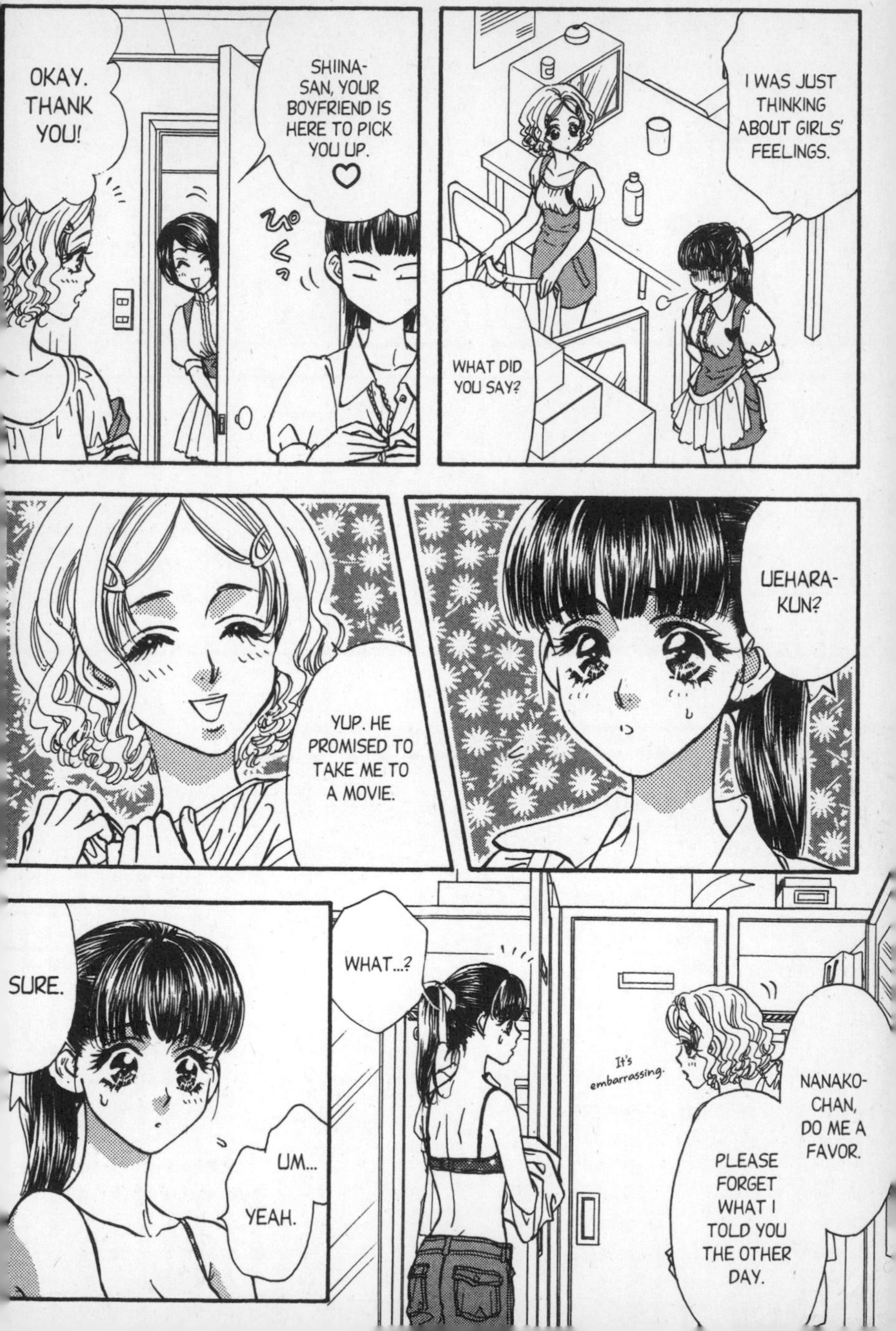
I WAS JUST THINKING ABOUT GIRLS' FEELINGS.
WHAT DID YOU SAY?
SHIINA-SAN, YOUR BOYFRIEND IS HERE TO PICK YOU UP. ♡
ぴくっ
OKAY. THANK YOU!
UEHARA-KUN?
YUP. HE PROMISED TO TAKE ME TO A MOVIE.
NANAKO-CHAN, DO ME A FAVOR.
PLEASE FORGET WHAT I TOLD YOU THE OTHER DAY.
It's embarrassing.
WHAT...?
UM...
YEAH.
SURE.

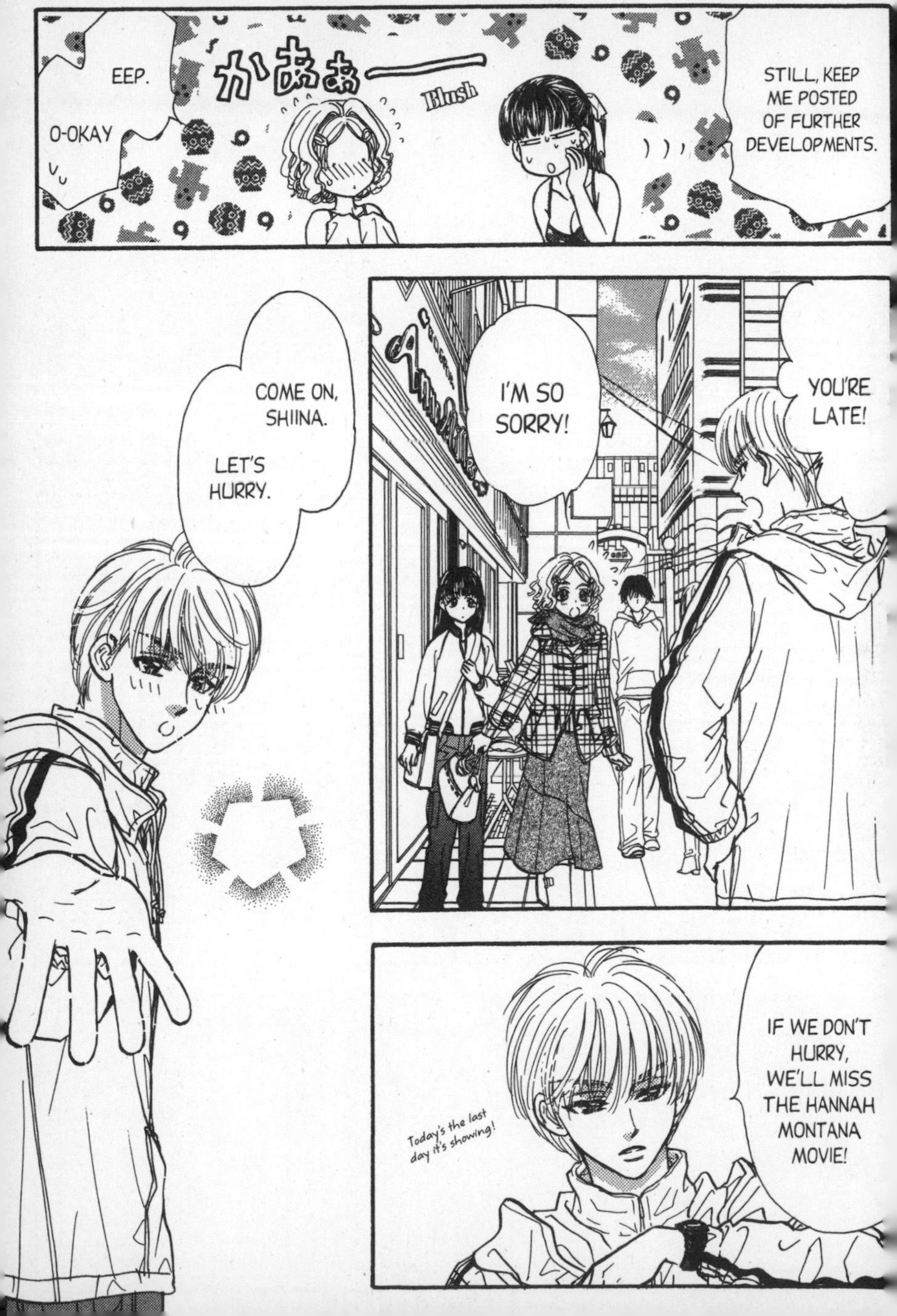
STILL, KEEP ME POSTED OF FURTHER DEVELOPMENTS.
かああーー
Blush
EEP.
O-OKAY
YOU'RE LATE!
I'M SO SORRY!
IF WE DON'T HURRY, WE'LL MISS THE HANNAH MONTANA MOVIE!
Today's the last day it's showing!
COME ON, SHIINA.
LET'S HURRY.

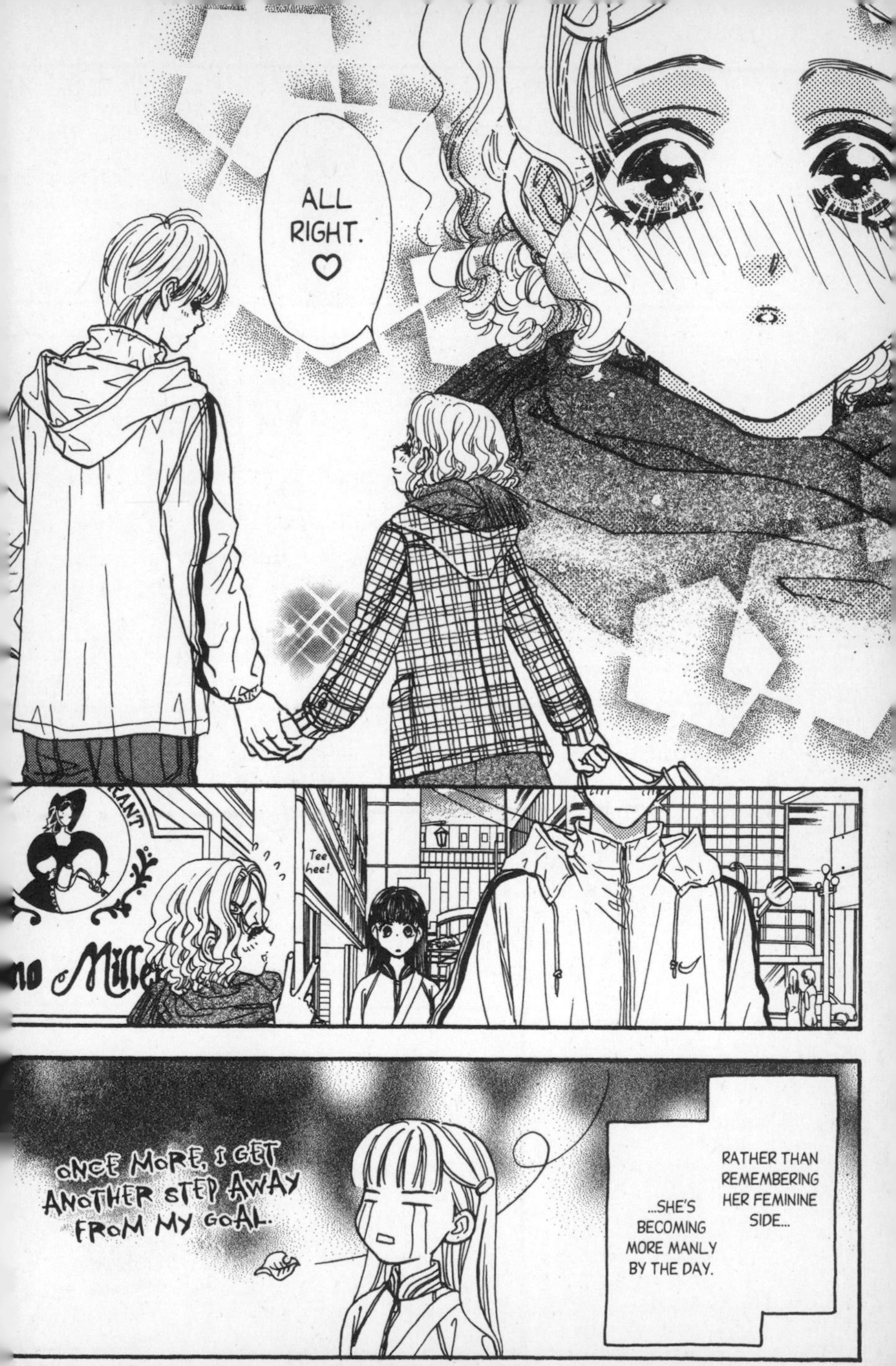
ALL RIGHT. ♡
Tee hee!
RATHER THAN REMEMBERING HER FEMININE SIDE...
...SHE'S BECOMING MORE MANLY BY THE DAY.
ONCE MORE, I GET ANOTHER STEP AWAY FROM MY GOAL.

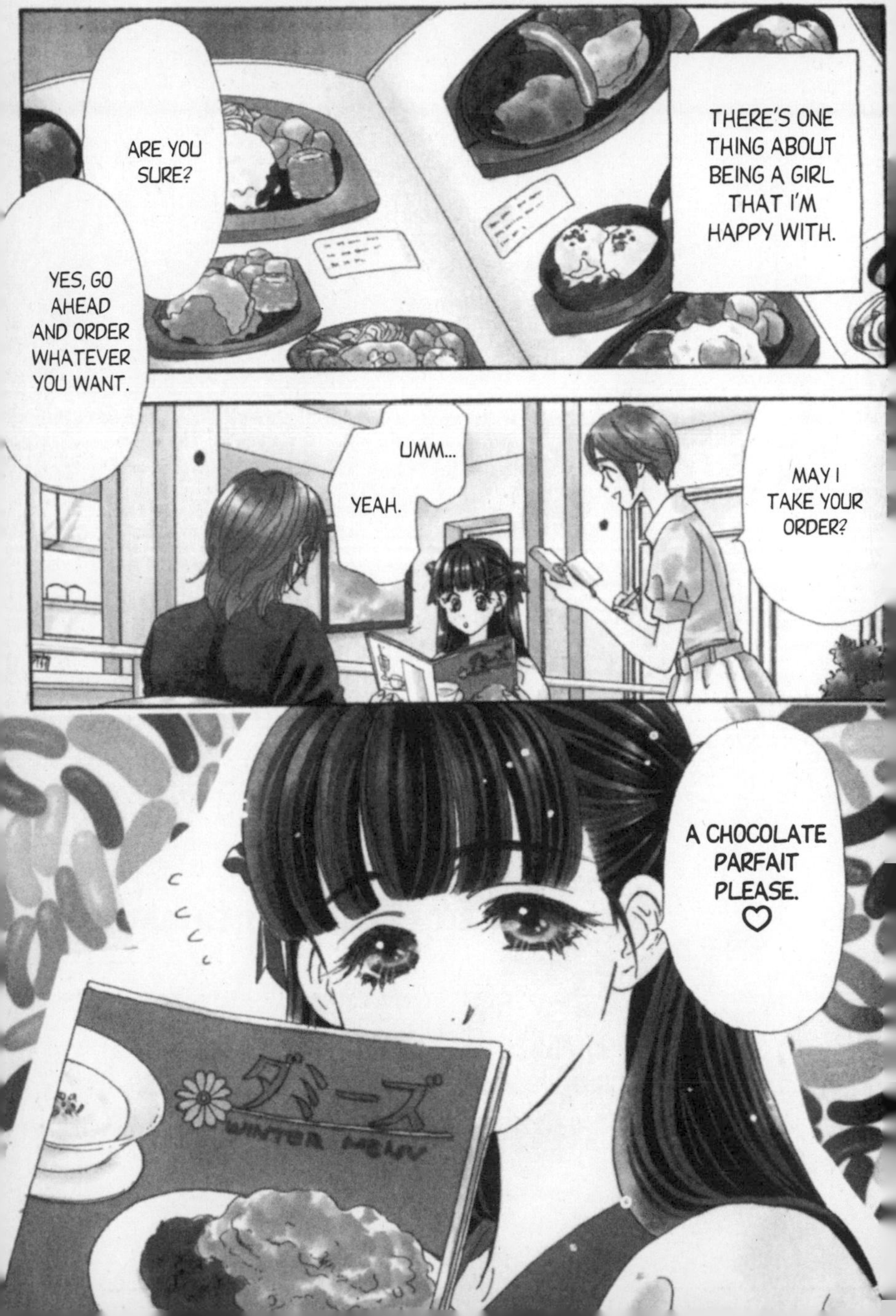
THERE'S ONE THING ABOUT BEING A GIRL THAT I'M HAPPY WITH.
ARE YOU SURE?
YES, GO AHEAD AND ORDER WHATEVER YOU WANT.
MAY I TAKE YOUR ORDER?
UMM... YEAH.
A CHOCOLATE PARFAIT PLEASE. ♡

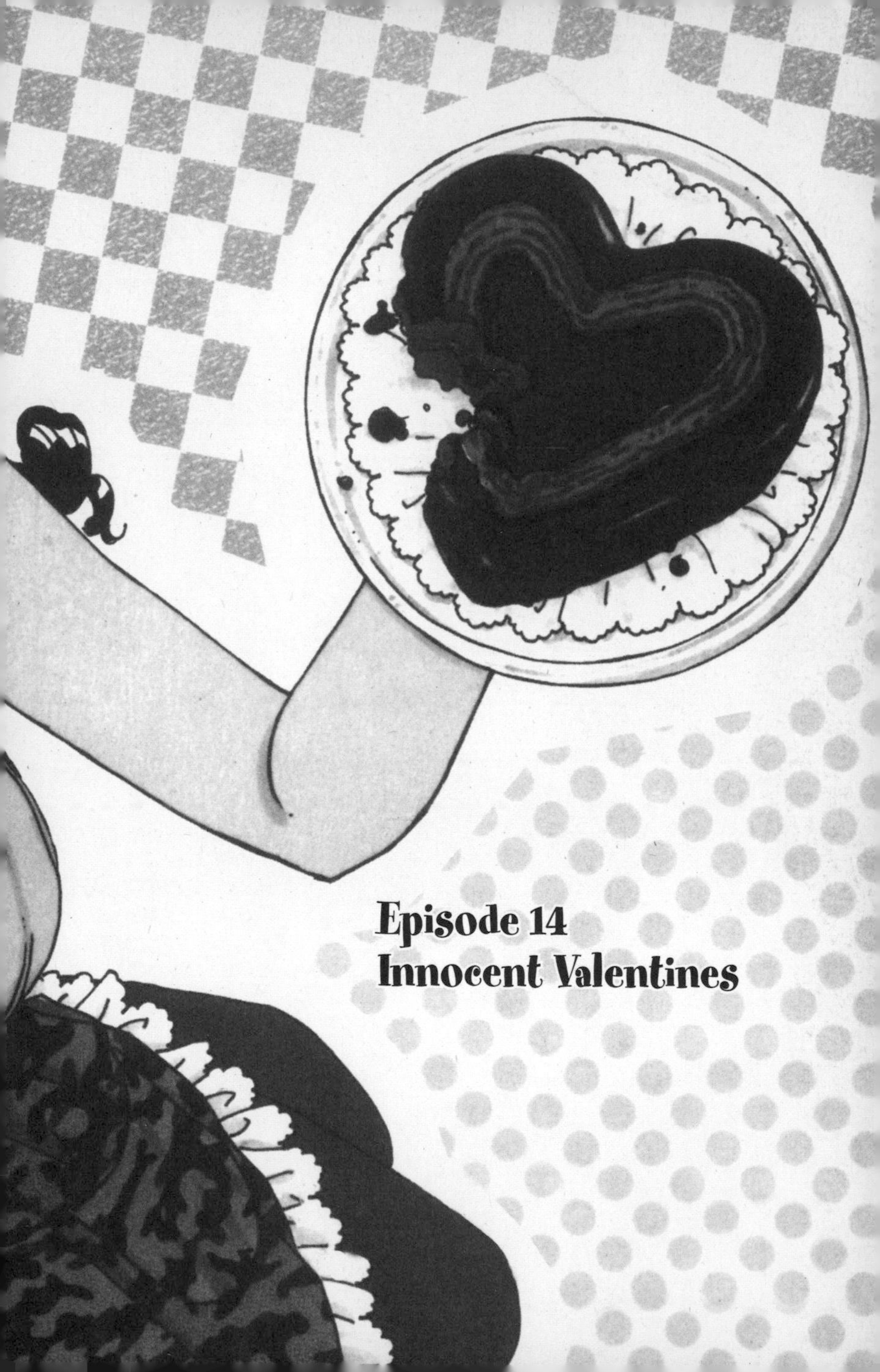

Episode 14
Innocent Valentines

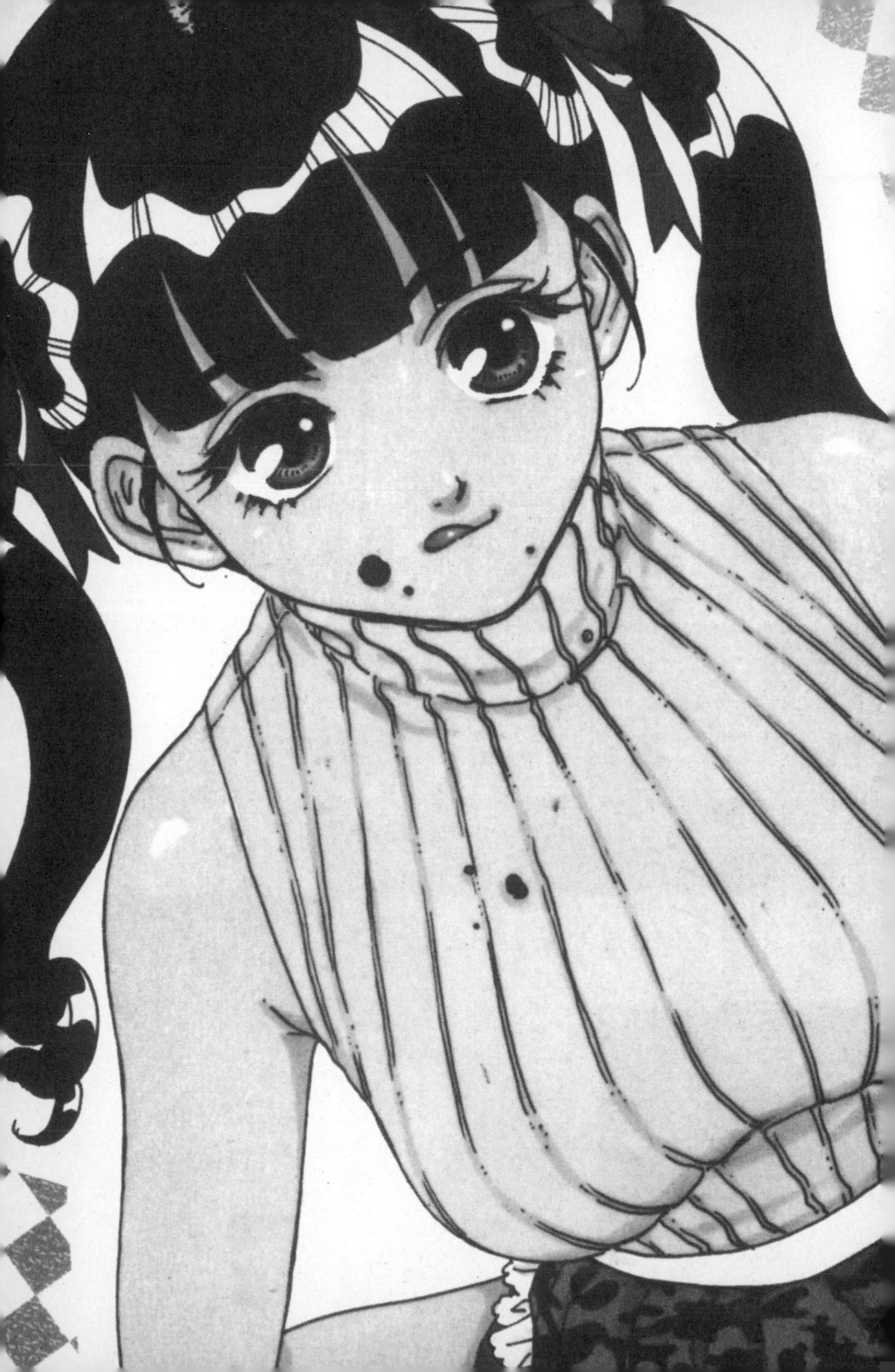

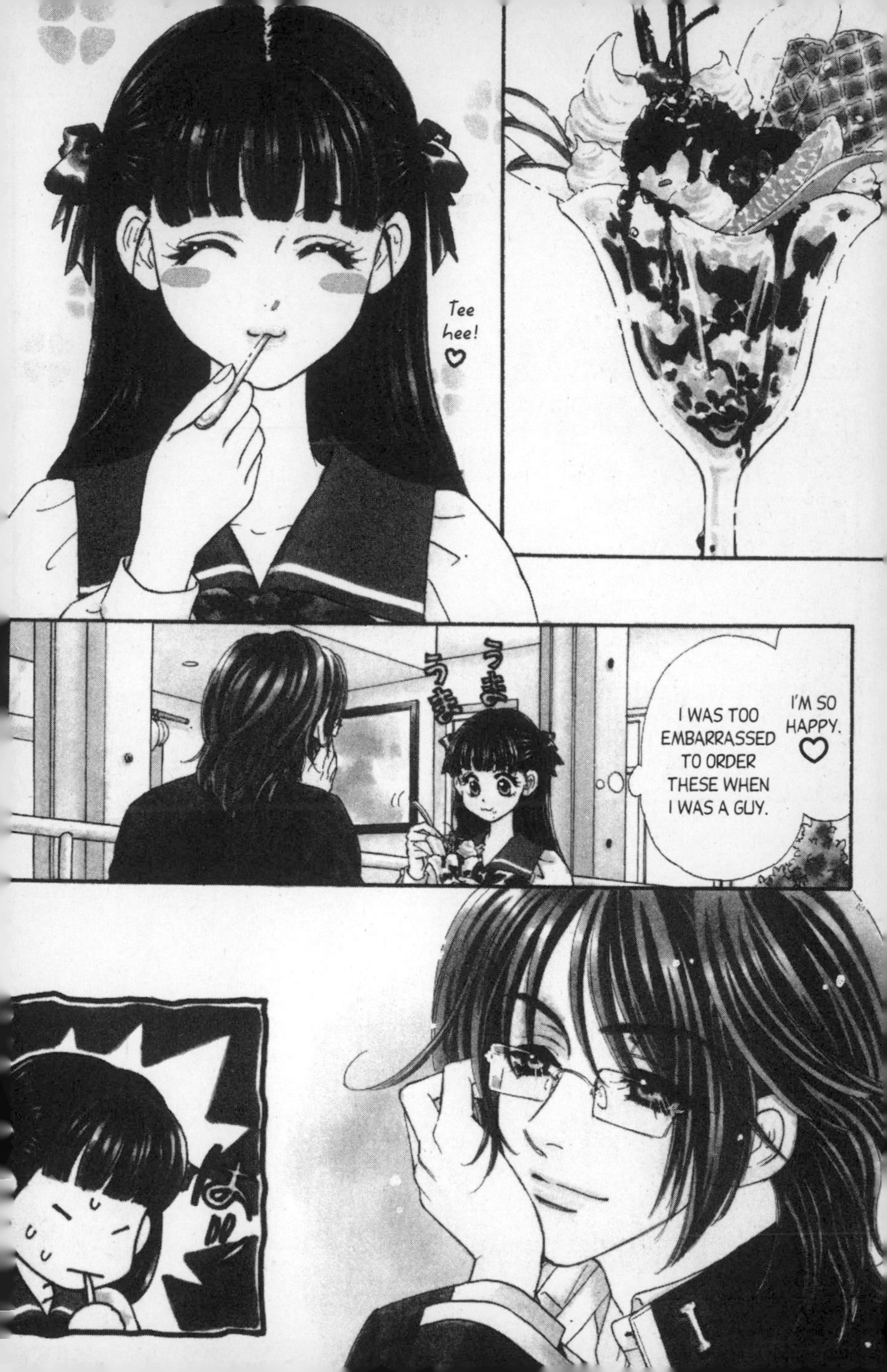
Tee hee! ♡
I'M SO HAPPY. ♡
I WAS TOO EMBARRASSED TO ORDER THESE WHEN I WAS A GUY.
うま うま

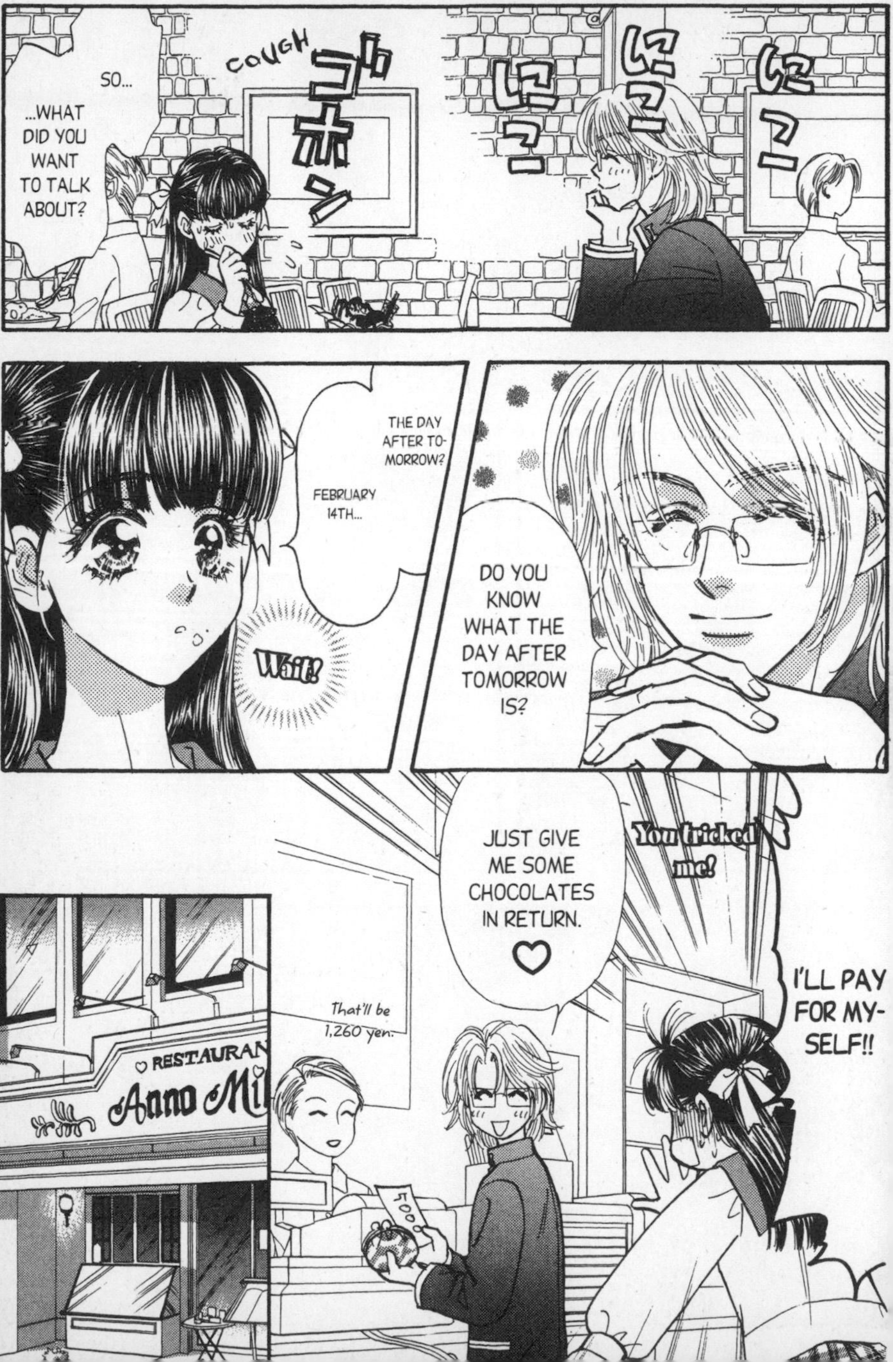
にこー
にこー
ゴホン
COUGH
SO...
...WHAT DID YOU WANT TO TALK ABOUT?
DO YOU KNOW WHAT THE DAY AFTER TOMORROW IS?
THE DAY AFTER TO-MORROW?
FEBRUARY 14TH...
Wait!
You tricked me!
I'LL PAY FOR MY-SELF!!
JUST GIVE ME SOME CHOCOLATES IN RETURN. ♥
That'll be 1,260 yen.
RESTAURAN
Anno Mil

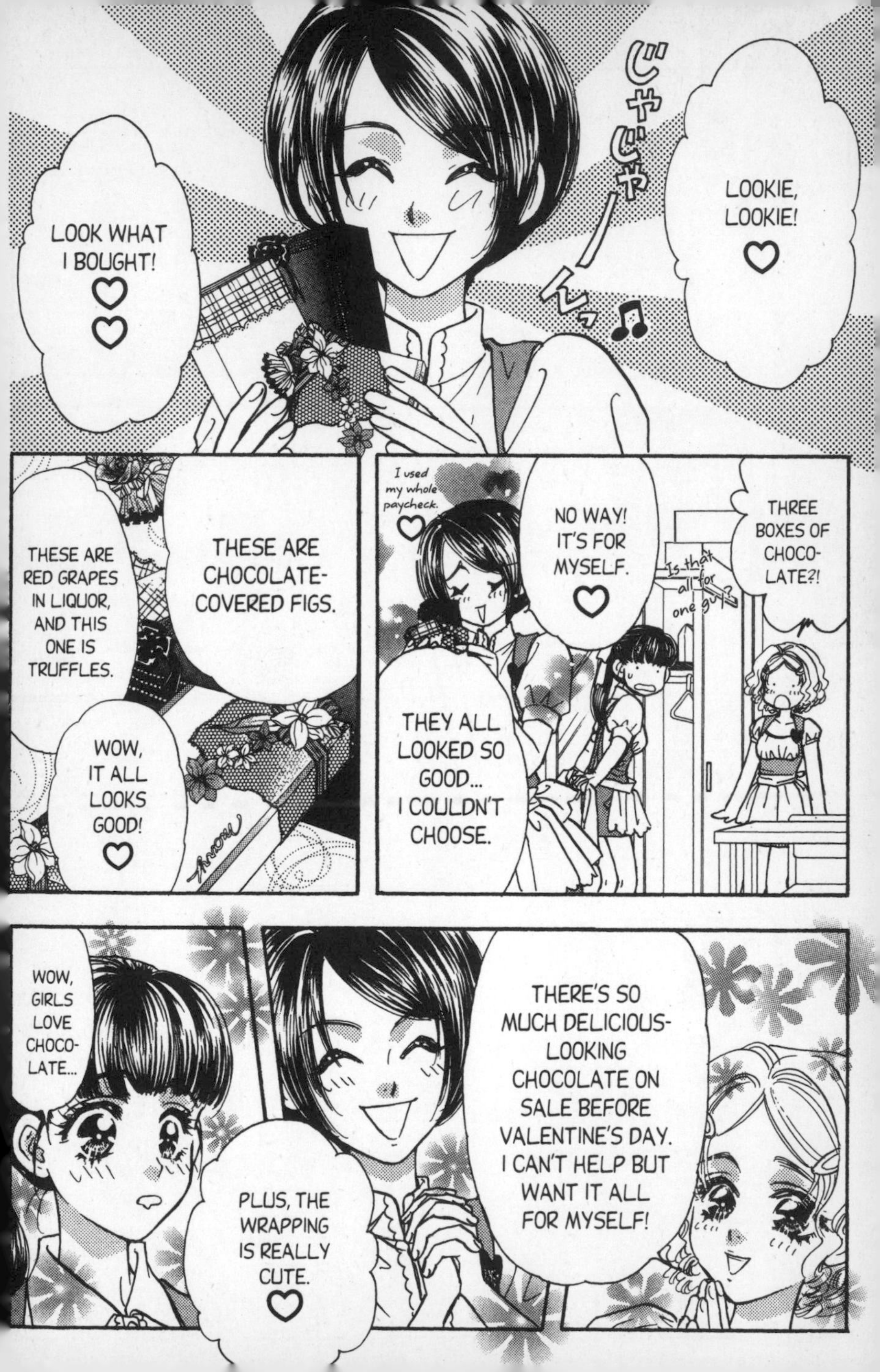
LOOKIE, LOOKIE! ♡
じゃじゃーん♪
LOOK WHAT I BOUGHT! ♡ ♡
THREE BOXES OF CHOCO-LATE?!
Is that all for one guy?
NO WAY! IT'S FOR MYSELF. ♡
I used my whole paycheck. ♡
THEY ALL LOOKED SO GOOD... I COULDN'T CHOOSE.
THESE ARE CHOCOLATE-COVERED FIGS.
THESE ARE RED GRAPES IN LIQUOR, AND THIS ONE IS TRUFFLES.
WOW, IT ALL LOOKS GOOD! ♡
THERE'S SO MUCH DELICIOUS-LOOKING CHOCOLATE ON SALE BEFORE VALENTINE'S DAY. I CAN'T HELP BUT WANT IT ALL FOR MYSELF!
PLUS, THE WRAPPING IS REALLY CUTE. ♡
WOW, GIRLS LOVE CHOCO-LATE...

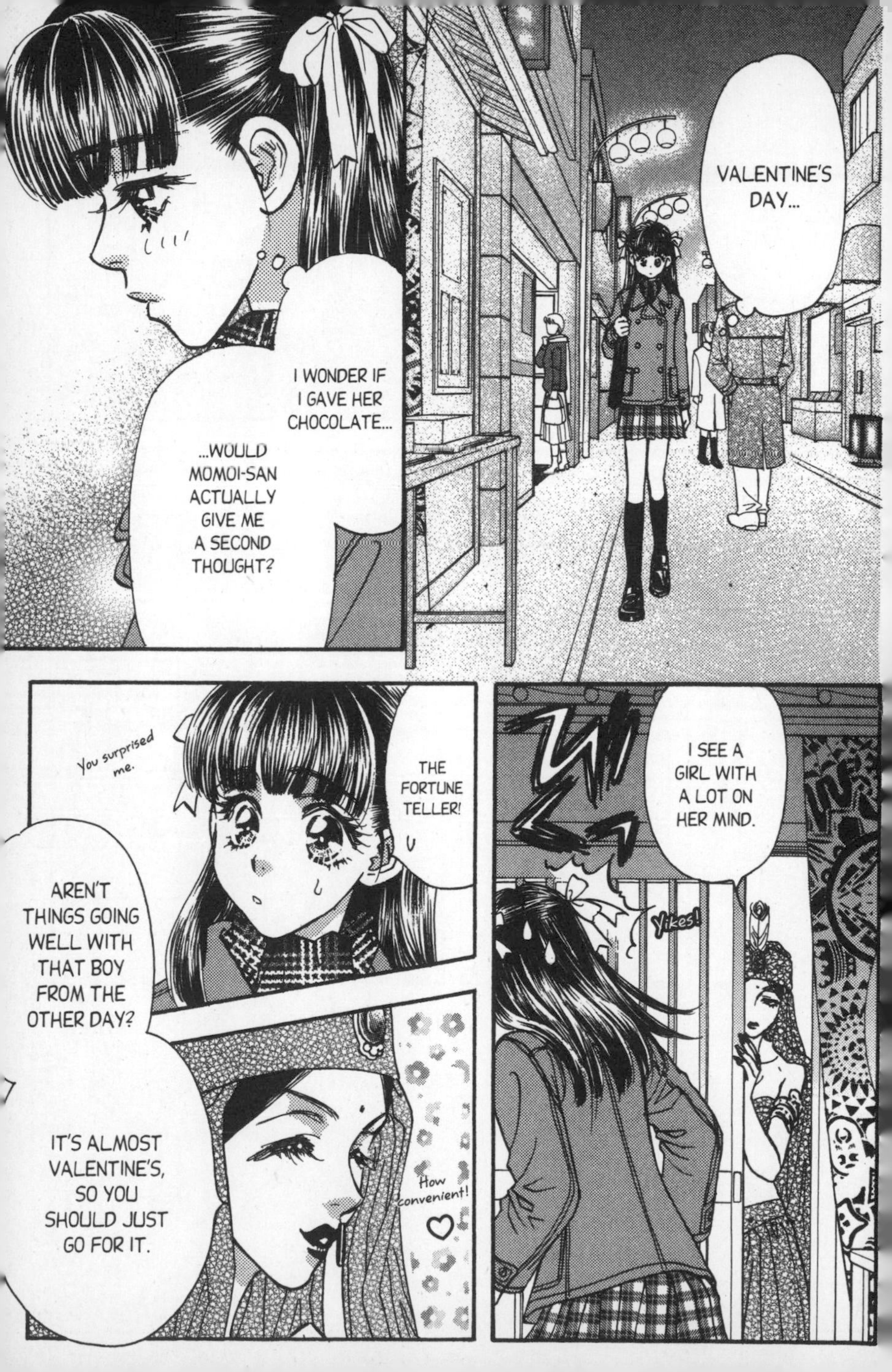
VALENTINE'S DAY...
I WONDER IF I GAVE HER CHOCOLATE...
...WOULD MOMOI-SAN ACTUALLY GIVE ME A SECOND THOUGHT?
I SEE A GIRL WITH A LOT ON HER MIND.
Yikes!
THE FORTUNE TELLER!
You surprised me.
AREN'T THINGS GOING WELL WITH THAT BOY FROM THE OTHER DAY?
IT'S ALMOST VALENTINE'S, SO YOU SHOULD JUST GO FOR IT.
How convenient!

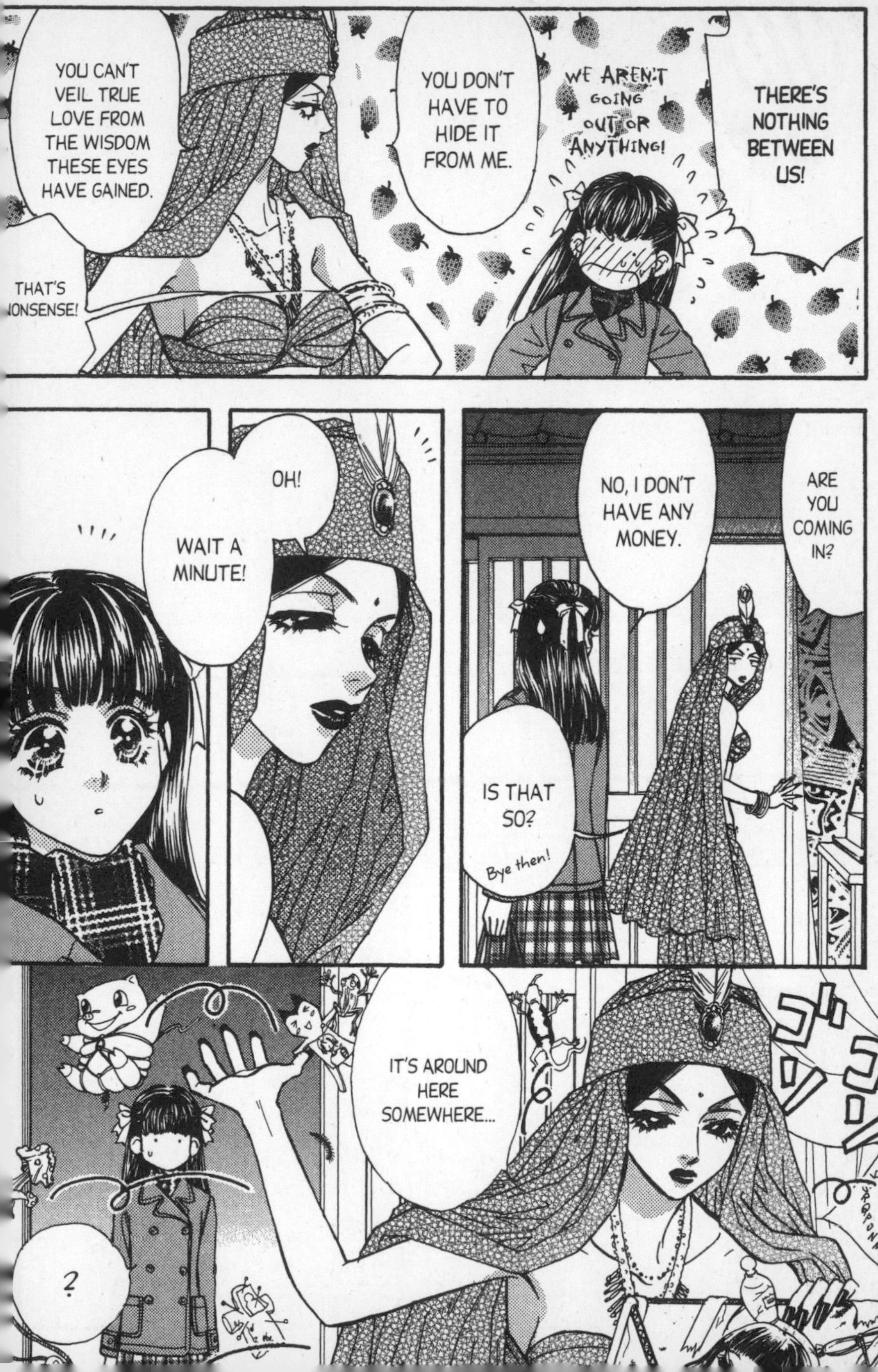
THERE'S NOTHING BETWEEN US!
WE AREN'T GOING OUT OR ANYTHING!
YOU DON'T HAVE TO HIDE IT FROM ME.
YOU CAN'T VEIL TRUE LOVE FROM THE WISDOM THESE EYES HAVE GAINED.
THAT'S NONSENSE!
ARE YOU COMING IN?
NO, I DON'T HAVE ANY MONEY.
IS THAT SO?
Bye then!
OH!
WAIT A MINUTE!
IT'S AROUND HERE SOMEWHERE...
?

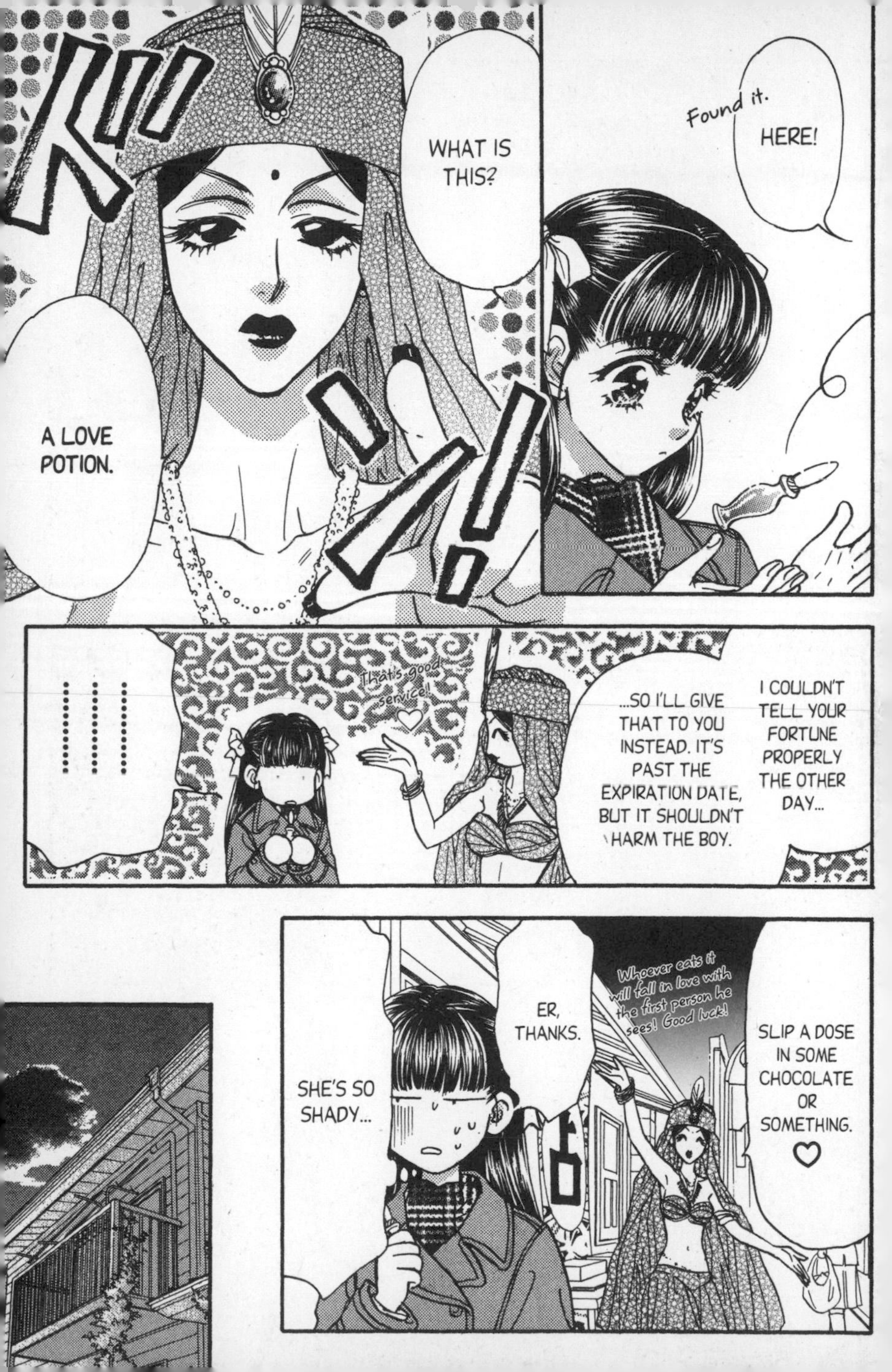
Found it.
HERE!
WHAT IS THIS?
A LOVE POTION.
I COULDN'T TELL YOUR FORTUNE PROPERLY THE OTHER DAY...
...SO I'LL GIVE THAT TO YOU INSTEAD. IT'S PAST THE EXPIRATION DATE, BUT IT SHOULDN'T HARM THE BOY.
That's good service! ♡
......
SLIP A DOSE IN SOME CHOCOLATE OR SOMETHING. ♡
Whoever eats it will fall in love with the first person he sees! Good luck!
ER, THANKS.
SHE'S SO SHADY...

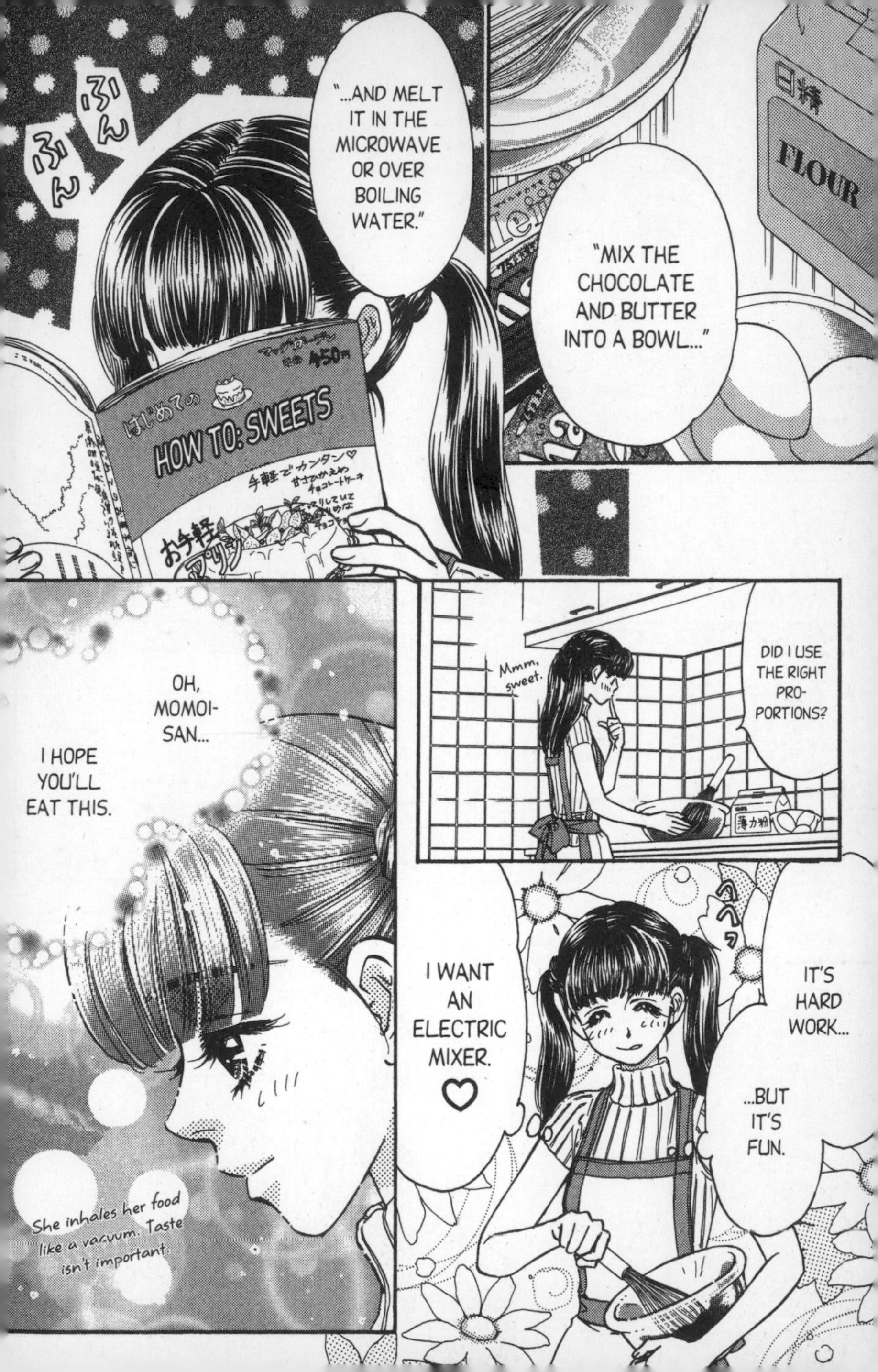
日清
FLOUR
"MIX THE CHOCOLATE AND BUTTER INTO A BOWL..."
"...AND MELT IT IN THE MICROWAVE OR OVER BOILING WATER."
ふん ふん
はじめての
HOW TO: SWEETS
手軽でカンタン♡
DID I USE THE RIGHT PRO-PORTIONS?
Mmm, sweet.
IT'S HARD WORK...
...BUT IT'S FUN.
I WANT AN ELECTRIC MIXER. ♡
OH, MOMOI-SAN...
I HOPE YOU'LL EAT THIS.
She inhales her food like a vacuum. Taste isn't important.

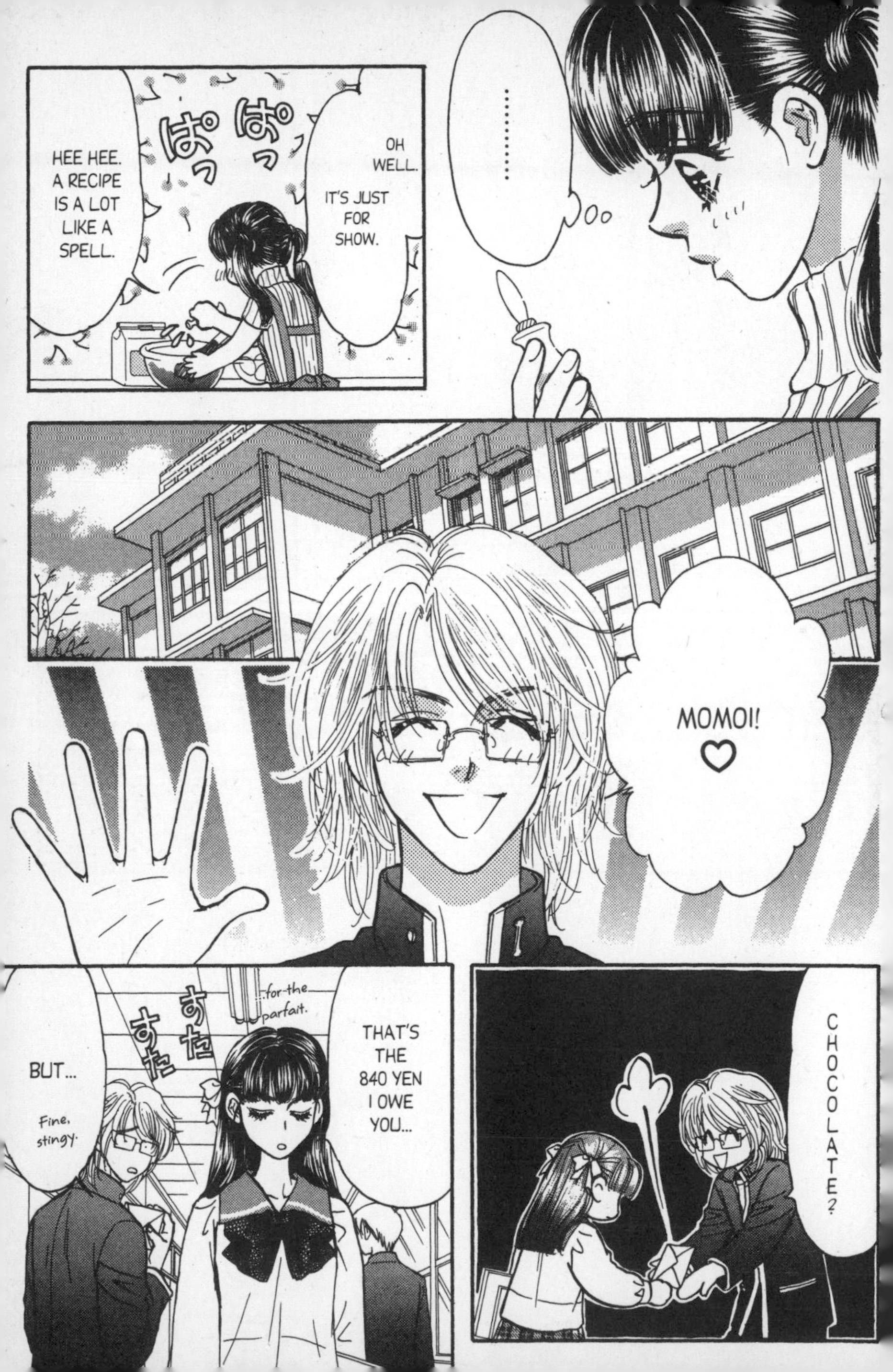
……
OH WELL.
IT'S JUST FOR SHOW.
ぱっぱっ
HEE HEE. A RECIPE IS A LOT LIKE A SPELL.
MOMOI! ♡
CHOCOLATE?
THAT'S THE 840 YEN I OWE YOU...
...for the parfait.
すたすた
BUT...
Fine, stingy.

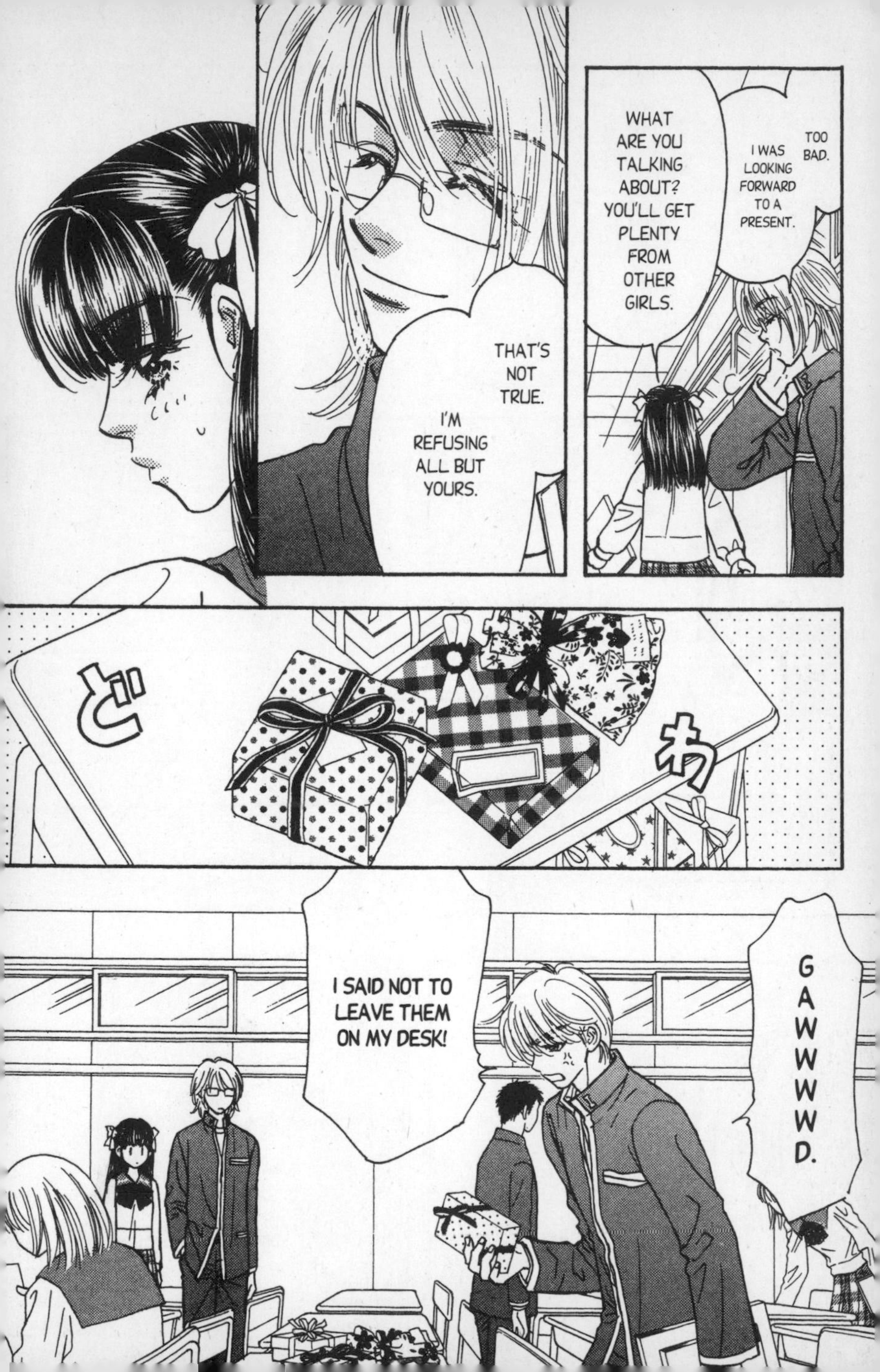
TOO BAD.
I WAS LOOKING FORWARD TO A PRESENT.
WHAT ARE YOU TALKING ABOUT? YOU'LL GET PLENTY FROM OTHER GIRLS.
THAT'S NOT TRUE.
I'M REFUSING ALL BUT YOURS.
どわ
GAWWWWD.
I SAID NOT TO LEAVE THEM ON MY DESK!

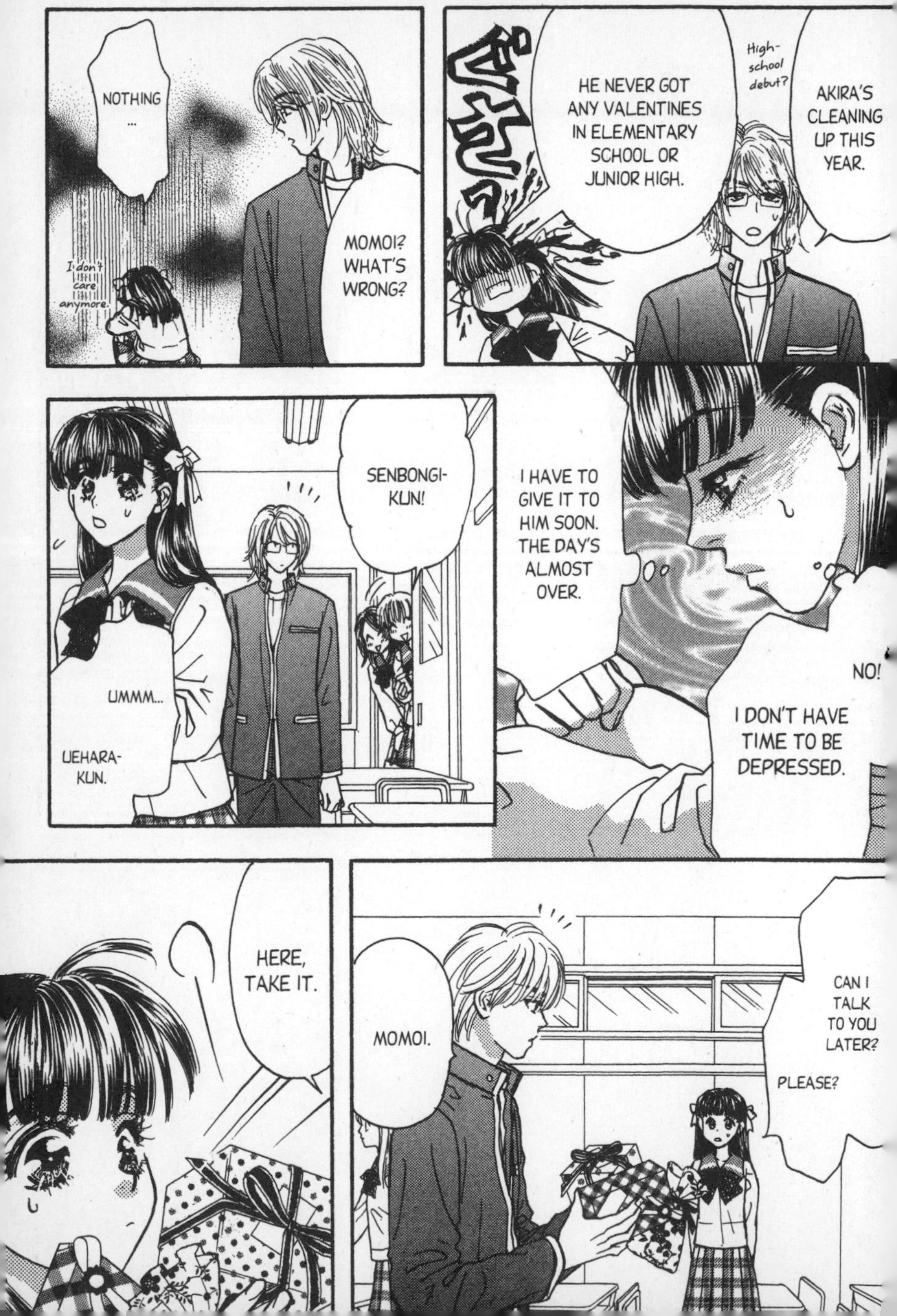
AKIRA'S CLEANING UP THIS YEAR.
High-school debut?
HE NEVER GOT ANY VALENTINES IN ELEMENTARY SCHOOL OR JUNIOR HIGH.
MOMOI? WHAT'S WRONG?
NOTHING ...
I don't care anymore.
NO!
I DON'T HAVE TIME TO BE DEPRESSED.
I HAVE TO GIVE IT TO HIM SOON. THE DAY'S ALMOST OVER.
SENBONGI-KUN!
UMMM...
UEHARA-KUN.
CAN I TALK TO YOU LATER?
PLEASE?
MOMOI.
HERE, TAKE IT.

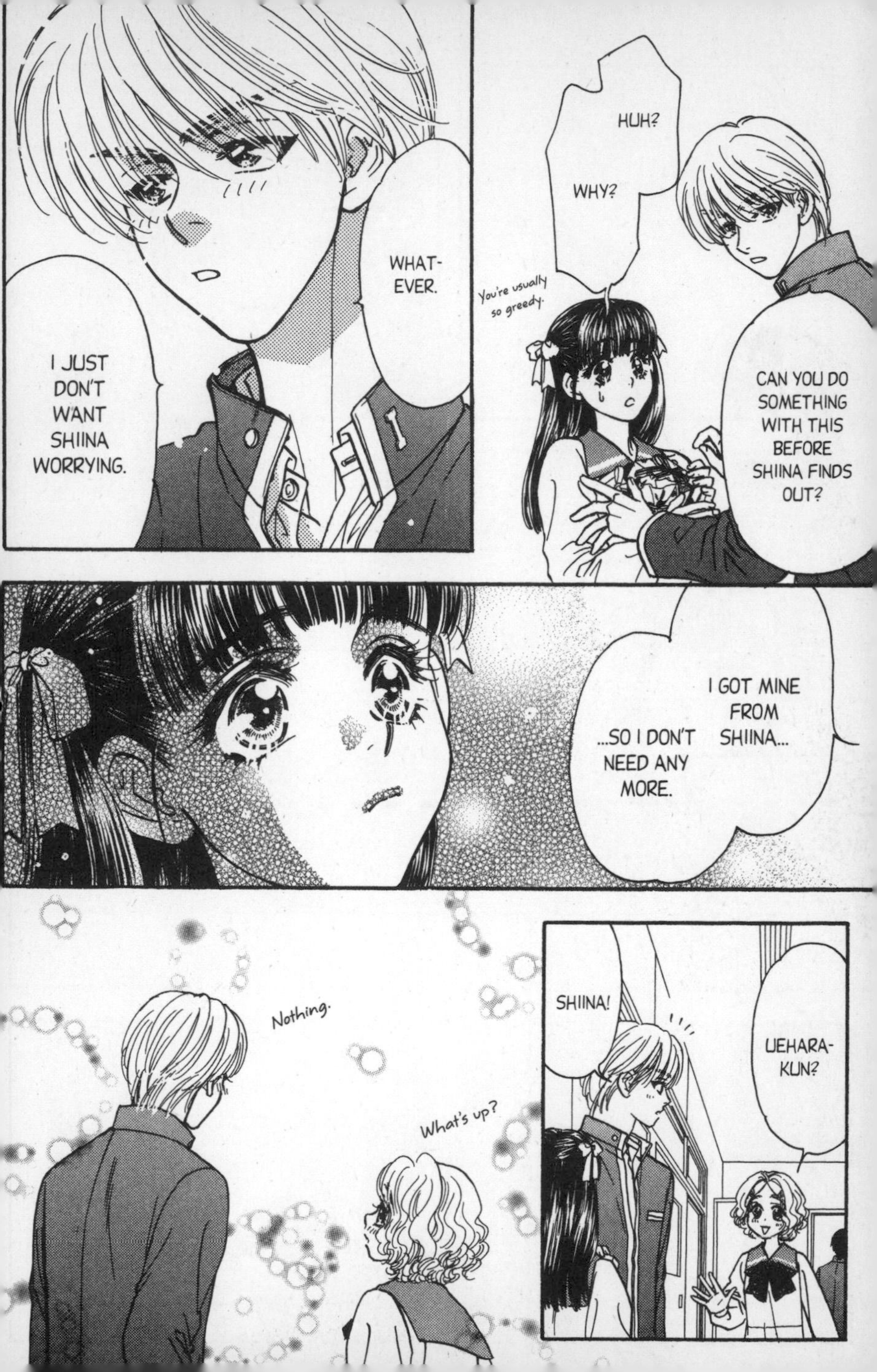
CAN YOU DO SOMETHING WITH THIS BEFORE SHIINA FINDS OUT?
HUH?
WHY?
You're usually so greedy.
WHAT-EVER.
I JUST DON'T WANT SHIINA WORRYING.
I GOT MINE FROM SHIINA...
...SO I DON'T NEED ANY MORE.
UEHARA-KUN?
SHIINA!
What's up?
Nothing.

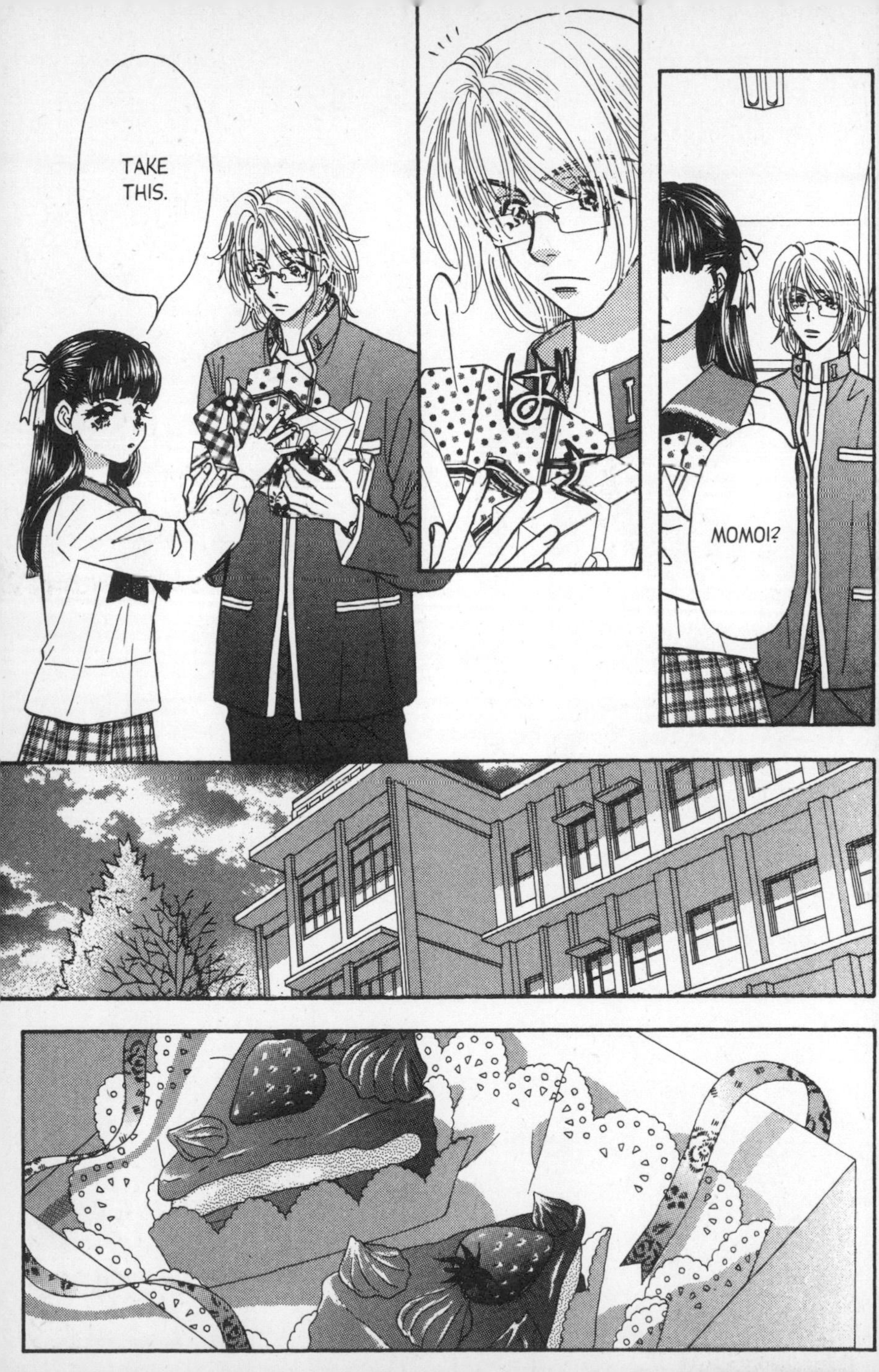
MOMOI?
TAKE THIS.

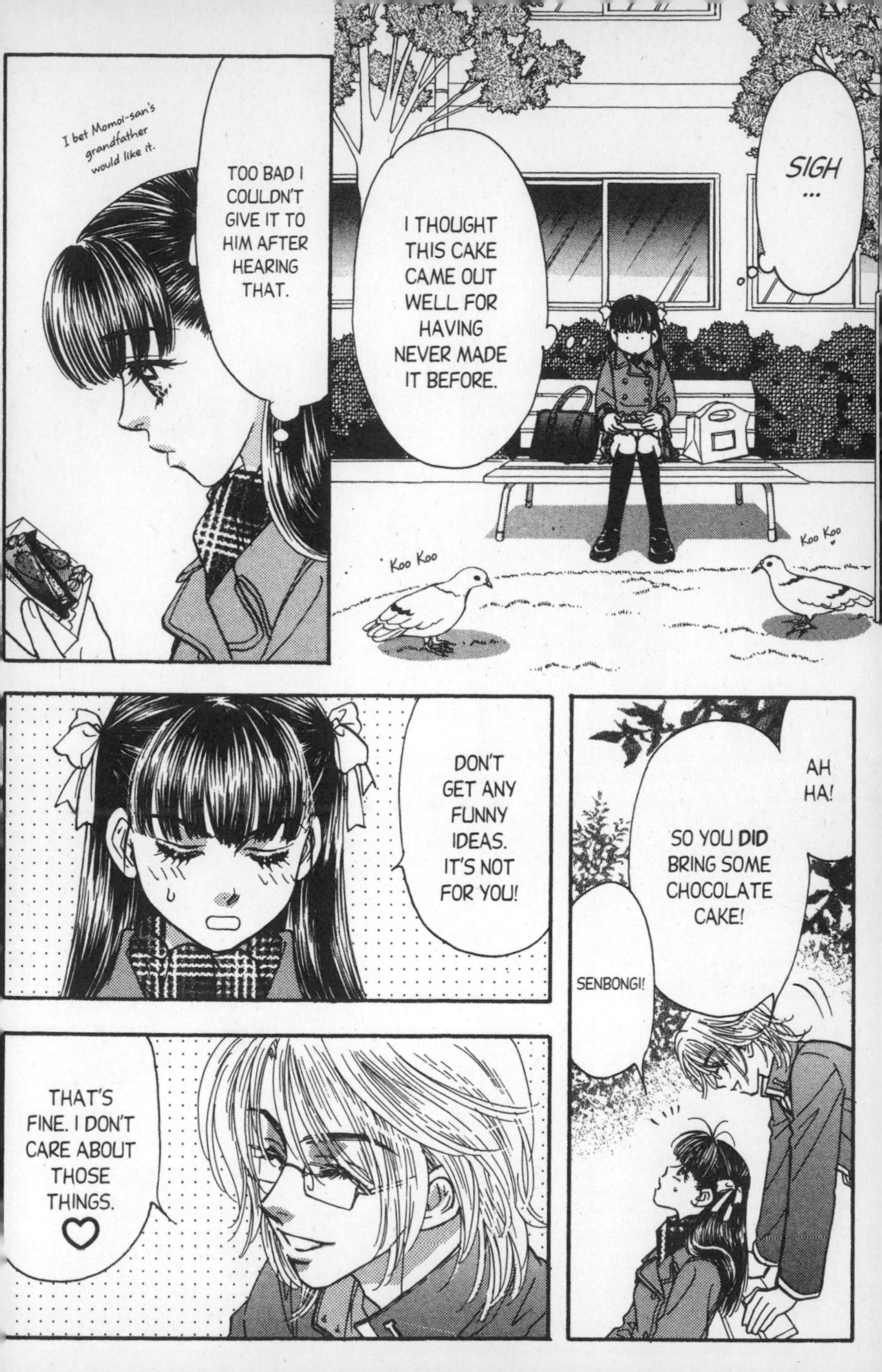
SIGH ...
I THOUGHT THIS CAKE CAME OUT WELL FOR HAVING NEVER MADE IT BEFORE.
Koo Koo
Koo Koo
TOO BAD I COULDN'T GIVE IT TO HIM AFTER HEARING THAT.
I bet Momoi-san's grandfather would like it.
AH HA! SO YOU **DID** BRING SOME CHOCOLATE CAKE!
SENBONGI!
DON'T GET ANY FUNNY IDEAS. IT'S NOT FOR YOU!
THAT'S FINE. I DON'T CARE ABOUT THOSE THINGS. ♥

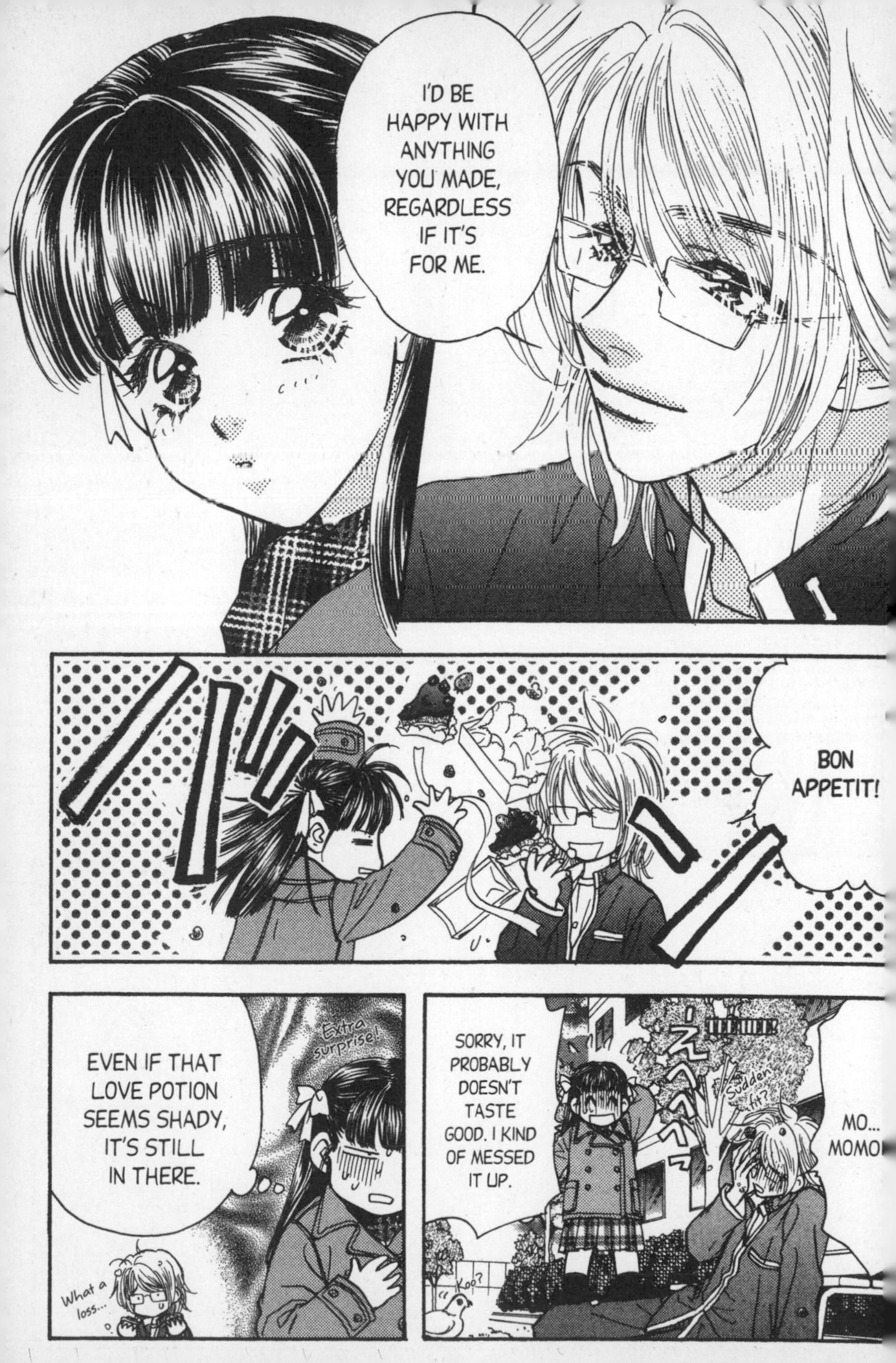
I'D BE HAPPY WITH ANYTHING YOU MADE, REGARDLESS IF IT'S FOR ME.
BON APPETIT!
MO... MOMO
Sudden fit?
SORRY, IT PROBABLY DOESN'T TASTE GOOD. I KIND OF MESSED IT UP.
Koo?
Extra surprise!
EVEN IF THAT LOVE POTION SEEMS SHADY, IT'S STILL IN THERE.
What a loss...

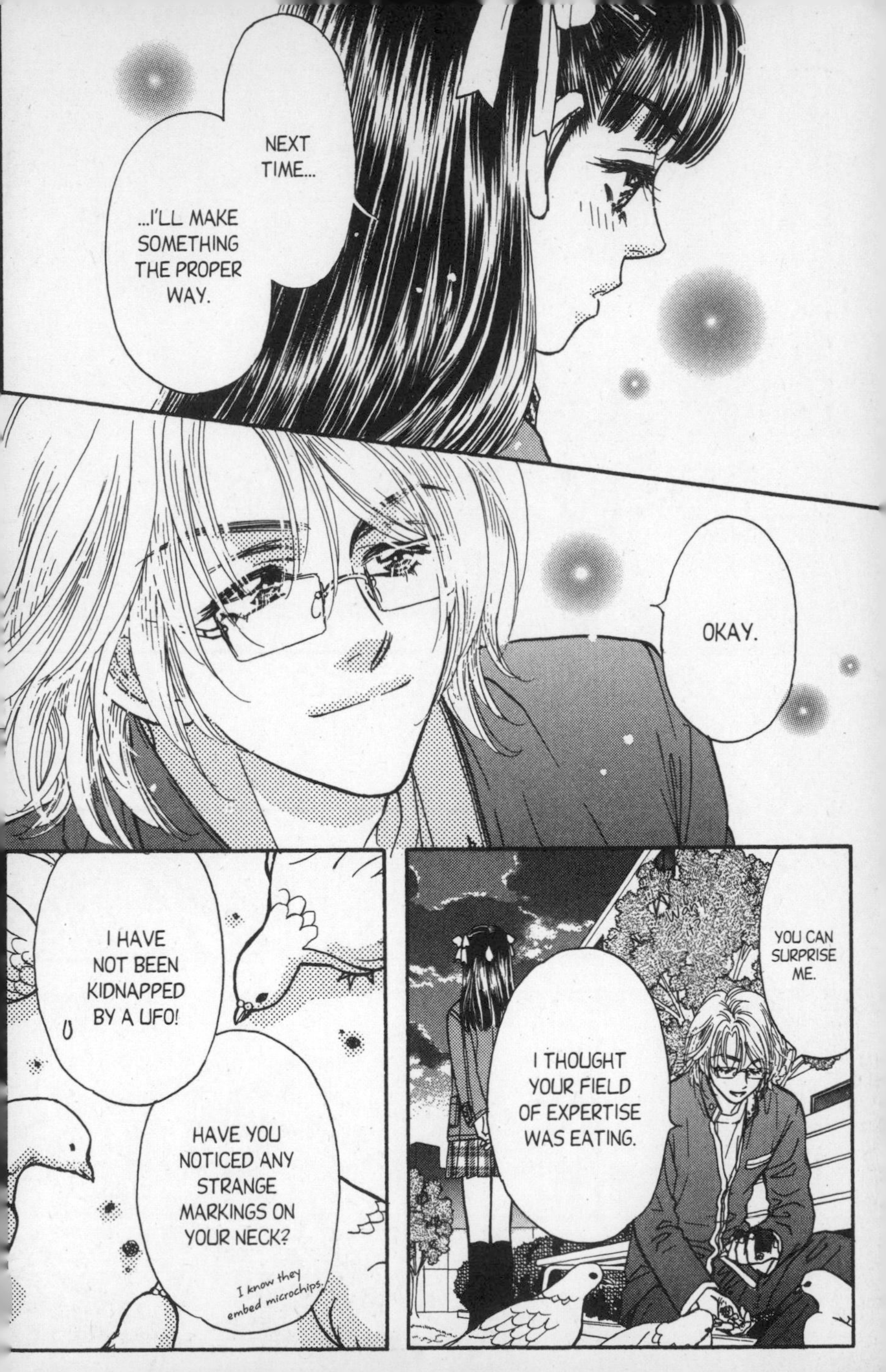
NEXT TIME...
...I'LL MAKE SOMETHING THE PROPER WAY.
OKAY.
YOU CAN SURPRISE ME.
I THOUGHT YOUR FIELD OF EXPERTISE WAS EATING.
I HAVE NOT BEEN KIDNAPPED BY A UFO!
HAVE YOU NOTICED ANY STRANGE MARKINGS ON YOUR NECK?
I know they embed microchips.

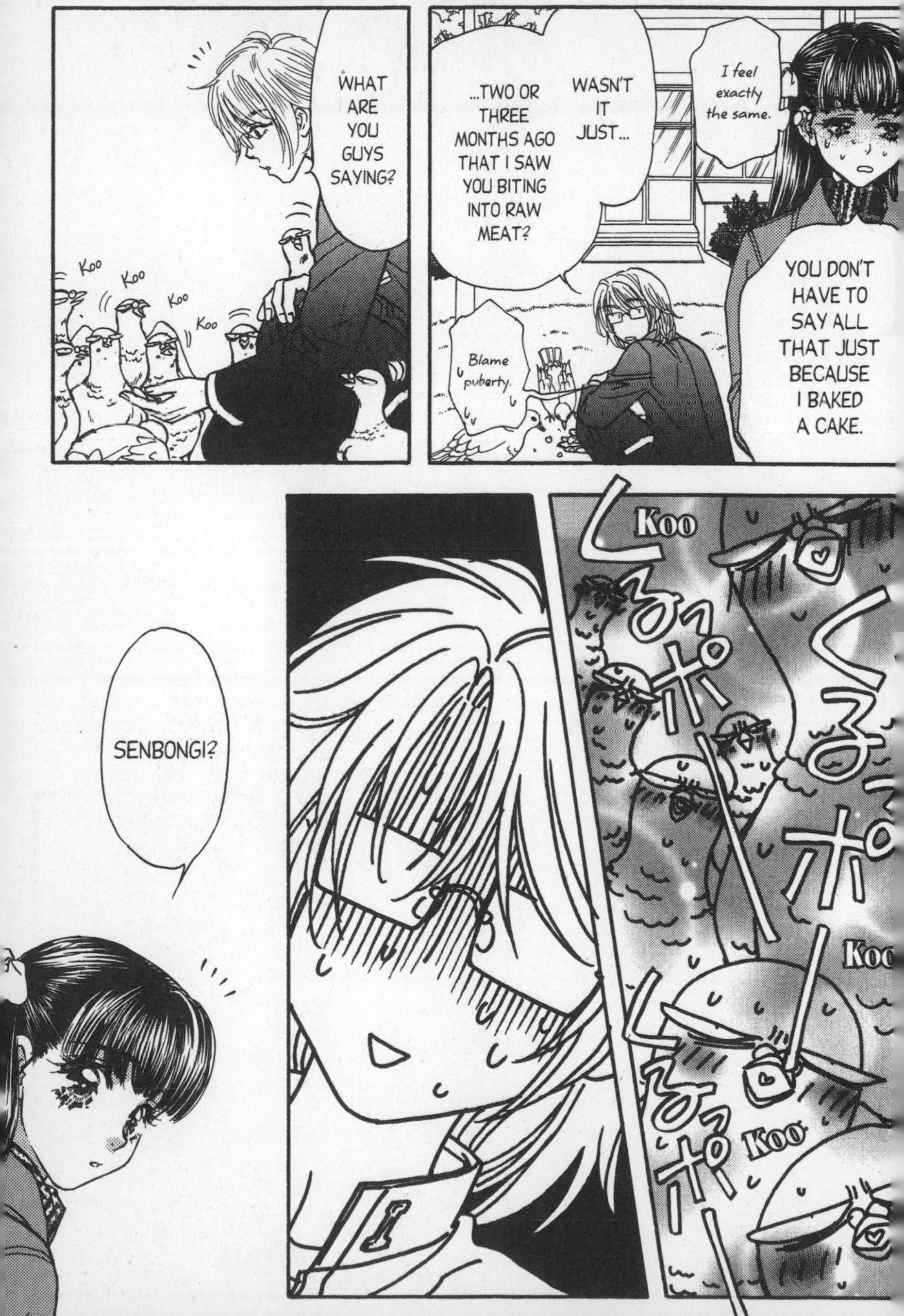
I feel exactly the same.
YOU DON'T HAVE TO SAY ALL THAT JUST BECAUSE I BAKED A CAKE.
WASN'T IT JUST...
...TWO OR THREE MONTHS AGO THAT I SAW YOU BITING INTO RAW MEAT?
Blame puberty.
WHAT ARE YOU GUYS SAYING?
Koo
Koo
Koo
Koo
Koo
くるっポ
くるっポ
Koo
くるっポ
Koo
SENBONGI?

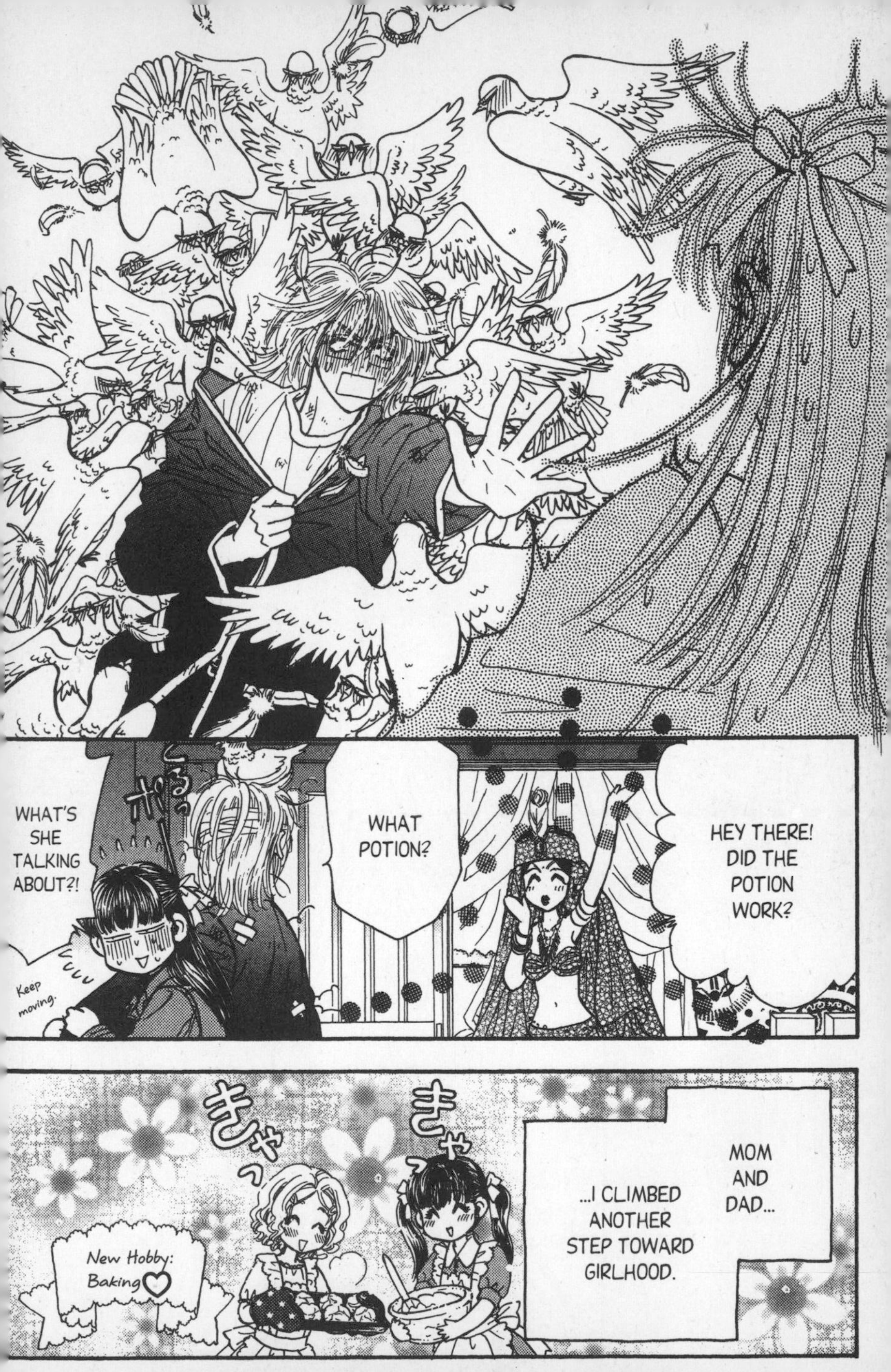
HEY THERE! DID THE POTION WORK?
WHAT POTION?
WHAT'S SHE TALKING ABOUT?!
Keep moving.
MOM AND DAD...
...I CLIMBED ANOTHER STEP TOWARD GIRLHOOD.
きゃっ
きゃっ
New Hobby: Baking♡

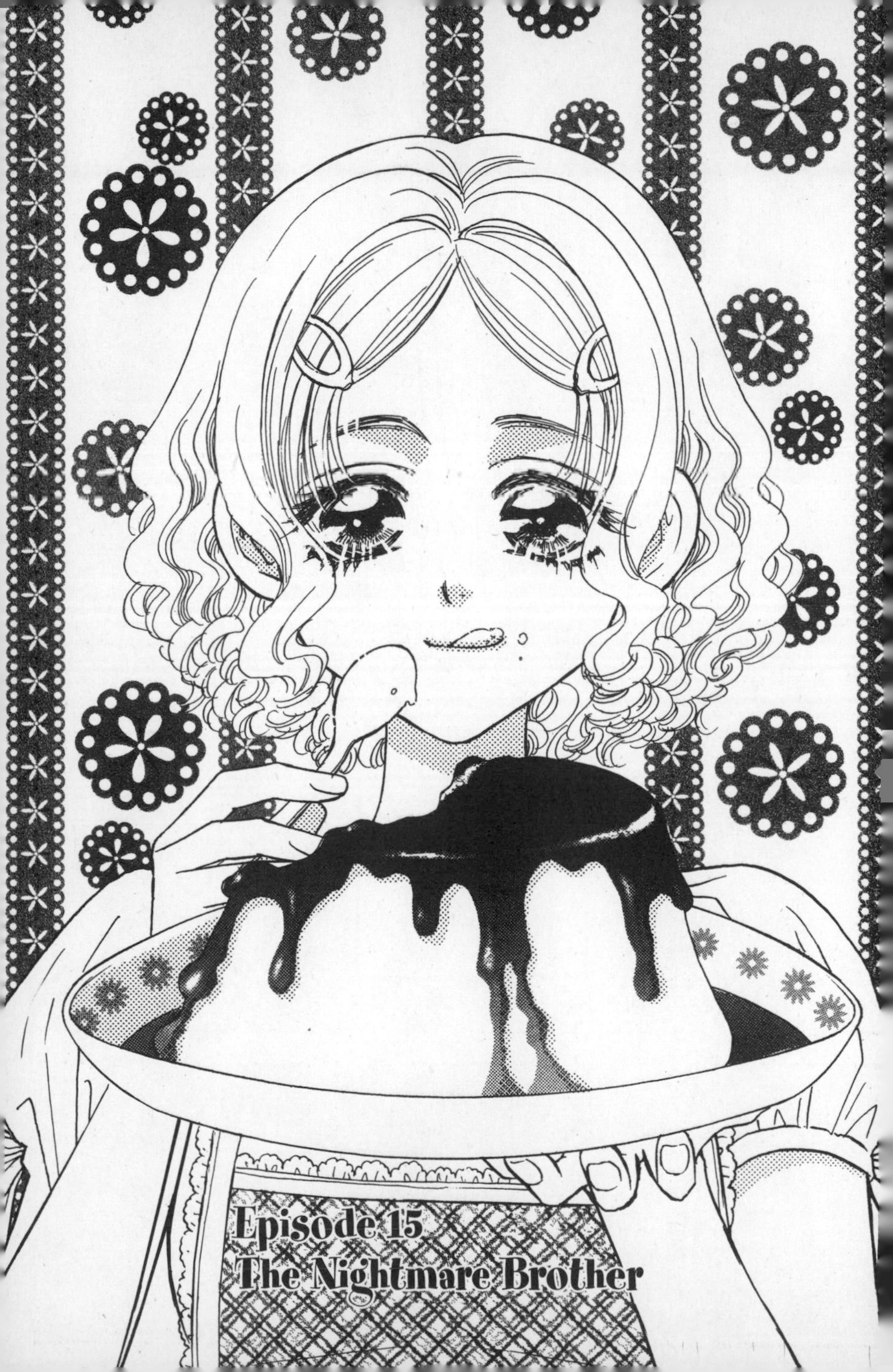
Episode 15
The Nightmare Brother

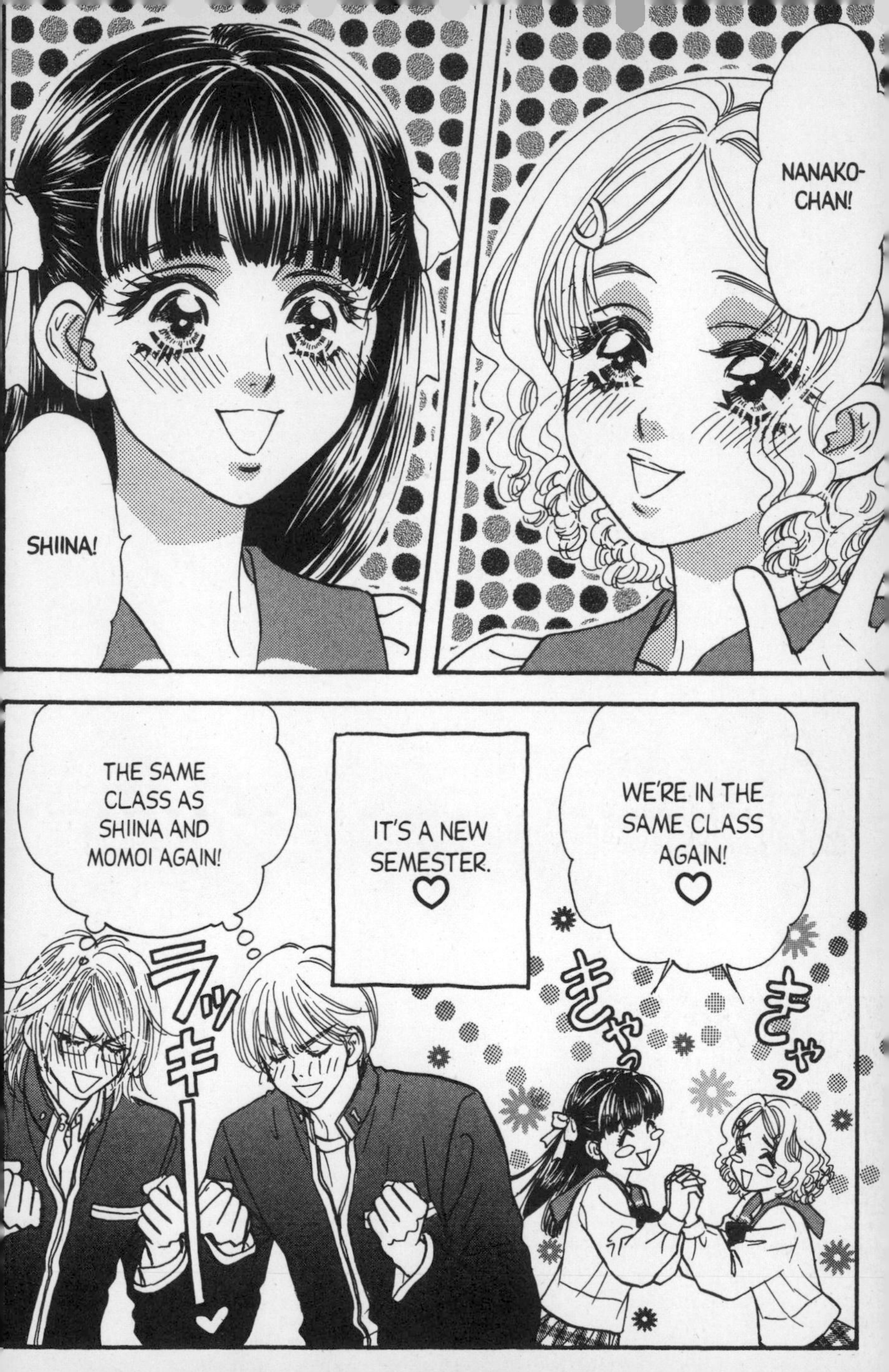
NANAKO-CHAN!
SHIINA!
WE'RE IN THE SAME CLASS AGAIN! ♡
きゃっ
きゃっ
IT'S A NEW SEMESTER. ♡
THE SAME CLASS AS SHIINA AND MOMOI AGAIN!
ラッキー

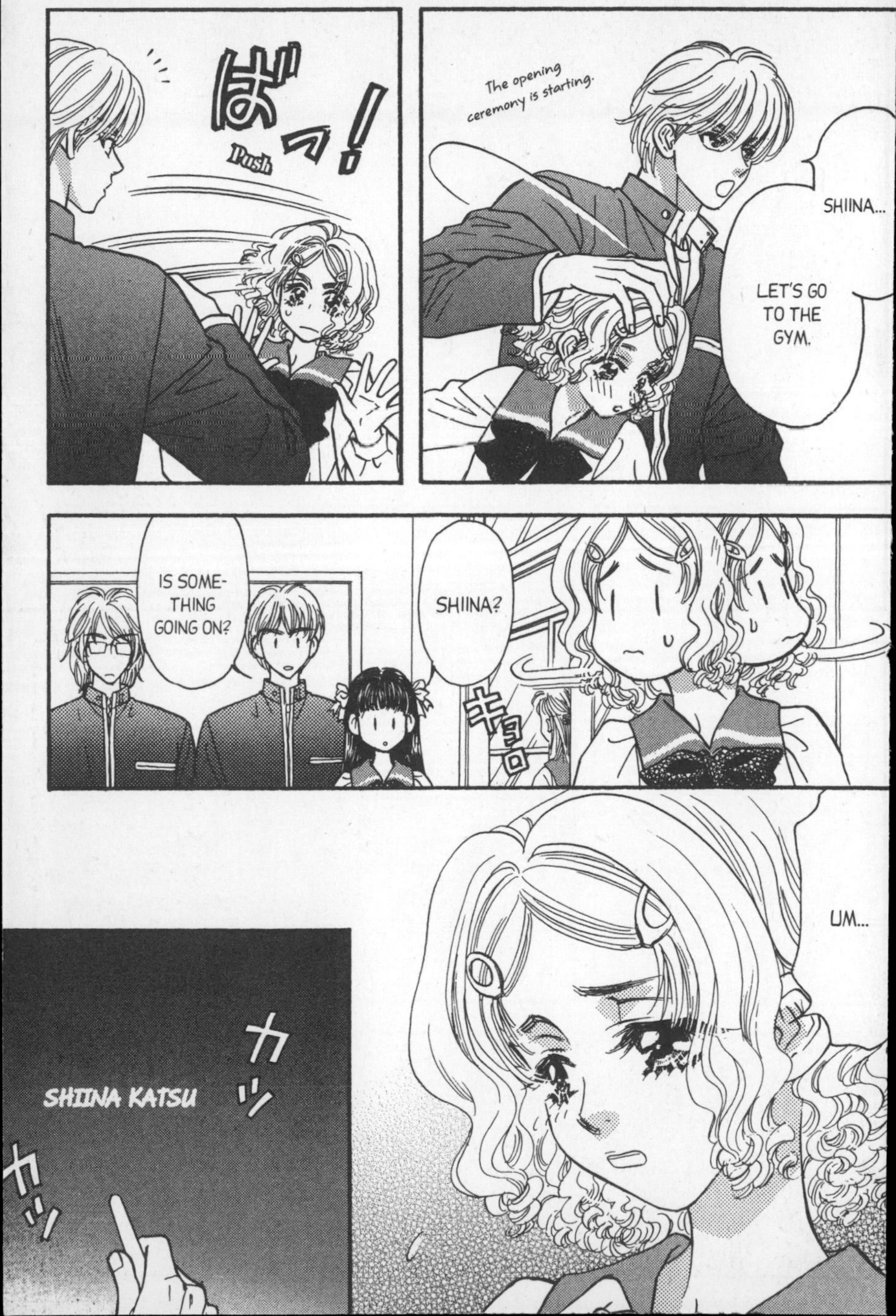
The opening ceremony is starting.
SHIINA...
LET'S GO TO THE GYM.
ばっ!
Push
キョロ
SHIINA?
IS SOME-THING GOING ON?
UM...
SHIINA KATSU
カッ

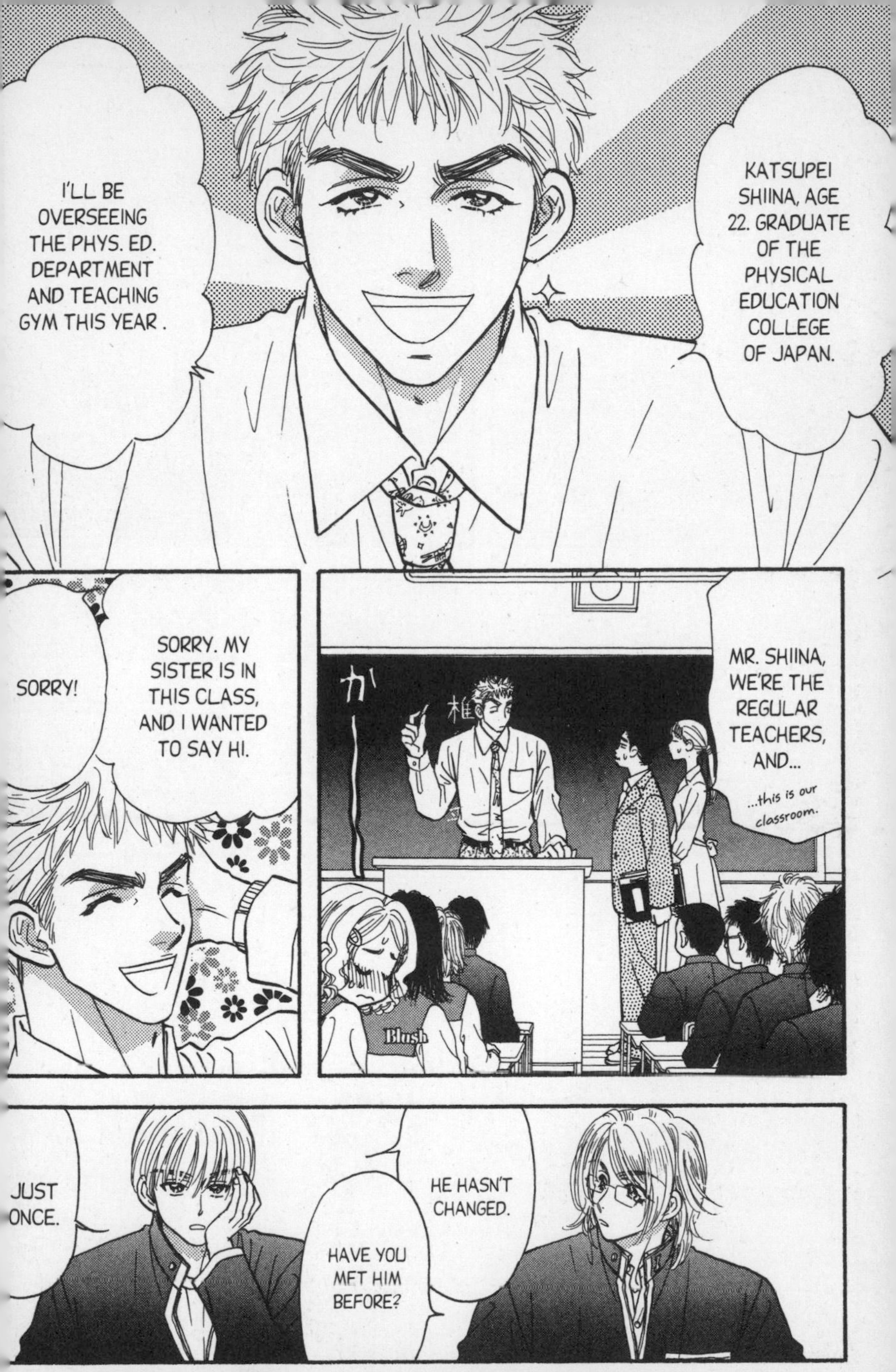
KATSUPEI SHIINA, AGE 22. GRADUATE OF THE PHYSICAL EDUCATION COLLEGE OF JAPAN.
I'LL BE OVERSEEING THE PHYS. ED. DEPARTMENT AND TEACHING GYM THIS YEAR.
MR. SHIINA, WE'RE THE REGULAR TEACHERS, AND...
...this is our classroom.
Blush
SORRY. MY SISTER IS IN THIS CLASS, AND I WANTED TO SAY HI.
SORRY!
HE HASN'T CHANGED.
HAVE YOU MET HIM BEFORE?
JUST ONCE.

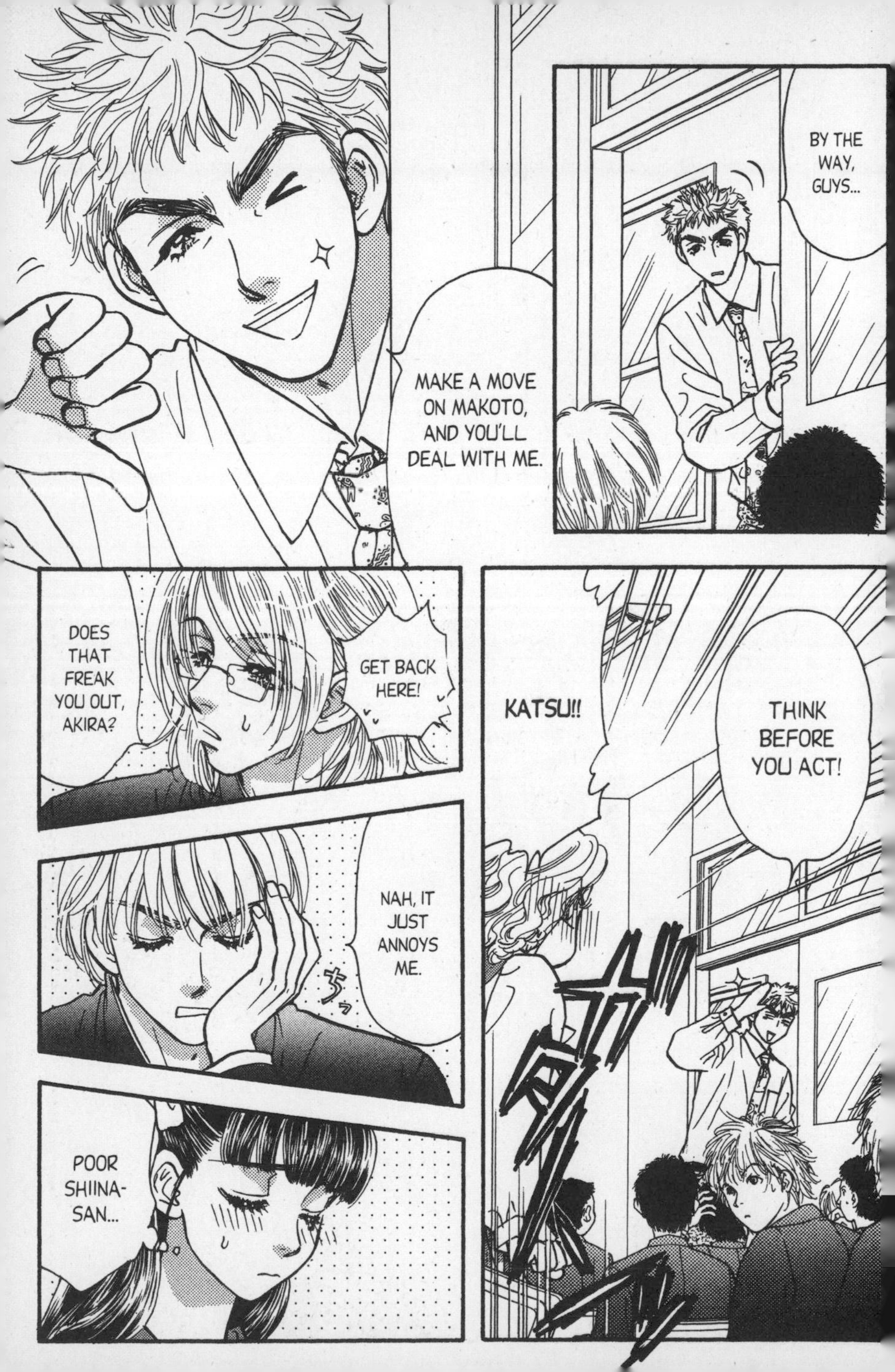
BY THE WAY, GUYS...
MAKE A MOVE ON MAKOTO, AND YOU'LL DEAL WITH ME.
THINK BEFORE YOU ACT!
KATSU!!
GET BACK HERE!
DOES THAT FREAK YOU OUT, AKIRA?
NAH, IT JUST ANNOYS ME.
POOR SHIINA-SAN...

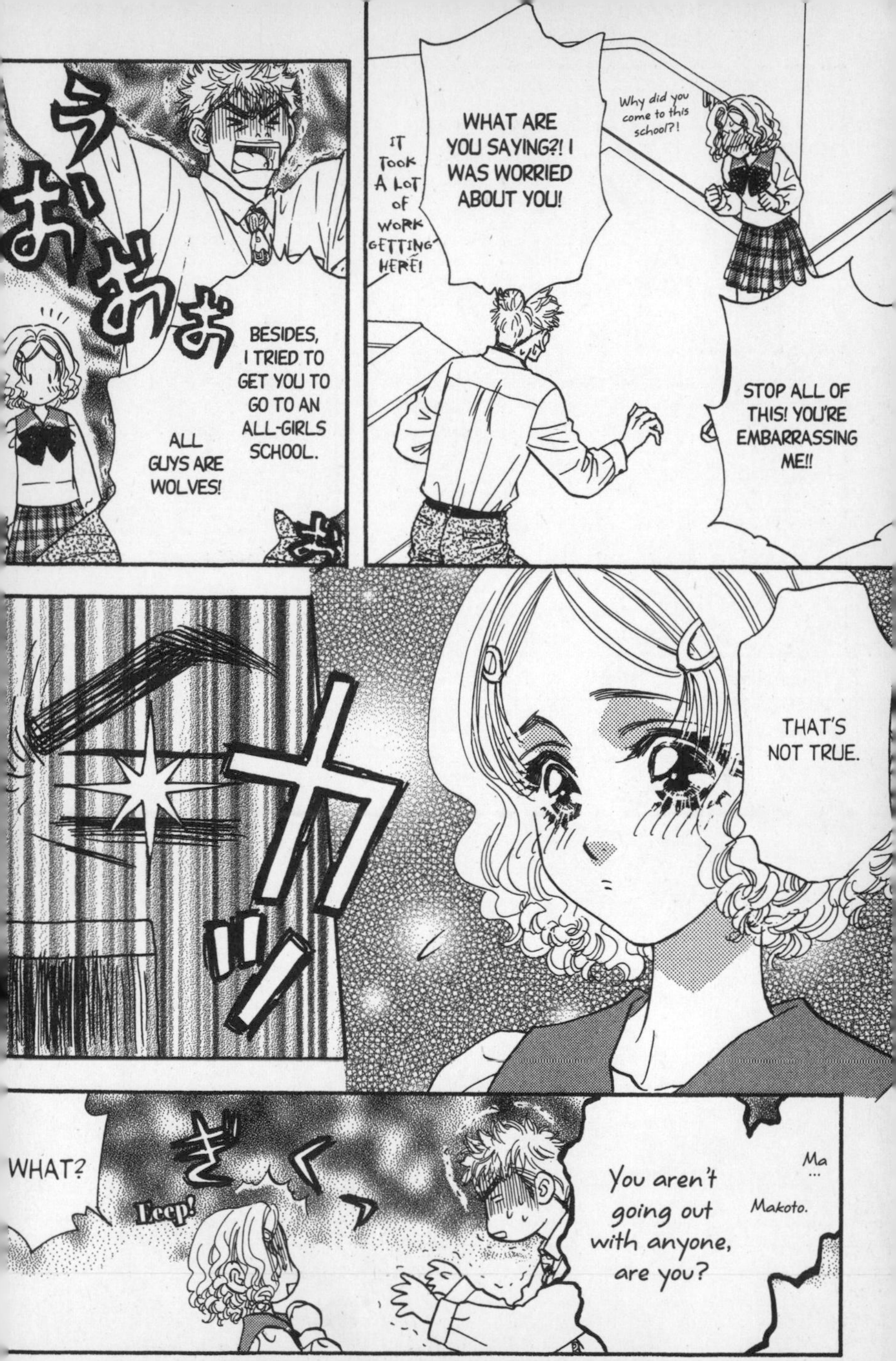
Why did you come to this school?!
WHAT ARE YOU SAYING?! I WAS WORRIED ABOUT YOU!
IT TOOK A LOT OF WORK GETTING HERE!
STOP ALL OF THIS! YOU'RE EMBARRASSING ME!!
うおおお
BESIDES, I TRIED TO GET YOU TO GO TO AN ALL-GIRLS SCHOOL.
ALL GUYS ARE WOLVES!
THAT'S NOT TRUE.
カッ
Ma...
Makoto.
You aren't going out with anyone, are you?
ぎくっ
Eeep!
WHAT?

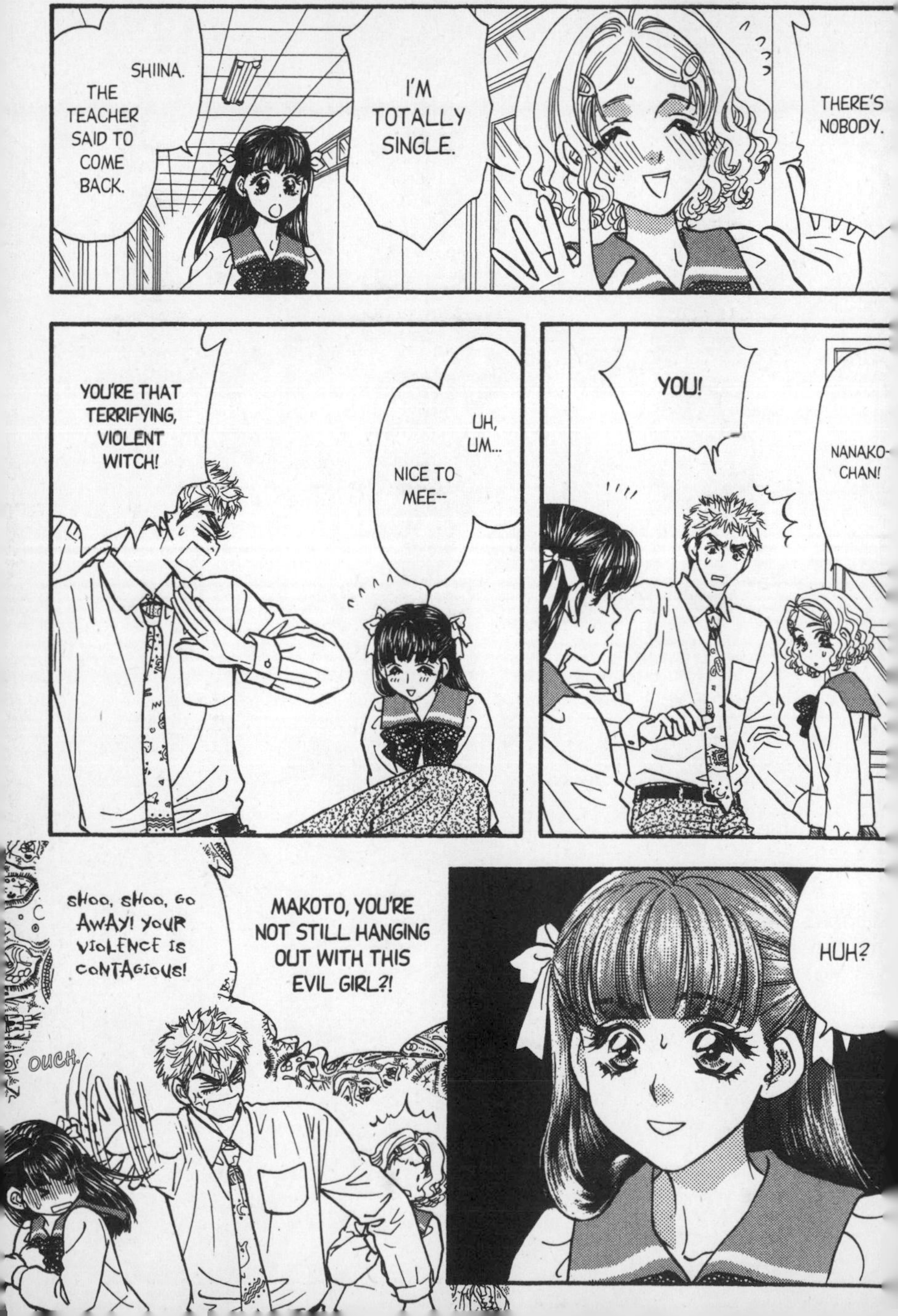
THERE'S NOBODY.
I'M TOTALLY SINGLE.
SHIINA. THE TEACHER SAID TO COME BACK.
NANAKO-CHAN!
YOU!
UH, UM...
NICE TO MEE--
YOU'RE THAT TERRIFYING, VIOLENT WITCH!
HUH?
MAKOTO, YOU'RE NOT STILL HANGING OUT WITH THIS EVIL GIRL?!
SHOO, SHOO, GO AWAY! YOUR VIOLENCE IS CONTAGIOUS!
OUCH.

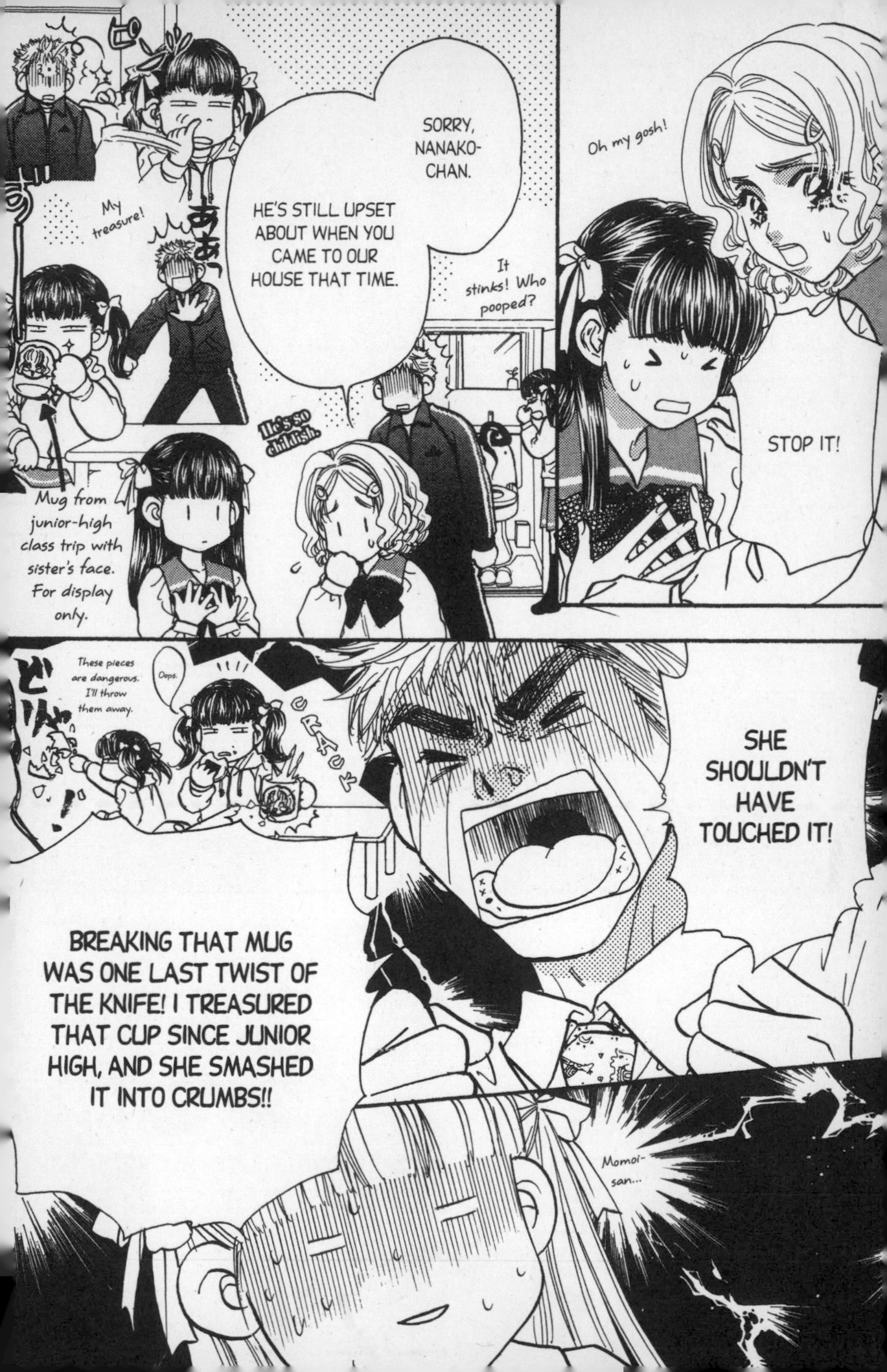
Oh my gosh!
STOP IT!
SORRY, NANAKO-CHAN.
HE'S STILL UPSET ABOUT WHEN YOU CAME TO OUR HOUSE THAT TIME.
It stinks! Who pooped?
He's so childish.
ああっ
My treasure!
Mug from junior-high class trip with sister's face. For display only.
SHE SHOULDN'T HAVE TOUCHED IT!
Oops.
These pieces are dangerous. I'll throw them away.
CRACK
BREAKING THAT MUG WAS ONE LAST TWIST OF THE KNIFE! I TREASURED THAT CUP SINCE JUNIOR HIGH, AND SHE SMASHED IT INTO CRUMBS!!
Momoi-san...

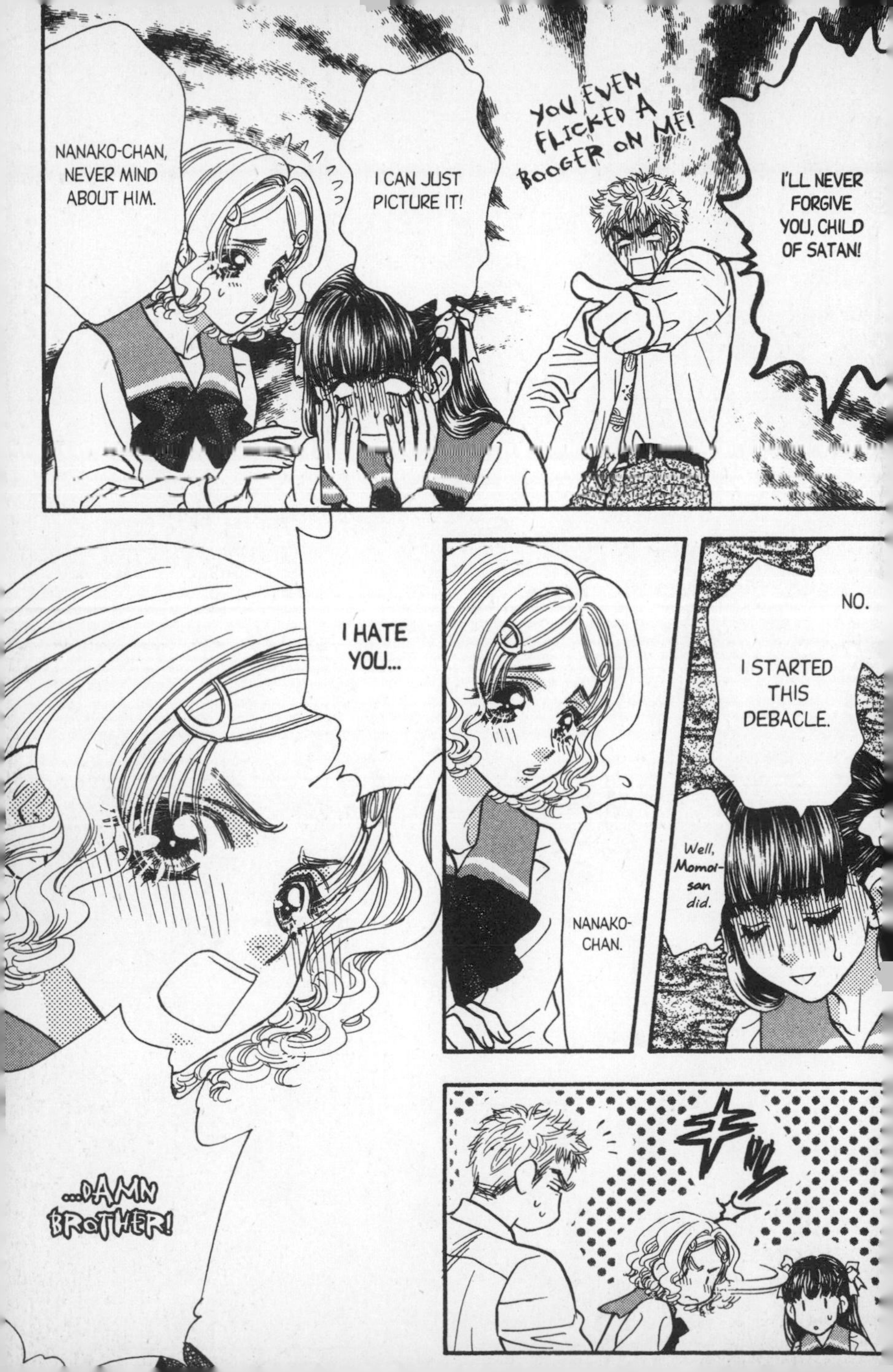
I'LL NEVER FORGIVE YOU, CHILD OF SATAN!
YOU EVEN FLICKED A BOOGER ON ME!
I CAN JUST PICTURE IT!
NANAKO-CHAN, NEVER MIND ABOUT HIM.
NO.
I STARTED THIS DEBACLE.
Well, Momoi-san did.
NANAKO-CHAN.
I HATE YOU...
...DAMN BROTHER!

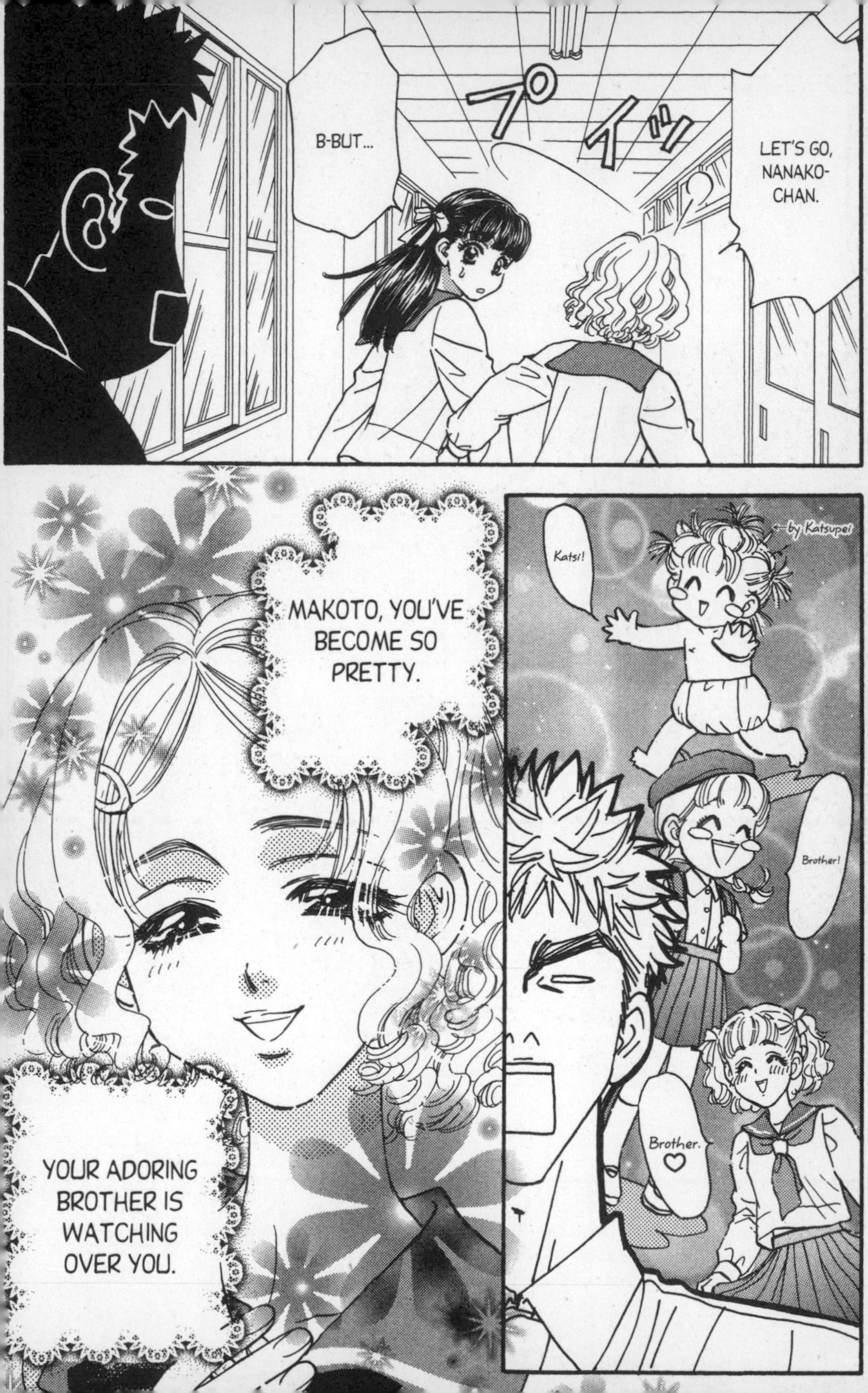
LET'S GO, NANAKO-CHAN.
プイッ
B-BUT...
←by Katsupei
Katsi!
Brother!
Brother. ♡
MAKOTO, YOU'VE BECOME SO PRETTY.
YOUR ADORING BROTHER IS WATCHING OVER YOU.

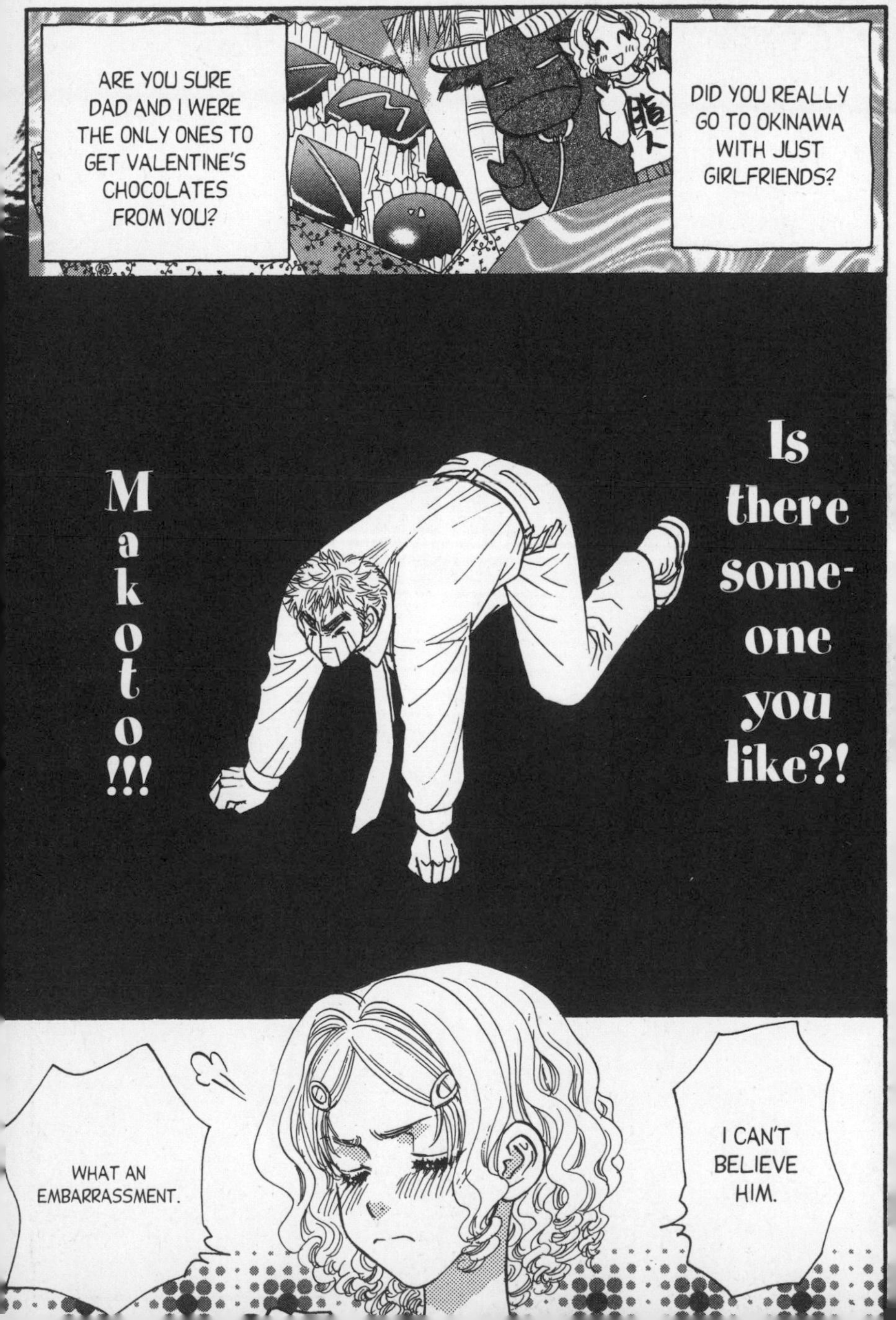
DID YOU REALLY GO TO OKINAWA WITH JUST GIRLFRIENDS?
ARE YOU SURE DAD AND I WERE THE ONLY ONES TO GET VALENTINE'S CHOCOLATES FROM YOU?
Is there some-one you like?!
Makoto!!!
I CAN'T BELIEVE HIM.
WHAT AN EMBARRASSMENT.

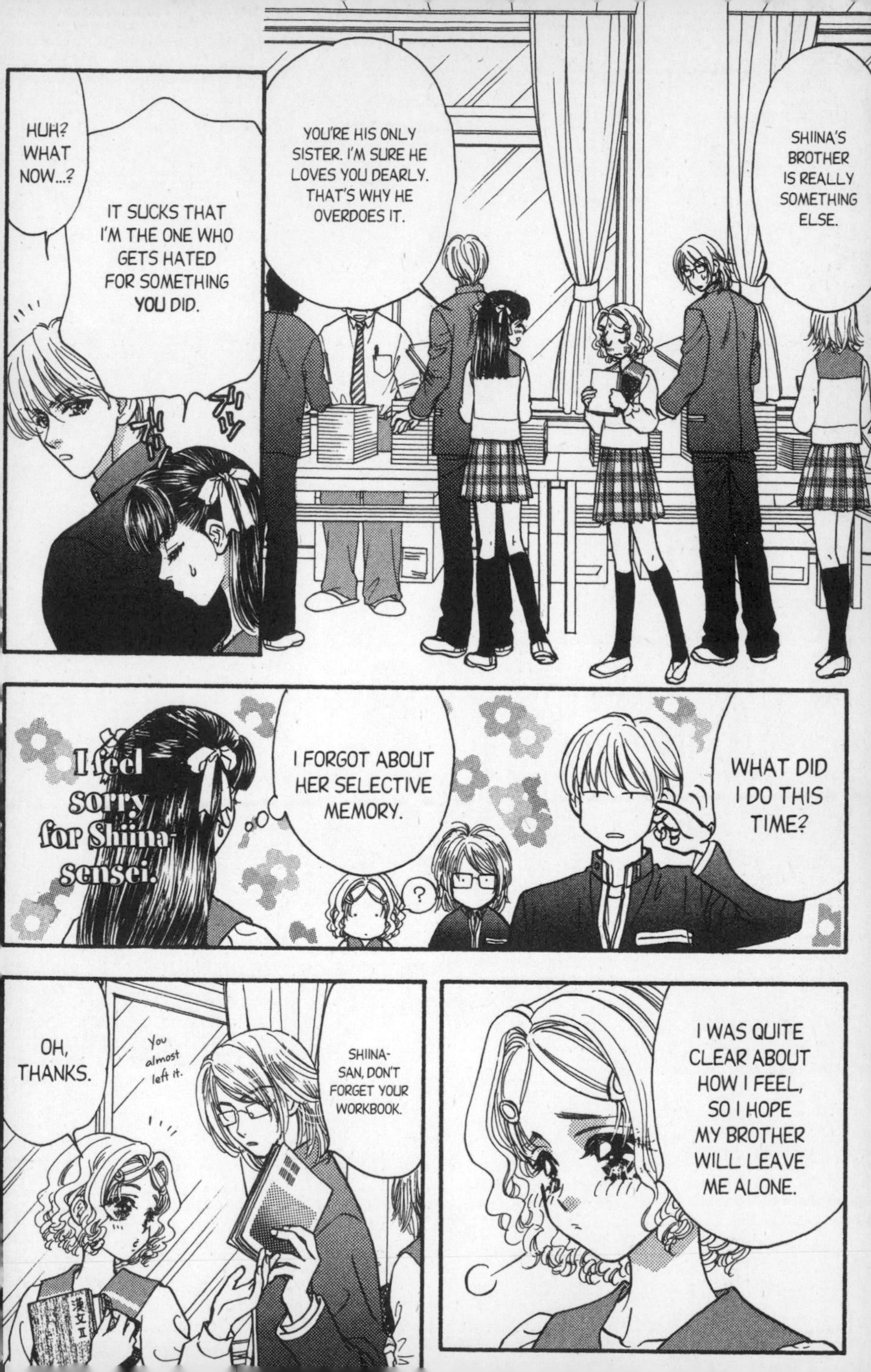
SHIINA'S BROTHER IS REALLY SOMETHING ELSE.
YOU'RE HIS ONLY SISTER. I'M SURE HE LOVES YOU DEARLY. THAT'S WHY HE OVERDOES IT.
HUH? WHAT NOW...?
IT SUCKS THAT I'M THE ONE WHO GETS HATED FOR SOMETHING YOU DID.
WHAT DID I DO THIS TIME?
?
I FORGOT ABOUT HER SELECTIVE MEMORY.
I feel sorry for Shiina-sensei.
I WAS QUITE CLEAR ABOUT HOW I FEEL, SO I HOPE MY BROTHER WILL LEAVE ME ALONE.
SHIINA-SAN, DON'T FORGET YOUR WORKBOOK.
You almost left it.
OH, THANKS.
漢文 II

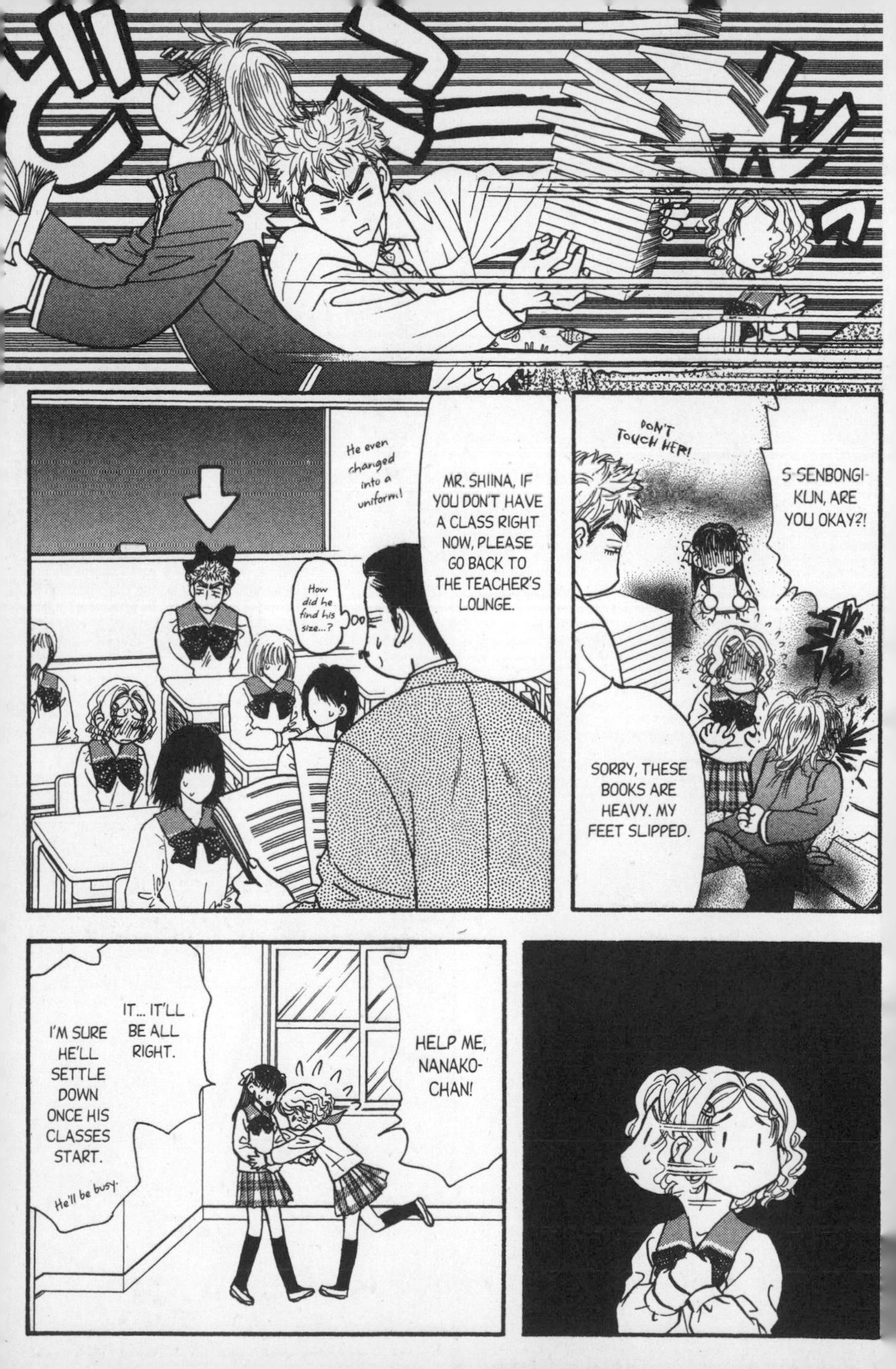
DON'T TOUCH HER!
S SENBONGI-KUN, ARE YOU OKAY?!
SORRY, THESE BOOKS ARE HEAVY. MY FEET SLIPPED.
MR. SHIINA, IF YOU DON'T HAVE A CLASS RIGHT NOW, PLEASE GO BACK TO THE TEACHER'S LOUNGE.
He even changed into a uniform!
How did he find his size...?
HELP ME, NANAKO-CHAN!
IT... IT'LL BE ALL RIGHT.
I'M SURE HE'LL SETTLE DOWN ONCE HIS CLASSES START.
He'll be busy.

SHHH!

Mmmf--

SHI--

BUT DON'T YOU SEE?

WHAT WILL I DO IF MY BROTHER FINDS OUT I'M GOING OUT WITH UEHARA-KUN?

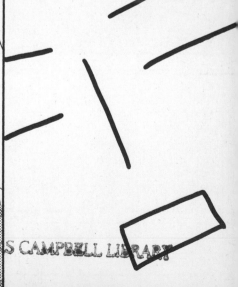

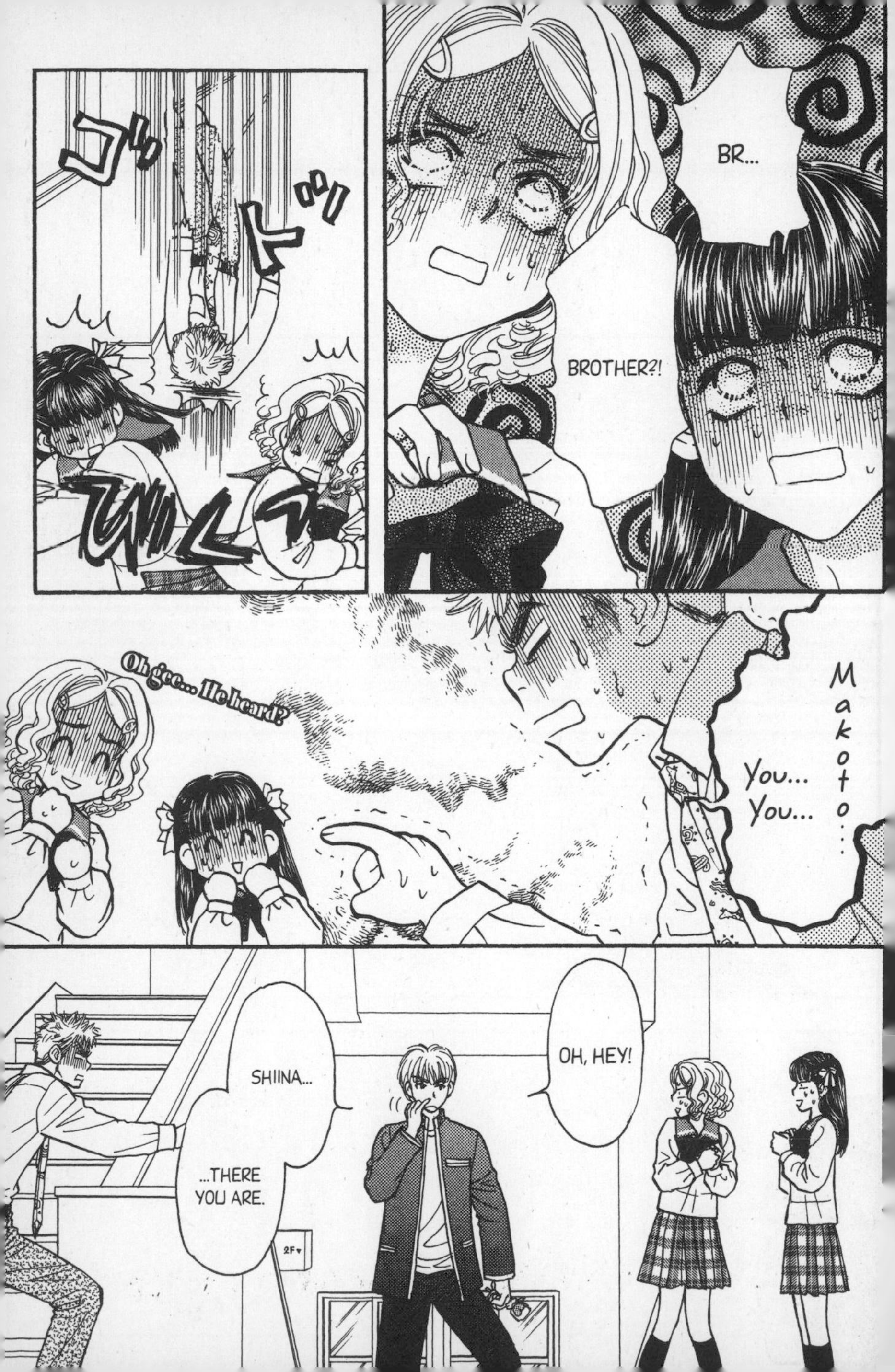
BR...
BROTHER?!
Makoto...
You...
You...
Oh gee... He heard?
OH, HEY!
SHIINA...
...THERE YOU ARE.
2F

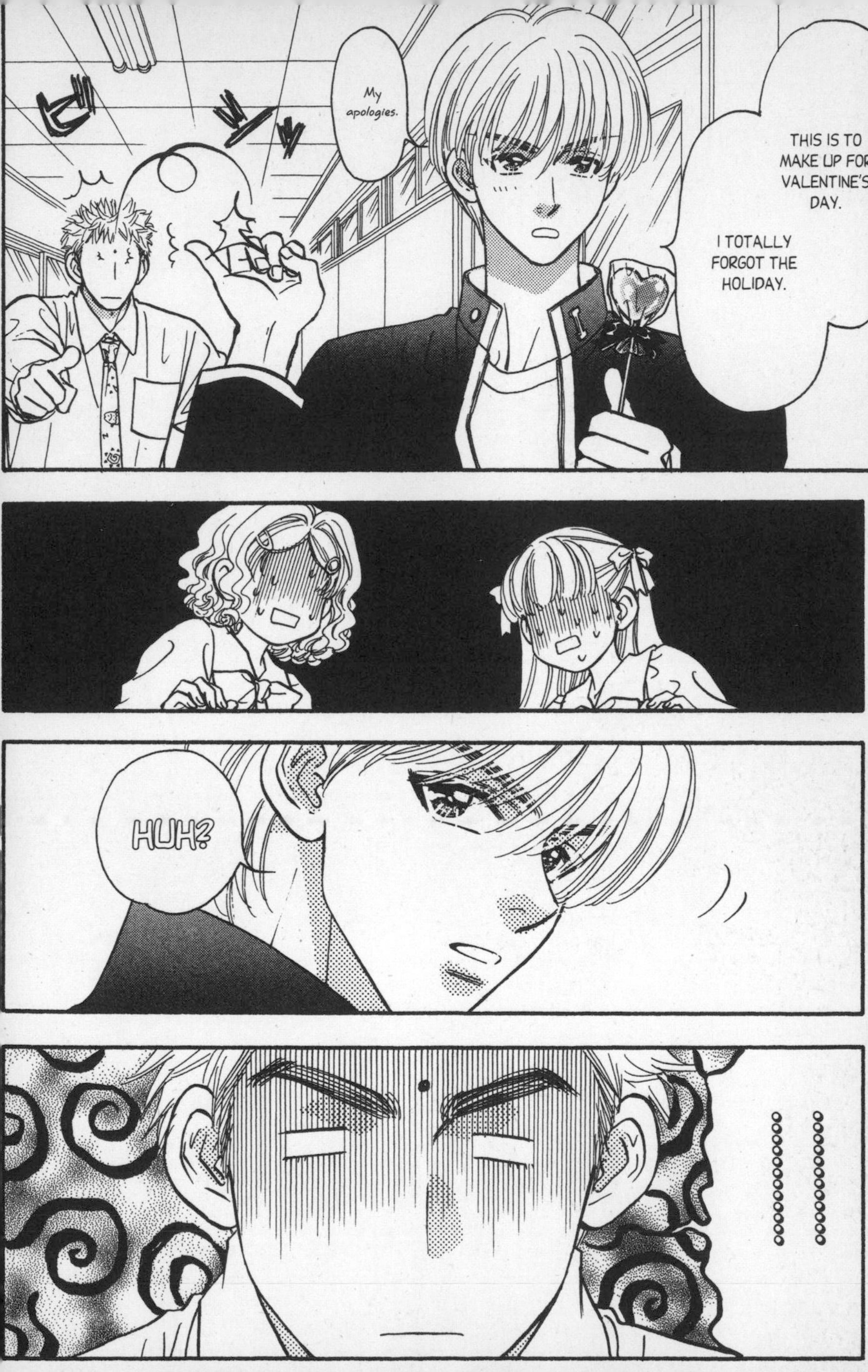
THIS IS TO MAKE UP FOR VALENTINE'S DAY.
I TOTALLY FORGOT THE HOLIDAY.
My apologies.
HUH?
OOOOOOOOOOOO
OOOOOOOOOOOO

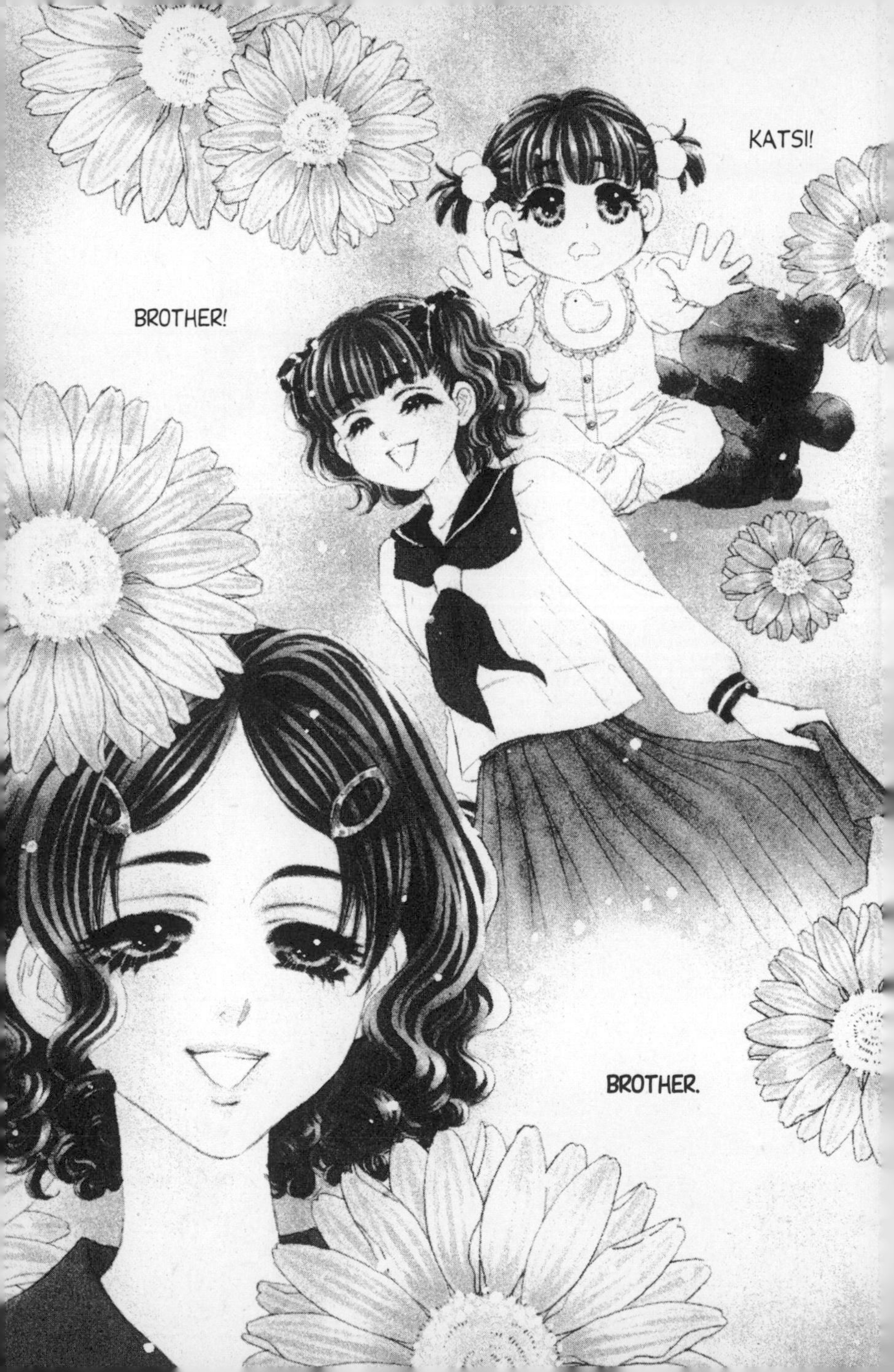
KATSI!
BROTHER!
BROTHER.

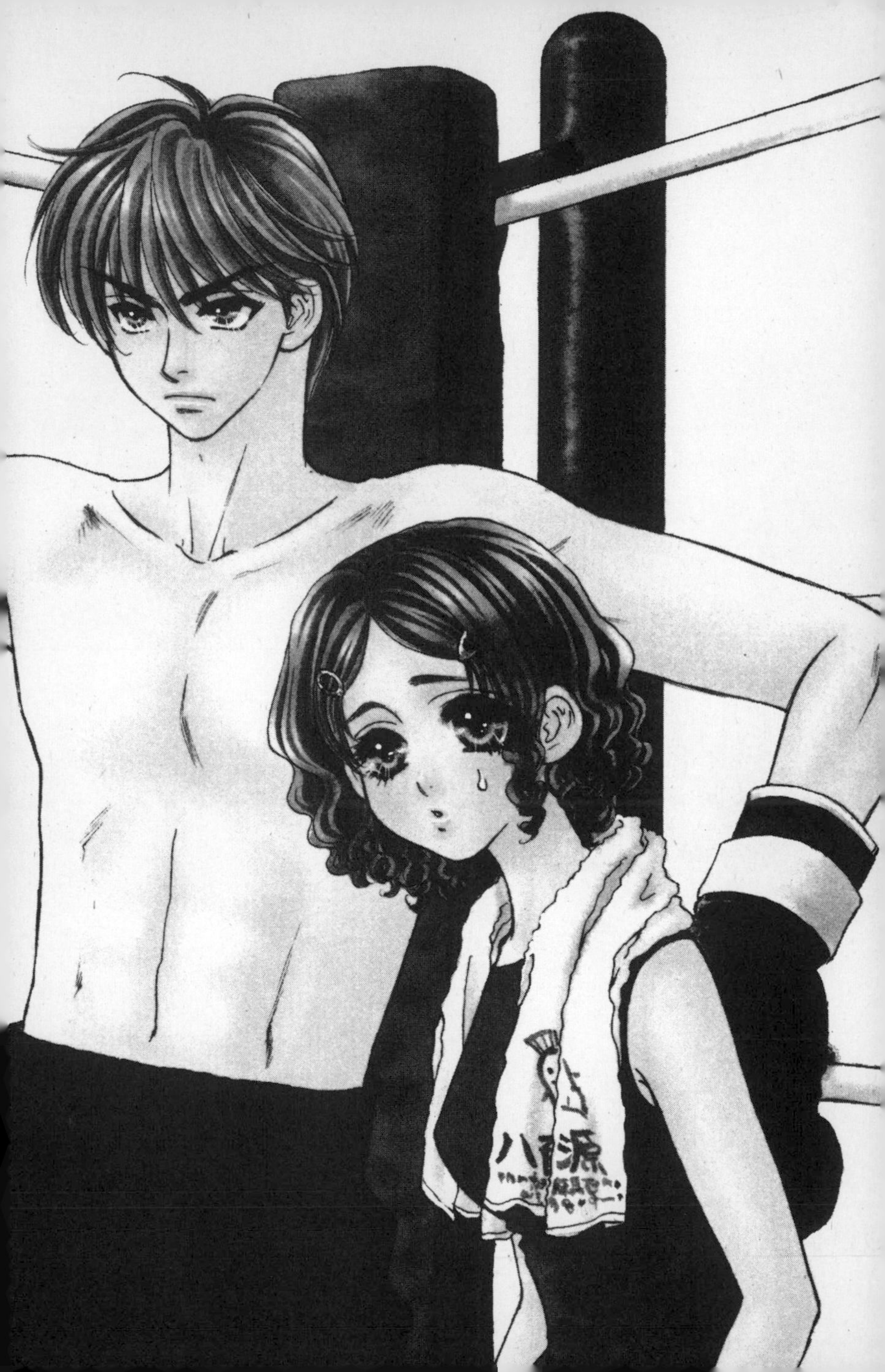

Episode 16
Brain Fever

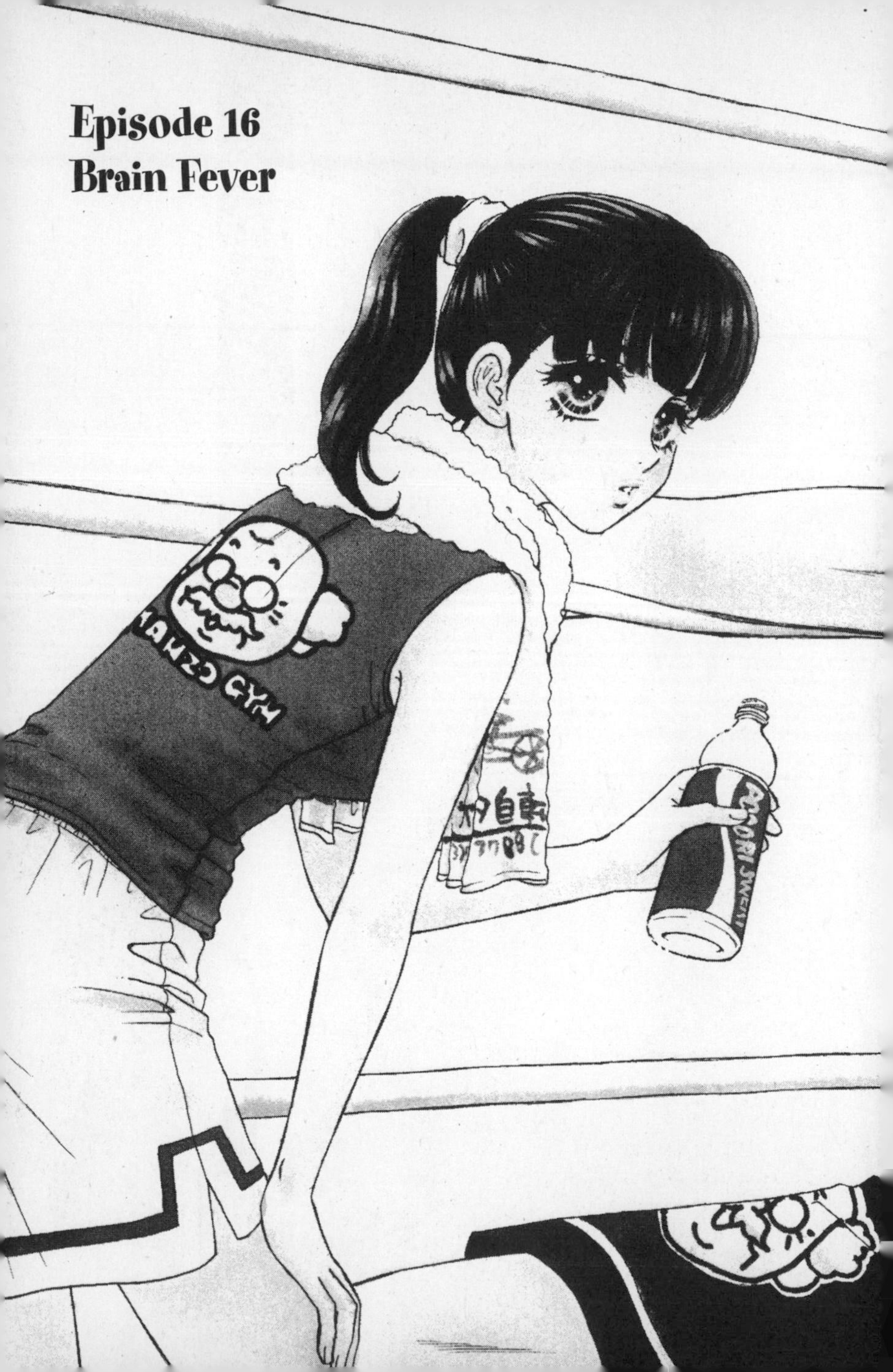

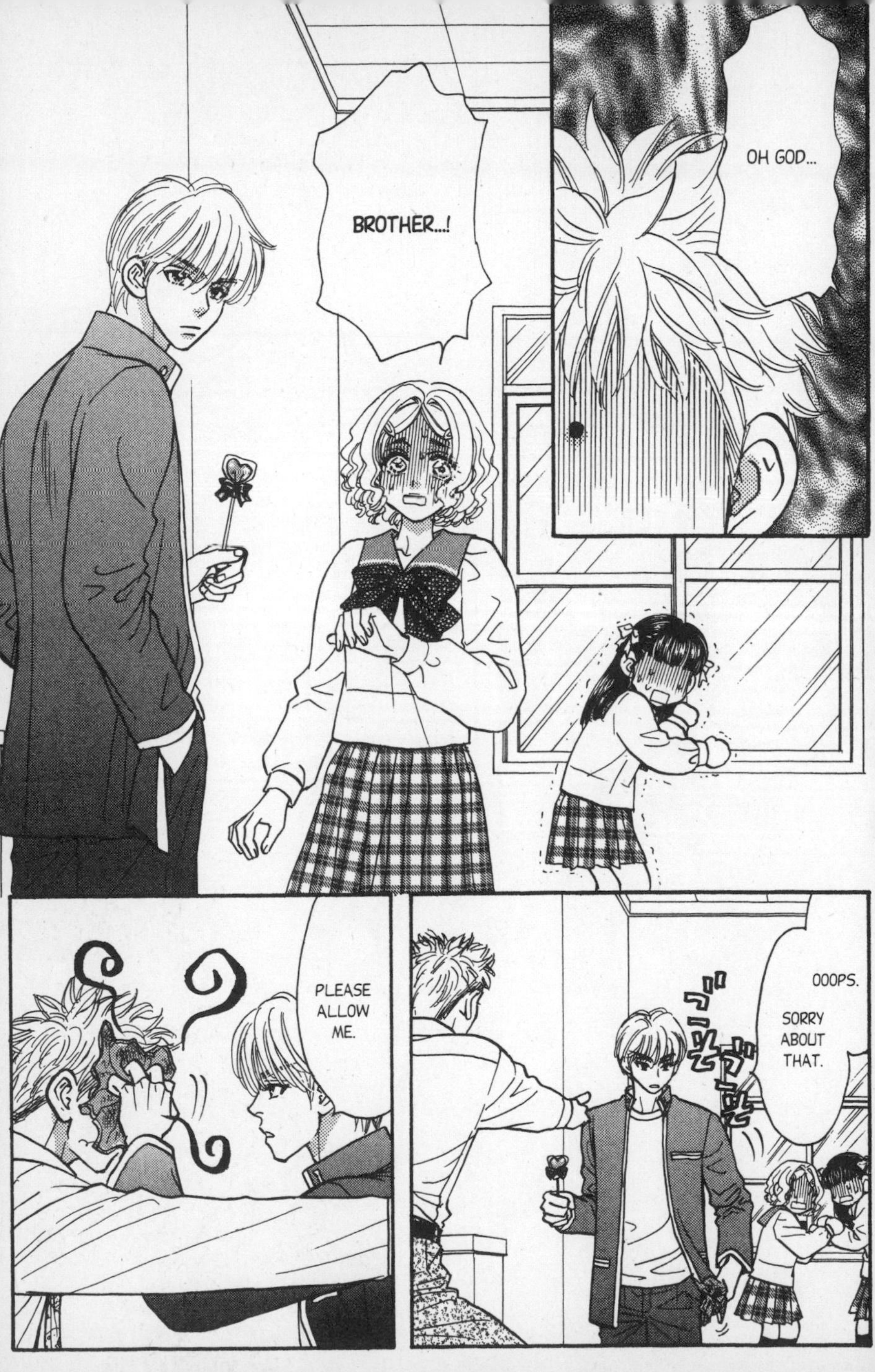
OH GOD...
BROTHER...!
OOOPS.
SORRY ABOUT THAT.
PLEASE ALLOW ME.

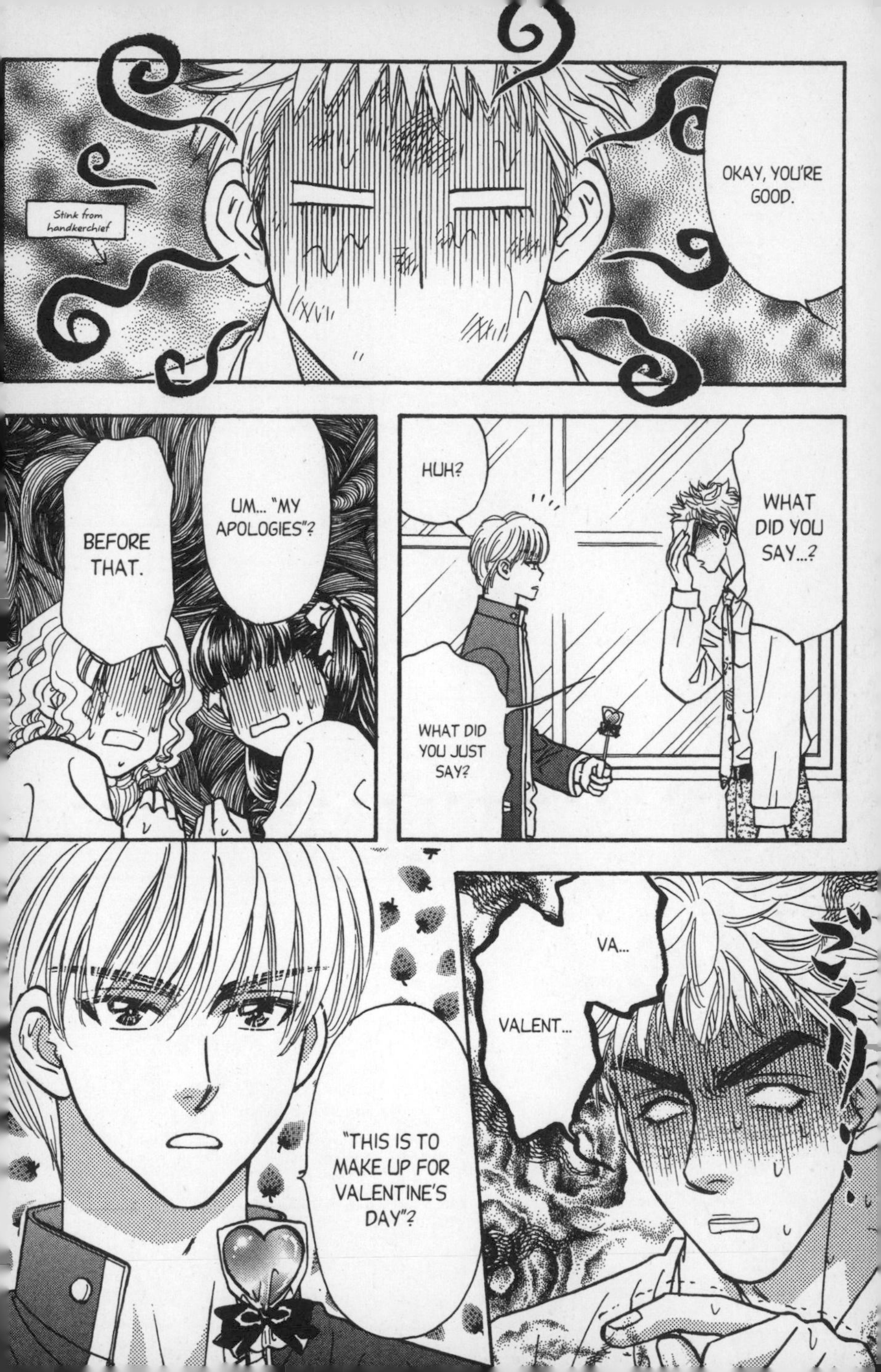
OKAY, YOU'RE GOOD.
Stink from handkerchief
WHAT DID YOU SAY...?
HUH?
WHAT DID YOU JUST SAY?
UM... "MY APOLOGIES"?
BEFORE THAT.
VA...
VALENT...
"THIS IS TO MAKE UP FOR VALENTINE'S DAY"?

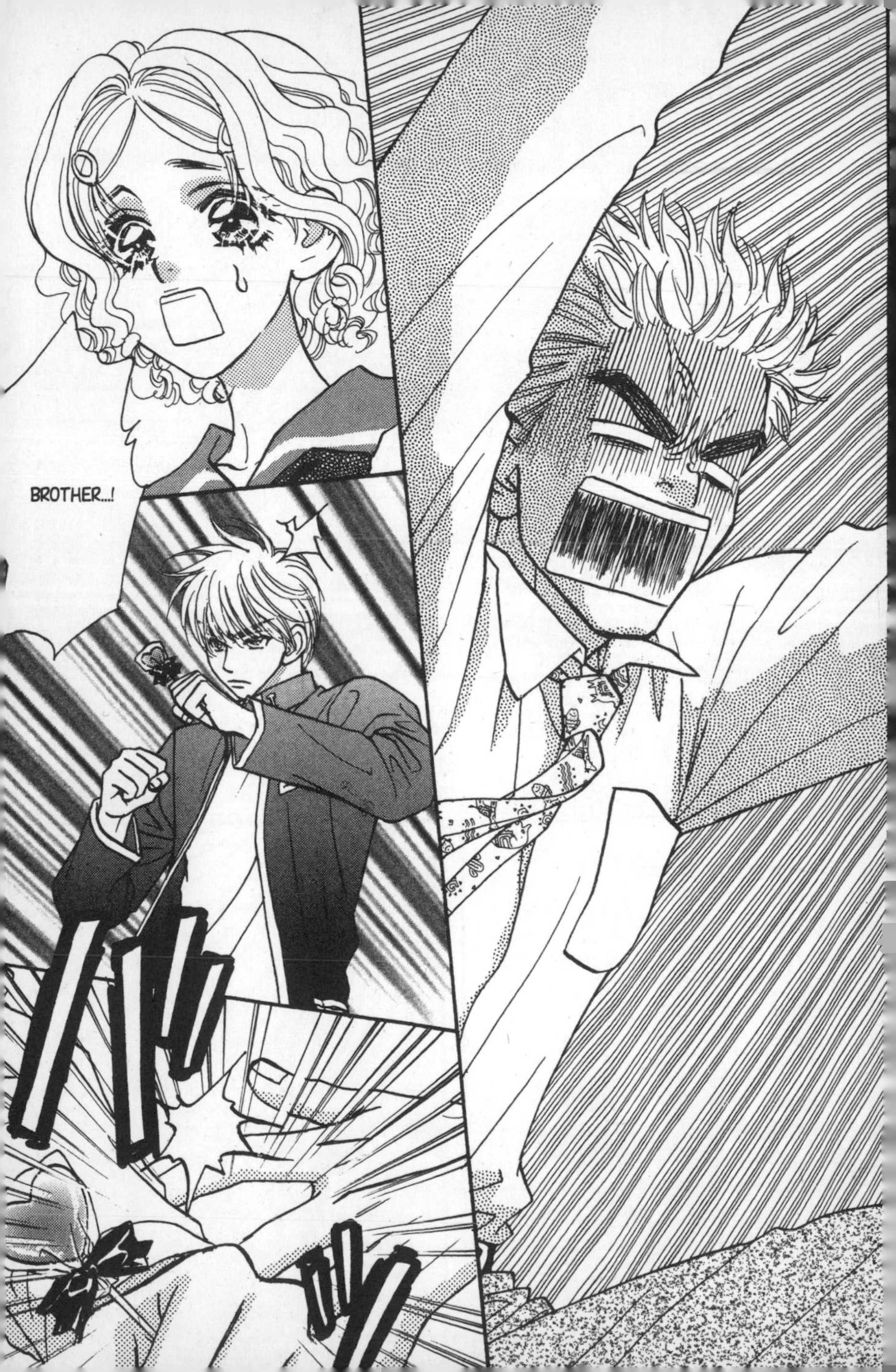
BROTHER...!

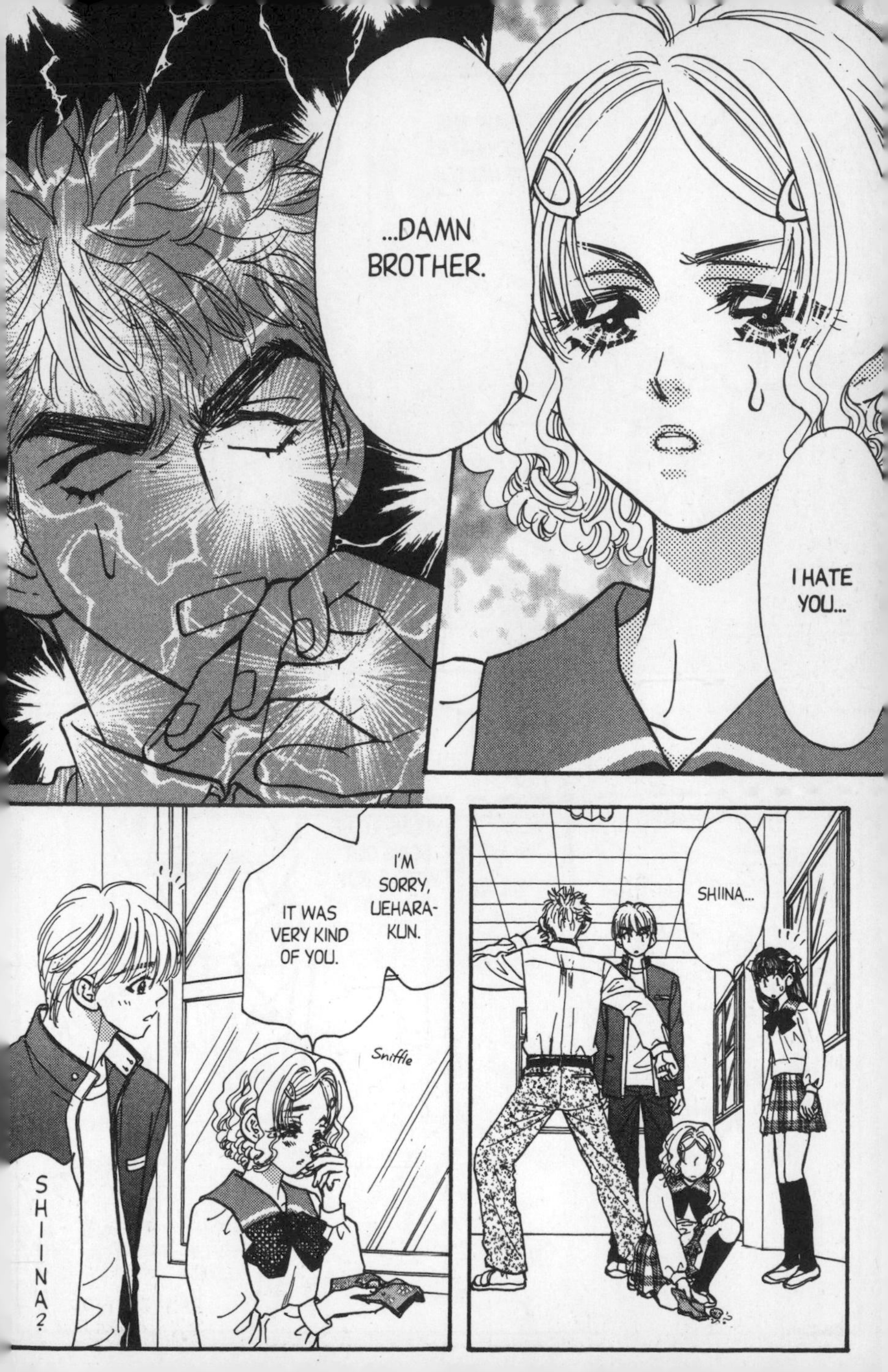
...DAMN BROTHER.
I HATE YOU...
SHIINA...
I'M SORRY, UEHARA-KUN.
IT WAS VERY KIND OF YOU.
Sniffle
SHIINA?

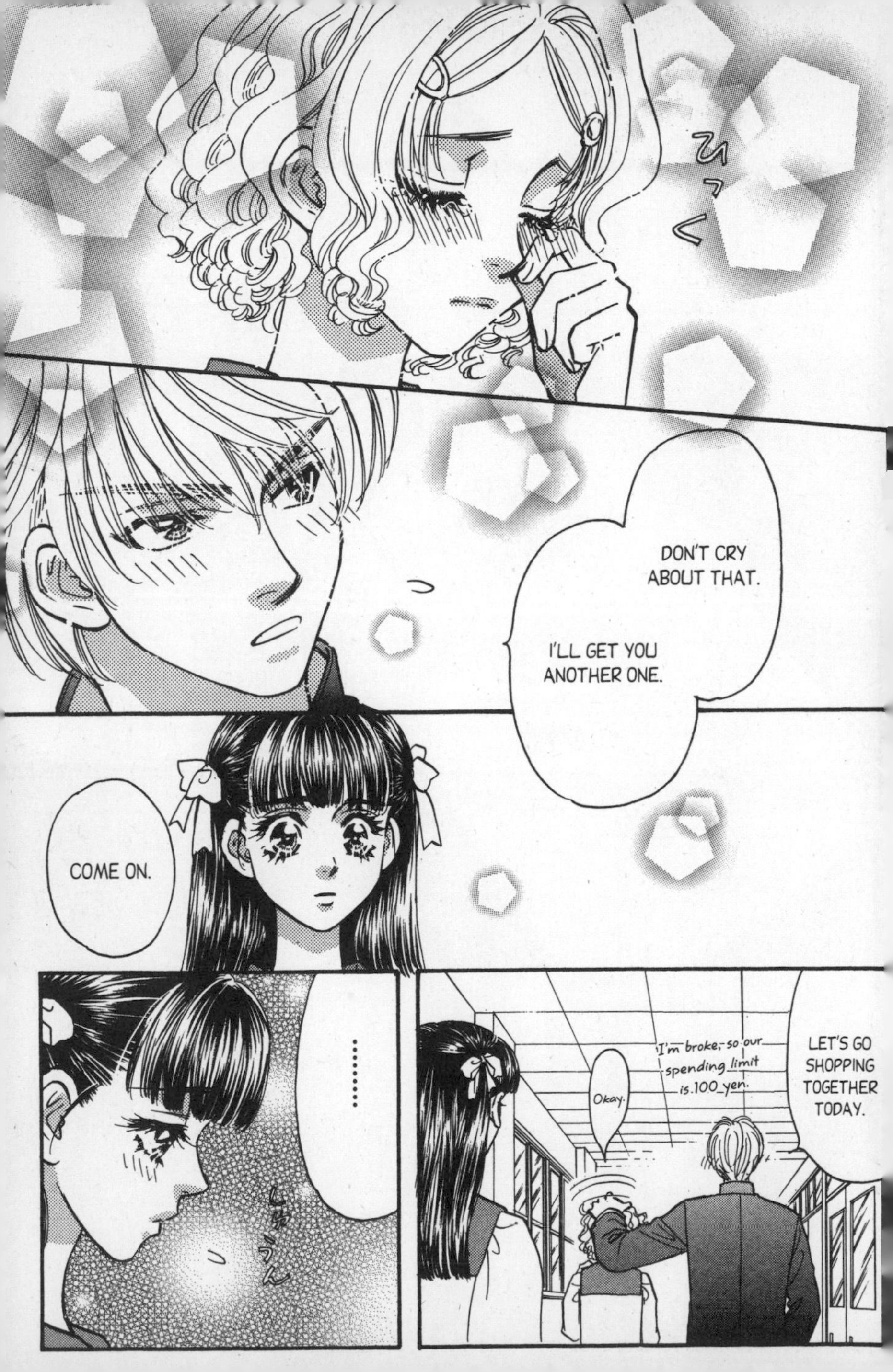
ひっく
DON'T CRY ABOUT THAT.
I'LL GET YOU ANOTHER ONE.
COME ON.
LET'S GO SHOPPING TOGETHER TODAY.
I'm broke, so our spending limit is 100 yen.
Okay.
....

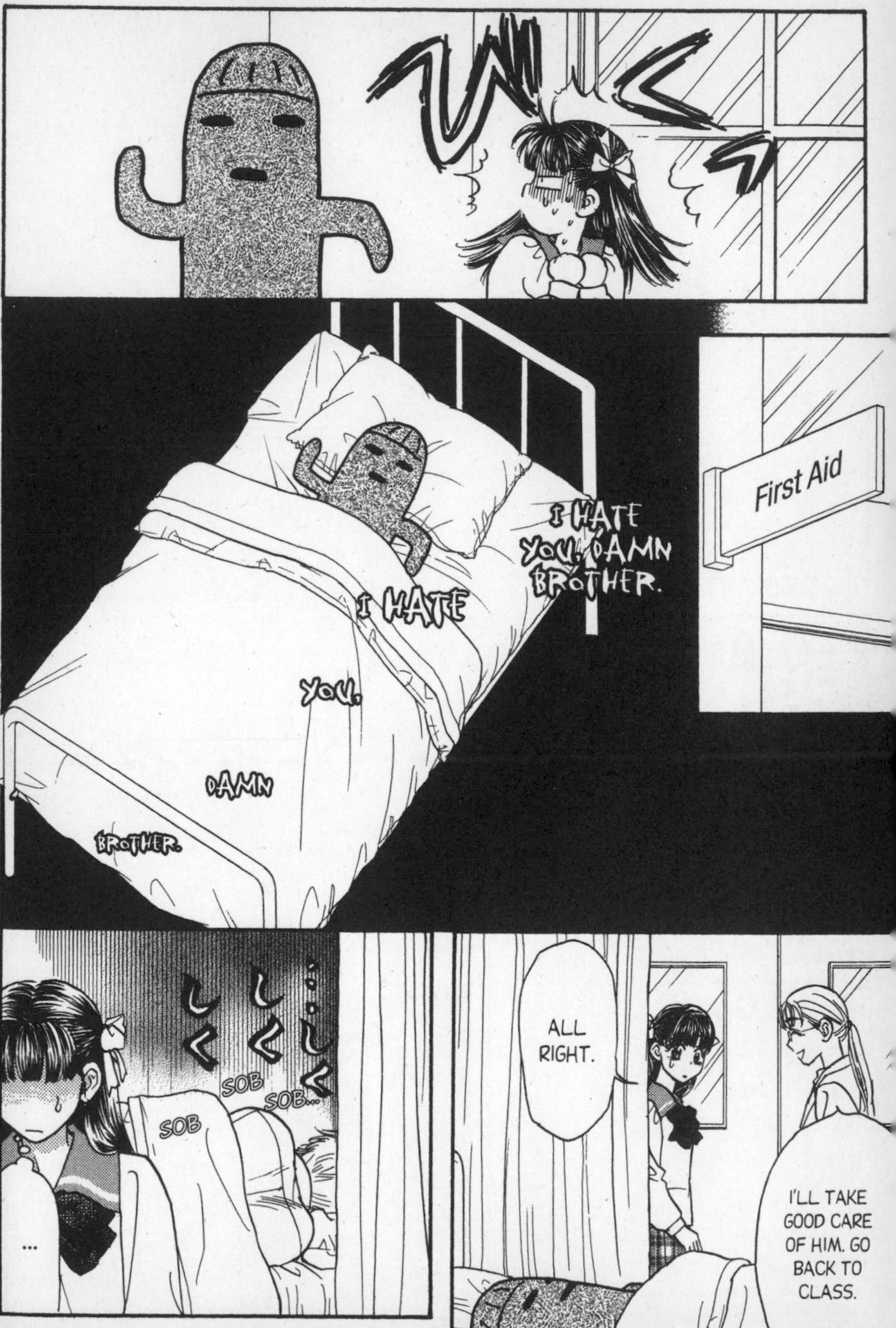
First Aid
I HATE YOU, DAMN BROTHER.
I HATE
YOU.
DAMN
BROTHER.
I'LL TAKE GOOD CARE OF HIM. GO BACK TO CLASS.
ALL RIGHT.
SOB
SOB...
SOB
...

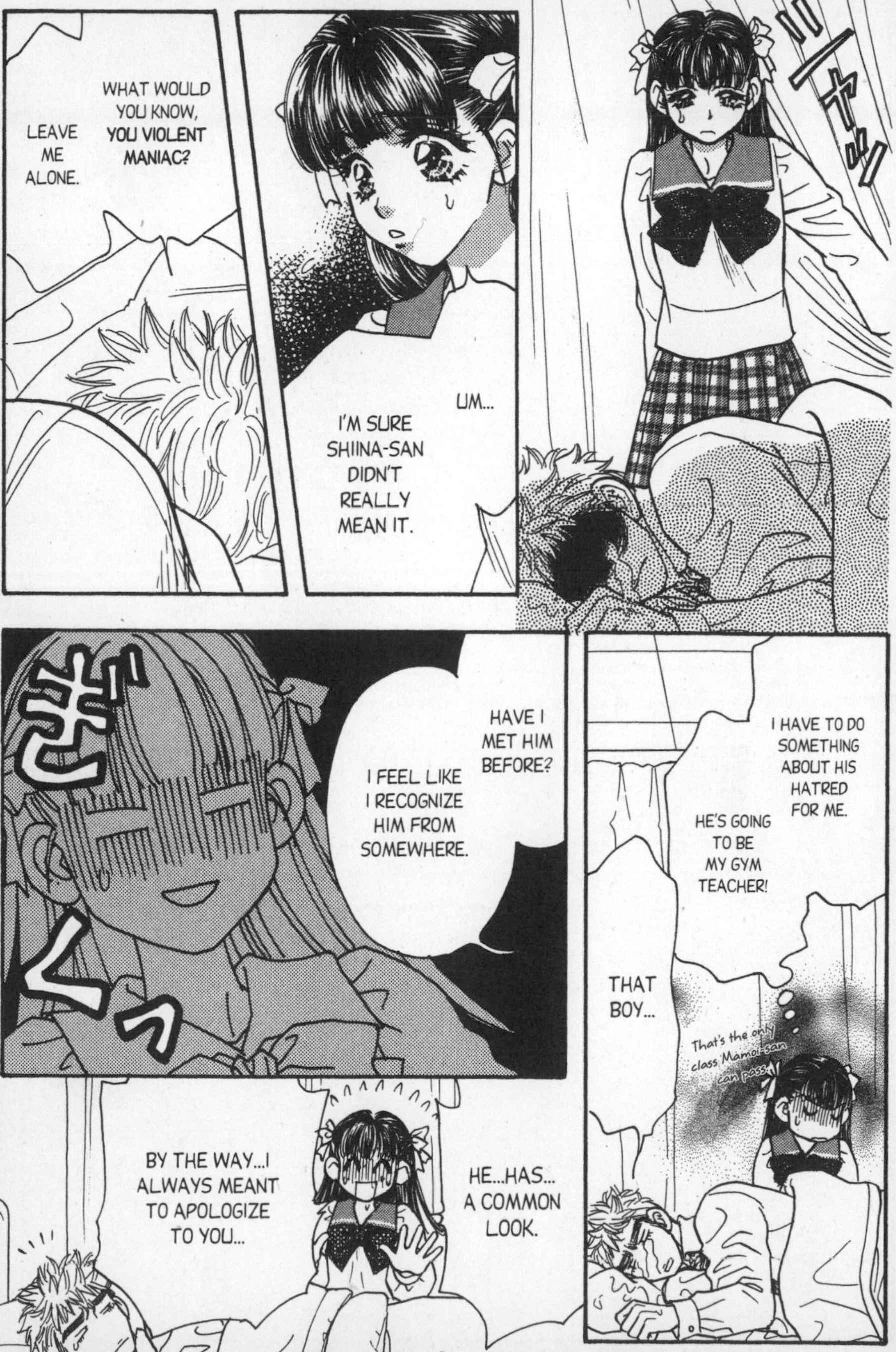
シャッ
UM...
I'M SURE SHIINA-SAN DIDN'T REALLY MEAN IT.
WHAT WOULD YOU KNOW, YOU VIOLENT MANIAC?
LEAVE ME ALONE.
I HAVE TO DO SOMETHING ABOUT HIS HATRED FOR ME.
HE'S GOING TO BE MY GYM TEACHER!
THAT BOY...
That's the only class Mamoi-san can pass.
ぎくっ
HAVE I MET HIM BEFORE?
I FEEL LIKE I RECOGNIZE HIM FROM SOMEWHERE.
HE...HAS... A COMMON LOOK.
BY THE WAY...I ALWAYS MEANT TO APOLOGIZE TO YOU...

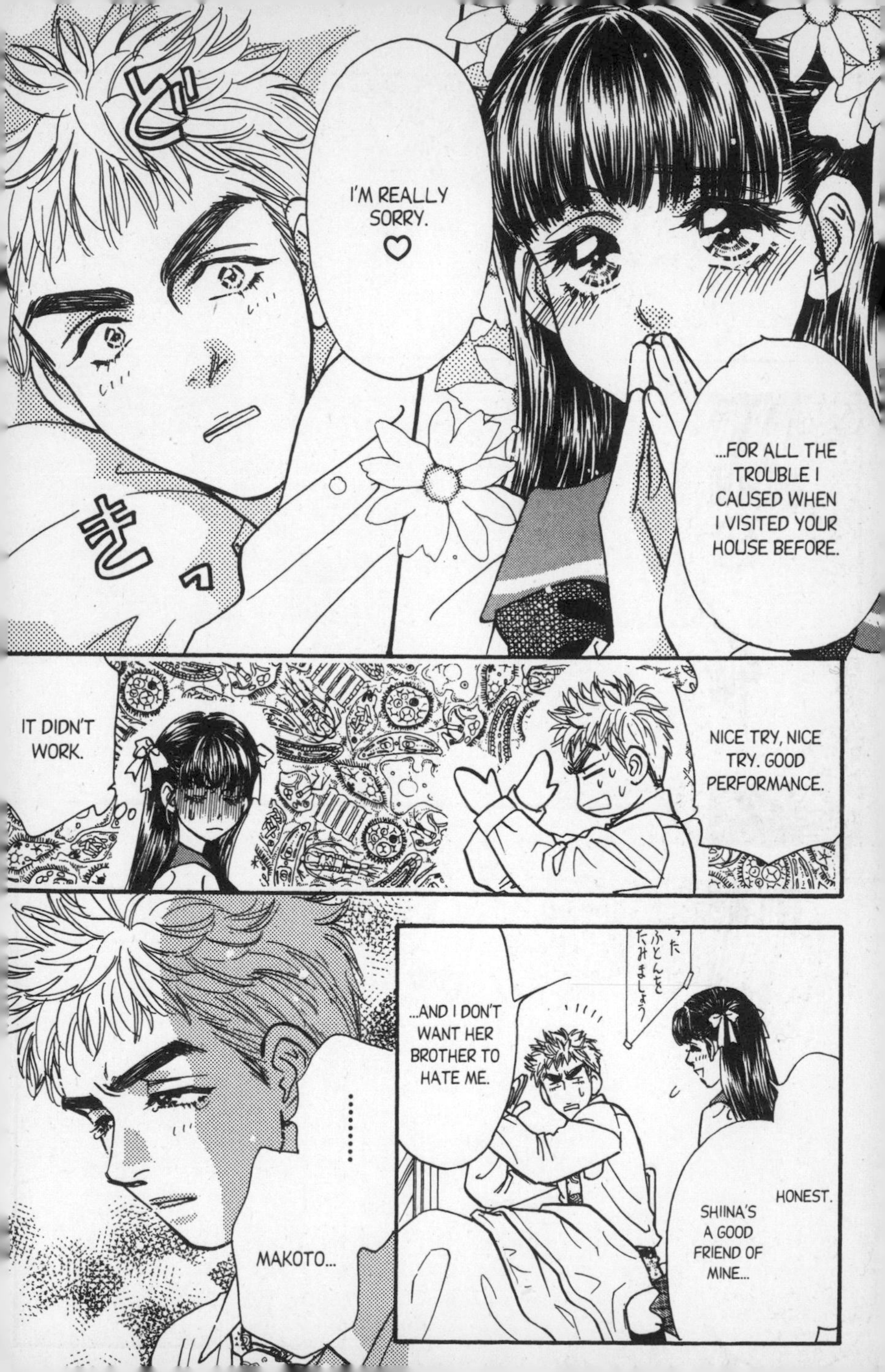
I'M REALLY SORRY. ♡
...FOR ALL THE TROUBLE I CAUSED WHEN I VISITED YOUR HOUSE BEFORE.
ど
きっ
NICE TRY, NICE TRY. GOOD PERFORMANCE.
IT DIDN'T WORK.
HONEST. SHIINA'S A GOOD FRIEND OF MINE...
...AND I DON'T WANT HER BROTHER TO HATE ME.
......
MAKOTO...

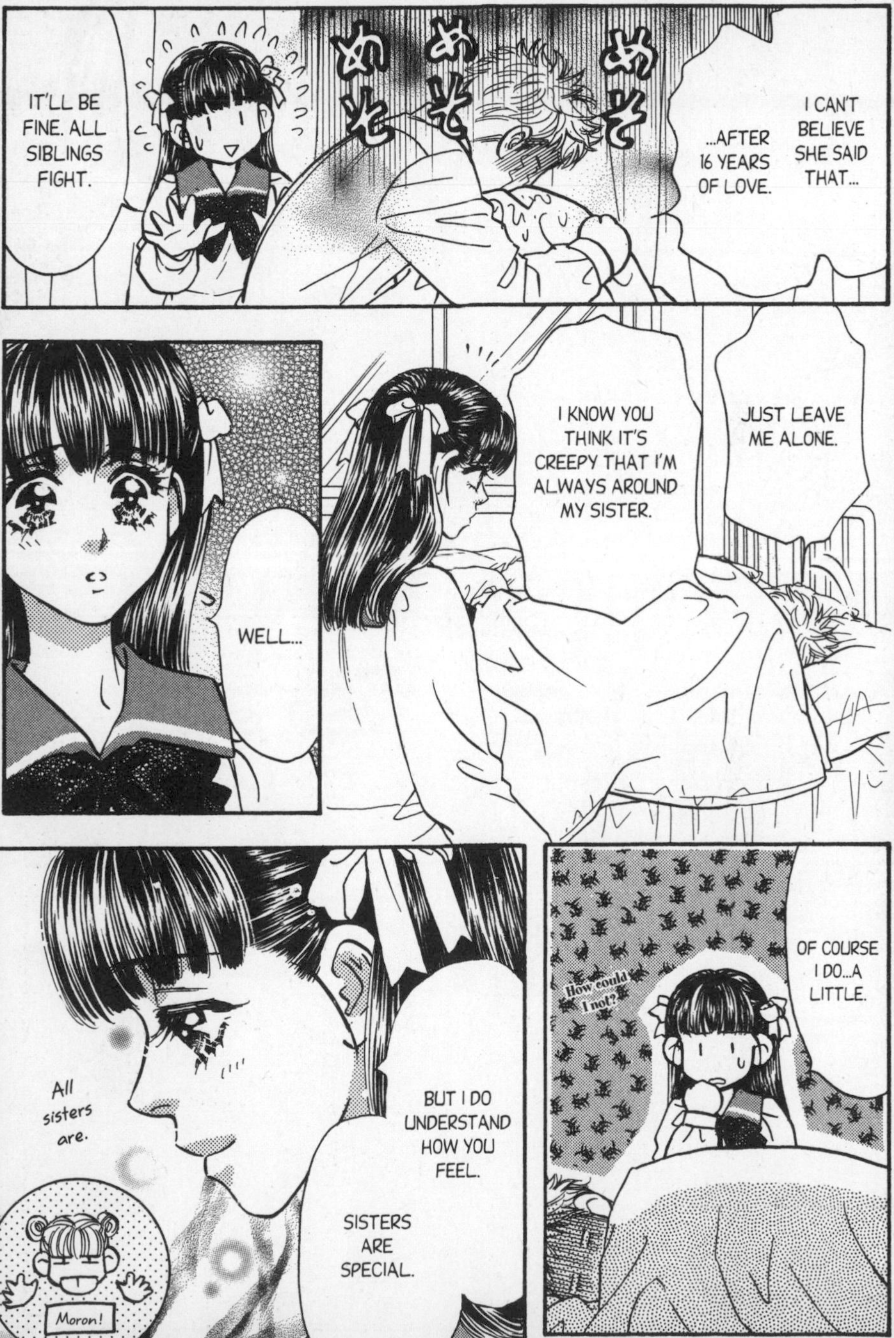

I CAN'T BELIEVE SHE SAID THAT...
...AFTER 16 YEARS OF LOVE.
めそ
めそ
めそ
IT'LL BE FINE. ALL SIBLINGS FIGHT.
JUST LEAVE ME ALONE.
I KNOW YOU THINK IT'S CREEPY THAT I'M ALWAYS AROUND MY SISTER.
WELL...
OF COURSE I DO...A LITTLE.
How could I not?
BUT I DO UNDERSTAND HOW YOU FEEL.
SISTERS ARE SPECIAL.
All sisters are.
Moron!

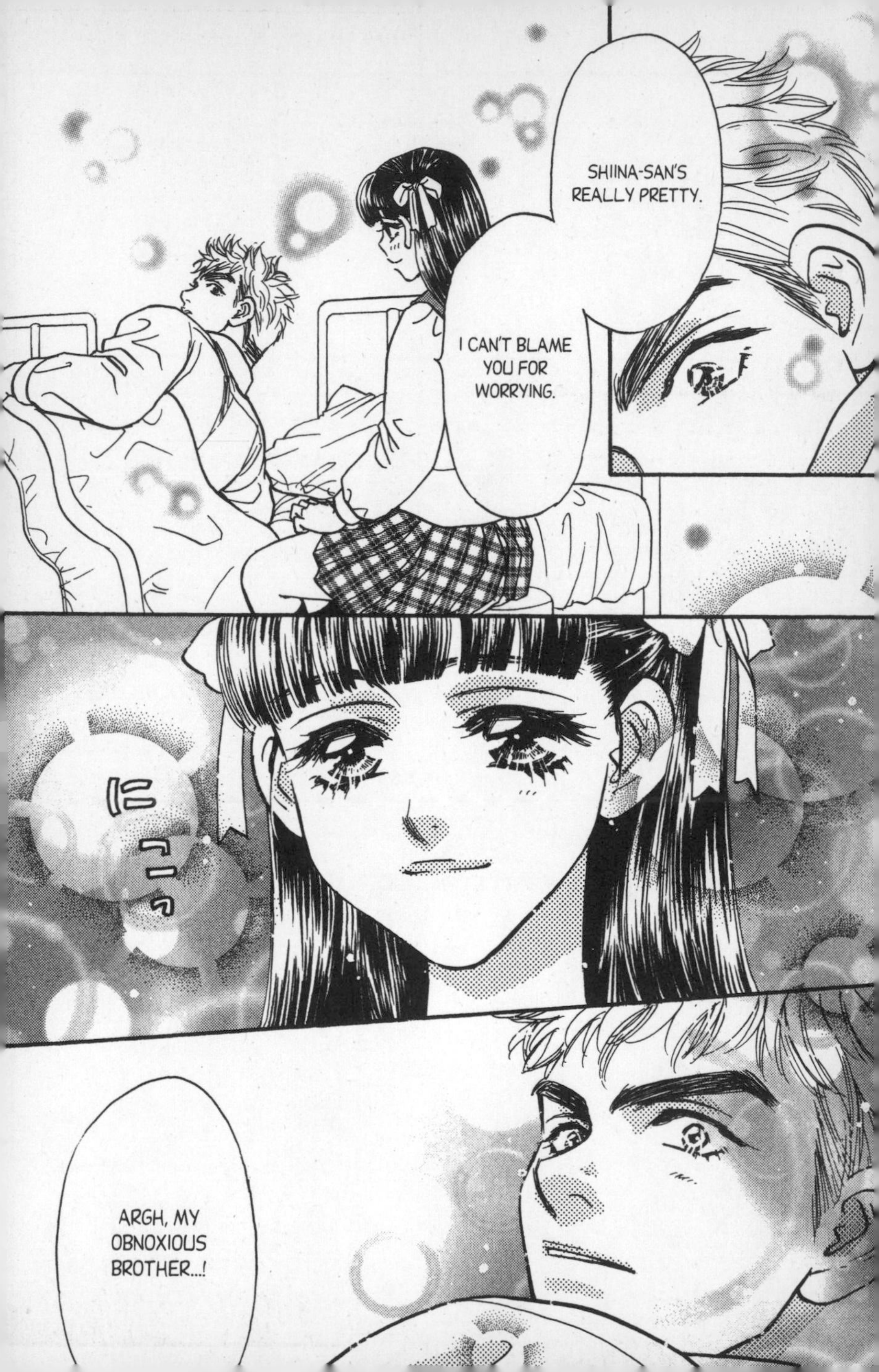
SHIINA-SAN'S REALLY PRETTY.
I CAN'T BLAME YOU FOR WORRYING.
ニコッ
ARGH, MY OBNOXIOUS BROTHER...!

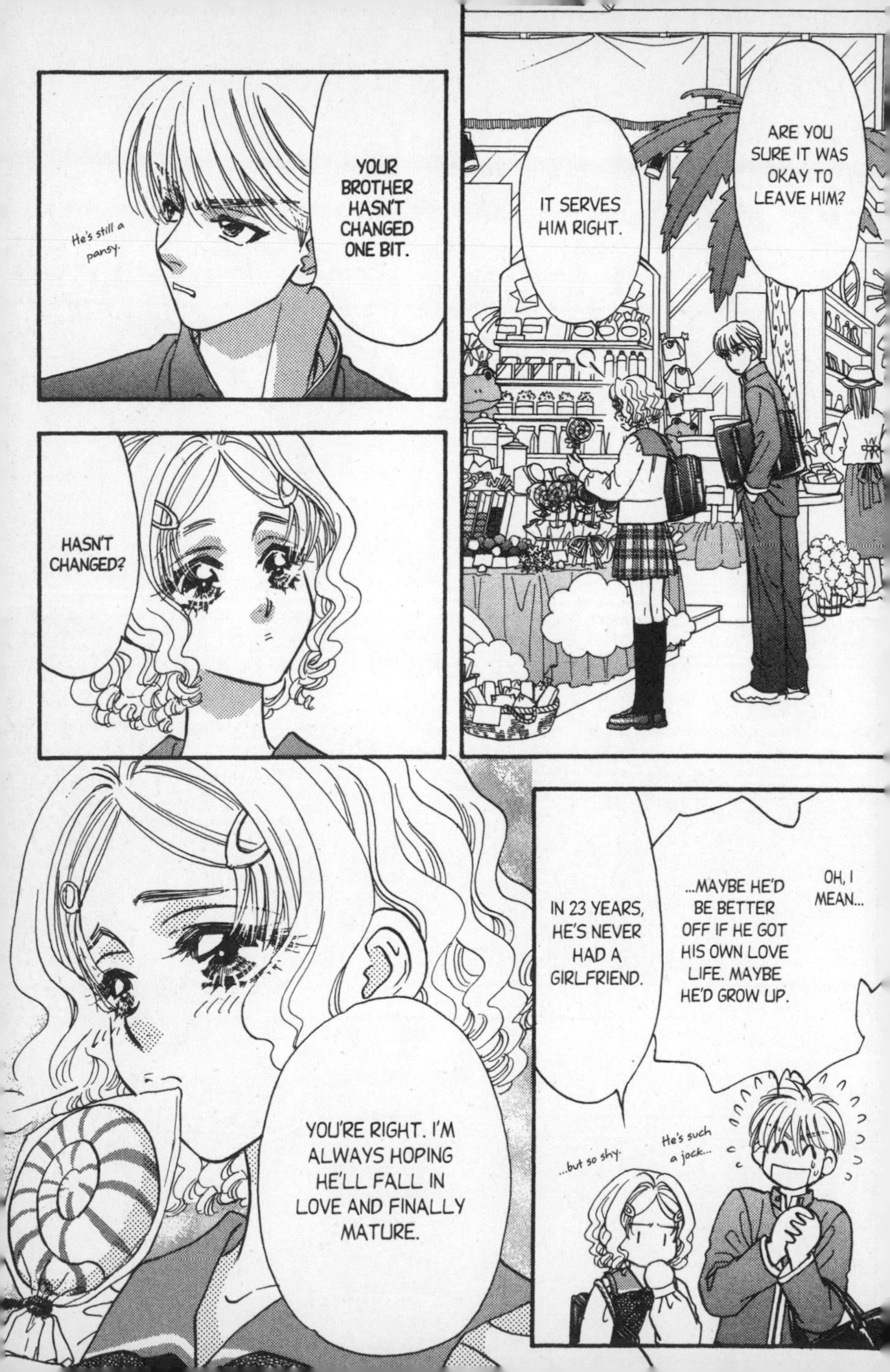

ARE YOU SURE IT WAS OKAY TO LEAVE HIM?
IT SERVES HIM RIGHT.
YOUR BROTHER HASN'T CHANGED ONE BIT.
He's still a pansy.
HASN'T CHANGED?
OH, I MEAN...
...MAYBE HE'D BE BETTER OFF IF HE GOT HIS OWN LOVE LIFE. MAYBE HE'D GROW UP.
IN 23 YEARS, HE'S NEVER HAD A GIRLFRIEND.
He's such a jock...
...but so shy.
YOU'RE RIGHT. I'M ALWAYS HOPING HE'LL FALL IN LOVE AND FINALLY MATURE.

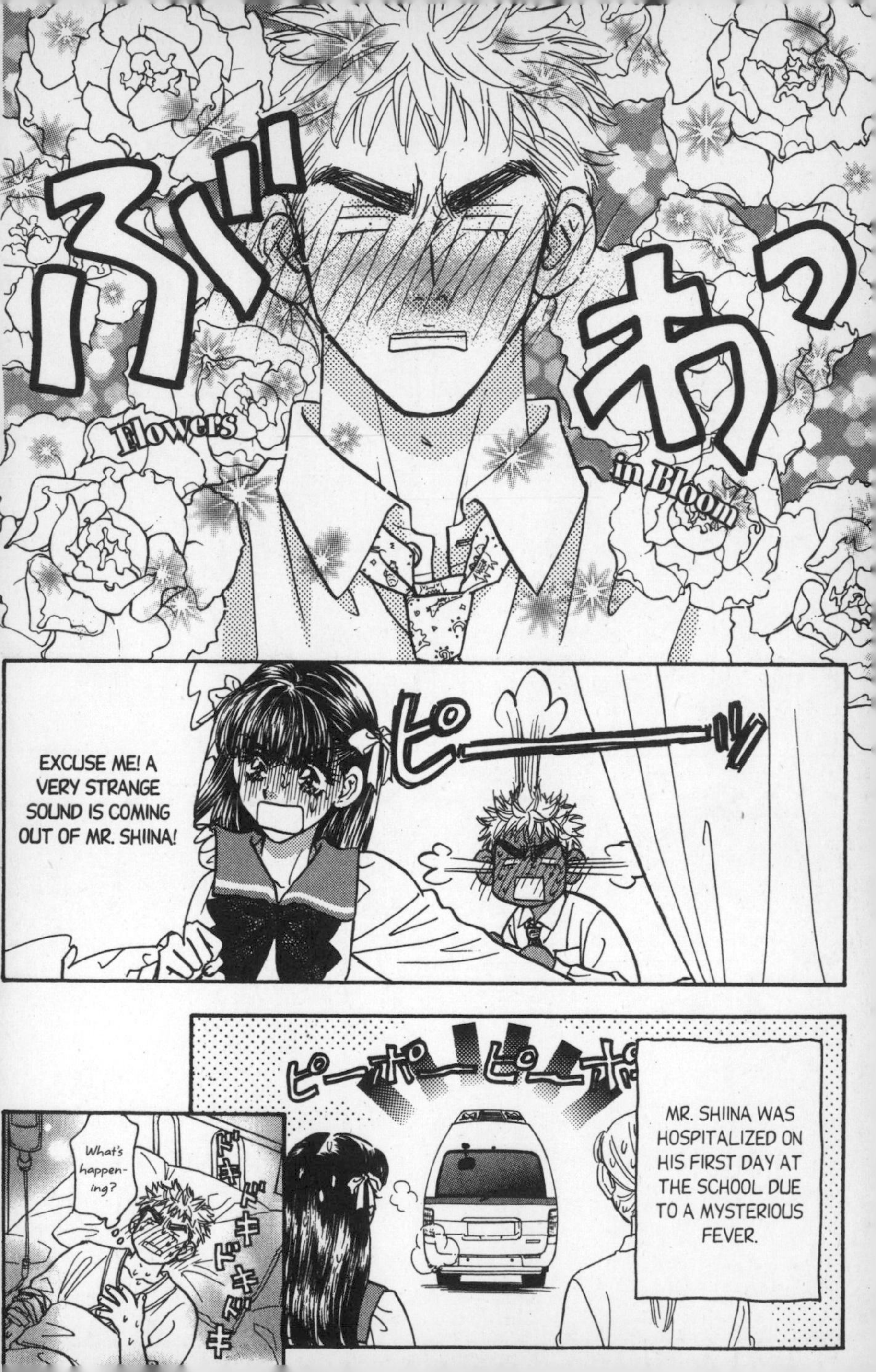
Flowers
in Bloom
ピーーッ
EXCUSE ME! A VERY STRANGE SOUND IS COMING OUT OF MR. SHIINA!
MR. SHIINA WAS HOSPITALIZED ON HIS FIRST DAY AT THE SCHOOL DUE TO A MYSTERIOUS FEVER.
What's happen-ing?

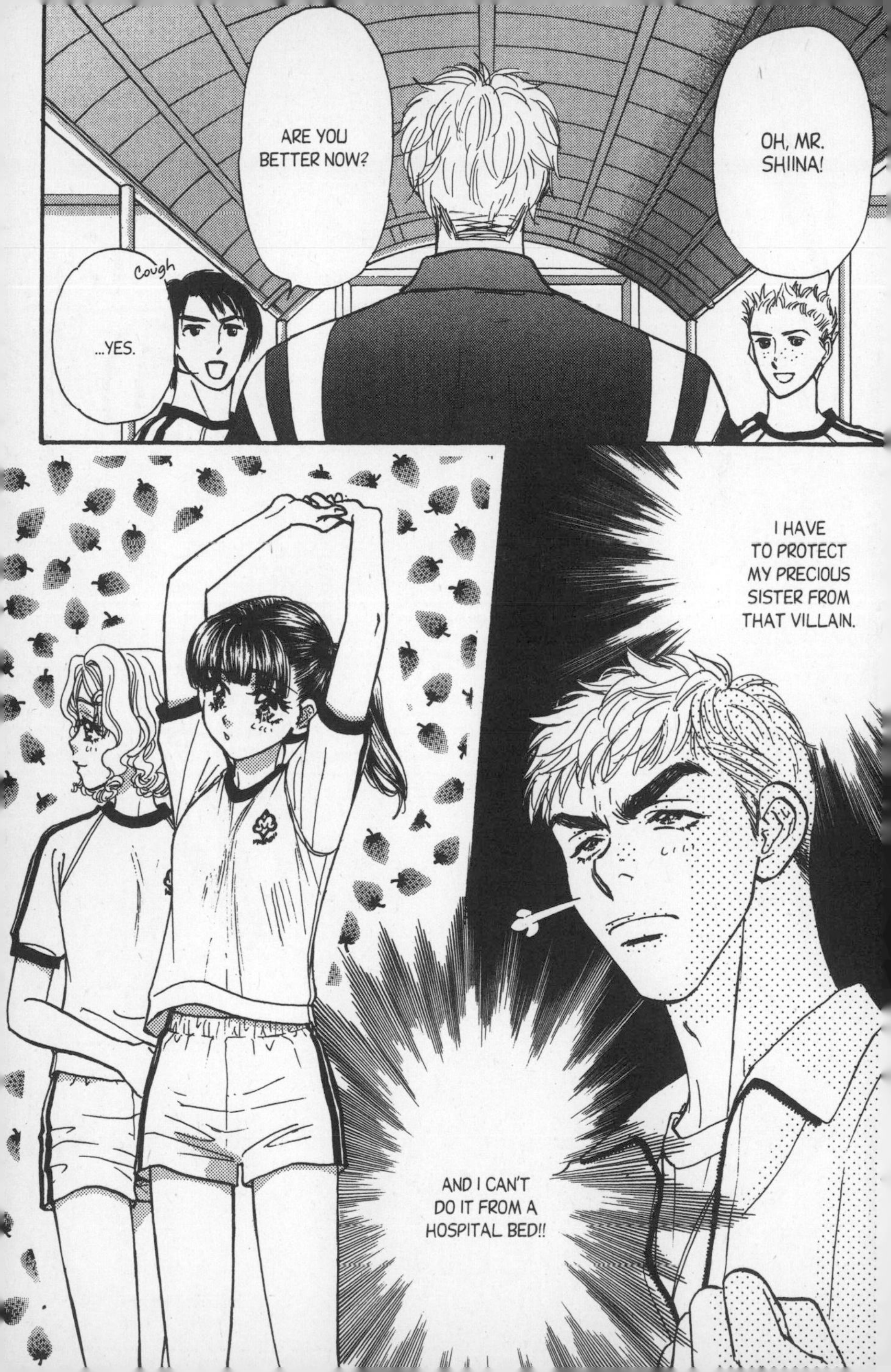
OH, MR. SHIINA!
ARE YOU BETTER NOW?
Cough
...YES.
I HAVE TO PROTECT MY PRECIOUS SISTER FROM THAT VILLAIN.
AND I CAN'T DO IT FROM A HOSPITAL BED!!

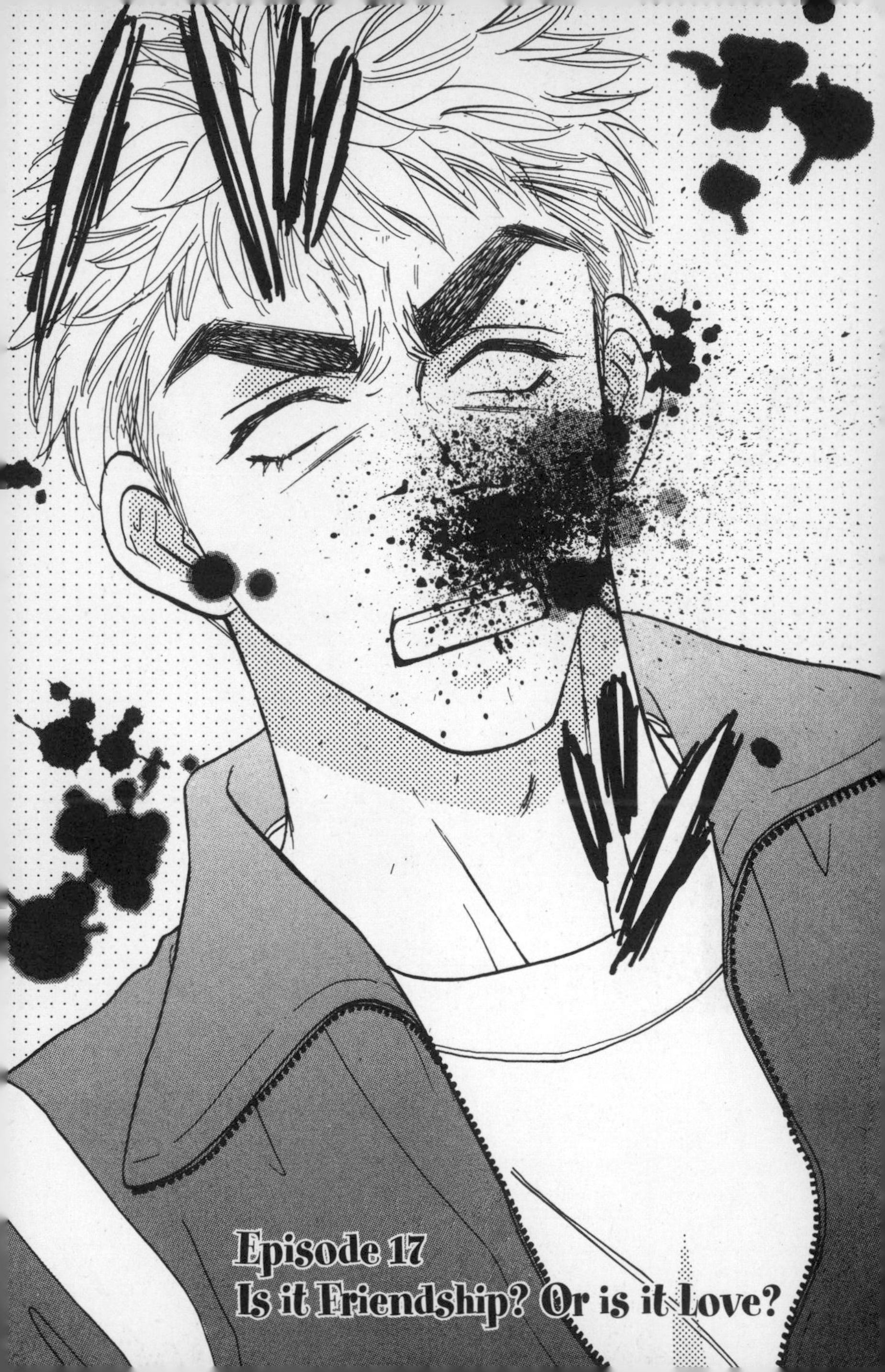

Episode 17
Is it Friendship? Or is it Love?

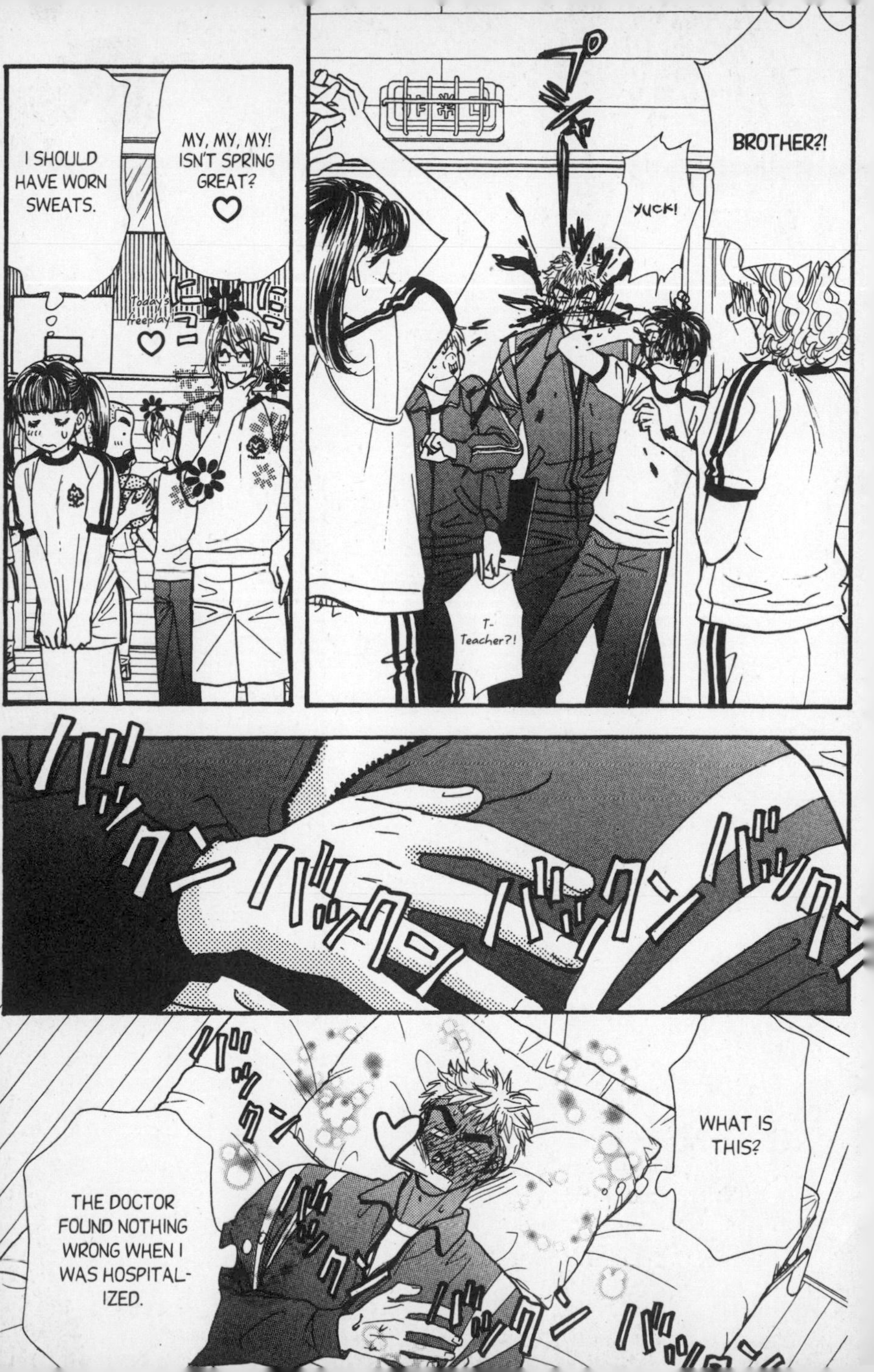
BROTHER?!
YUCK!
T-Teacher?!
MY, MY, MY! ISN'T SPRING GREAT? ♡
I SHOULD HAVE WORN SWEATS.
Today's freeplay! ♡
WHAT IS THIS?
THE DOCTOR FOUND NOTHING WRONG WHEN I WAS HOSPITAL-IZED.

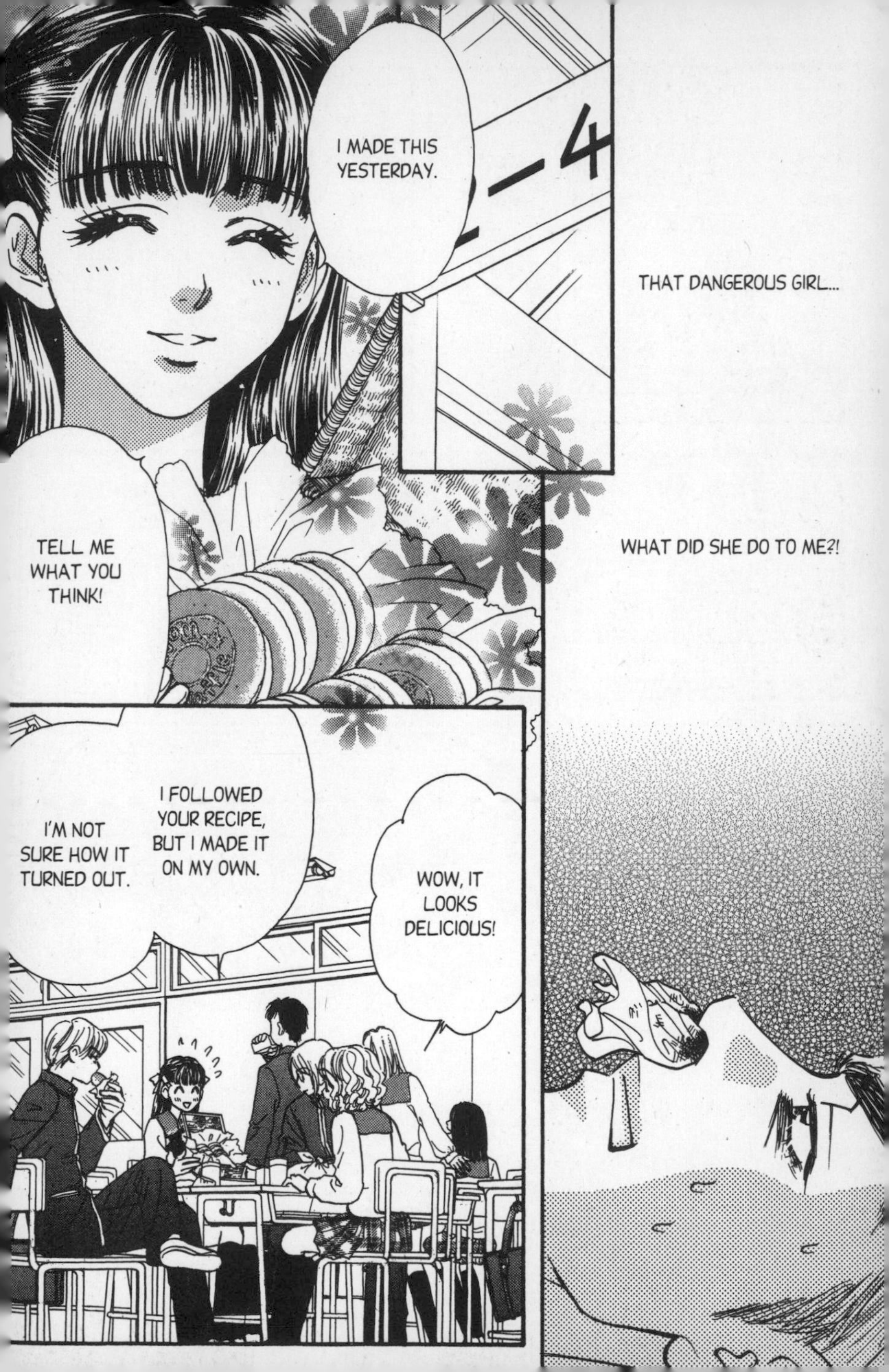

THAT DANGEROUS GIRL...
WHAT DID SHE DO TO ME?!
I MADE THIS YESTERDAY.
TELL ME WHAT YOU THINK!
WOW, IT LOOKS DELICIOUS!
I FOLLOWED YOUR RECIPE, BUT I MADE IT ON MY OWN.
I'M NOT SURE HOW IT TURNED OUT.

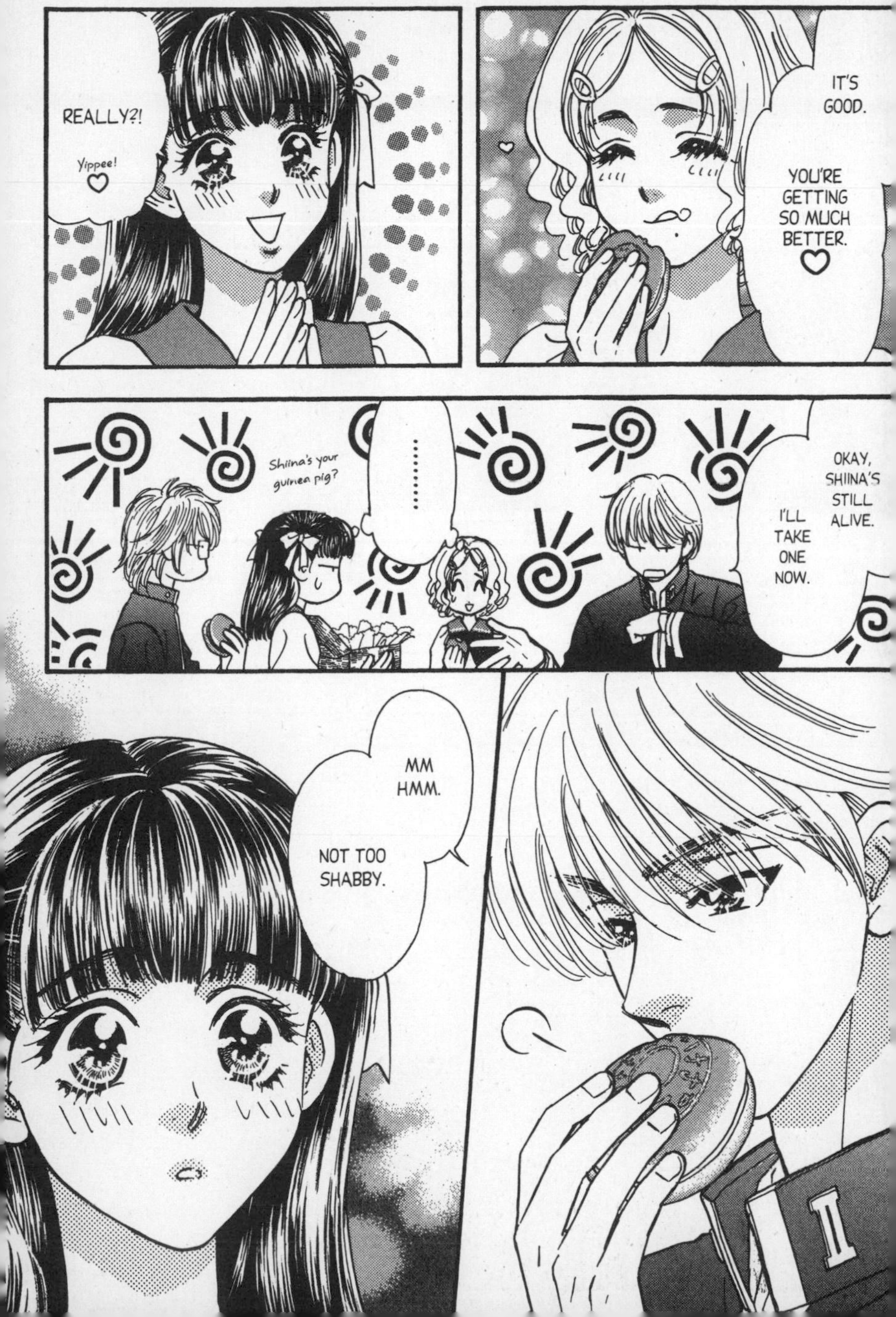
IT'S GOOD.
YOU'RE GETTING SO MUCH BETTER. ♡
REALLY?!
Yippee! ♡
OKAY, SHIINA'S STILL ALIVE.
I'LL TAKE ONE NOW.
......
Shiina's your guinea pig?
MM HMM.
NOT TOO SHABBY.

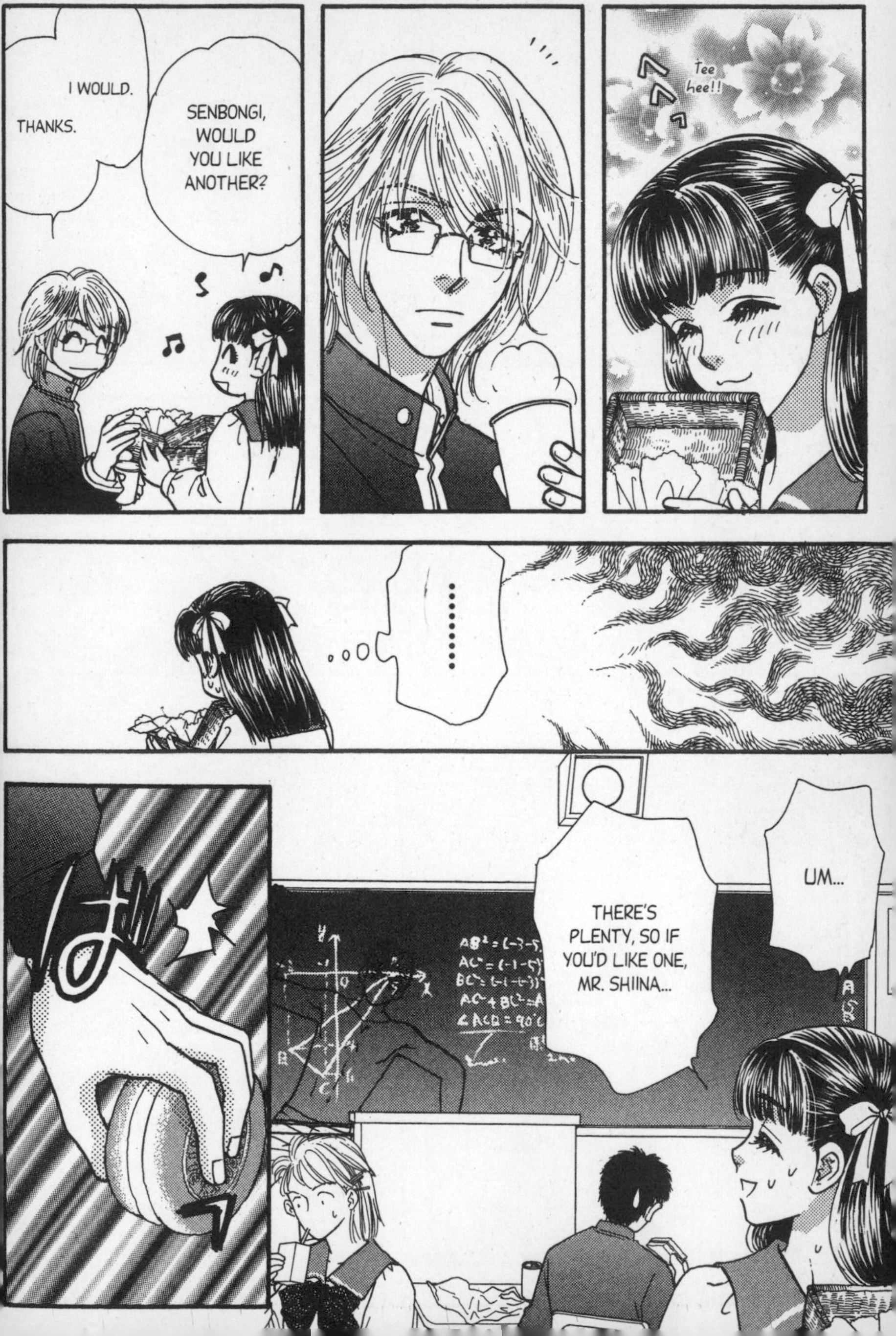
Tee hee!!
SENBONGI, WOULD YOU LIKE ANOTHER?
I WOULD. THANKS.
......
UM...
THERE'S PLENTY, SO IF YOU'D LIKE ONE, MR. SHIINA...

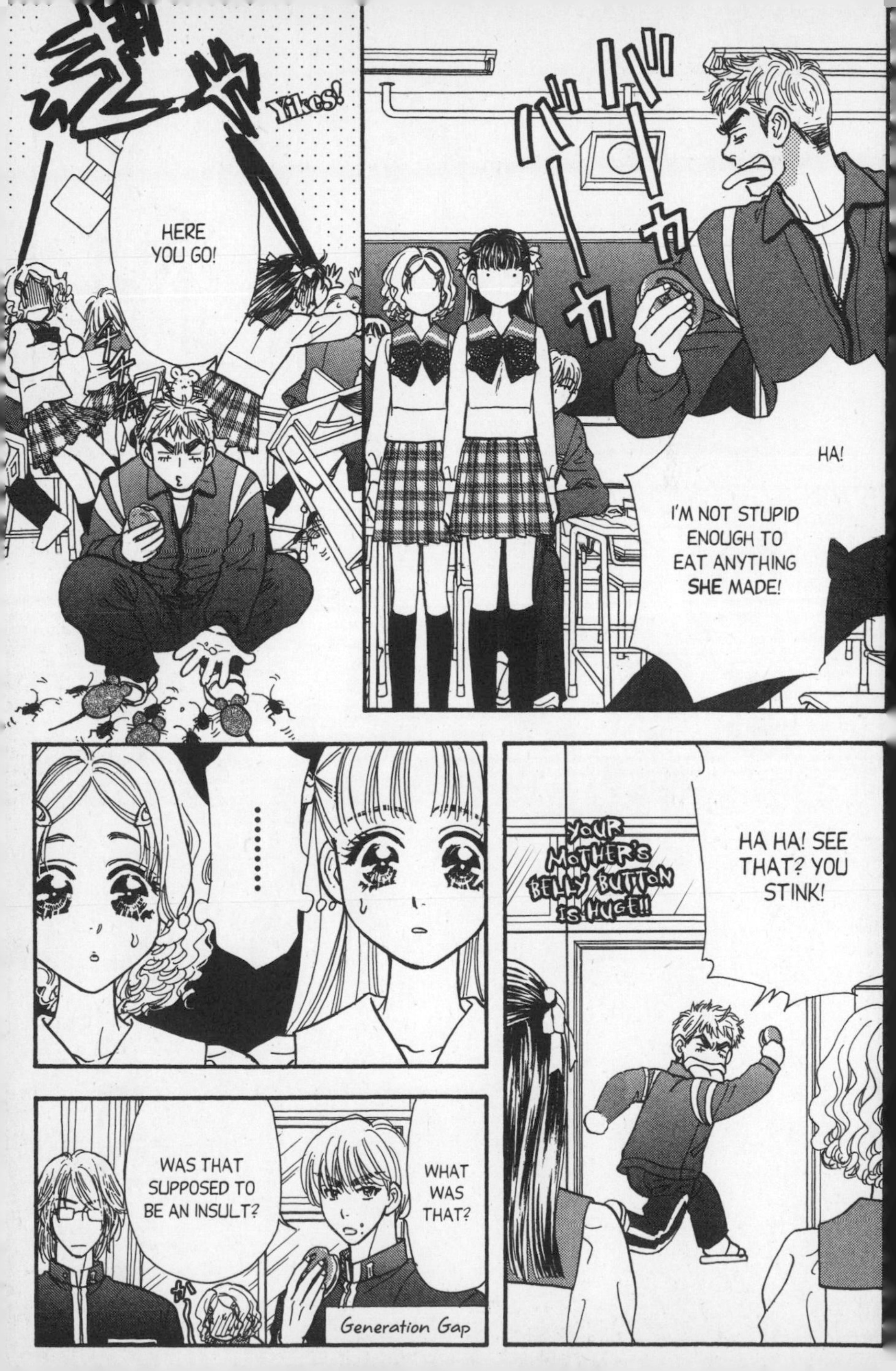
HA!
I'M NOT STUPID ENOUGH TO EAT ANYTHING SHE MADE!
Yikes!
HERE YOU GO!
HA HA! SEE THAT? YOU STINK!
YOUR MOTHER'S BELLY BUTTON IS HUGE!!
……
WHAT WAS THAT?
WAS THAT SUPPOSED TO BE AN INSULT?
Generation Gap

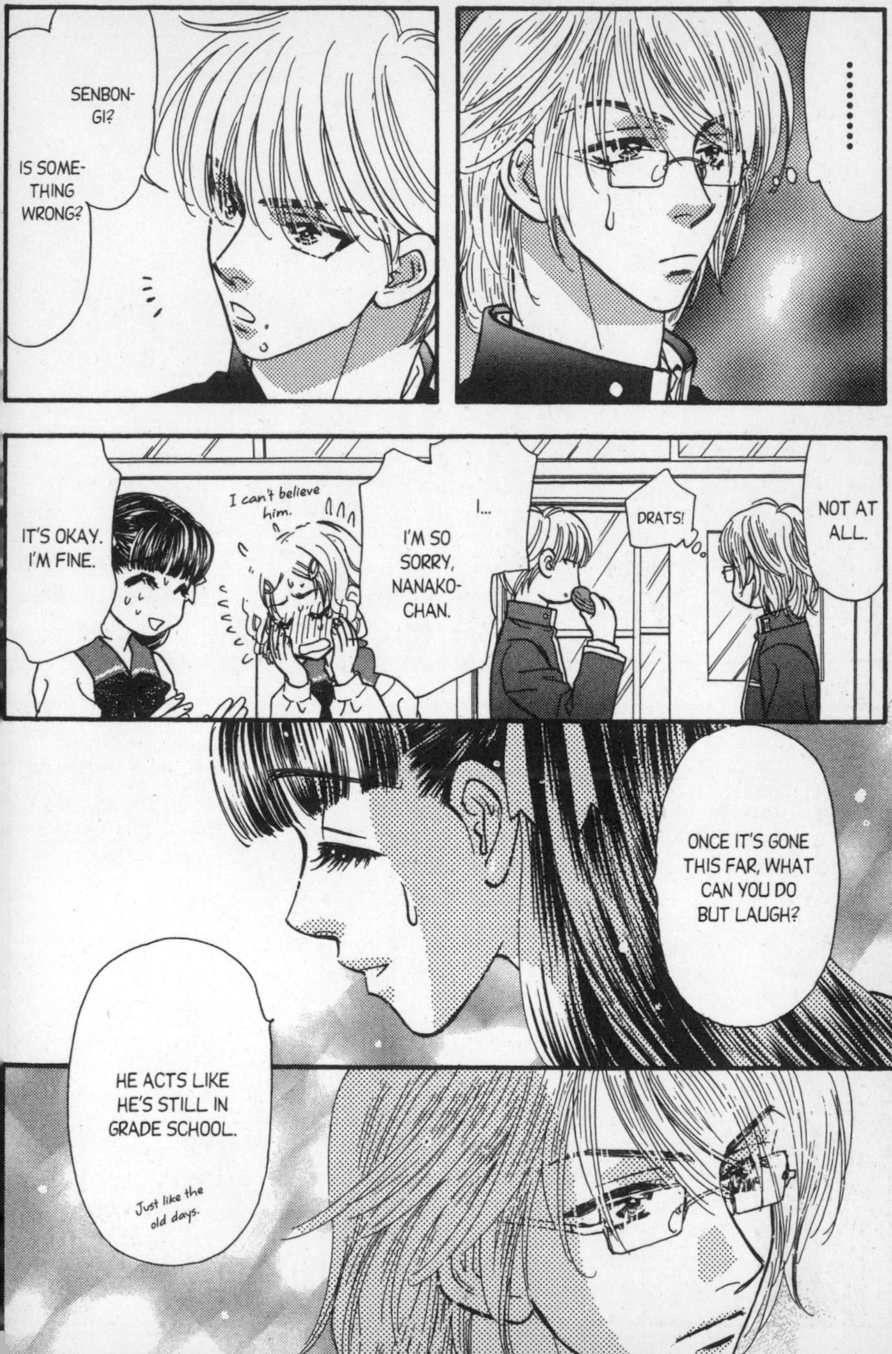

......
SENBON-GI?
IS SOME-THING WRONG?
NOT AT ALL.
DRATS!
I...
I'M SO SORRY, NANAKO-CHAN.
I can't believe him.
IT'S OKAY. I'M FINE.
ONCE IT'S GONE THIS FAR, WHAT CAN YOU DO BUT LAUGH?
HE ACTS LIKE HE'S STILL IN GRADE SCHOOL.
Just like the old days.

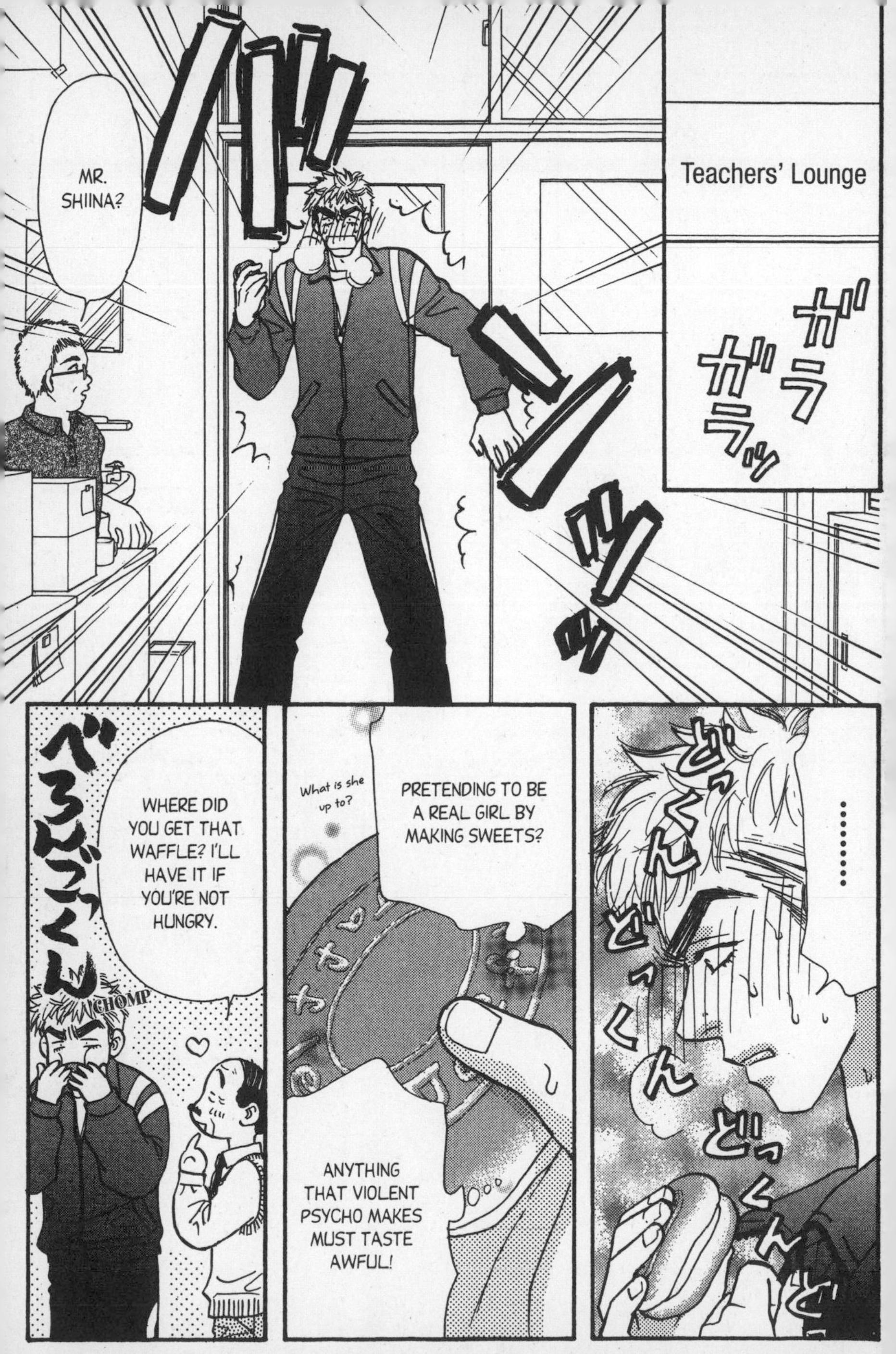

Teachers' Lounge
ガラガラッ
MR. SHIINA?
....
What is she up to?
PRETENDING TO BE A REAL GIRL BY MAKING SWEETS?
ANYTHING THAT VIOLENT PSYCHO MAKES MUST TASTE AWFUL!
WHERE DID YOU GET THAT WAFFLE? I'LL HAVE IT IF YOU'RE NOT HUNGRY.
CHOMP

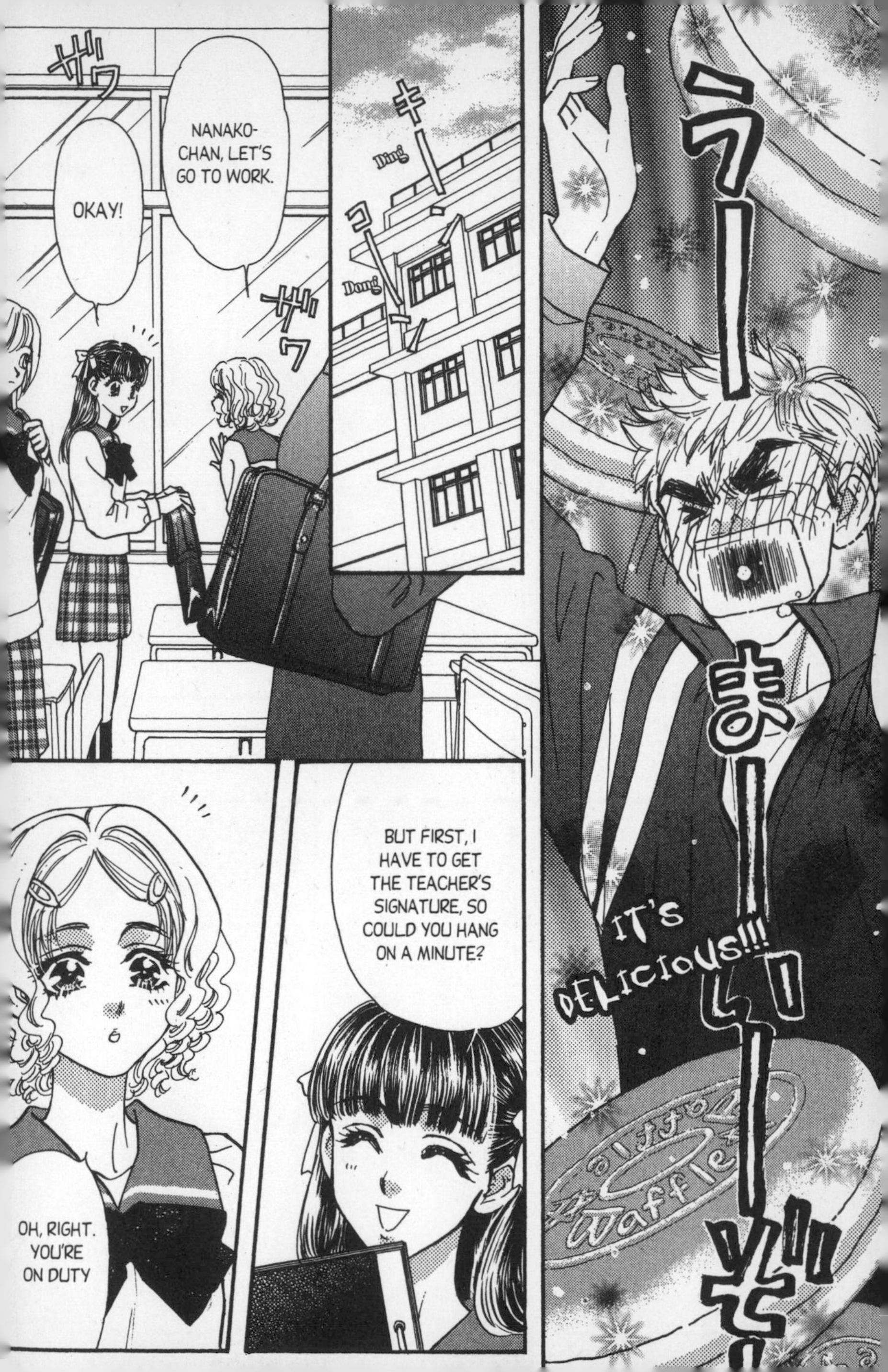

IT'S DELICIOUS!!!
Waffle
Ding
Dong
NANAKO-CHAN, LET'S GO TO WORK.
OKAY!
BUT FIRST, I HAVE TO GET THE TEACHER'S SIGNATURE, SO COULD YOU HANG ON A MINUTE?
OH, RIGHT. YOU'RE ON DUTY

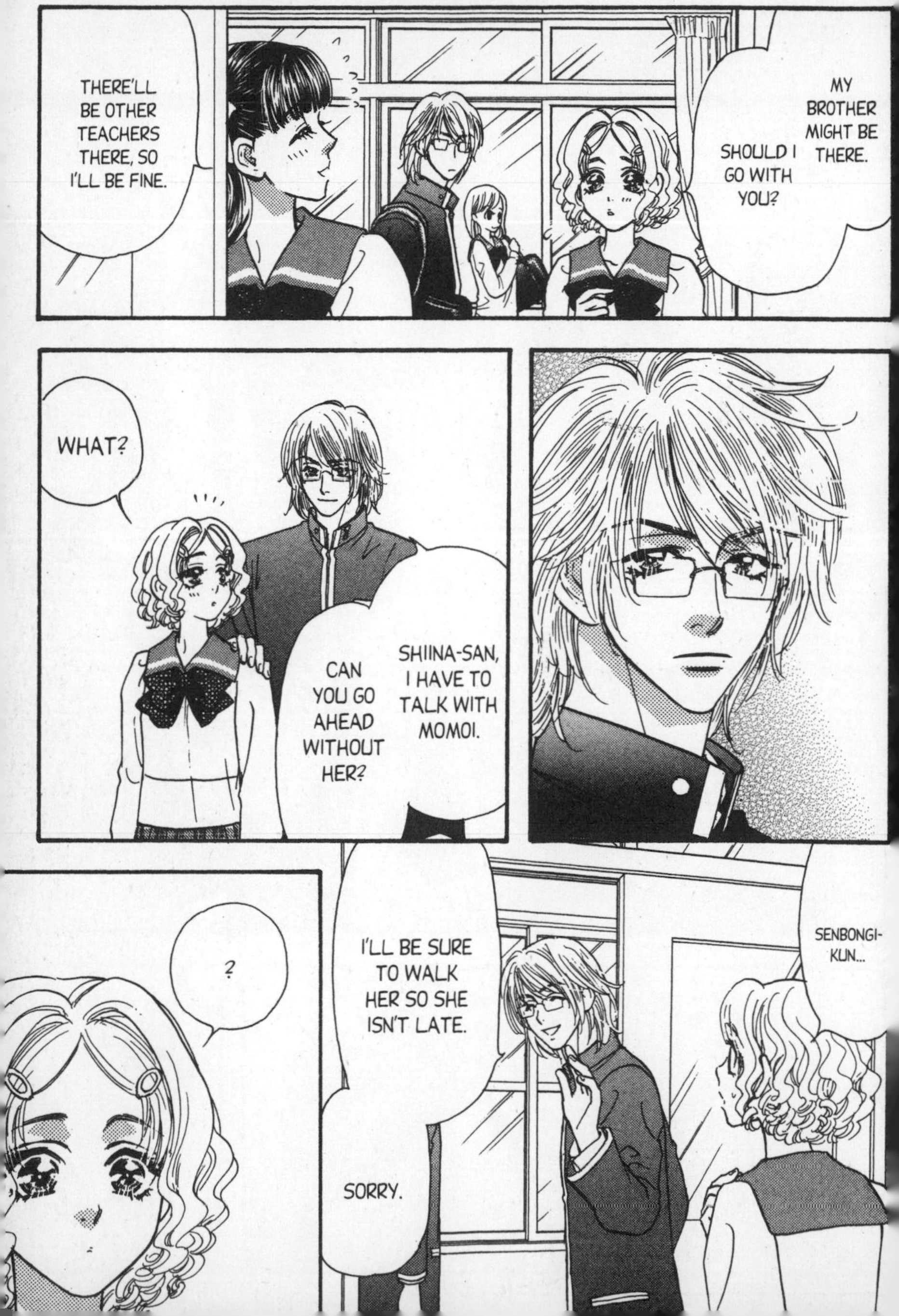
MY BROTHER MIGHT BE THERE.
SHOULD I GO WITH YOU?
THERE'LL BE OTHER TEACHERS THERE, SO I'LL BE FINE.
SHIINA-SAN, I HAVE TO TALK WITH MOMOI.
CAN YOU GO AHEAD WITHOUT HER?
WHAT?
SENBONGI-KUN...
I'LL BE SURE TO WALK HER SO SHE ISN'T LATE.
SORRY.
?

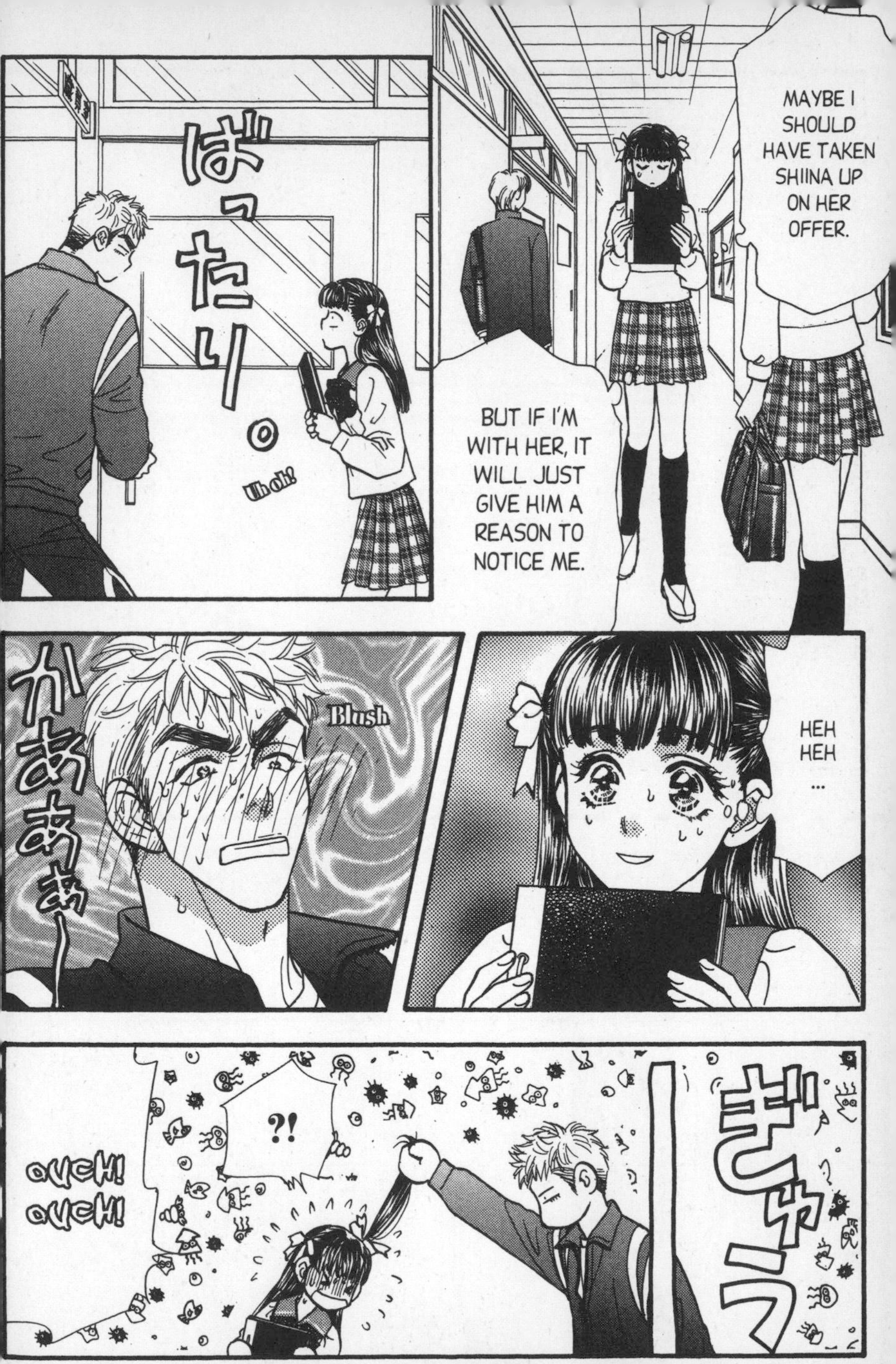
MAYBE I SHOULD HAVE TAKEN SHIINA UP ON HER OFFER.
BUT IF I'M WITH HER, IT WILL JUST GIVE HIM A REASON TO NOTICE ME.
ばったり
Uh oh!
HEH HEH ...
かあああぁ
Blush
ぎゅう
?!
OUCH! OUCH!

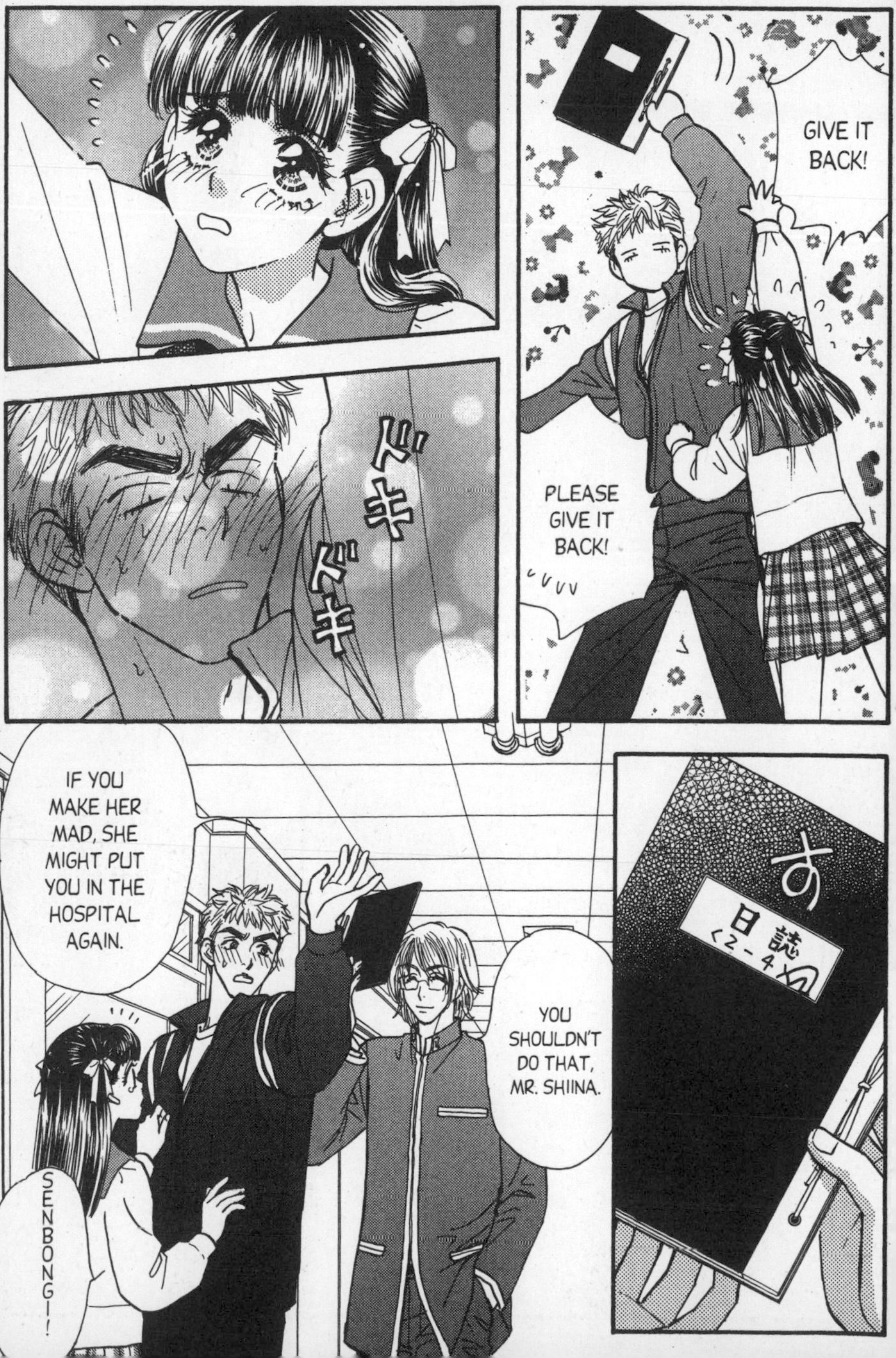
GIVE IT BACK!
PLEASE GIVE IT BACK!
ドキドキ
お
日誌
<2-4>
YOU SHOULDN'T DO THAT, MR. SHIINA.
IF YOU MAKE HER MAD, SHE MIGHT PUT YOU IN THE HOSPITAL AGAIN.
SENBONGI!!

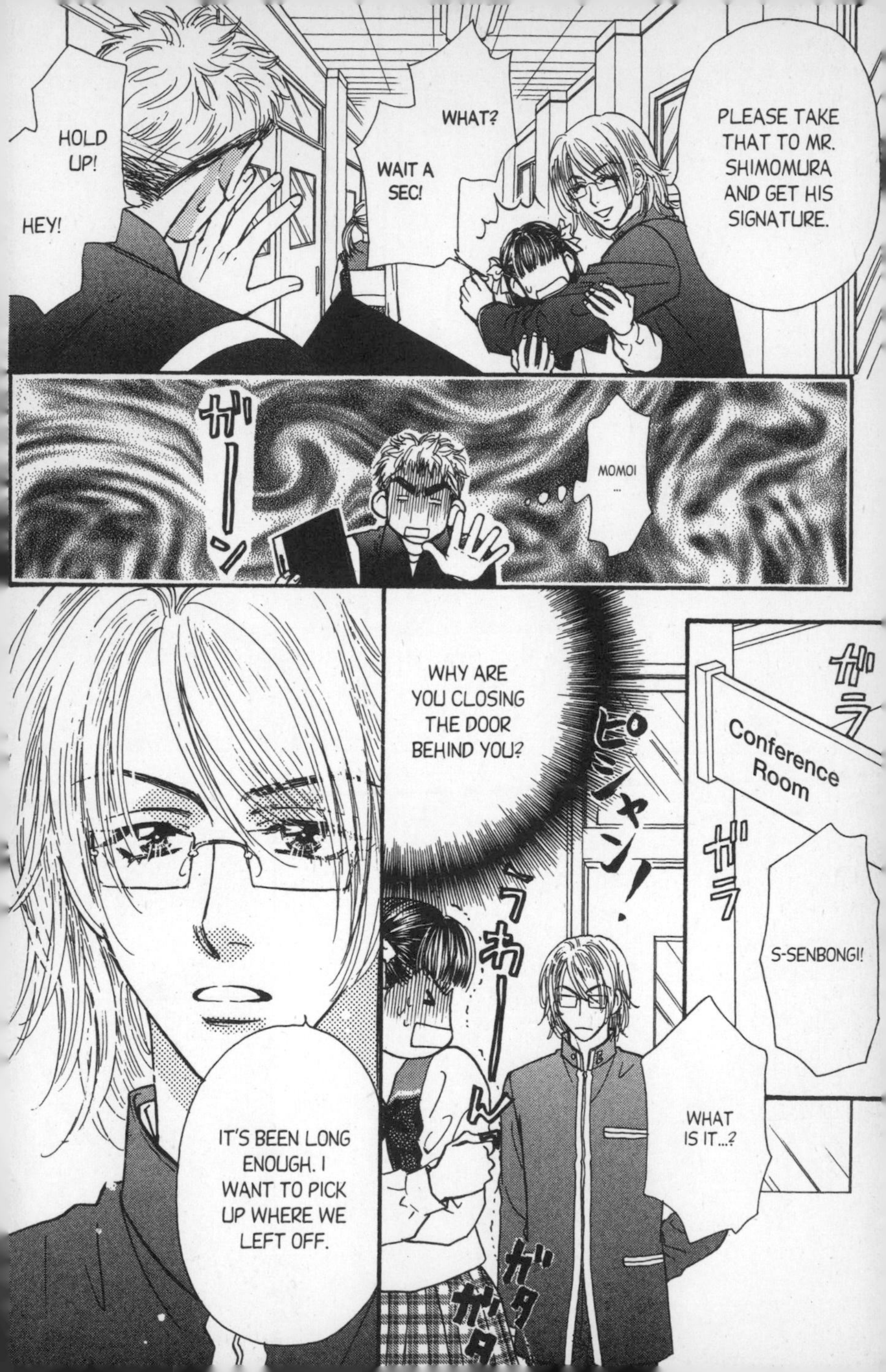
PLEASE TAKE THAT TO MR. SHIMOMURA AND GET HIS SIGNATURE.
WHAT?
WAIT A SEC!
HOLD UP!
HEY!
MOMOI ...
ガーン
ガラ
Conference Room
ガラ
S-SENBONGI!
WHAT IS IT...?
ピシャン!
WHY ARE YOU CLOSING THE DOOR BEHIND YOU?
うわーん
ガタ
ガタ
IT'S BEEN LONG ENOUGH. I WANT TO PICK UP WHERE WE LEFT OFF.

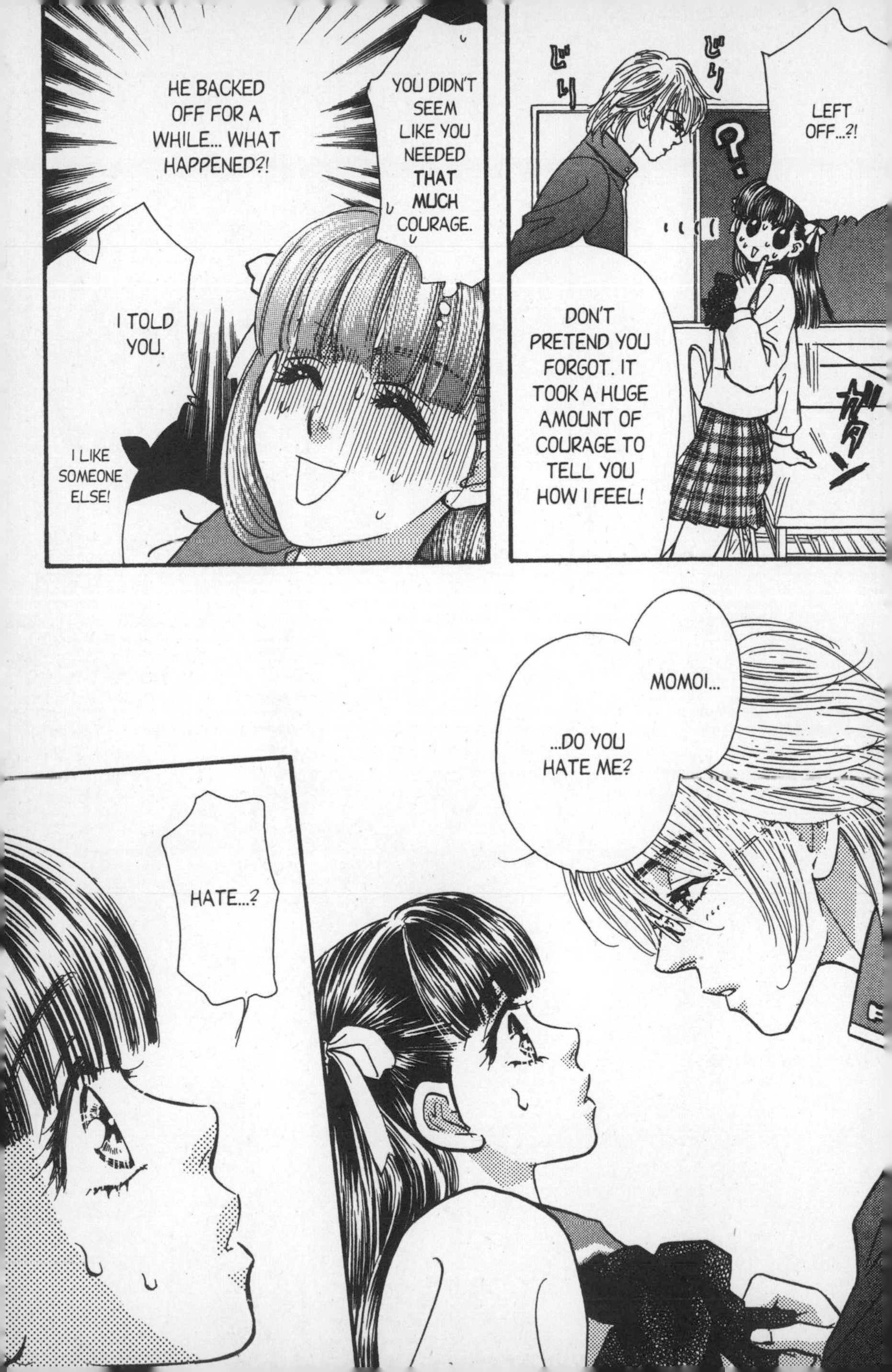

LEFT OFF...?!
DON'T PRETEND YOU FORGOT. IT TOOK A HUGE AMOUNT OF COURAGE TO TELL YOU HOW I FEEL!
YOU DIDN'T SEEM LIKE YOU NEEDED THAT MUCH COURAGE.
HE BACKED OFF FOR A WHILE... WHAT HAPPENED?!
I TOLD YOU.
I LIKE SOMEONE ELSE!
MOMOI... ...DO YOU HATE ME?
HATE...?

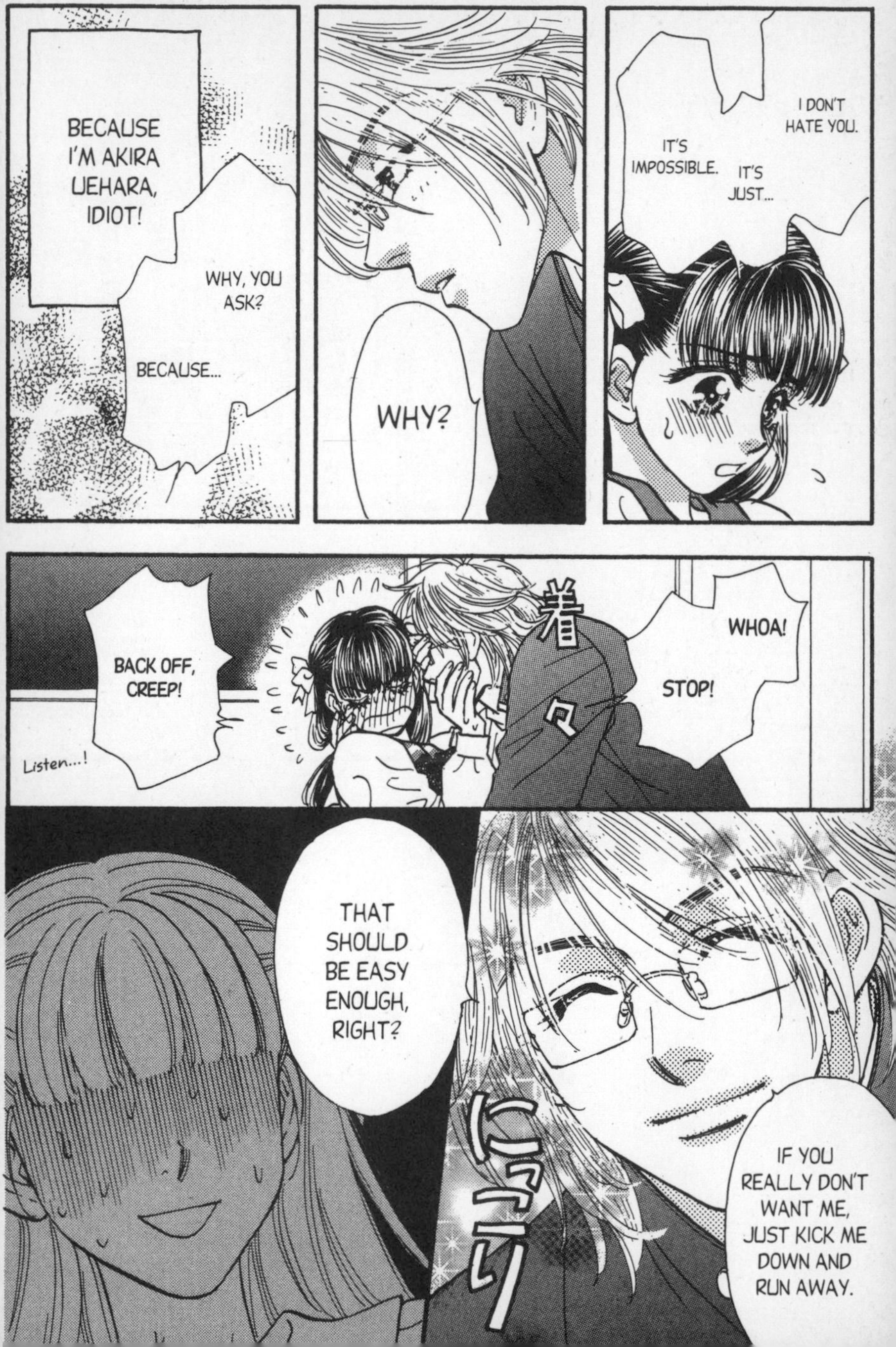
I DON'T HATE YOU.
IT'S JUST...
IT'S IMPOSSIBLE.
WHY?
WHY, YOU ASK?
BECAUSE...
BECAUSE I'M AKIRA UEHARA, IDIOT!
WHOA!
STOP!
着々
BACK OFF, CREEP!
Listen...!
IF YOU REALLY DON'T WANT ME, JUST KICK ME DOWN AND RUN AWAY.
THAT SHOULD BE EASY ENOUGH, RIGHT?

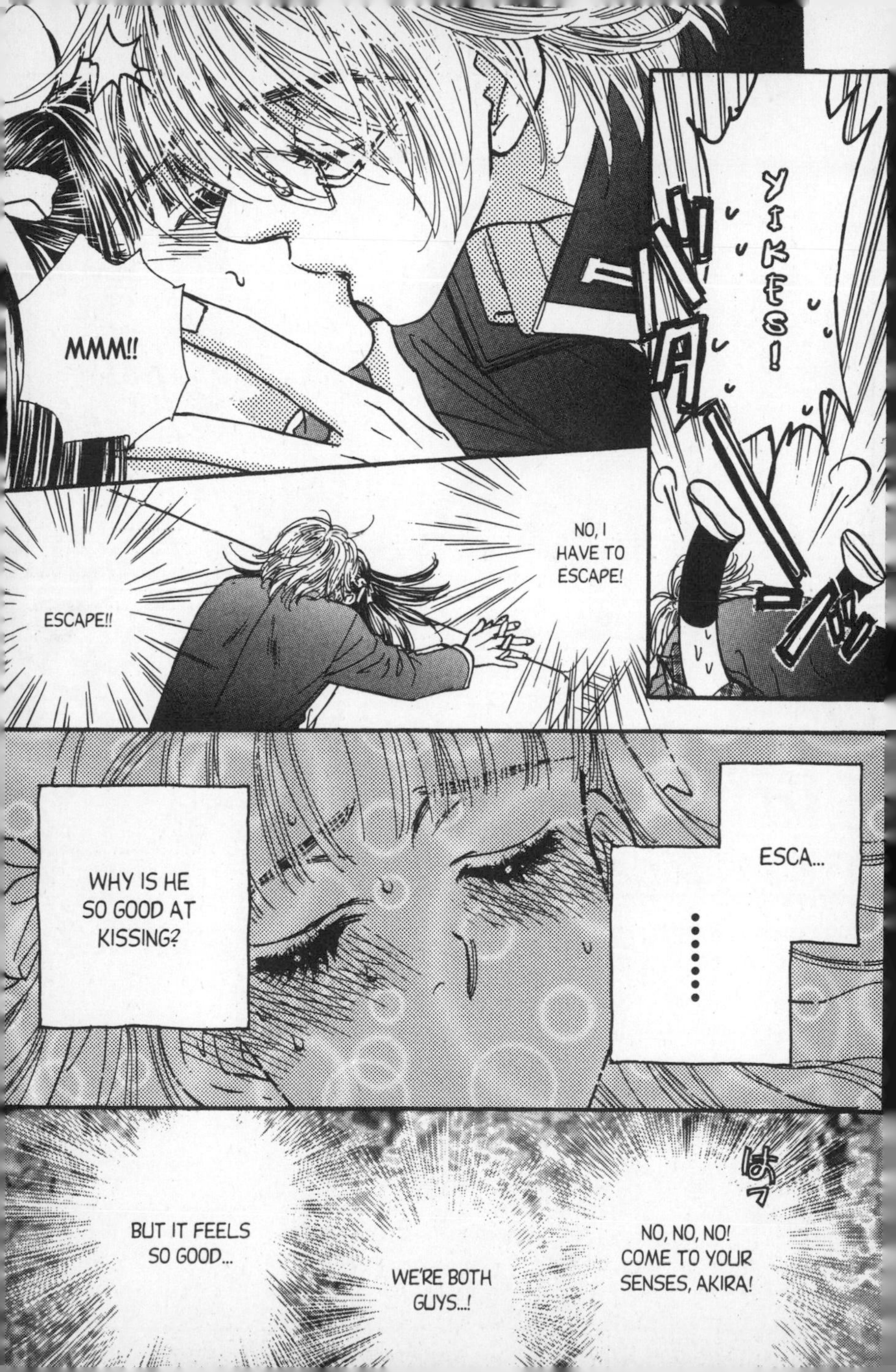
MMM!!
YIKES!
NO, I HAVE TO ESCAPE!
ESCAPE!!
ESCA...
......
WHY IS HE SO GOOD AT KISSING?
はっ
NO, NO, NO! COME TO YOUR SENSES, AKIRA!
WE'RE BOTH GUYS...!
BUT IT FEELS SO GOOD...

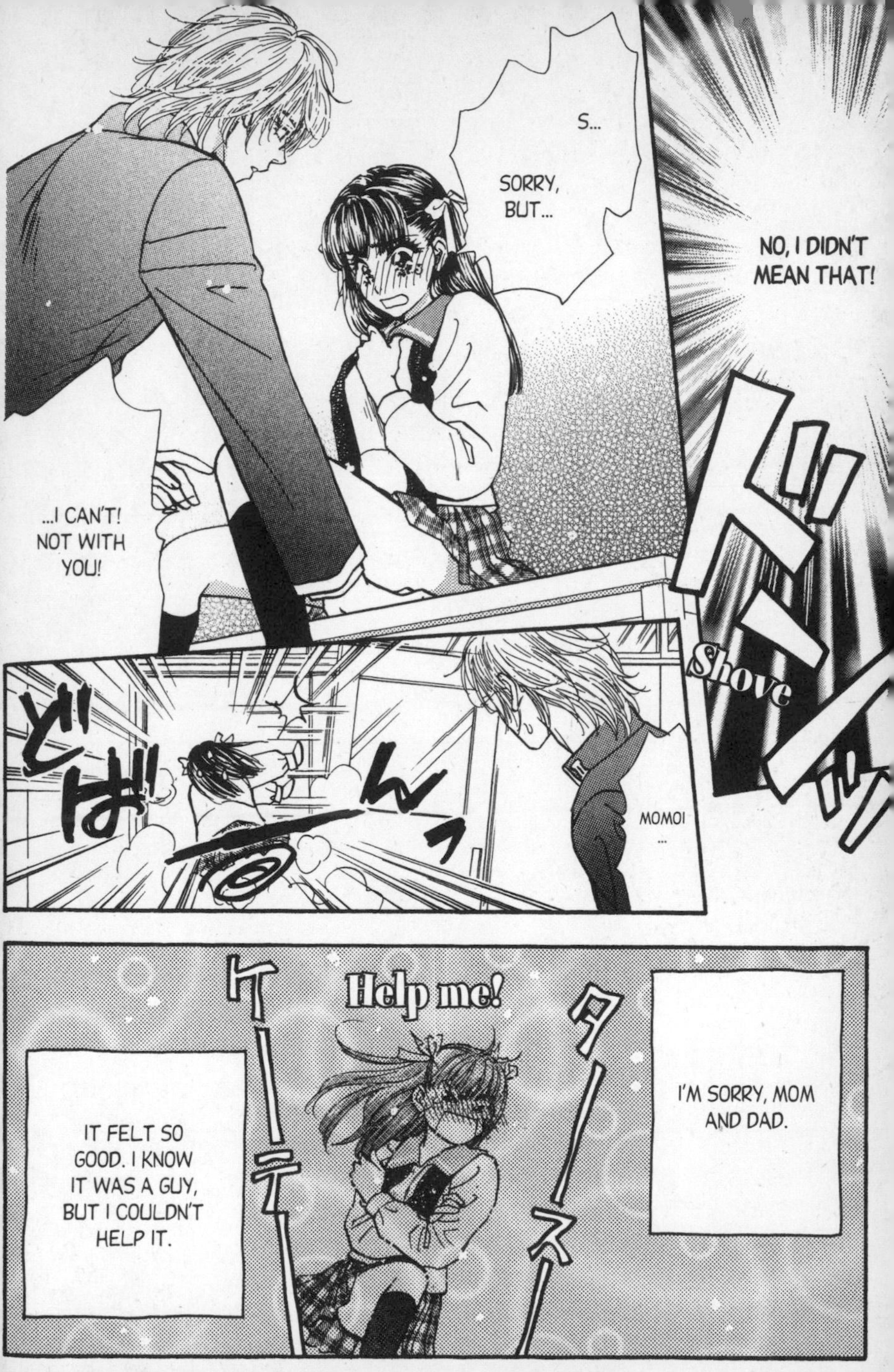
S...
SORRY, BUT...
...I CAN'T! NOT WITH YOU!
NO, I DIDN'T MEAN THAT!
Shove
MOMOI ...
I'M SORRY, MOM AND DAD.
Help me!
IT FELT SO GOOD. I KNOW IT WAS A GUY, BUT I COULDN'T HELP IT.

Episode 19
Viva! Bear Trap!!

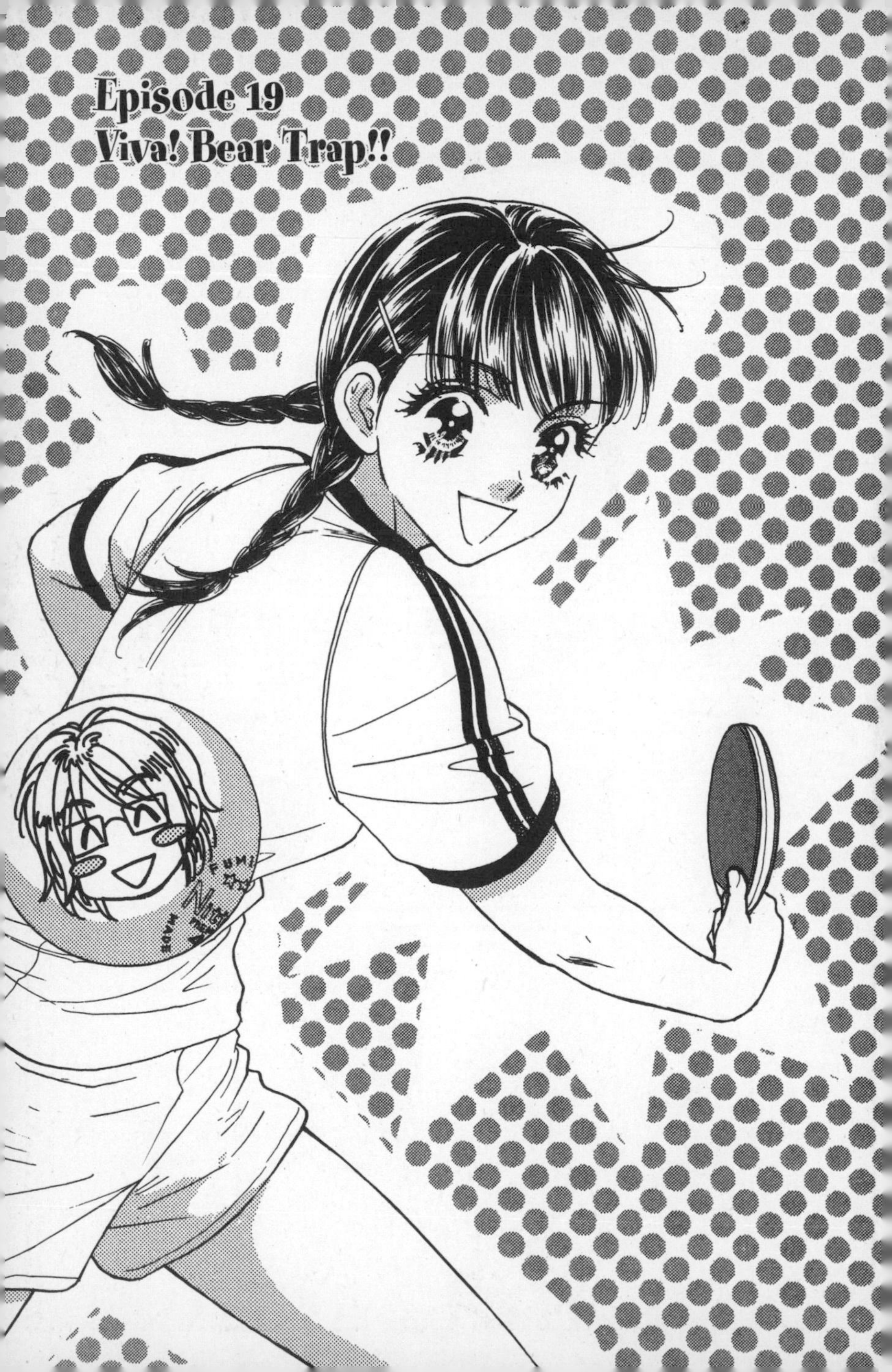

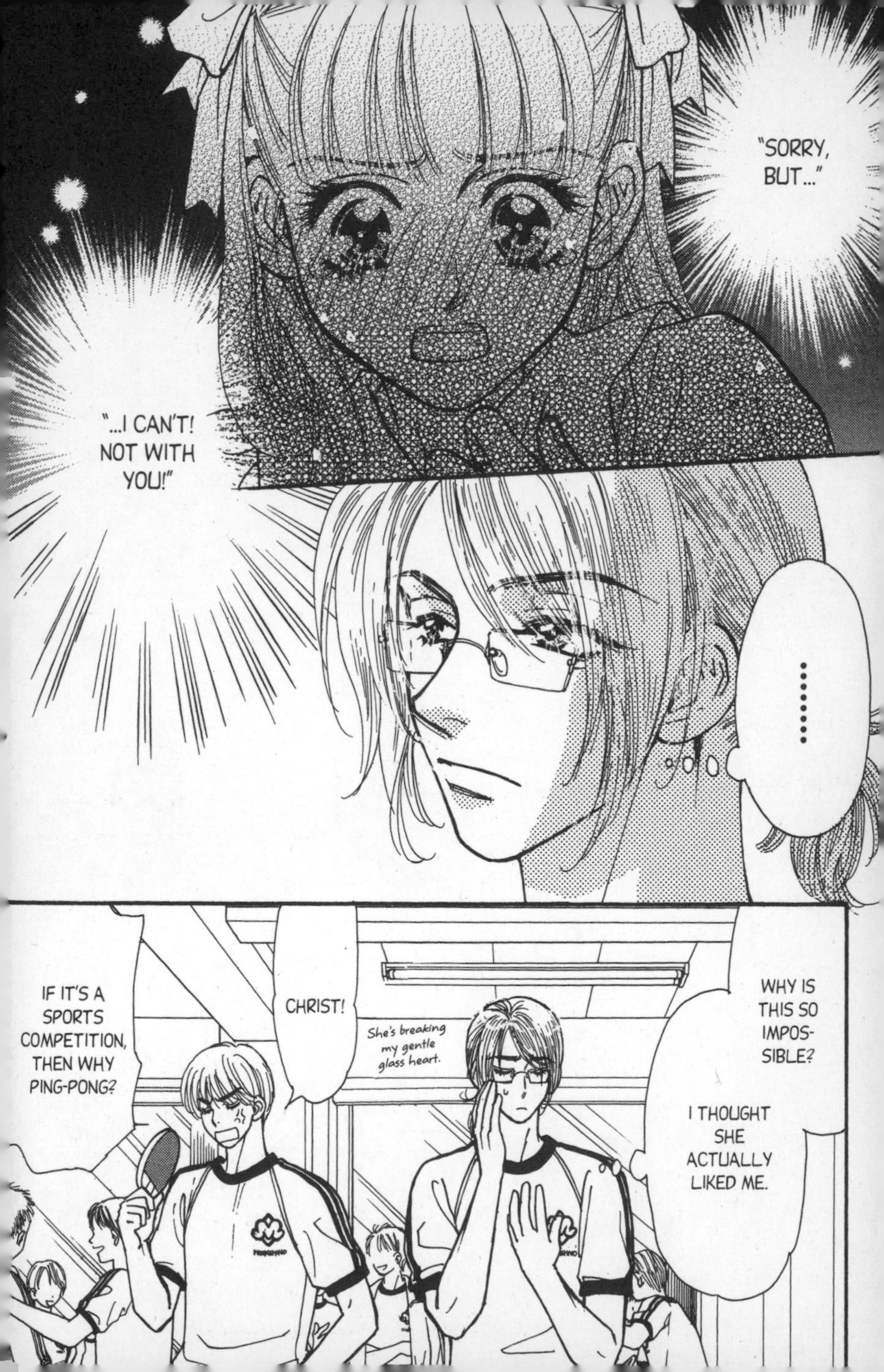
"SORRY, BUT..."
"...I CAN'T! NOT WITH YOU!"
......
WHY IS THIS SO IMPOS-SIBLE?
I THOUGHT SHE ACTUALLY LIKED ME.
She's breaking my gentle glass heart.
CHRIST!
IF IT'S A SPORTS COMPETITION, THEN WHY PING-PONG?

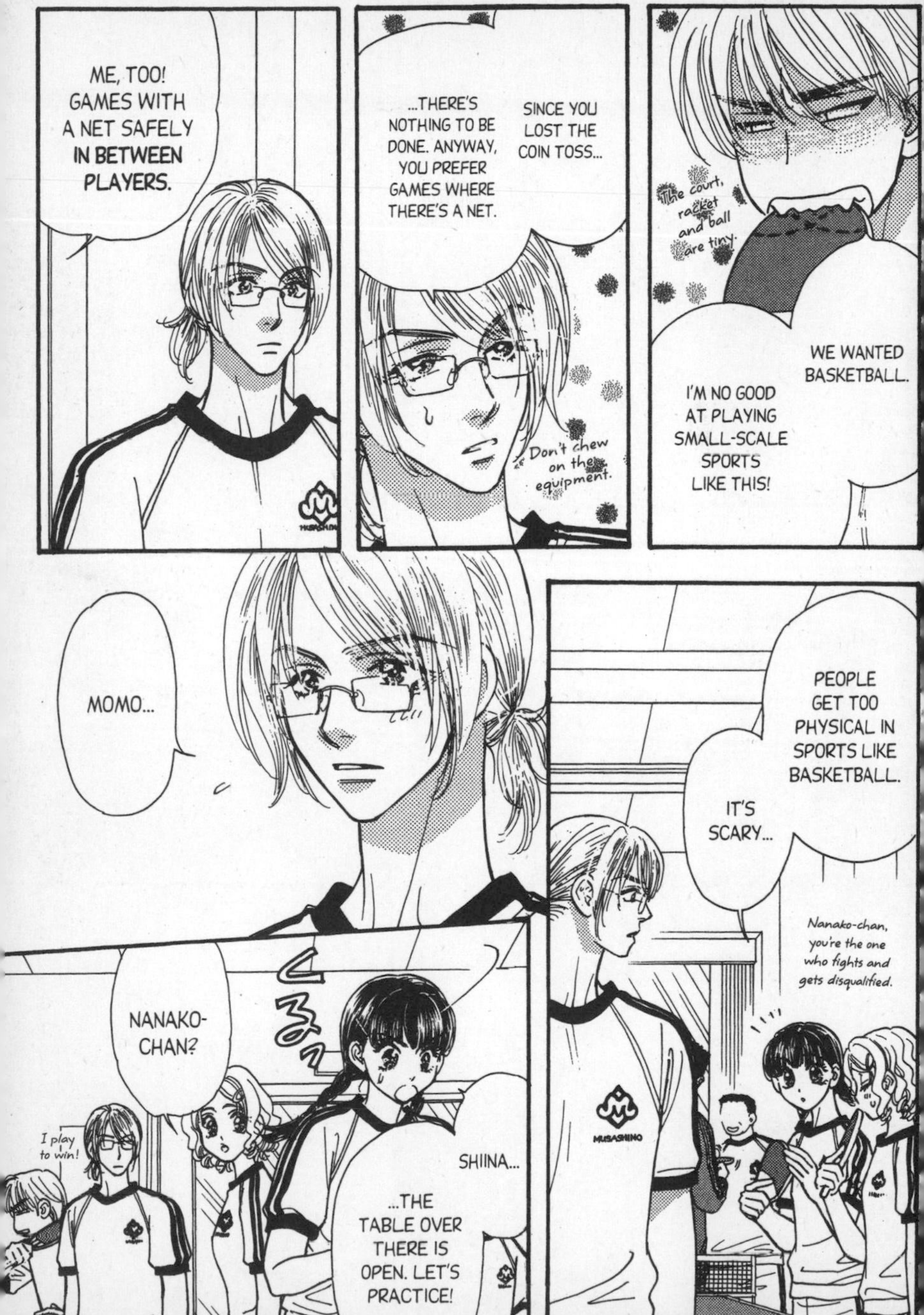
The court, racket and ball are tiny.
WE WANTED BASKETBALL.
I'M NO GOOD AT PLAYING SMALL-SCALE SPORTS LIKE THIS!
SINCE YOU LOST THE COIN TOSS...
...THERE'S NOTHING TO BE DONE. ANYWAY, YOU PREFER GAMES WHERE THERE'S A NET.
Don't chew on the equipment.
ME, TOO! GAMES WITH A NET SAFELY IN BETWEEN PLAYERS.
PEOPLE GET TOO PHYSICAL IN SPORTS LIKE BASKETBALL.
IT'S SCARY...
Nanako-chan, you're the one who fights and gets disqualified.
MOMO...
NANAKO-CHAN?
SHIINA...
...THE TABLE OVER THERE IS OPEN. LET'S PRACTICE!
I play to win!

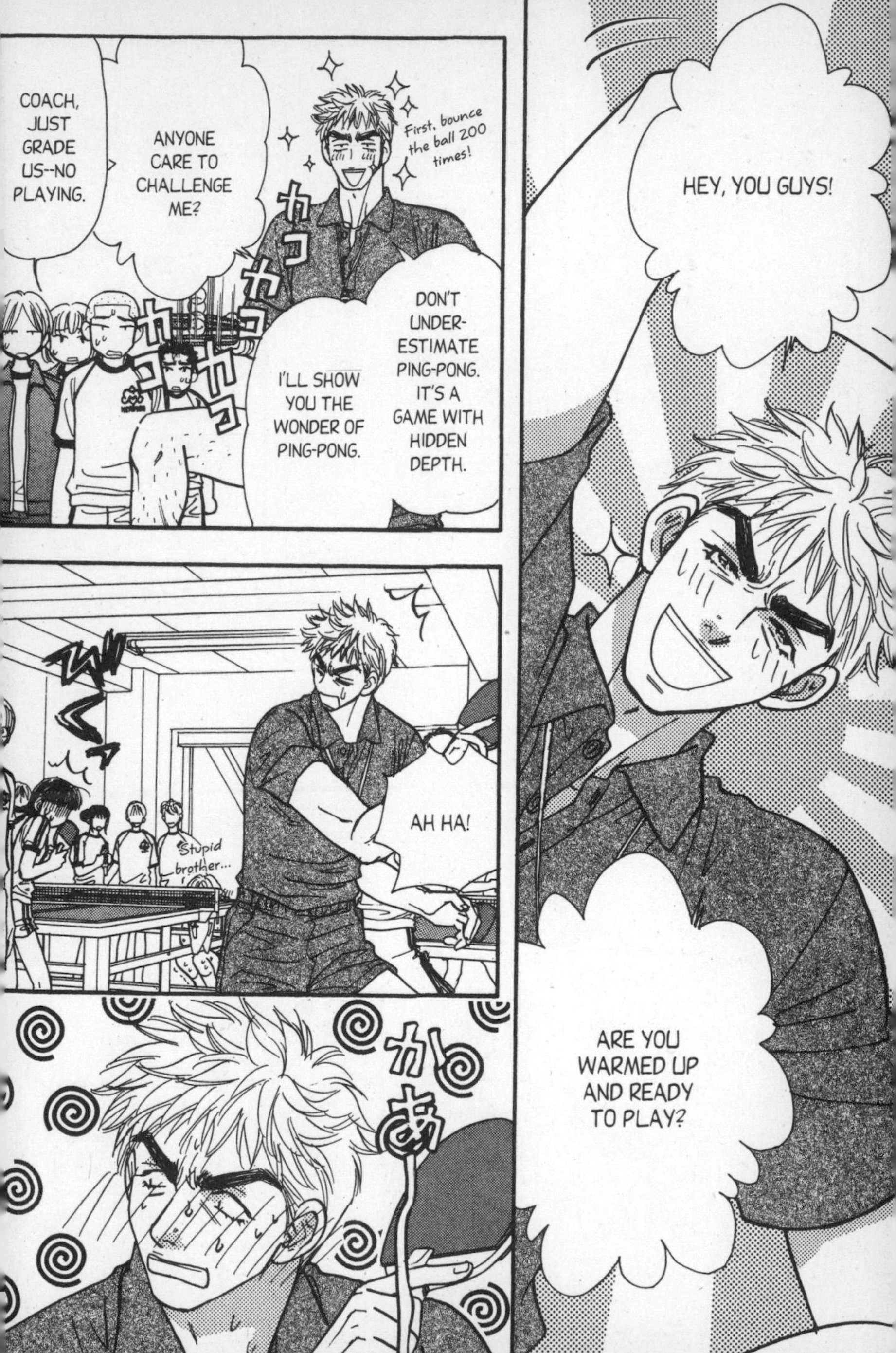
HEY, YOU GUYS!
ARE YOU WARMED UP AND READY TO PLAY?
DON'T UNDER-ESTIMATE PING-PONG. IT'S A GAME WITH HIDDEN DEPTH.
I'LL SHOW YOU THE WONDER OF PING-PONG.
First, bounce the ball 200 times!
ANYONE CARE TO CHALLENGE ME?
COACH, JUST GRADE US--NO PLAYING.
AH HA!
Stupid brother...

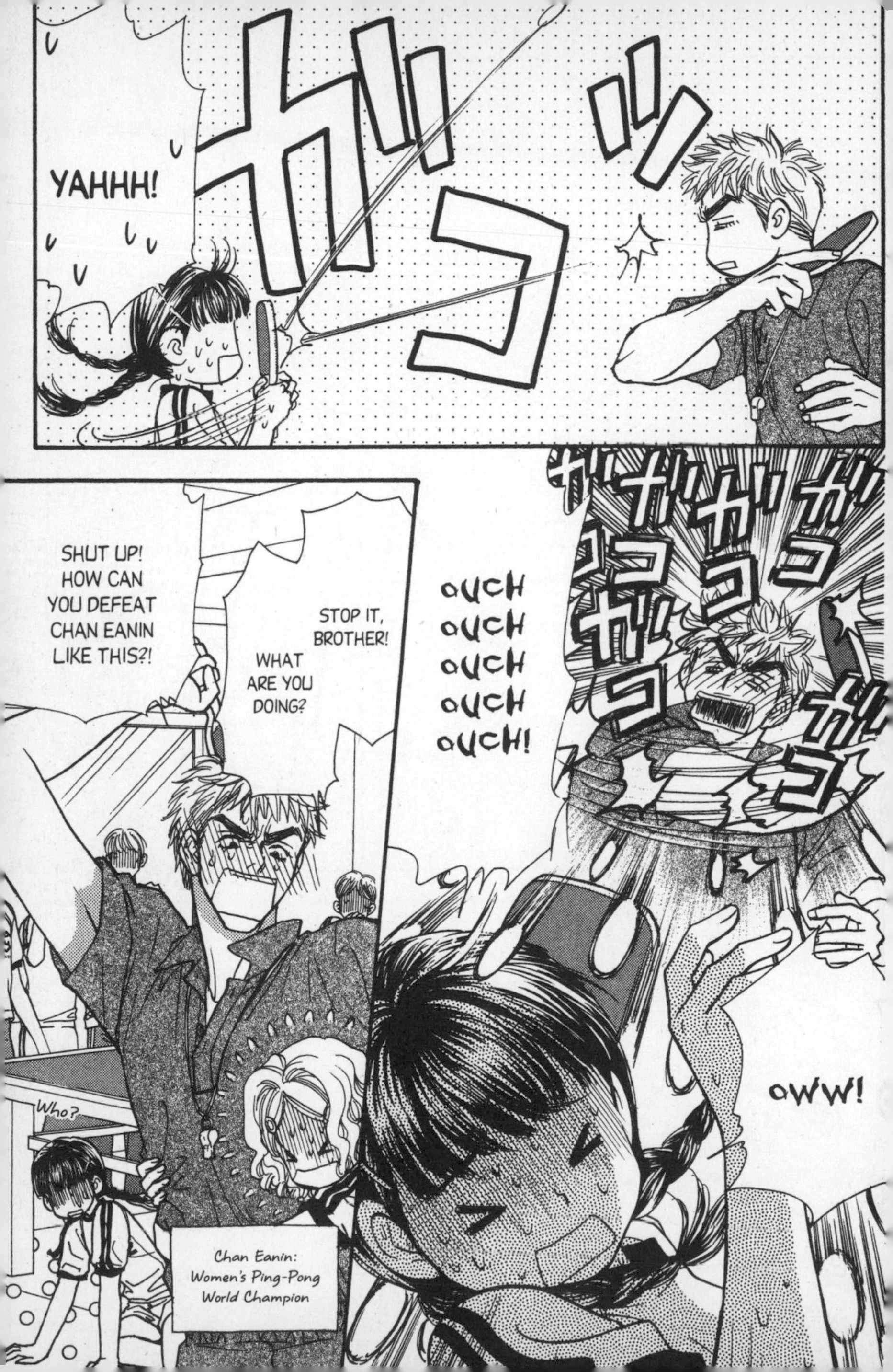
YAHHH!
OUCH OUCH OUCH OUCH OUCH!
OWW!
STOP IT, BROTHER!
WHAT ARE YOU DOING?
SHUT UP! HOW CAN YOU DEFEAT CHAN EANIN LIKE THIS?!
Who?
Chan Eanin: Women's Ping-Pong World Champion

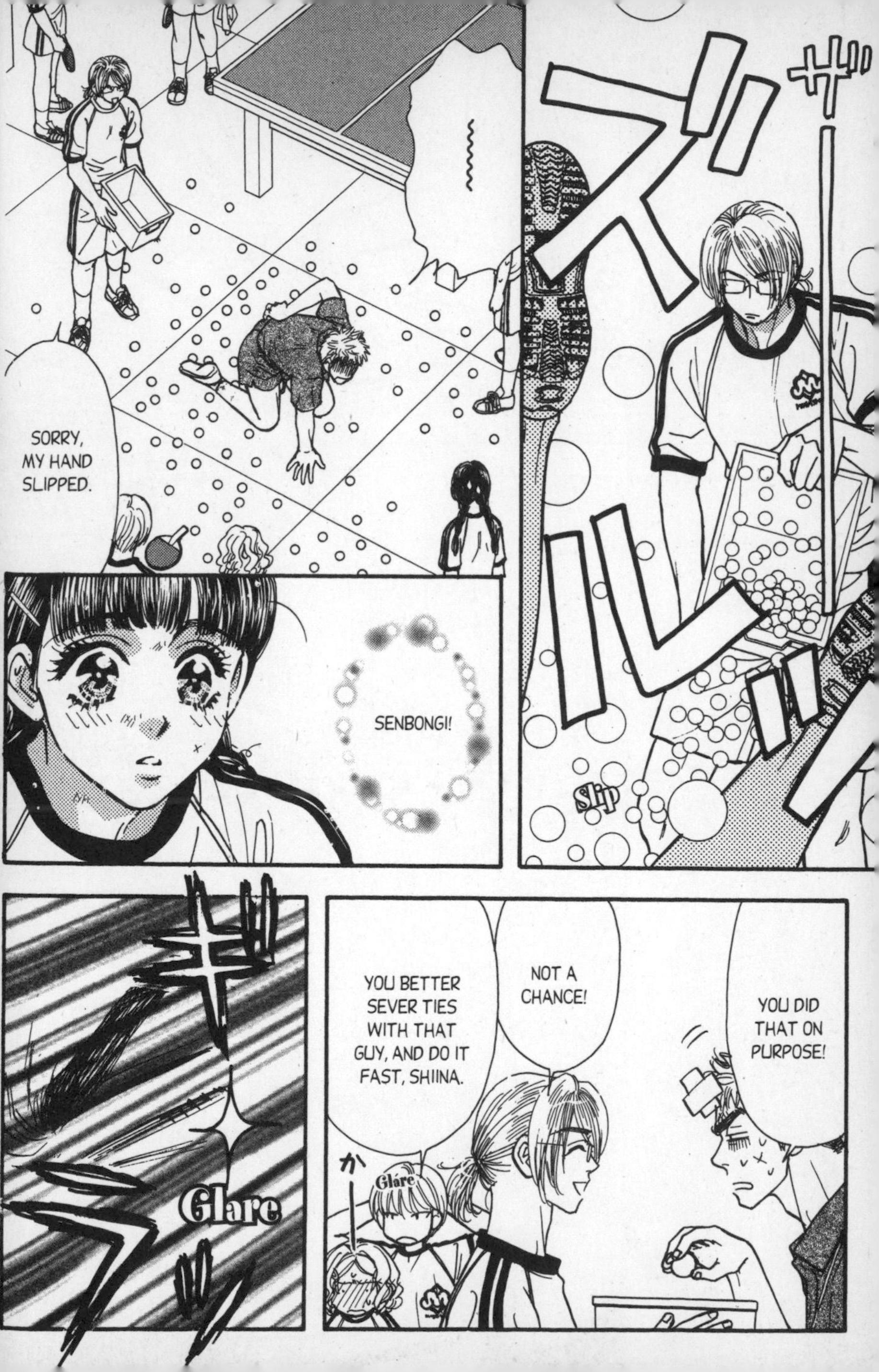
Slip
SORRY, MY HAND SLIPPED.
SENBONGI!
YOU DID THAT ON PURPOSE!
NOT A CHANCE!
YOU BETTER SEVER TIES WITH THAT GUY, AND DO IT FAST, SHIINA.
Glare
Glare

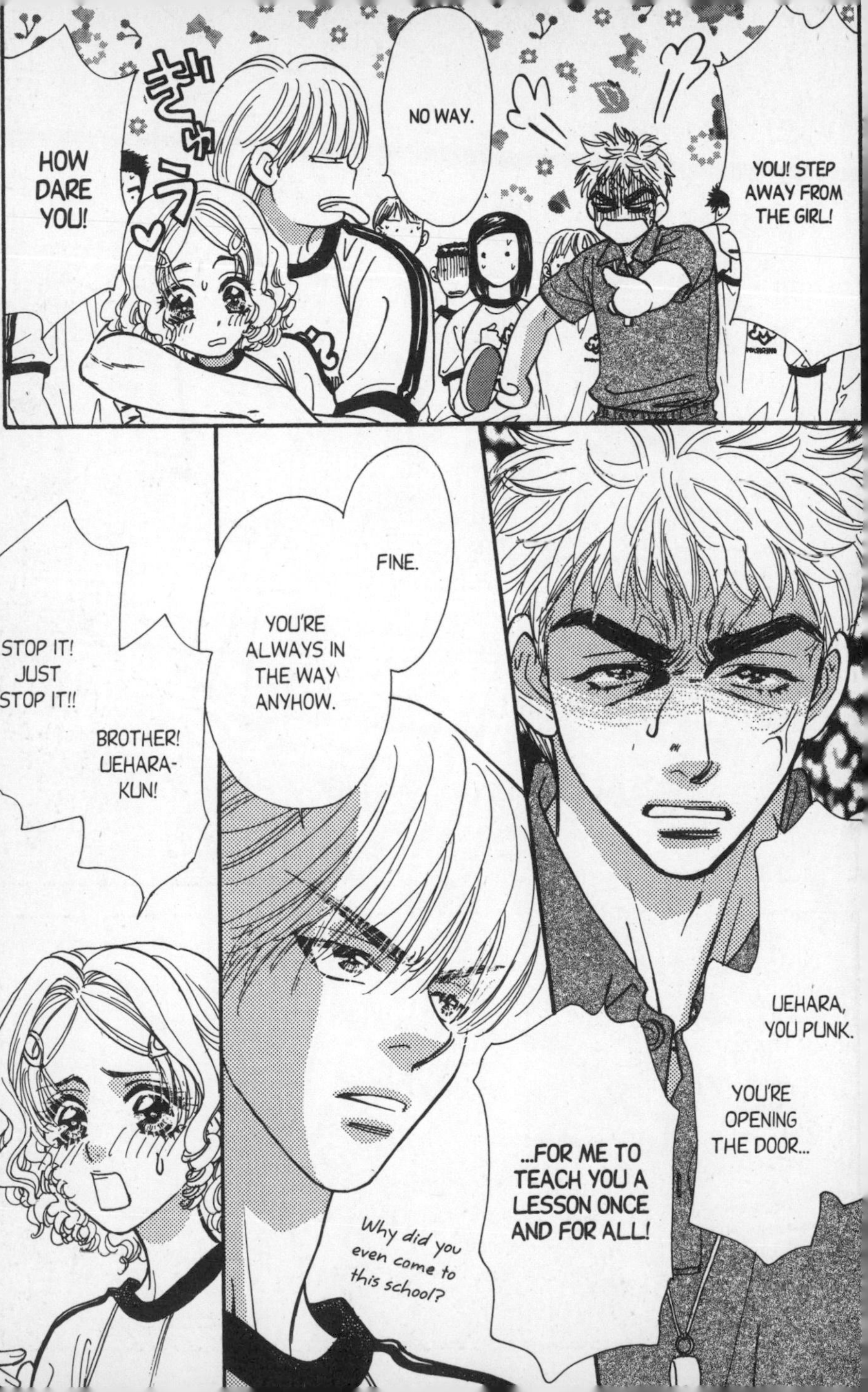
YOU! STEP AWAY FROM THE GIRL!
NO WAY.
HOW DARE YOU!
UEHARA, YOU PUNK.
YOU'RE OPENING THE DOOR...
...FOR ME TO TEACH YOU A LESSON ONCE AND FOR ALL!
FINE.
YOU'RE ALWAYS IN THE WAY ANYHOW.
Why did you even come to this school?
STOP IT! JUST STOP IT!!
BROTHER! UEHARA-KUN!

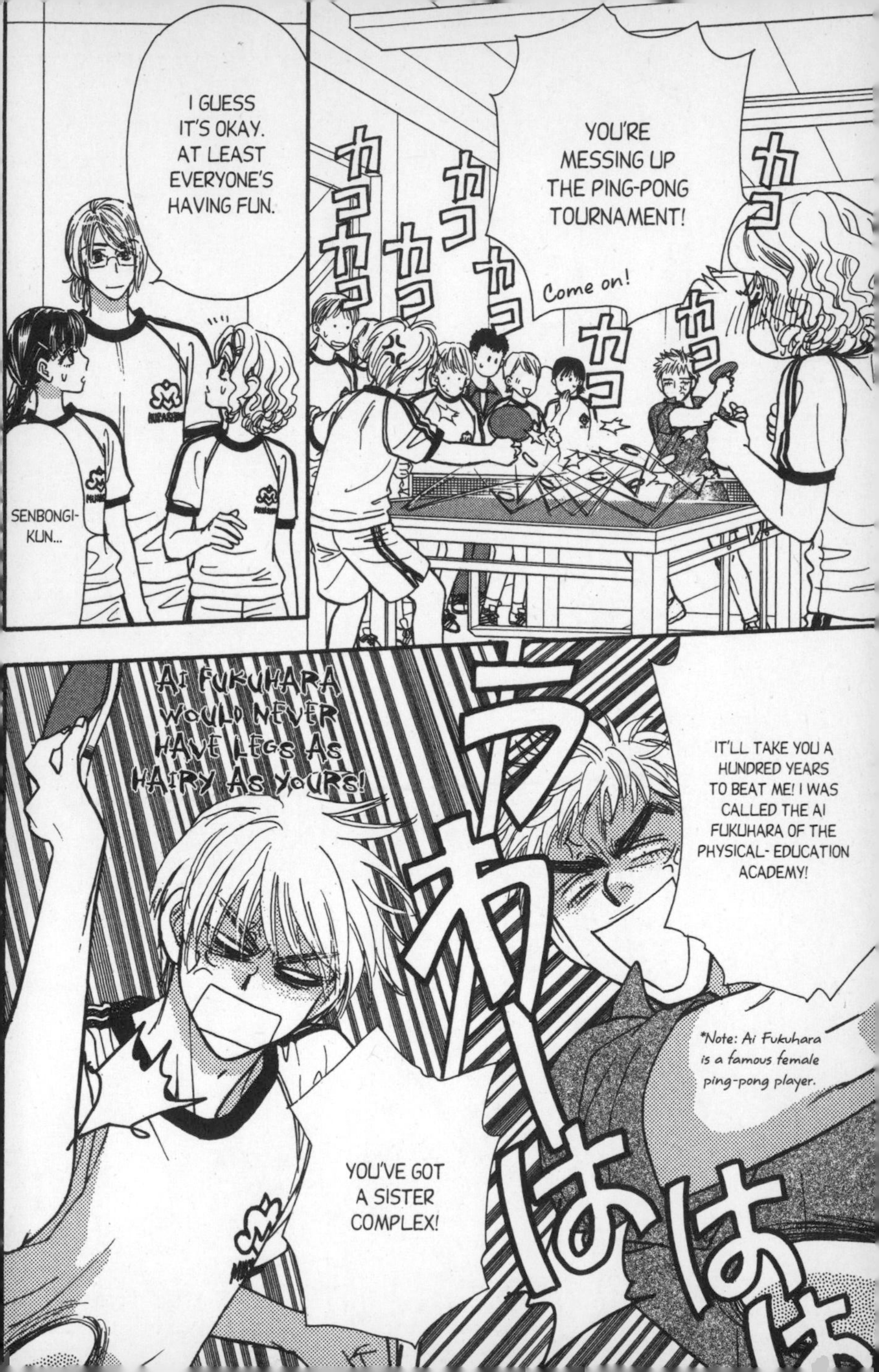

YOU'RE MESSING UP THE PING-PONG TOURNAMENT!
カッ
カッ
カッ カッ
Come on!
カッ カッ
カッ カッ カッ
I GUESS IT'S OKAY. AT LEAST EVERYONE'S HAVING FUN.
SENBONGI-KUN...
IT'LL TAKE YOU A HUNDRED YEARS TO BEAT ME! I WAS CALLED THE AI FUKUHARA OF THE PHYSICAL- EDUCATION ACADEMY!
*Note: Ai Fukuhara is a famous female ping-pong player.
うわーははは
AI FUKUHARA WOULD NEVER HAVE LEGS AS HAIRY AS YOURS!
YOU'VE GOT A SISTER COMPLEX!

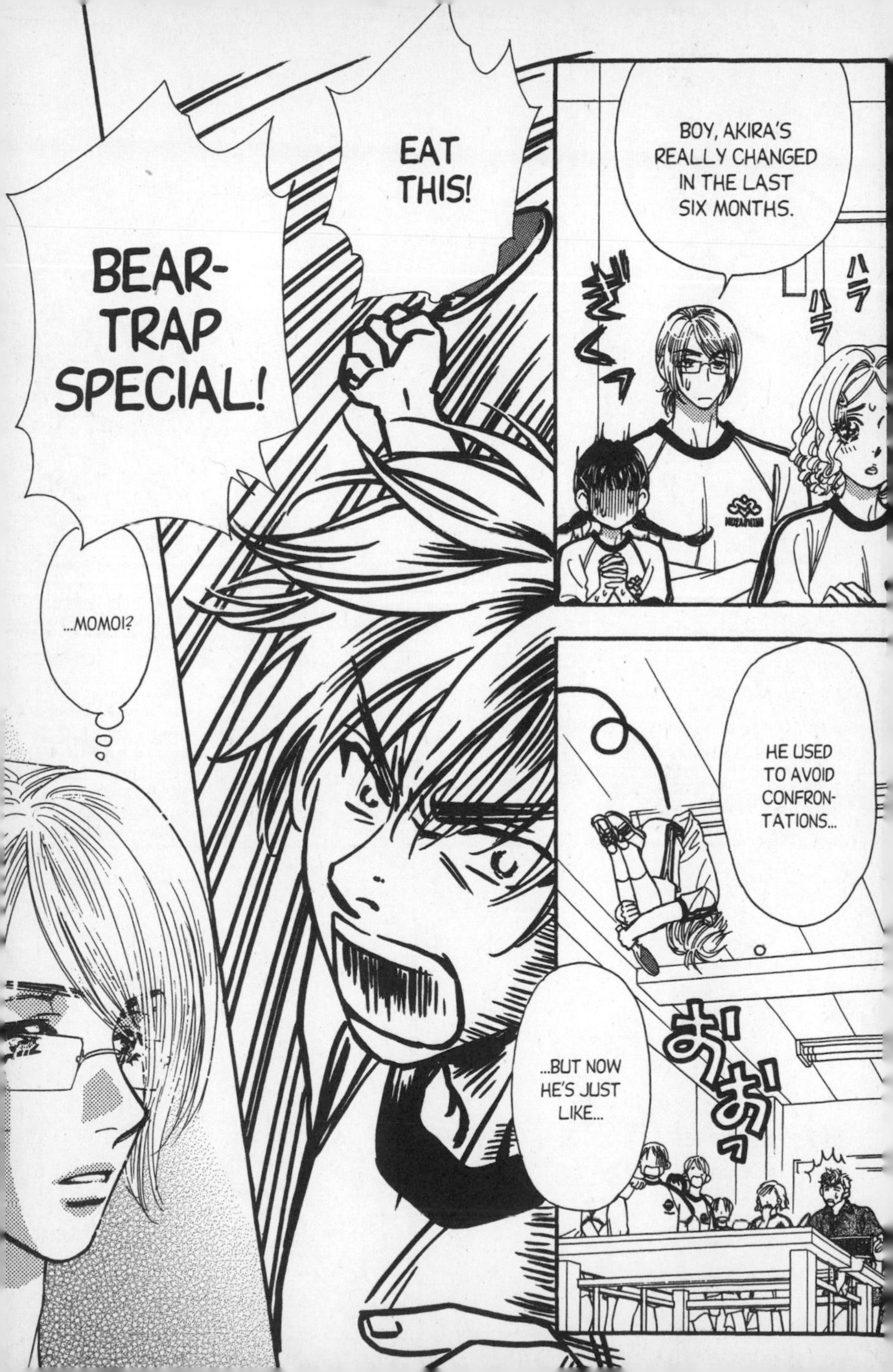
BOY, AKIRA'S REALLY CHANGED IN THE LAST SIX MONTHS.
ハラハラ
ぎくっ
HE USED TO AVOID CONFRONTATIONS...
...BUT NOW HE'S JUST LIKE...
おおっ
EAT THIS!
BEAR-TRAP SPECIAL!
...MOMOI?

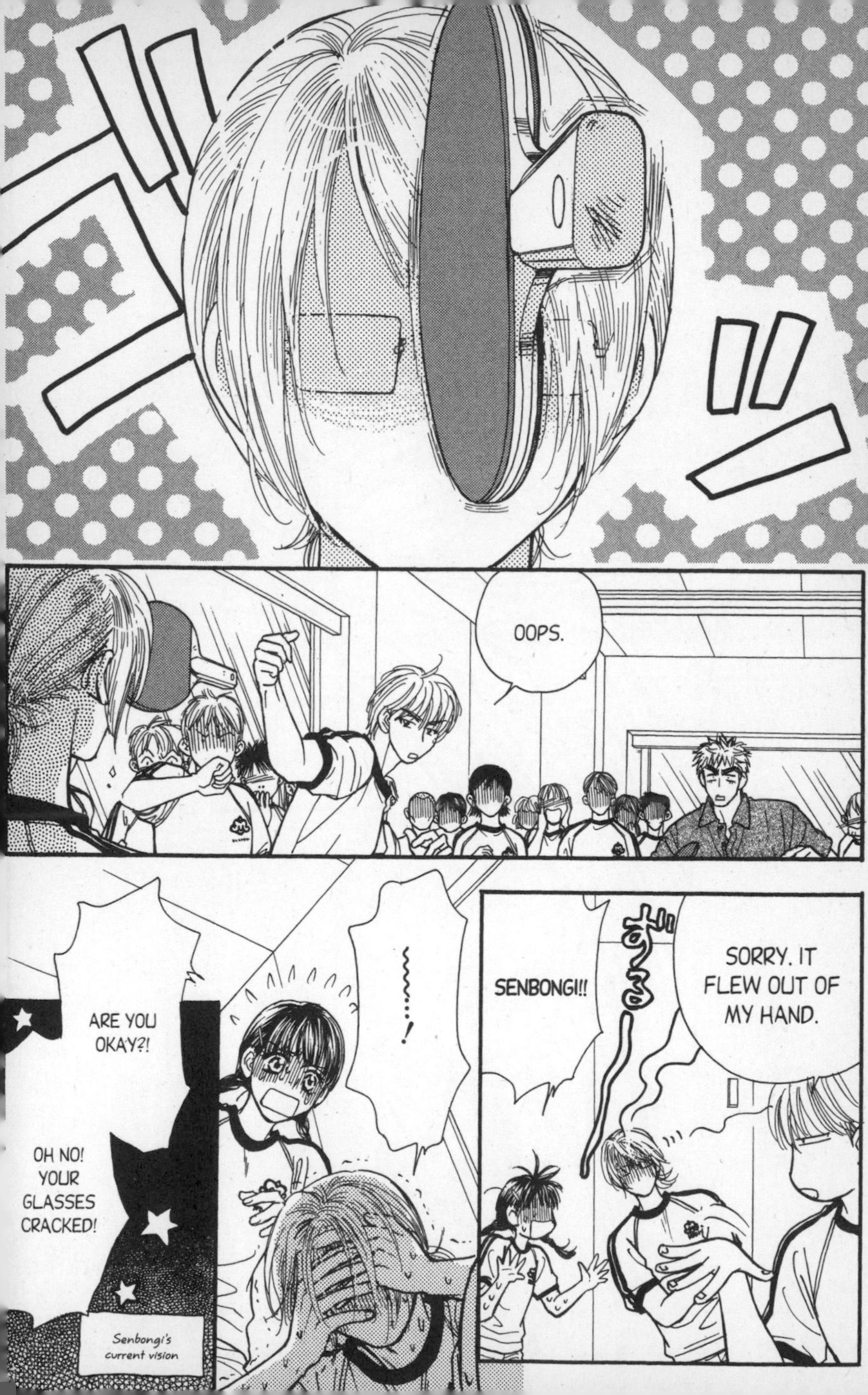
OOPS.
SORRY. IT FLEW OUT OF MY HAND.
SENBONGI!!
......!
ARE YOU OKAY?!
OH NO! YOUR GLASSES CRACKED!
Senbongi's current vision

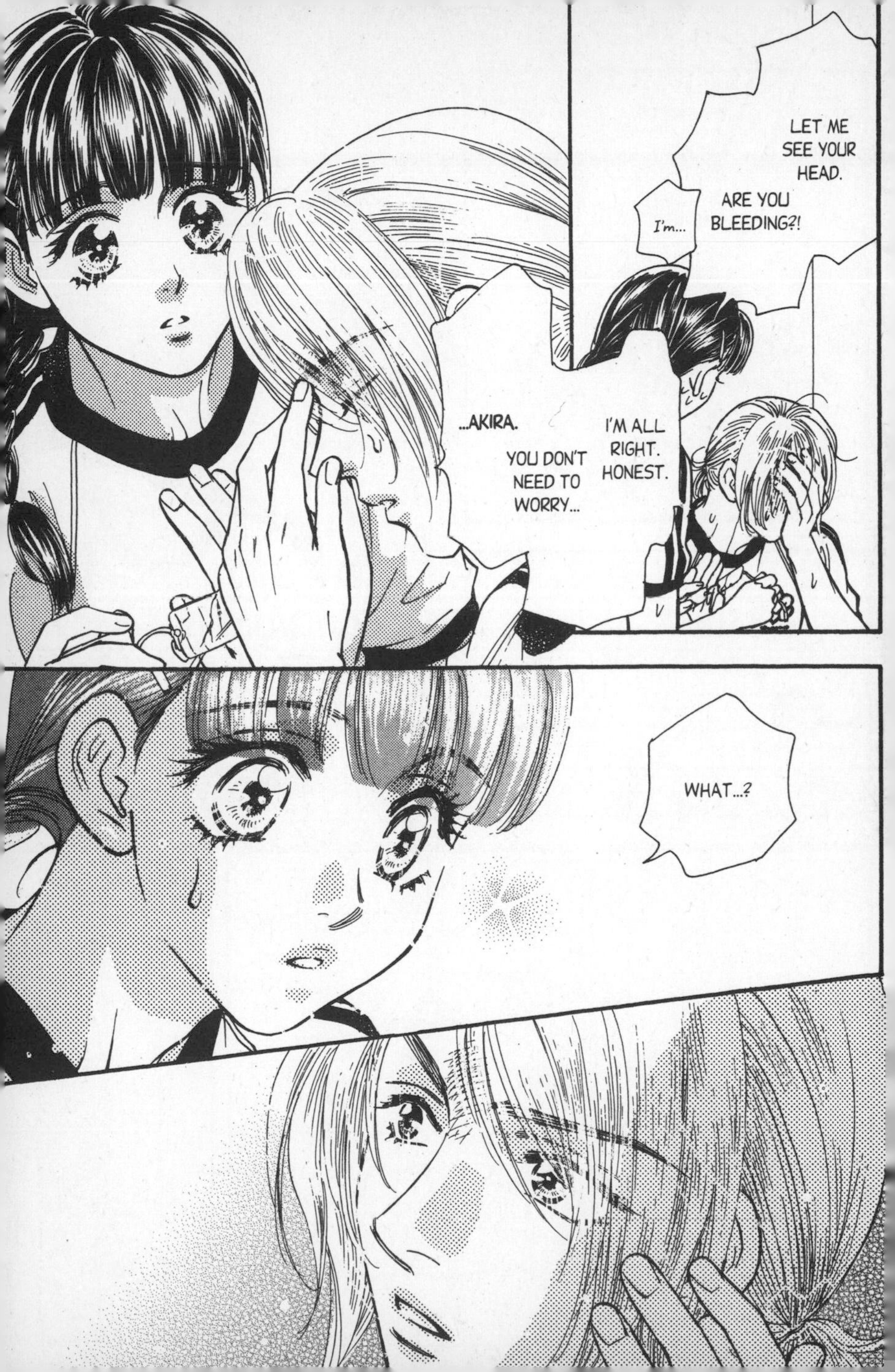
LET ME SEE YOUR HEAD.
ARE YOU BLEEDING?!
I'm...
I'M ALL RIGHT. HONEST.
...AKIRA.
YOU DON'T NEED TO WORRY...
WHAT...?

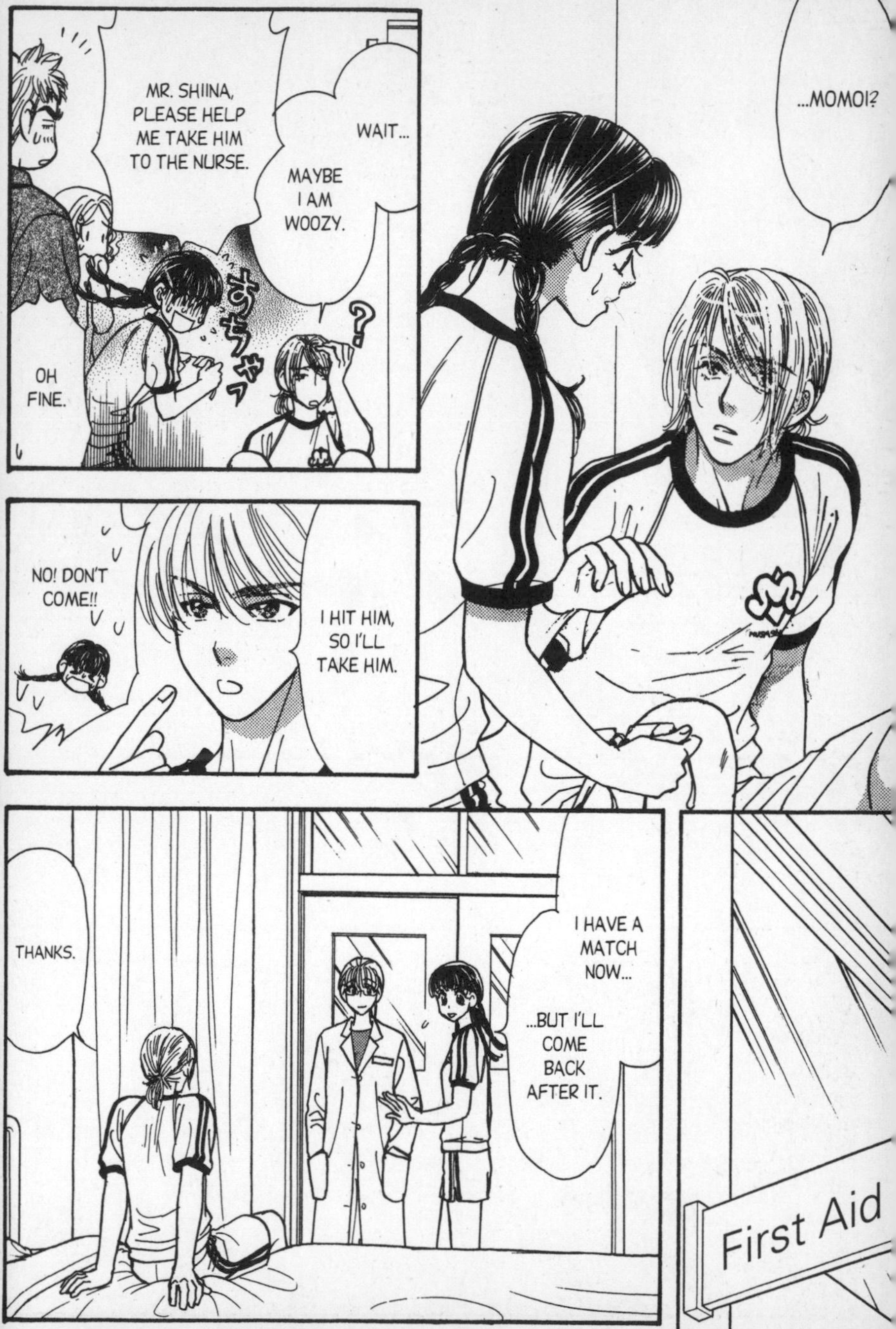
...MOMOI?
MR. SHIINA, PLEASE HELP ME TAKE HIM TO THE NURSE.
WAIT...
MAYBE I AM WOOZY.
OH FINE.
I HIT HIM, SO I'LL TAKE HIM.
NO! DON'T COME!!
First Aid
I HAVE A MATCH NOW...
...BUT I'LL COME BACK AFTER IT.
THANKS.

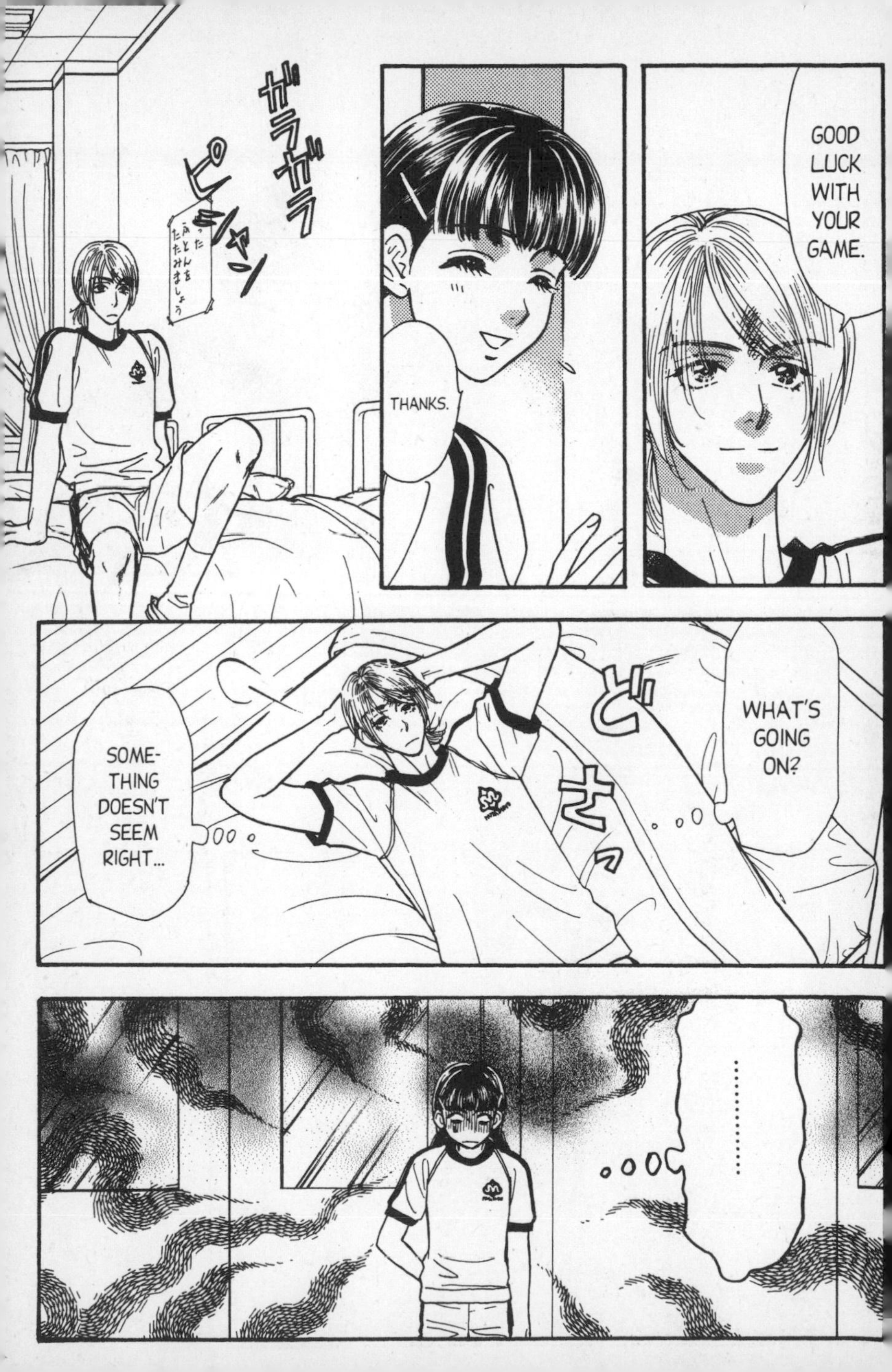
GOOD LUCK WITH YOUR GAME.
THANKS.
ガラガラ
ピシャン
WHAT'S GOING ON?
どさっ
SOME-THING DOESN'T SEEM RIGHT...
......

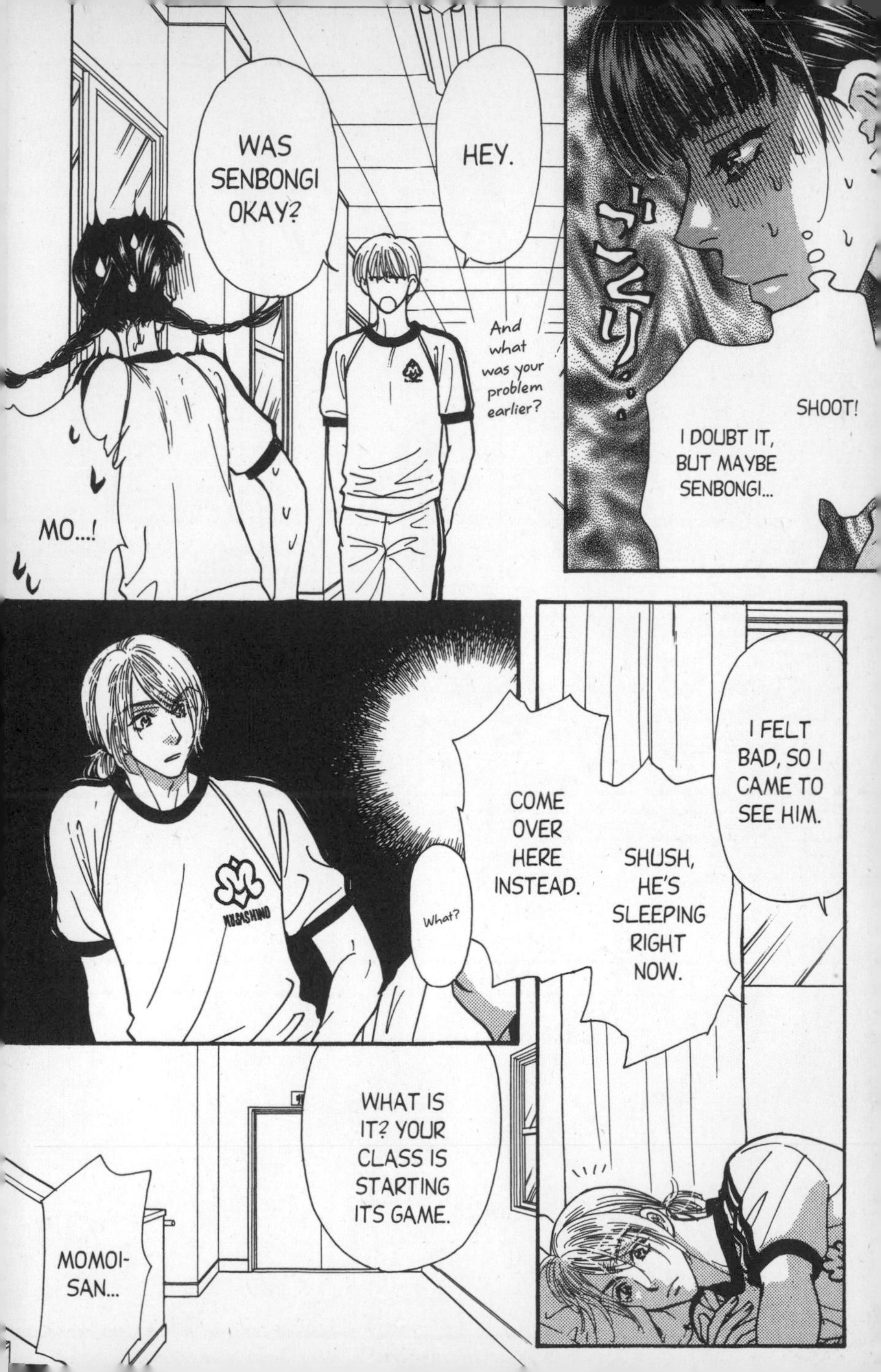
SHOOT!
I DOUBT IT, BUT MAYBE SENBONGI...
HEY.
WAS SENBONGI OKAY?
And what was your problem earlier?
MO...!
I FELT BAD, SO I CAME TO SEE HIM.
SHUSH, HE'S SLEEPING RIGHT NOW.
COME OVER HERE INSTEAD.
What?
WHAT IS IT? YOUR CLASS IS STARTING ITS GAME.
MOMOI-SAN...

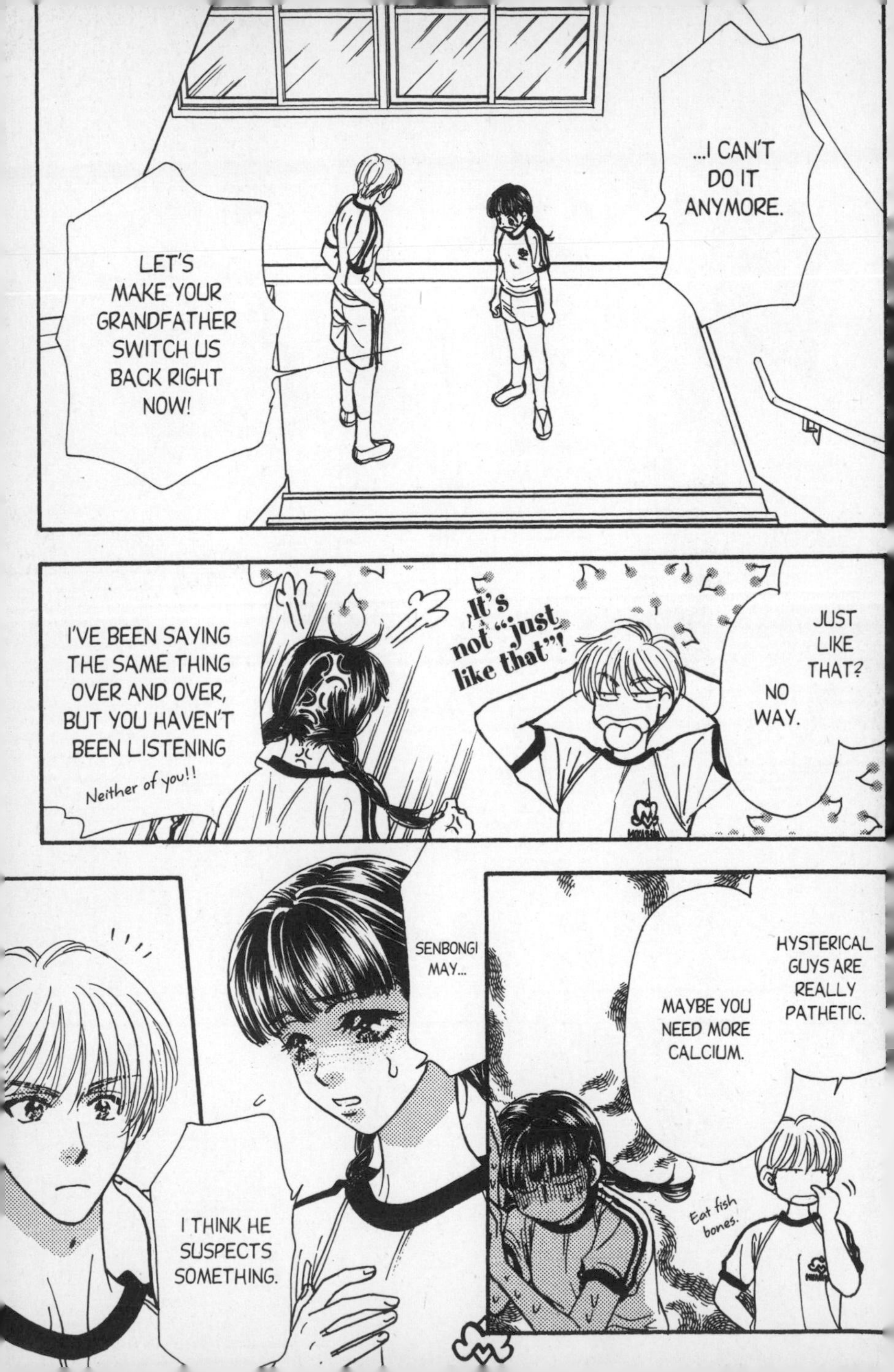
...I CAN'T DO IT ANYMORE.
LET'S MAKE YOUR GRANDFATHER SWITCH US BACK RIGHT NOW!
JUST LIKE THAT?
NO WAY.
It's not "just like that"!
I'VE BEEN SAYING THE SAME THING OVER AND OVER, BUT YOU HAVEN'T BEEN LISTENING
Neither of you!!
HYSTERICAL GUYS ARE REALLY PATHETIC.
MAYBE YOU NEED MORE CALCIUM.
Eat fish bones.
SENBONGI MAY...
I THINK HE SUSPECTS SOMETHING.

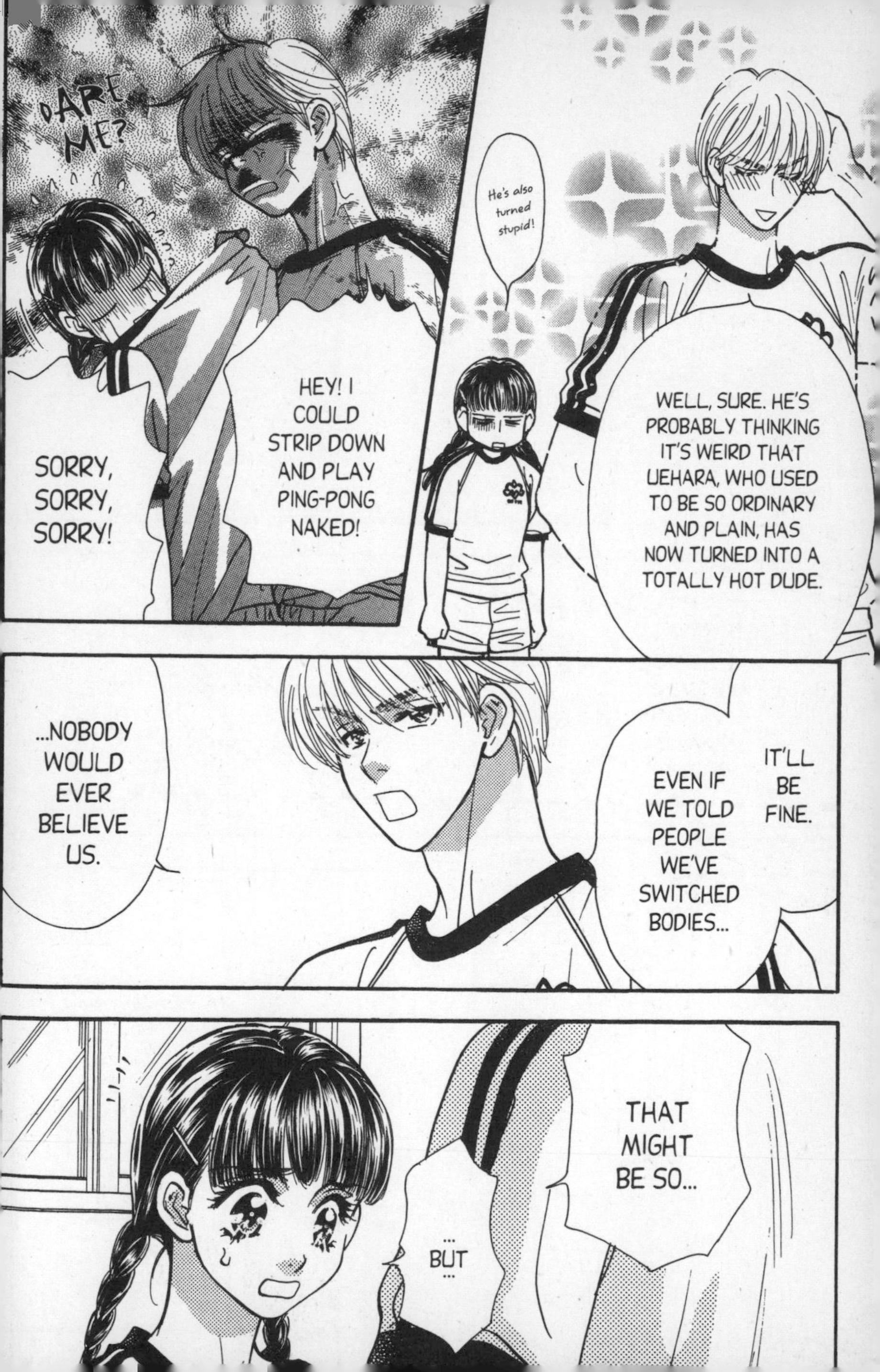
WELL, SURE. HE'S PROBABLY THINKING IT'S WEIRD THAT UEHARA, WHO USED TO BE SO ORDINARY AND PLAIN, HAS NOW TURNED INTO A TOTALLY HOT DUDE.
He's also turned stupid!
DARE ME?
HEY! I COULD STRIP DOWN AND PLAY PING-PONG NAKED!
SORRY, SORRY, SORRY!
IT'LL BE FINE.
EVEN IF WE TOLD PEOPLE WE'VE SWITCHED BODIES...
...NOBODY WOULD EVER BELIEVE US.
THAT MIGHT BE SO...
...BUT...

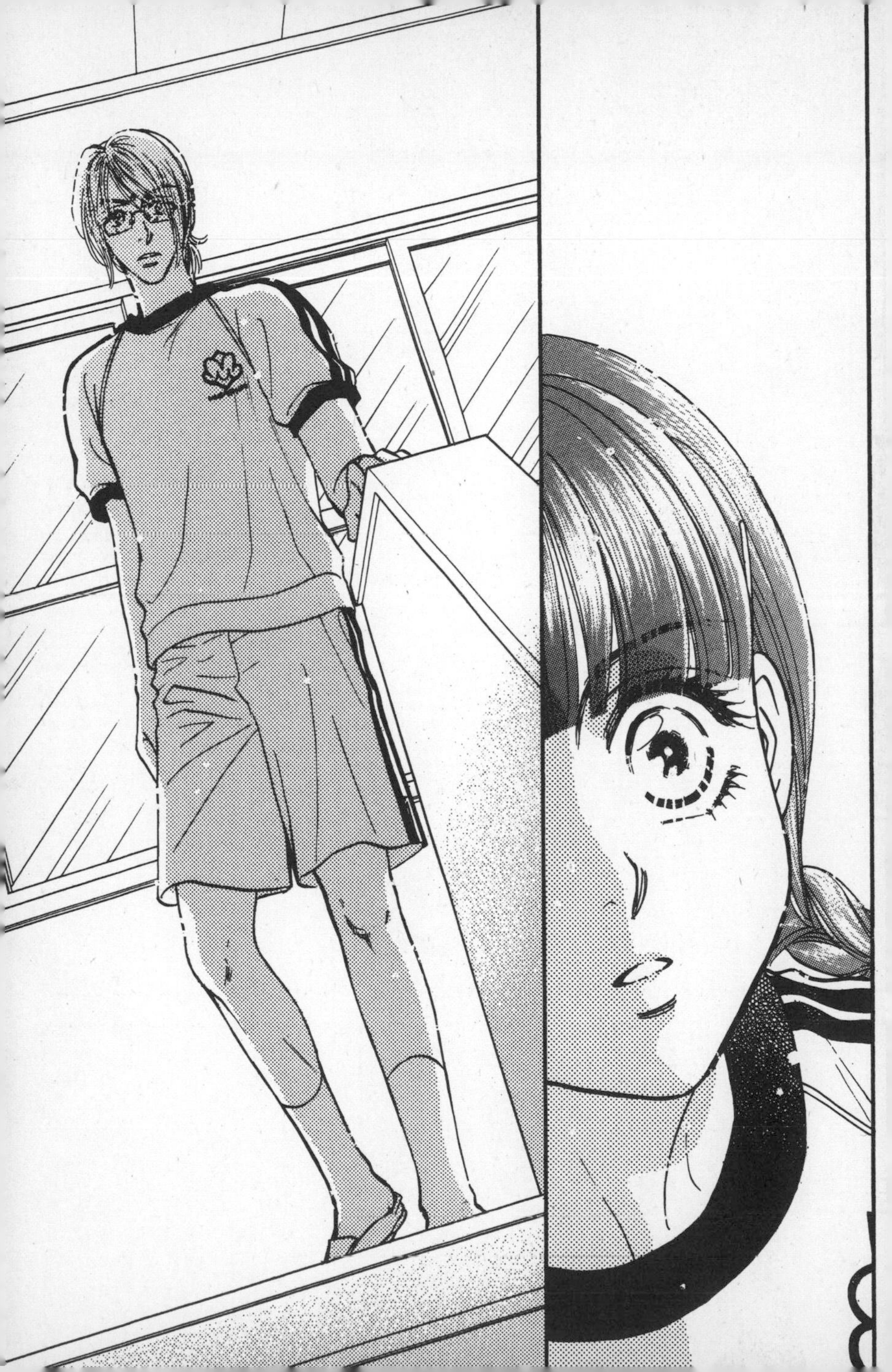

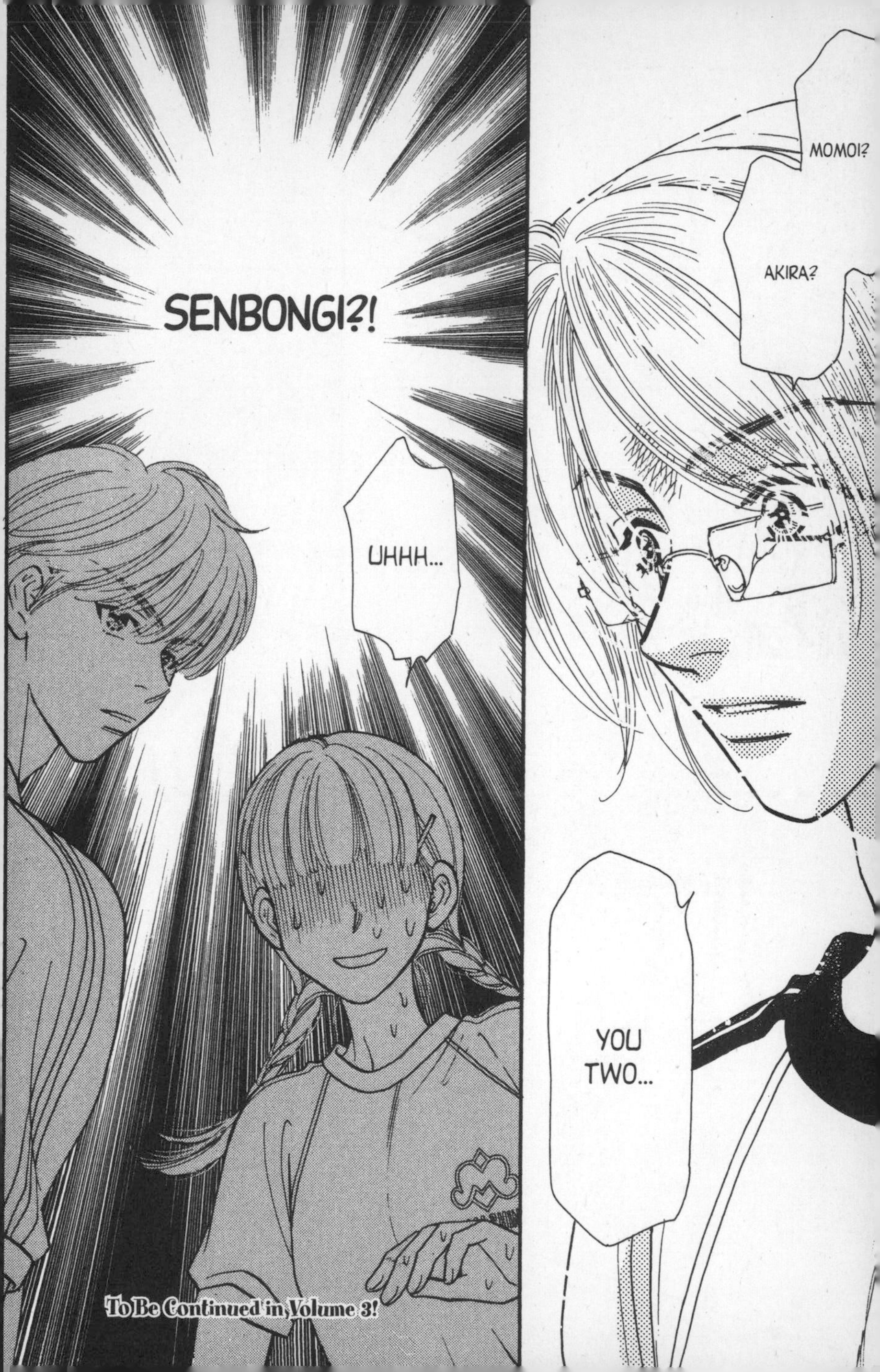
MOMOI?
AKIRA?
YOU TWO...
SENBONGI?!
UHHH...
To Be Continued in Volume 3!

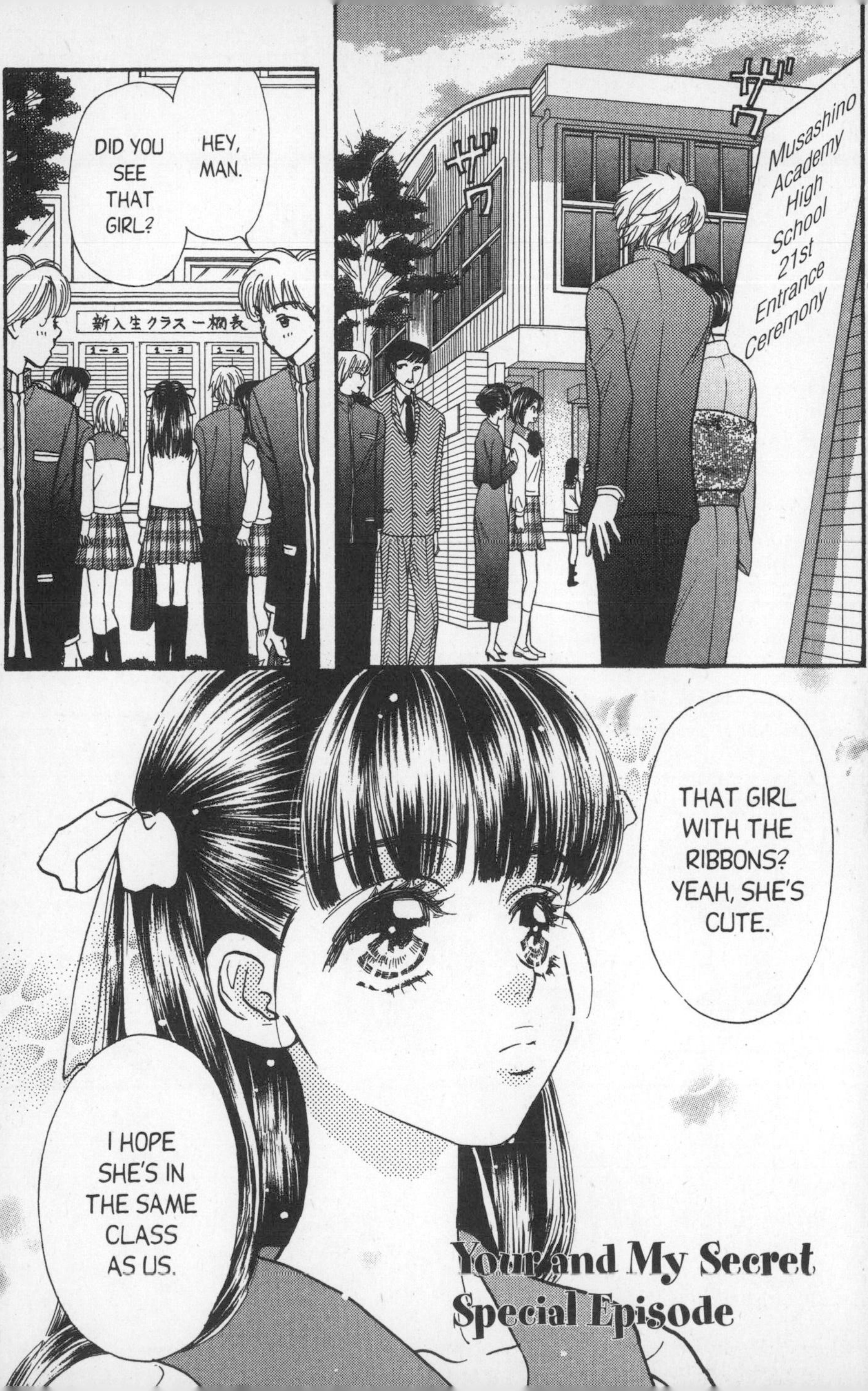
ザワ
ザワ
Musashino Academy High School 21st Entrance Ceremony
HEY, MAN.
DID YOU SEE THAT GIRL?
新入生クラス一欄表
1-2
1-3
1-4
THAT GIRL WITH THE RIBBONS? YEAH, SHE'S CUTE.
I HOPE SHE'S IN THE SAME CLASS AS US.
Your and My Secret
Special Episode

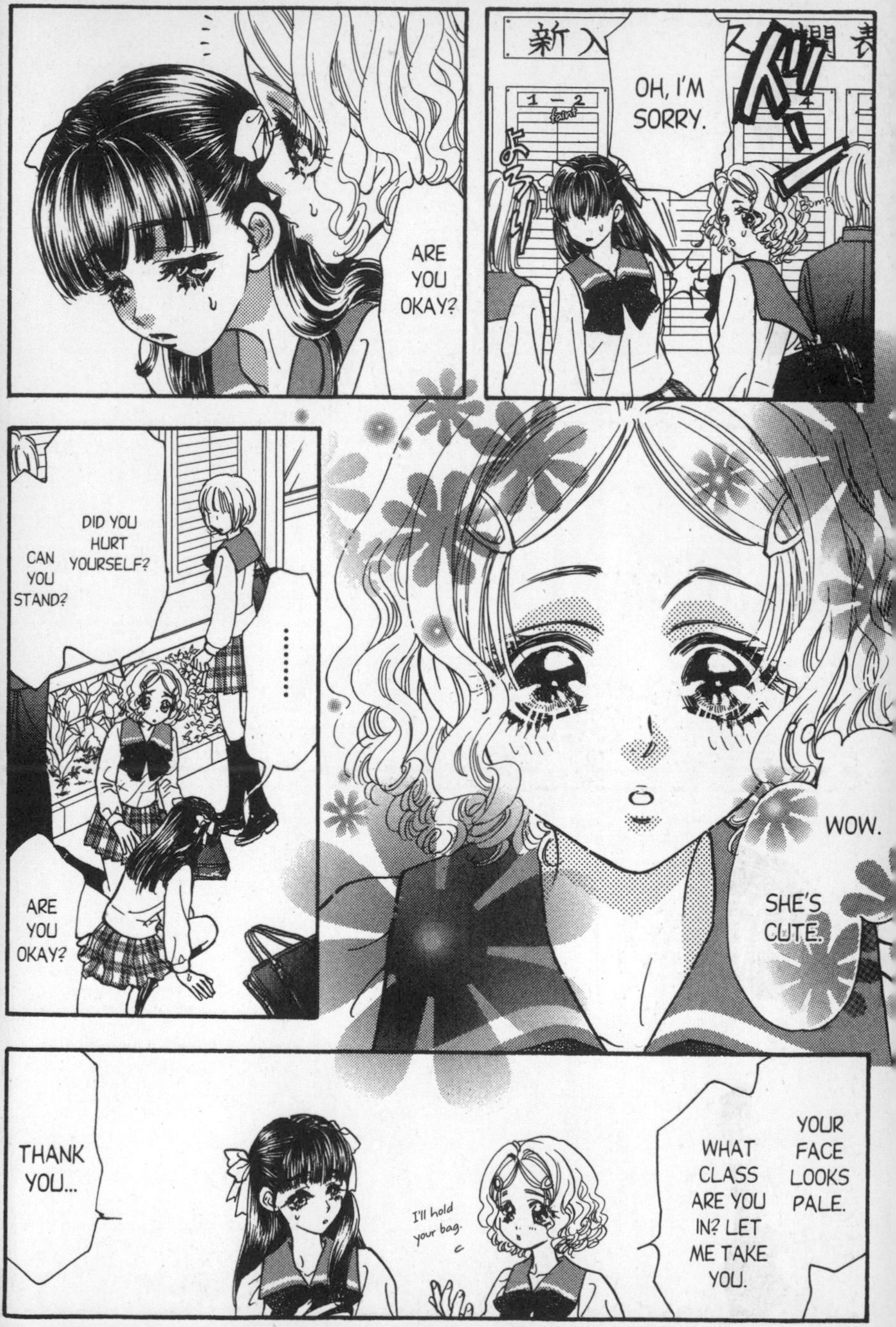
faint
OH, I'M SORRY.
Bump
ARE YOU OKAY?
WOW.
SHE'S CUTE.
DID YOU HURT YOURSELF?
CAN YOU STAND?
......
ARE YOU OKAY?
YOUR FACE LOOKS PALE.
WHAT CLASS ARE YOU IN? LET ME TAKE YOU.
I'll hold your bag.
THANK YOU...

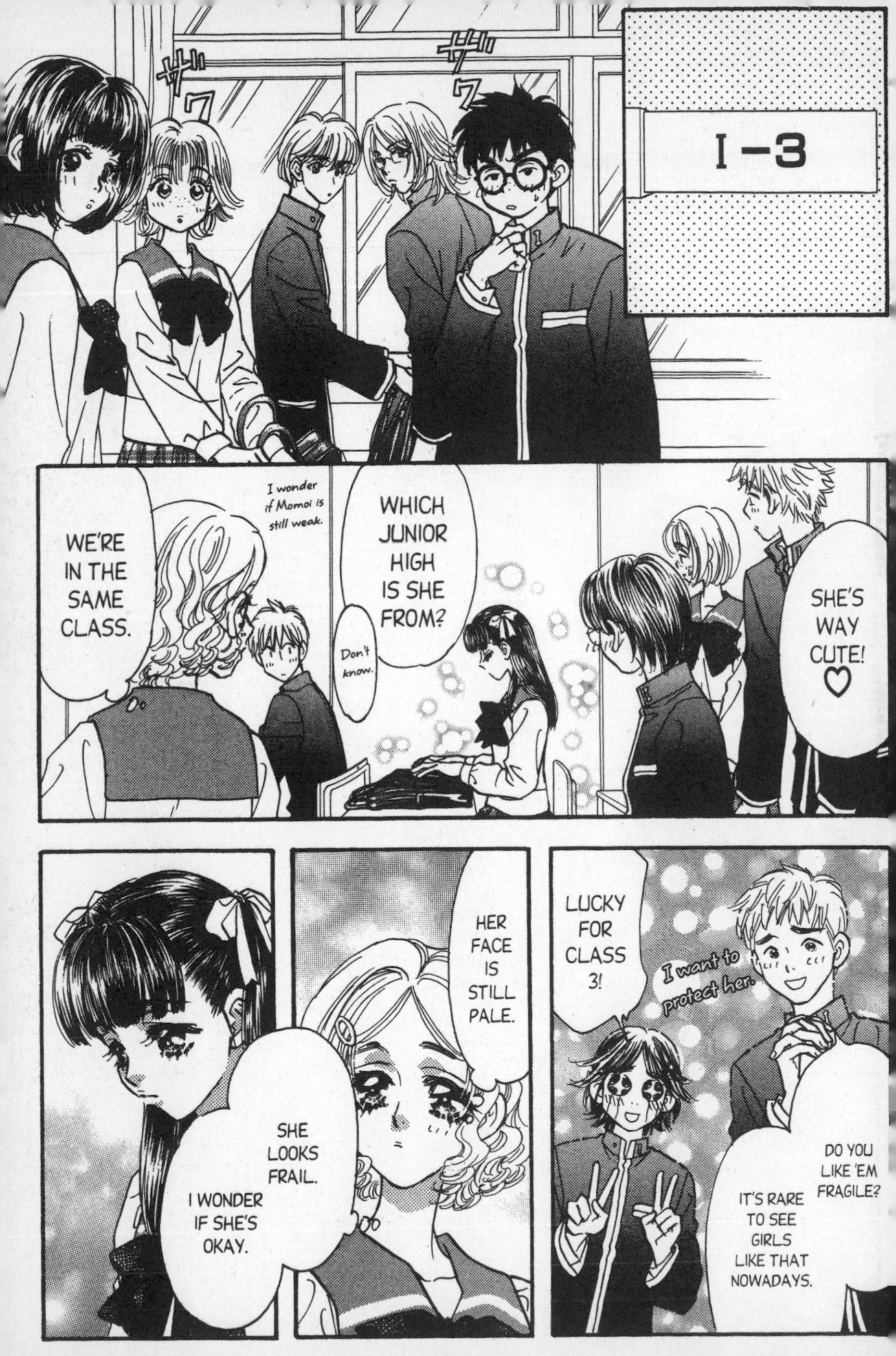
I-3
ザワ
ザワ
SHE'S WAY CUTE! ♡
WHICH JUNIOR HIGH IS SHE FROM?
Don't know.
I wonder if Momoi is still weak.
WE'RE IN THE SAME CLASS.
LUCKY FOR CLASS 3!
I want to protect her.
DO YOU LIKE 'EM FRAGILE?
IT'S RARE TO SEE GIRLS LIKE THAT NOWADAYS.
HER FACE IS STILL PALE.
SHE LOOKS FRAIL.
I WONDER IF SHE'S OKAY.

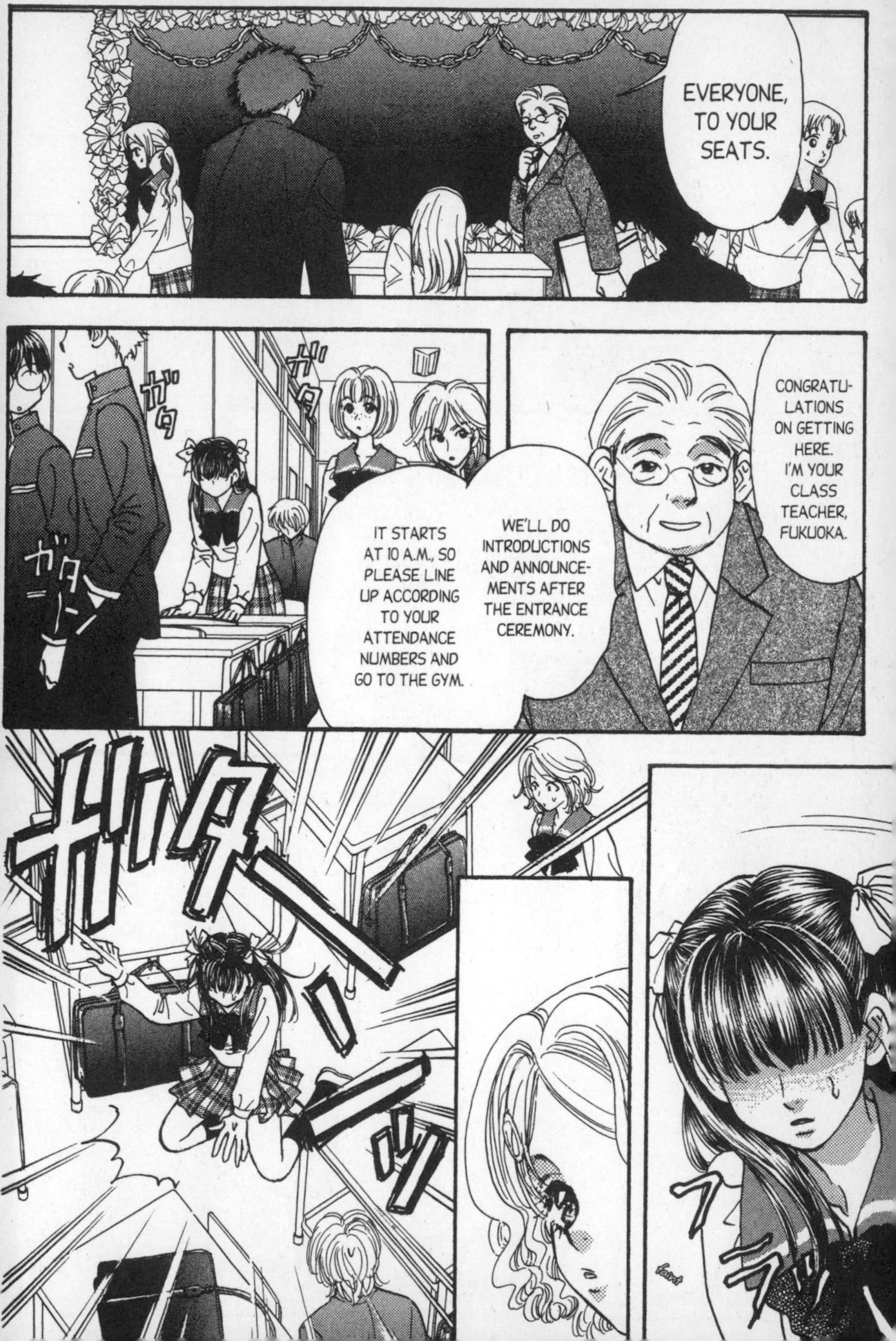
EVERYONE, TO YOUR SEATS.
CONGRATULATIONS ON GETTING HERE. I'M YOUR CLASS TEACHER, FUKUOKA.
WE'LL DO INTRODUCTIONS AND ANNOUNCEMENTS AFTER THE ENTRANCE CEREMONY.
ガタ
ガタ
IT STARTS AT 10 A.M., SO PLEASE LINE UP ACCORDING TO YOUR ATTENDANCE NUMBERS AND GO TO THE GYM.
ガターン
faint

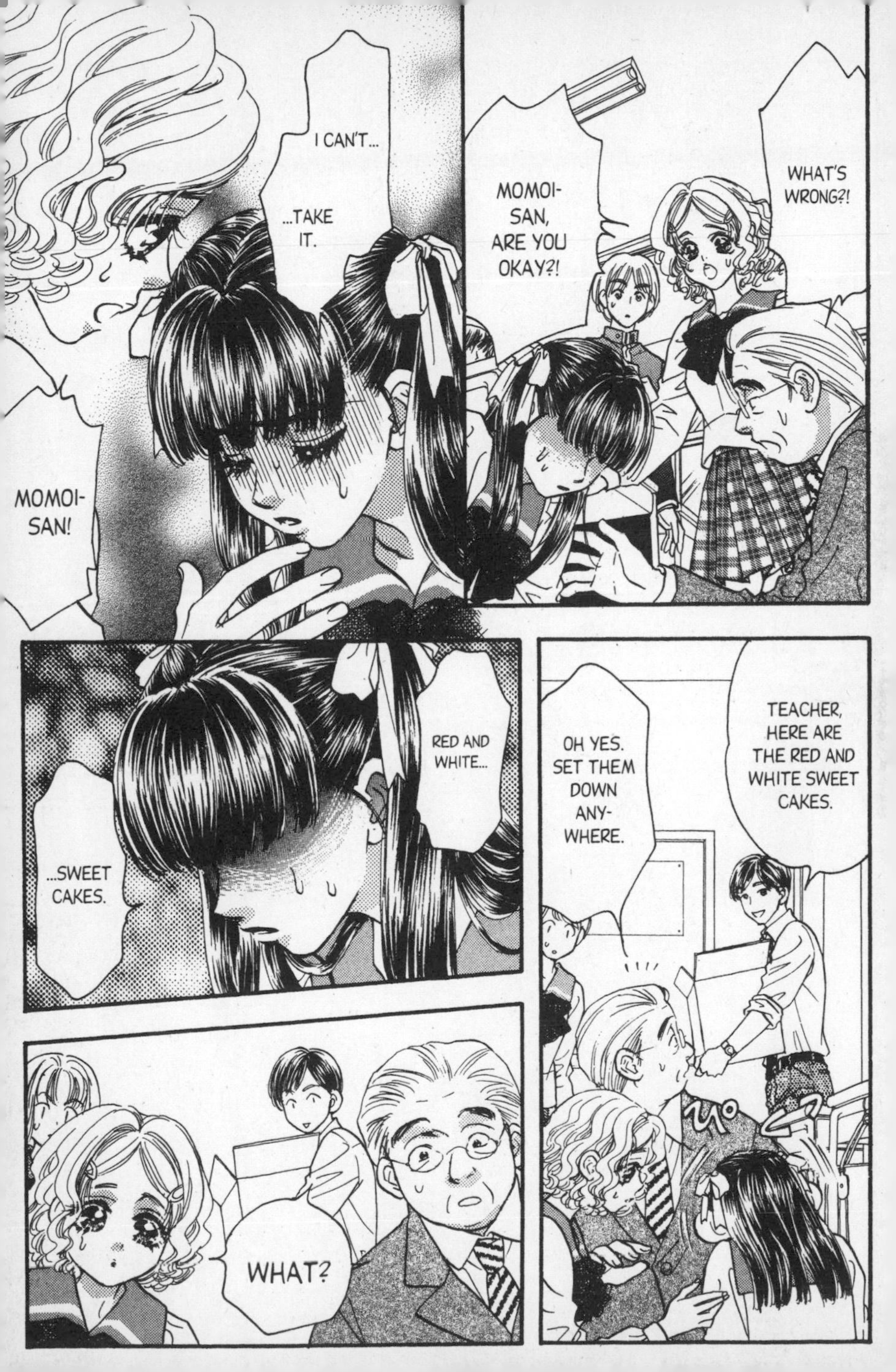
WHAT'S WRONG?!
MOMOI-SAN, ARE YOU OKAY?!
I CAN'T...
...TAKE IT.
MOMOI-SAN!
TEACHER, HERE ARE THE RED AND WHITE SWEET CAKES.
OH YES. SET THEM DOWN ANY-WHERE.
RED AND WHITE...
...SWEET CAKES.
WHAT?

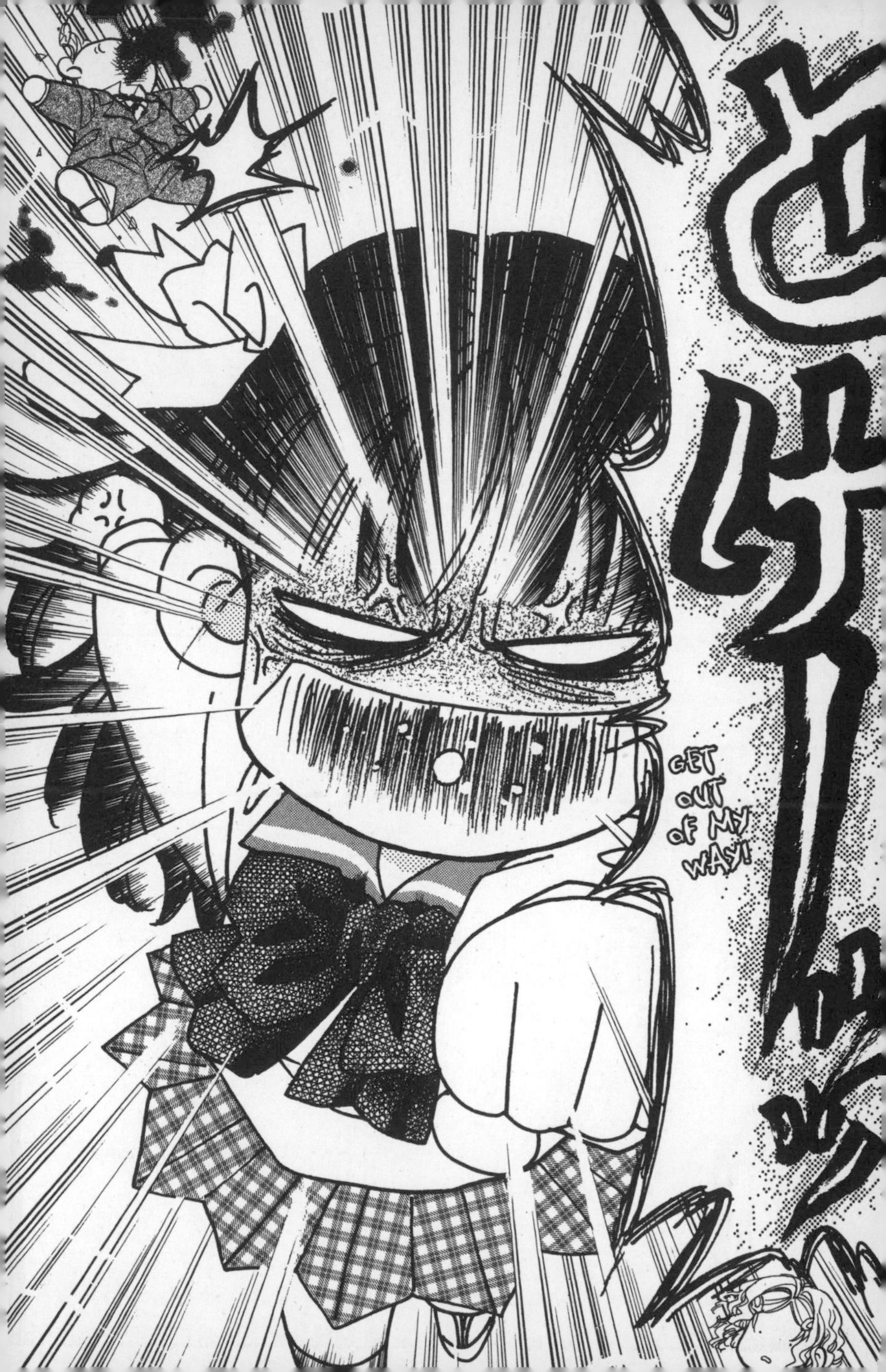
GET OUT OF MY WAY!

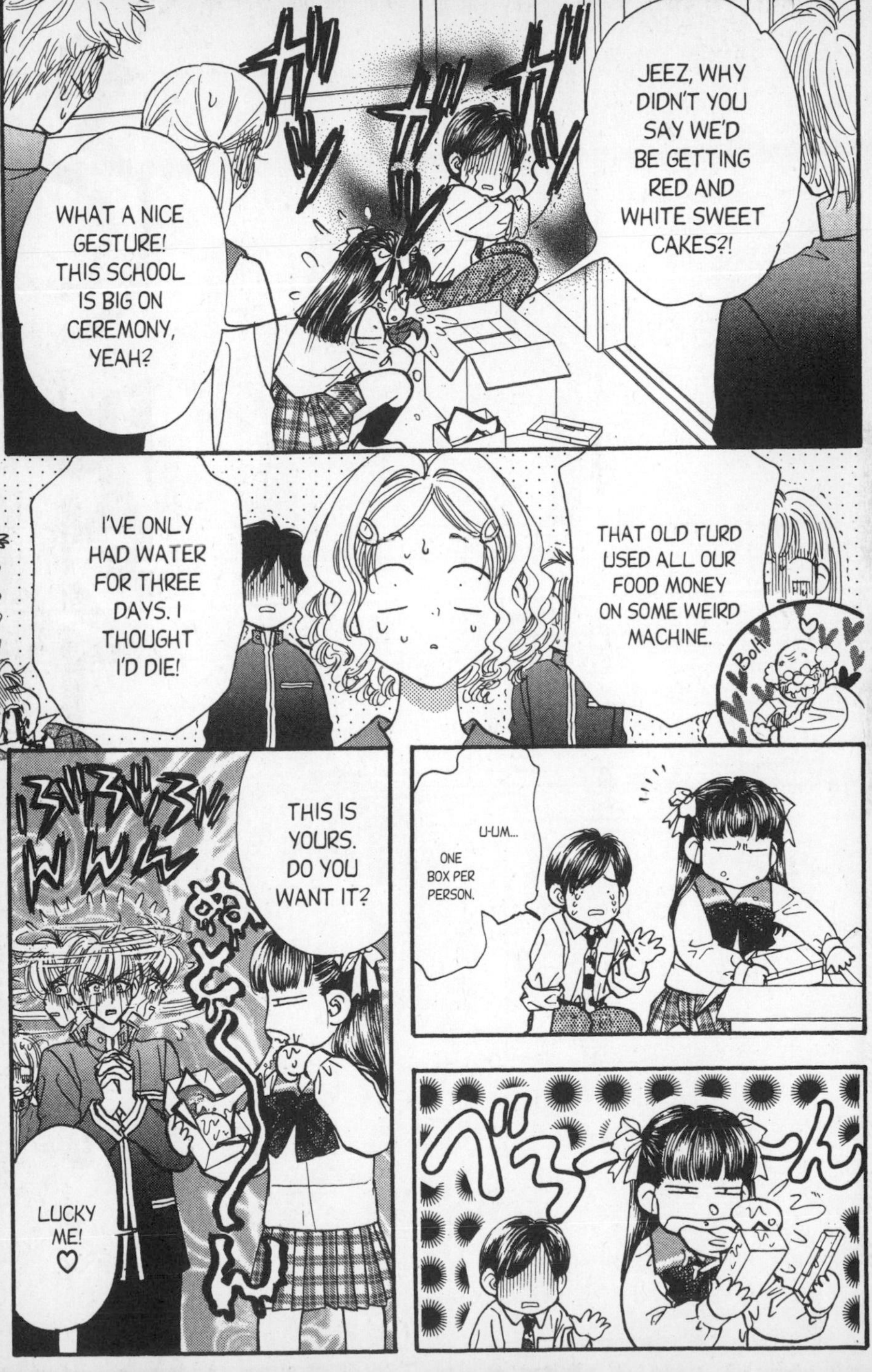
JEEZ, WHY DIDN'T YOU SAY WE'D BE GETTING RED AND WHITE SWEET CAKES?!
WHAT A NICE GESTURE! THIS SCHOOL IS BIG ON CEREMONY, YEAH?
THAT OLD TURD USED ALL OUR FOOD MONEY ON SOME WEIRD MACHINE.
Bolt
I'VE ONLY HAD WATER FOR THREE DAYS. I THOUGHT I'D DIE!
U-UM...
ONE BOX PER PERSON.
THIS IS YOURS. DO YOU WANT IT?
LUCKY ME! ♡
べろーん

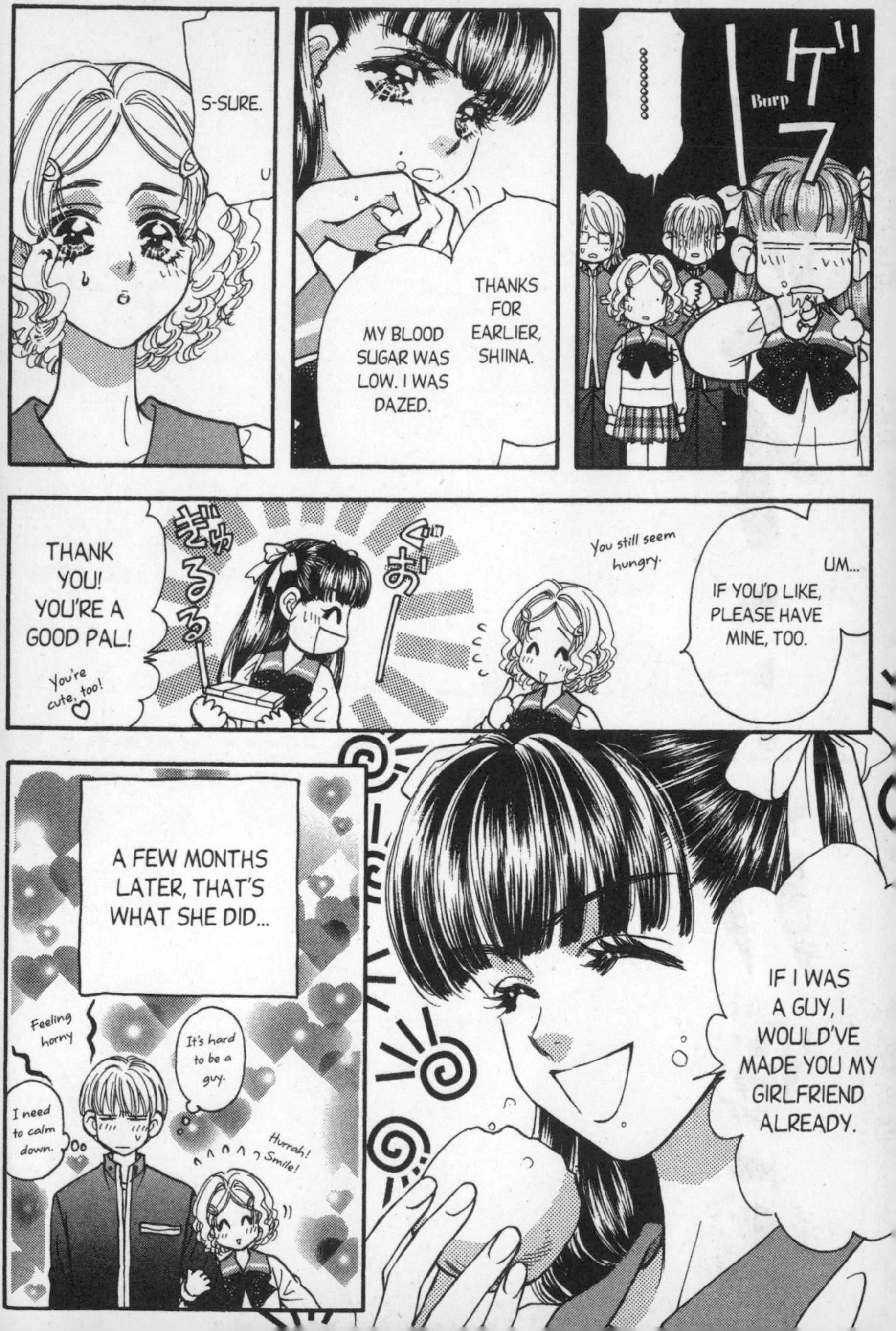
......
ゲフ
Burp
THANKS FOR EARLIER, SHIINA.
MY BLOOD SUGAR WAS LOW. I WAS DAZED.
S-SURE.
UM... IF YOU'D LIKE, PLEASE HAVE MINE, TOO.
You still seem hungry.
ぐぉー
ぎゅるる
THANK YOU! YOU'RE A GOOD PAL!
You're cute, too! ♡
IF I WAS A GUY, I WOULD'VE MADE YOU MY GIRLFRIEND ALREADY.
A FEW MONTHS LATER, THAT'S WHAT SHE DID...
Hurrah! Smile!
It's hard to be a guy.
Feeling horny
I need to calm down.

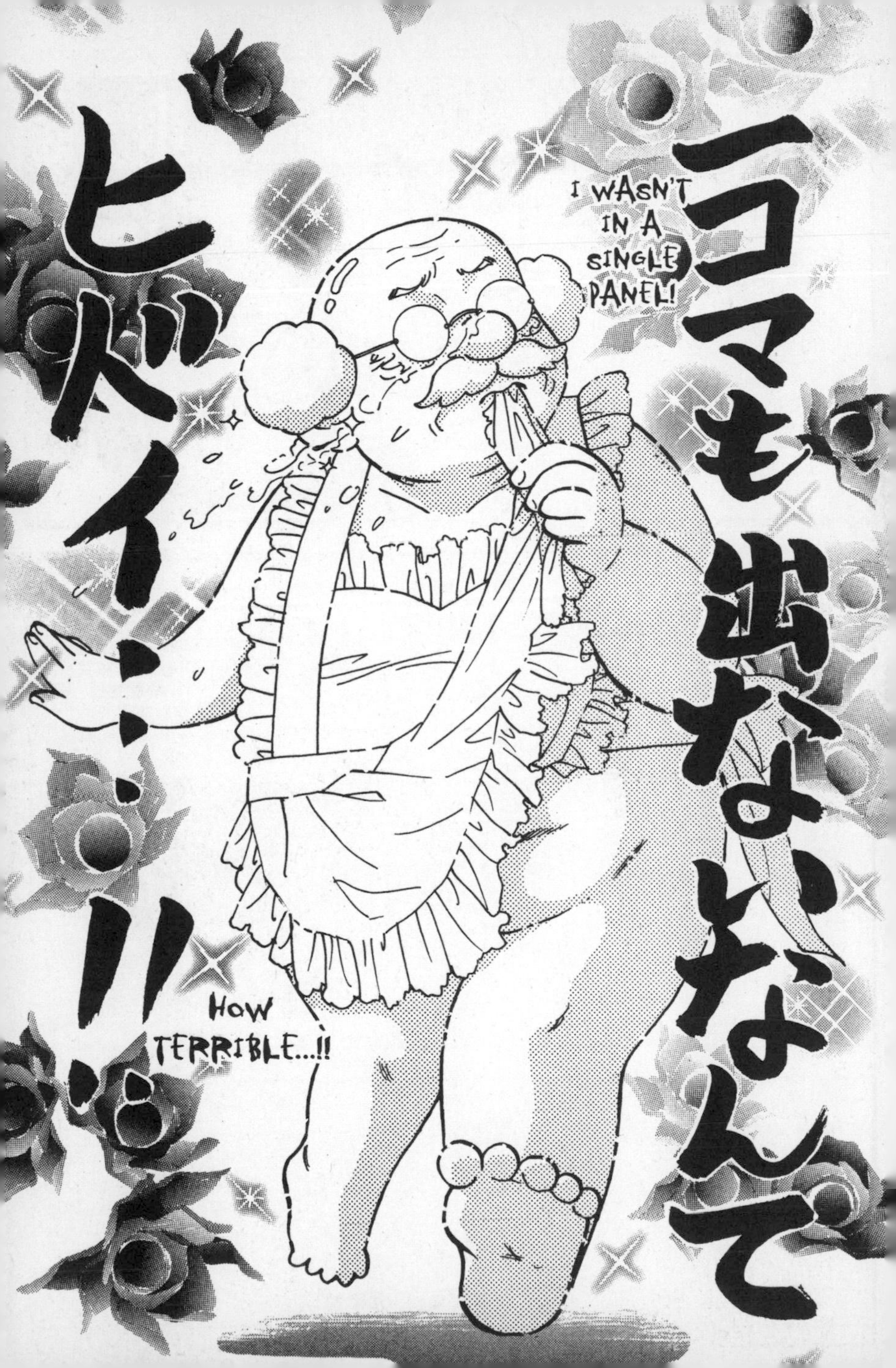

コマも出ないなんて
I WASN'T IN A SINGLE PANEL!
ヒドイッ!!
HOW TERRIBLE...!!

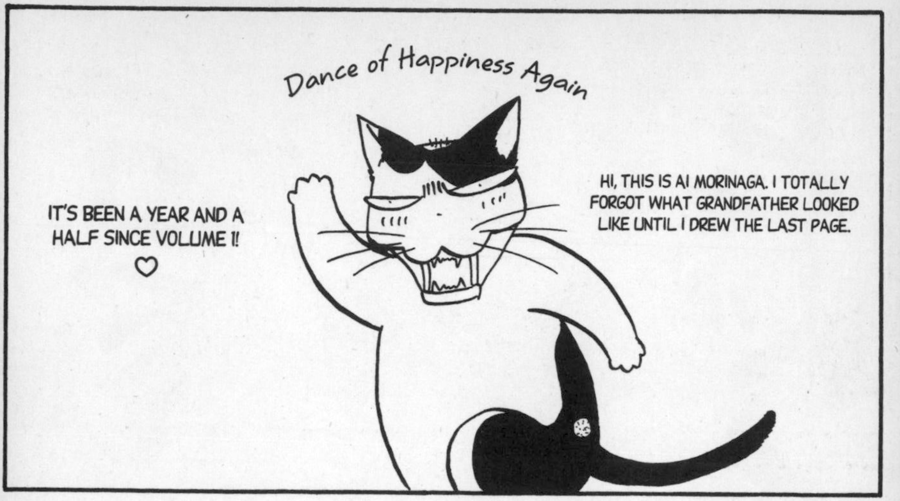
Dance of Happiness Again
HI, THIS IS AI MORINAGA. I TOTALLY FORGOT WHAT GRANDFATHER LOOKED LIKE UNTIL I DREW THE LAST PAGE.
IT'S BEEN A YEAR AND A HALF SINCE VOLUME 1! ♡

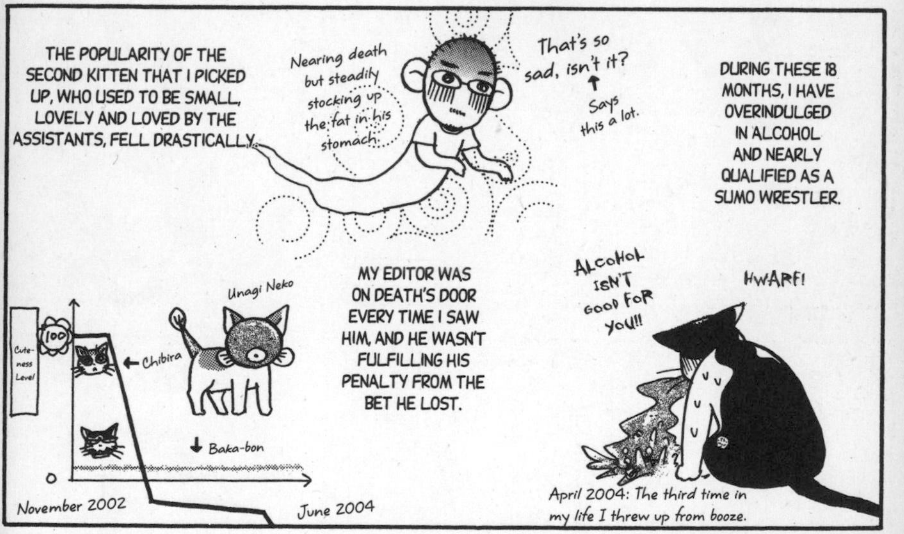
DURING THESE 18 MONTHS, I HAVE OVERINDULGED IN ALCOHOL AND NEARLY QUALIFIED AS A SUMO WRESTLER.
That's so sad, isn't it?
Says this a lot.
Nearing death but steadily stocking up the fat in his stomach
THE POPULARITY OF THE SECOND KITTEN THAT I PICKED UP, WHO USED TO BE SMALL, LOVELY AND LOVED BY THE ASSISTANTS, FELL DRASTICALLY.
HWARF!
ALCOHOL ISN'T GOOD FOR YOU!!
April 2004: The third time in my life I threw up from booze.
MY EDITOR WAS ON DEATH'S DOOR EVERY TIME I SAW HIM, AND HE WASN'T FULFILLING HIS PENALTY FROM THE BET HE LOST.
Unagi Neko
Chibira
Baka-bon
100
Cute-ness Level
0
November 2002
June 2004

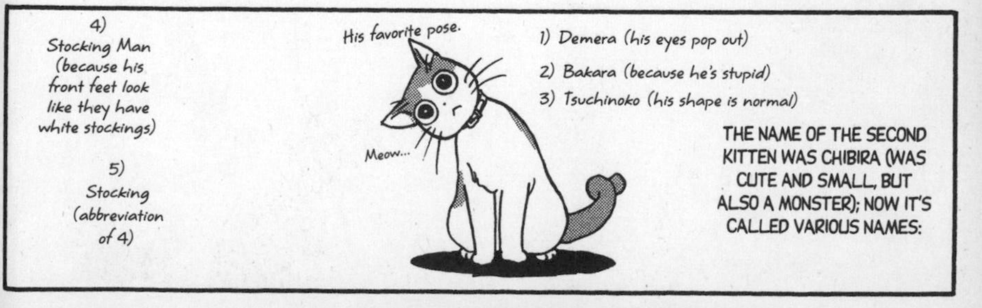
THE NAME OF THE SECOND KITTEN WAS CHIBIRA (WAS CUTE AND SMALL, BUT ALSO A MONSTER); NOW IT'S CALLED VARIOUS NAMES:
1) Demera (his eyes pop out)
2) Bakara (because he's stupid)
3) Tsuchinoko (his shape is normal)
His favorite pose.
Meow...
4) Stocking Man (because his front feet look like they have white stockings)
5) Stocking (abbreviation of 4)

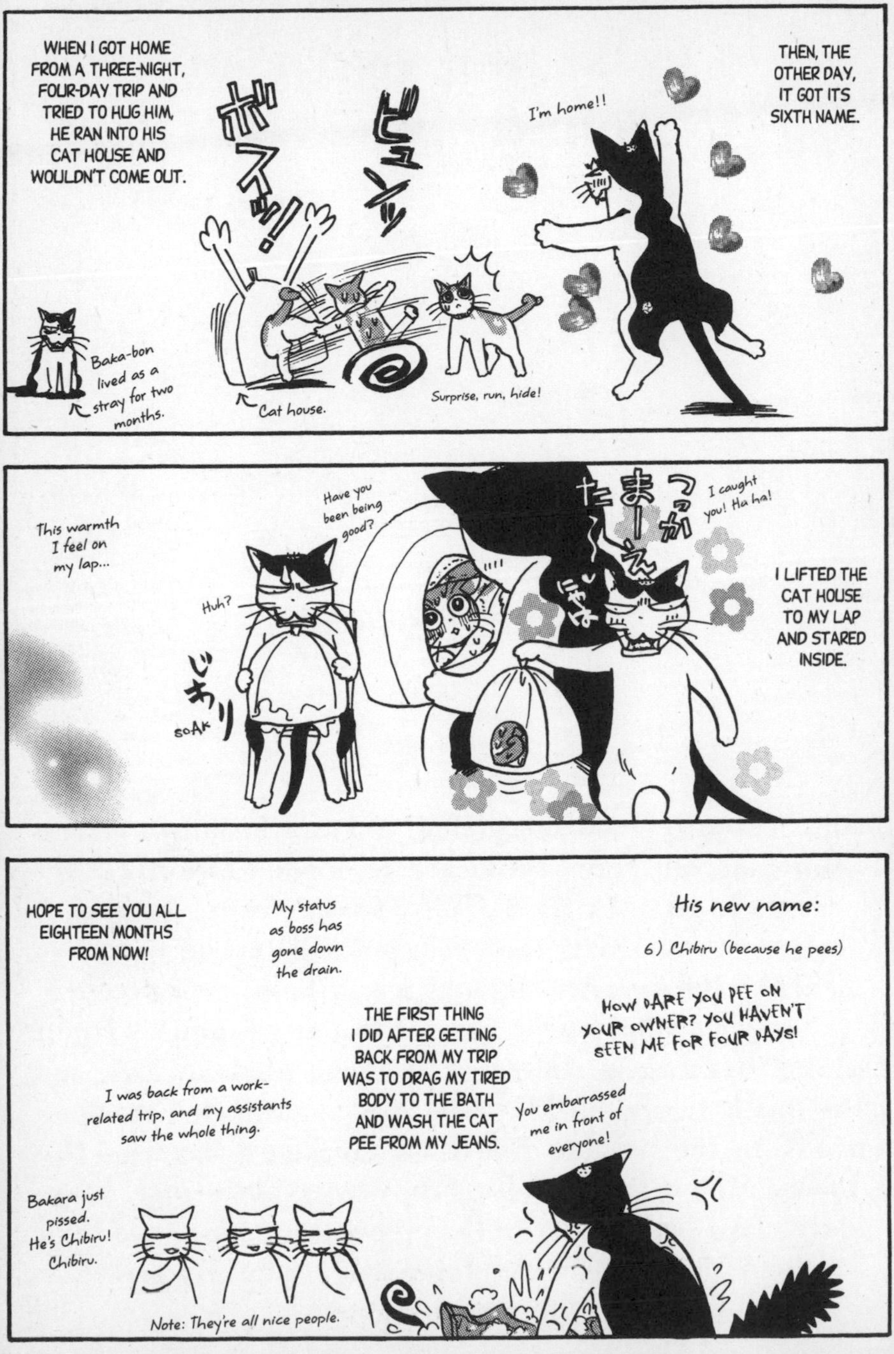
THEN, THE OTHER DAY, IT GOT ITS SIXTH NAME.
I'm home!!
ピュンッ
ボスッ!
Surprise, run, hide!
WHEN I GOT HOME FROM A THREE-NIGHT, FOUR-DAY TRIP AND TRIED TO HUG HIM, HE RAN INTO HIS CAT HOUSE AND WOULDN'T COME OUT.
Cat house.
Baka-bon lived as a stray for two months.
I LIFTED THE CAT HOUSE TO MY LAP AND STARED INSIDE.
I caught you! Ha ha!
にゃは
Have you been being good?
This warmth I feel on my lap...
Huh?
じわり
SOAK
His new name:
6) Chibiru (because he pees)
HOW DARE YOU PEE ON YOUR OWNER? YOU HAVEN'T SEEN ME FOR FOUR DAYS!
You embarrassed me in front of everyone!
THE FIRST THING I DID AFTER GETTING BACK FROM MY TRIP WAS TO DRAG MY TIRED BODY TO THE BATH AND WASH THE CAT PEE FROM MY JEANS.
My status as boss has gone down the drain.
HOPE TO SEE YOU ALL EIGHTEEN MONTHS FROM NOW!
I was back from a work-related trip, and my assistants saw the whole thing.
Bakara just pissed. He's Chibiru! Chibiru.
Note: They're all nice people.

In the next volume of Your & My Secret:

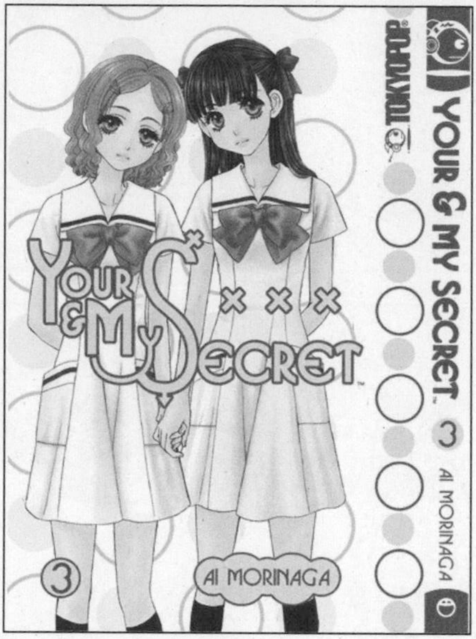
TOKYOPOP
YOUR & MY SECRET
3
AI MORINAGA
YOUR & MY SECRET
3
AI MORINAGA

Yup, Senbongi heard everything, and now he knows what's going on. But here's the kicker--he doesn't care and still wants to go out with Akira in Nanako's body! To make matters worse, Akira can't help noticing that he's getting girlier by the day. Are all those female hormones affecting the way his mind works...or is it that he's found his true calling? Regardless, Akira just wants his old body back, and he finally figures out the right way to motivate Grandpa into fixing the machine. But when Nanako catches wind that the machine is finally getting repaired, will she just sit by idly? Don't miss more of the preposterous fun (and the return of Grandpa!) in volume 3 of Your & My Secret!

Fruits Basket ™

By Natsuki Takaya

Volume 20

Can Tohru deal with the truth?

After running away from his feelings and everyone he knows, Kyo is back with the truth about his role in the death of Tohru's mother. But how will he react when Tohru says that she still loves him?

Winner of the American Anime Award for Best Manga!

The #1 selling shojo manga in America!

FOR MORE INFORMATION VISIT: WWW.TOKYOPOP.COM

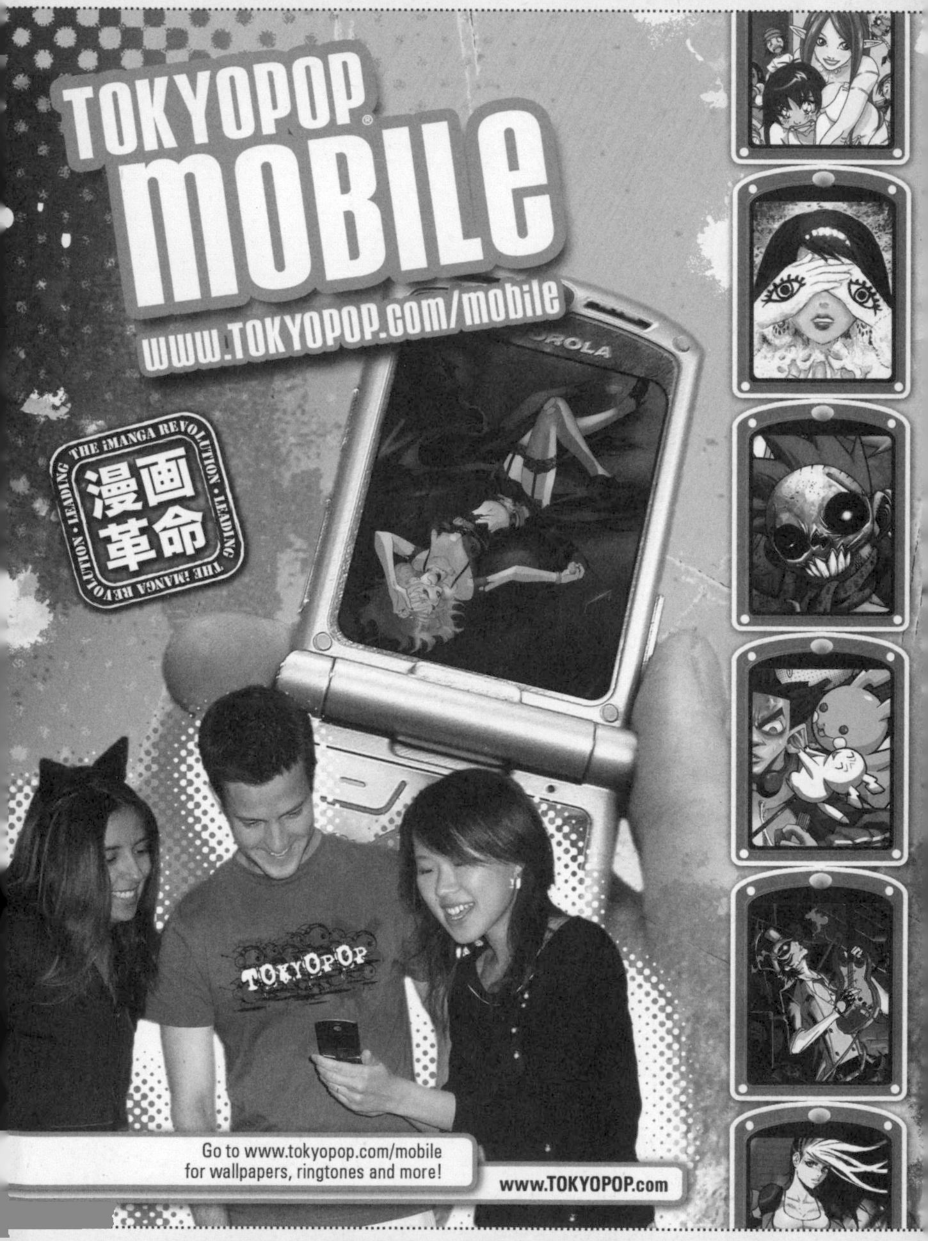
TOKYOPOP®
MOBILE
www.TOKYOPOP.com/mobile
THE iMANGA REVOLUTION • LEADING THE iMANGA REVOLUTION • LEADING
漫画革命
TOKYOPOP
Go to www.tokyopop.com/mobile
for wallpapers, ringtones and more!
www.TOKYOPOP.com

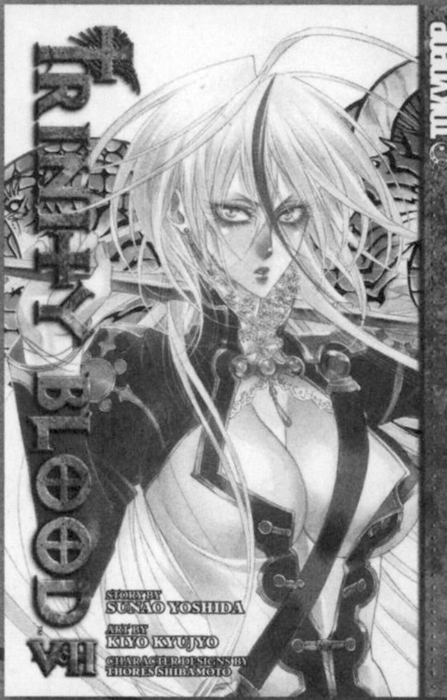
TRINITY BLOOD
TOKYOPOP
STORY BY SUNAO YOSHIDA
ART BY KIYO KYUJYO
CHARACTER DESIGNS BY THORES SHIBAMOTO
VII

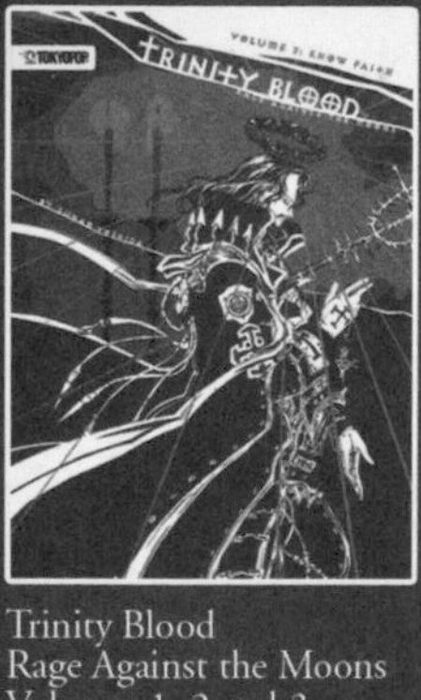
TOKYOPOP
TRINITY BLOOD

Trinity Blood
Rage Against the Moons
Volumes 1, 2 and 3

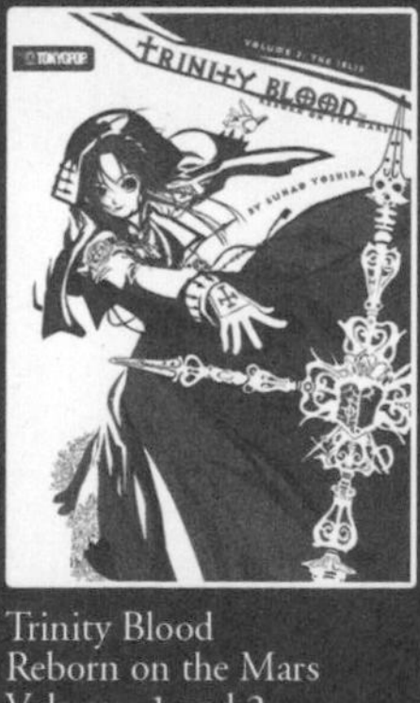
TOKYOPOP
TRINITY BLOOD

Trinity Blood
Reborn on the Mars
Volumes 1 and 2

Hotel AFRICA™

VOLUME TWO
By Hee Jung Park

Anything can happen at the Hotel Africa

Tales of heartbreak, irony, and redemption are in store when you check in a second time to the Hotel Africa. Continue along with Elvis as he reveals more tales of the desolate hotel and its strange guests.

INCLUDES ORIGINAL COLOR ART!

ART NOT FINAL

hee jung park's
fever

one

Also available from Hee Jung Park
Fever

Once you go to Fever, you will never be the same...

Too Long

A girl who attracts suicide victims, a shy record store customer, and the star of a rock band... what could these three have in common? Find out in this moving collection of short stories.

Too Long

© Hee-Jung Park

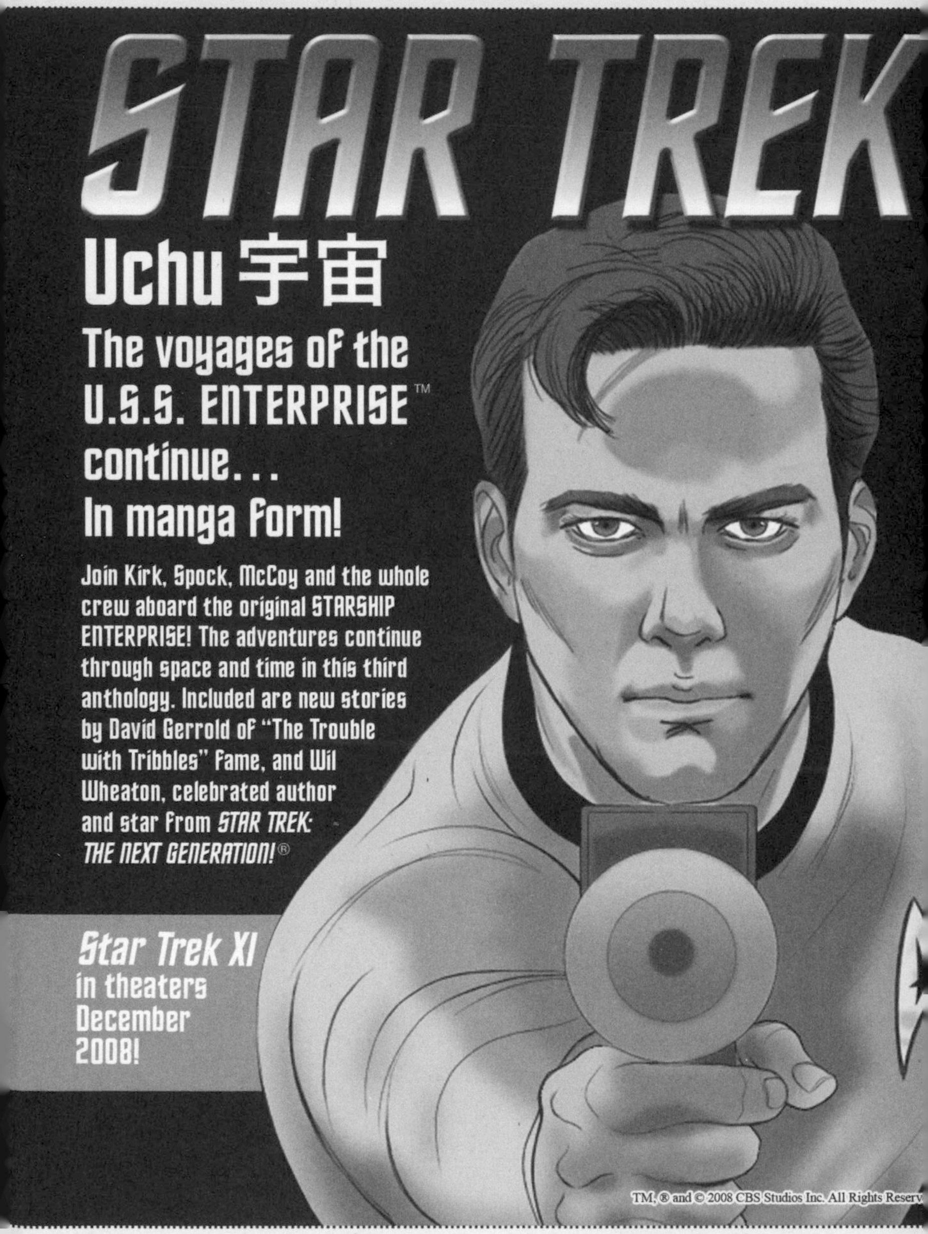
STAR TREK
Uchu 宇宙
The voyages of the U.S.S. ENTERPRISE™ continue...
In manga form!
Join Kirk, Spock, McCoy and the whole crew aboard the original STARSHIP ENTERPRISE! The adventures continue through space and time in this third anthology. Included are new stories by David Gerrold of "The Trouble with Tribbles" fame, and Wil Wheaton, celebrated author and star from STAR TREK: THE NEXT GENERATION!®
Star Trek XI in theaters December 2008!
TM, ® and © 2008 CBS Studios Inc. All Rights Reserv

JYU-OH-SEI™

獣王星

DARE TO VISIT THE PLANET OF THE BEAST KING

Young twins Thor and Rai are kidnapped from their space station colony and dropped on the forsaken planet known to the universe as the Planet of the Beast King. Can they survive this harsh world infested with giant carnivorous plants and populated with criminal outcasts? And how will they be able to escape the planet when the only way off is to become the new Beast King?!

© 1993, 2006, 2008 Natsumi Itsuki / HAKUSENSHA, Inc.

STOP!

This is the back of the book.
You wouldn't want to spoil a great ending!

This book is printed "manga-style," in the authentic Japanese right-to-left format. Since none of the artwork has been flipped or altered, readers get to experience the story just as the creator intended. You've been asking for it, so TOKYOPOP® delivered: authentic, hot-off-the-press, and far more fun!

DIRECTIONS

If this is your first time reading manga-style, here's a quick guide to help you understand how it works.

It's easy... just start in the top right panel and follow the numbers. Have fun, and look for more 100% authentic manga from TOKYOPOP®!

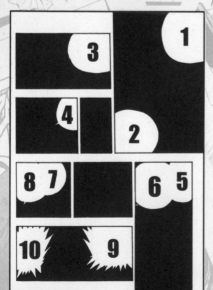